BLACK CULTURE AND THE NEW DEAL

BLACK CULTURE

AND THE NEW DEAL

The Quest for Civil Rights in the Roosevelt Era

LAUREN REBECCA SKLAROFF

The University *of* North Carolina Press
Chapel Hill

© 2009
THE UNIVERSITY
OF NORTH CAROLINA
PRESS

Designed by Kim Bryant
Set in Arnhem by Tseng
Information Systems, Inc.
Manufactured in the
United States of America

The paper in this book
meets the guidelines for
permanence and durability
of the Committee on
Production Guidelines
for Book Longevity of
the Council on Library
Resources.

The University of North
Carolina Press has been a
member of the Green Press
Initiative since 2003.

Library of Congress Cataloging-in-Publication Data
Sklaroff, Lauren Rebecca.
Black culture and the New Deal : the quest for civil
rights in the Roosevelt era / Lauren Rebecca Sklaroff.
p. cm.
Includes bibliographical references and index.
ISBN 978-0-8078-3312-4 (cloth : alk. paper)
1. African Americans—Intellectual life—20th century.
2. African Americans—Civil rights—History—20th
century. 3. New Deal, 1933–1939. 4. United States—
Politics and government—1933–1945. 5. United
States—Race relations—Political aspects—History—
20th century. 6. Social change—United States—
History—20th century. 7. United States—Cultural
policy—History—20th century. 8. Art and state—
United States—History—20th century. I. Title.
E185.6.S62 2009
323.1196073—dc22
2009018548

Earlier versions of parts of this book were previously
published: Sklaroff, Lauren R., "Constructing G.I. Joe
Louis: Cultural Solutions to the 'Negro Problem' during
World War II," *Journal of American History* 89, no. 3
(2002): 958–83; and Sklaroff, Lauren R., "Variety for the
Servicemen: The *Jubilee* Radio Show and the Paradox
of Racializing Radio during World War II," *American
Quarterly* 56, no. 4 (2004): 945–73, © The Johns Hopkins
University Press. Used with permission.

13 12 11 10 09   5 4 3 2 1

for JIM
   with MUCH LOVE

CONTENTS

Acknowledgments *xi*

Introduction *1*

1 | Ambivalent Inclusion *15*

2 | Hooked on Classics *33*

3 | The Editor's Dilemma *81*

4 | Constructing G.I. Joe Louis *123*

5 | Variety for the Servicemen *159*

6 | Projecting Unity *193*

Epilogue *241*

Notes 253
Bibliography 287
Index 301

ILLUSTRATIONS

Hallie Flanagan, national director of the FTP *38*

New York City FTP Negro Unit theater and stage
     workers *48*

Clarence Muse, Los Angeles FTP Negro Unit
     director *49*

Scene from *Walk Together, Chillun* *58*

Cast of *Swing Mikado* *67*

Four Jitterbugs from *Swing Mikado* *71*

Eleanor Roosevelt and Colonel Harrington *76*

Jitterbugs dance in the aisle at New York *Swing
     Mikado* *77*

Joe Louis demonstrates boxing technique to
     soldiers *128*

Elmer Davis, director of the OWI *130*

Joe Louis and his fellow soldiers *147*

Joe Louis boxes Elza Thompson *149*

Enlistment poster featuring Joe Louis *154*

Staff of the AFRS (c. 1942) *164*

Tom Lewis, commander of the AFRS *165*

Black infantrymen in training, Fort Belvoir *168*

Major Mann Holiner, producer of *Jubilee* *176*

Ernest Whitman, Lena Horne, and Eddie Green *181*

Lena Horne in *Stormy Weather* (1943) *187*

Bing Crosby and Eddie Green *190*

Hattie McDaniel and Mary McLeod Bethune *210*

Ethel Waters in *Cabin in the Sky* (1943) *213*

Lena Horne and Bill Robinson in *Stormy Weather*
     (1943) *217*

Multiethnic platoon in *Bataan* (1943) *223*

Scene from *Sahara* (1943) featuring Rex Ingram *225*

Cast of *Lifeboat* (1944) featuring Canada Lee *229*

ACKNOWLEDGMENTS

In his classic, *Charlotte's Web*, E. B. White writes, "It is not often that some-one comes along who is a true friend and a good writer" (184). I am unusu-ally fortunate to have so many people in my life that fit this description. While a graduate student at the University of Virginia, I was lucky enough to have Nelson Lichtenstein as an adviser; the confidence Nelson had in my work, even at its earliest stages, continues to amaze me. I will never be able to thank him enough for always being my advocate and for his willing-ness to read everything I have sent his way.

In her exceptional scholarship and strong convictions, Grace Hale has also served as an important role model. I thank Grace for her honesty and for always urging me to pursue my interests—no matter how unconven-tional. Many others at Virginia provided valuable guidance, including Ed Ayers, Cindy Aron, Brian Owensby, Chuck McCurdy, and Eric Lott. Maire Murphy helped me navigate the often rough terrain of graduate school; years after we both have left Charlottesville, Maire remains a great friend who affirms my choices and is always willing to listen.

I had the wonderful opportunity to hold a Smithsonian predoctoral fel-lowship at the National Museum of American History and to work with many talented scholars. Charlie McGovern believed in this project in its most abstract iteration and guided me to many invaluable resources. A terrific mentor with an encyclopedic mind for all things popular culture, Charlie had an immeasurable impact on this project. I appreciate Pete Daniel for creating and sustaining an intellectually vibrant community at the Smithsonian and the many fellows who enlightened me through their scholarship and reassured me in times of frustration. In addition, I thank Fath Ruffins for her reliable advice and her astute sense of perspective.

I am grateful to the Department of History and Art History at George Mason University, where I held the J. N. G. Finley postdoctoral fellowship in 2003–4. At George Mason, I received remarkable guidance from the late Roy Rosenzweig, who, despite all of own his projects, always found time to read my work and provide suggestions. I also had the privilege of the late Larry Levine's insights; Larry read the manuscript in its entirety, and his extensive comments forced me to think very differently about the meaning of black culture.

I would like to thank editors Joanne Meyerowitz, of the *Journal of American History*, and Lucy Maddox and Marita Sturken, of *American Quarterly*, for their interest in my research and for placing earlier versions of portions of this work in such exciting forums so early in my professional career. Kathy Newman, George Roeder, and anonymous readers provided close, thoughtful readings of the manuscripts of my articles that informed my thinking throughout the book. This scholarship has been presented at conferences of the American Historical Association and the Organization of American Historians, and I appreciate Gary Gerstle, Lewis Erenberg, John Gennari, and Jonathan Holloway for their perspectives.

Most of my research was conducted in Washington, D.C., and I would like to thank the helpful staffs at the National Archives, the Library of Congress, the Archives Center at the National Museum of American History, and the Moorland-Spingarn Research Center at Howard University. In addition, I am grateful for the aid of archivists at the Franklin D. Roosevelt Library, which granted me the Eichelberger-Linzer Research Fellowship.

Since January of 2005, Columbia, South Carolina, has been my home, and the Department of History at the University of South Carolina has been exceptionally kind and welcoming. Christine Ames, Ronald Atkinson, Marjorie Spruill, and Connie Schultz made my move down south and the transition to a new job seem much less overwhelming. While serving as chair of the history department, Patrick Maney always had my best interest at heart, and I thank him for his enthusiasm toward my research. Our current chair, Lacy Ford, generously provided additional resources toward completion of this book. I am much obliged to Mark Smith, who has helped me stay on course, with an unflagging confidence in my scholarship and academic potential. I thank Pat Sullivan for all of her great advice on publishing this book and for challenging me to always reevaluate the meaning of the black freedom struggle. In addition, Dan Carter extended the great gift of his wisdom and friendship while cheerfully agreeing to read this manuscript—his suggestions have proved invaluable. Finally, I am so appreciative of Larry Glickman, an amazing colleague, friend, and mentor who offered sharp and constructive comments on my book.

I am indebted to the three research assistants who have been integral to the completion of this book. Rhett Cooper located background information on the most obscure figures, and her clever determination led librarians and archivists to find important materials beyond those I requested.

Becky Miller has been my angel of organization; in addition to all of the formatting, indexing, and filing, she offered useful insights on content and structure. Finally, I am thankful to Santi Thompson for procuring image permissions and reproductions. All of these individuals displayed enormous dedication to this project, and I am so fortunate to have worked with them.

At the University of North Carolina Press, Chuck Grench has supported this project for several years; I appreciate his sound advice and encouragement. I also extend thanks to Katy O'Brien, Paul Betz, John Wilson, Kim Bryant, and Dino Battista for all of their hard work in the publication process. Harvard Sitkoff and Jeffrey Sammons provided suggestive and thoughtful reader reports that improved the book dramatically.

In Columbia and elsewhere, dear friends have added clarity to the chaos. Thank you to everyone, particularly my mommy allies, who have given my life more balance and have tolerated my endless stressing about this book. I give special thanks to Sara Weinberg for her lovely photographs and for offering such continuous generosity. I could never have completed this without Wendy Wannamaker, who has cared for my children for the past four years. Wendy has given me a truly priceless gift—the ability to leave my house each day with complete peace of mind. I will always appreciate Wendy's remarkable love and patience, as well as her flexibility in providing additional care during this project's completion.

My family continues to express a strong interest in my book, which is amazing given the length of time that it has been "almost finished." Without their love, this book would never have been possible. Thank you to my aunt and uncle, Andrea and Marty Feigenbaum, for always wanting the best for me, and to my brother, Jonathan Sklaroff, for always making me laugh. I am so grateful to my mother-in-law, Diana Lamey, for her steady faith in my scholarship. Diana traveled to the Library of Congress to procure additional images, and I will always appreciate her attentiveness over the years, as she willingly listened to me ramble on about my work. In addition, this book is inspired by my grandmother, Myra Green, a fellow scholar who has all my love and admiration. I thank her for questioning me and challenging me, for her intellectual curiosity and integrity. My beloved, extraordinary grandfather, William Green, passed away as I was completing this project, and I am heartbroken that he will not be able to see the final product.

There are not enough words to describe how grateful I am to my parents, Ellen and Neil Sklaroff, who always knew that I could finish this book, even when I wavered. Their love and assurance through both exciting and frustrating moments has meant everything. My interest in the history of racial injustice as well as the meaning of art and literature is a direct reflection of my parents' values, and I appreciate them for exemplifying a thirst for knowledge and a dedication to critical inquiry.

My sons, Jack and Alex, bring sheer happiness to every day, and thinking of their adorable faces provides comfort during the often lonely and difficult writing process. While my work has undoubtedly reduced the number of my children's play dates and certainly the number of home-cooked meals, I hope my scholarship will instill in them a love of reading and a determination to pursue their passions. My husband, Jim Lamey, to whom this book is dedicated, has been my proofreader, research assistant, moving man, military historian, and unconditional supporter. I thank him for all of this, and for much, much more.

BLACK CULTURE AND THE NEW DEAL

INTRODUCTION

Four years after Franklin Roosevelt's death, Eleanor Roosevelt remembered her frustrations when racial issues, such as the antilynching bill and the abolition of the poll tax, reached her husband's desk. "Although Franklin was in favor of both measures, they never became 'must' legislation. When I would protest, he would simply say: 'First things come first, and I can't alienate certain votes I need for measures that are more important at the moment by pushing any measure that would entail a fight.'"[1] A powerful southern congressional bloc influenced the executive treatment of race relations during the Depression and World War II. To the chagrin of many civil rights leaders, the support of this southern contingency always outweighed the administration's commitment to endorsing measures that would explicitly improve political, economic, and social conditions for black Americans.[2]

Still, the federal government did not completely ignore civil rights in this politically explosive atmosphere. One important method that the Roosevelt administration employed to acknowledge African Americans and to involve them in the president's "New Deal" was through federally sponsored cultural programs. Initially conceived under the Works Progress Administration's (WPA) Federal Arts Project (FAP) and then continued under wartime agencies such as the Office of War Information (OWI) and the War Department, fine art and media-based programs represented an important strand of civil rights policy during the Roosevelt era. Through the publications of the Federal Writers' Project (FWP), the plays of the Federal Theatre Project (FTP), the endorsement of black celebrities such as Joe Louis, and the production of wartime films and radio shows, liberal administrators demonstrated a sustained commitment to addressing the concerns of black Americans when political pragmatism prevented official support for structural legislation. Beginning in the 1930s, government program administrators imagined that these cultural projects would provide a safe treatment of pressing political concerns and a foundation for the government's policies toward African Americans in the postwar period.

This history is undoubtedly complex. Not only did government program administrators further marginalize concrete civil rights legislation in adopting certain cultural policies, but each program encountered obstacles that would limit African Americans' power and representation. Black participants worked within the tightest of cultural spaces, facing the scrutiny of the House Un-American Activities Committee (HUAC), the racism and aesthetic inflexibility of many state directors, the political exigencies of war, and compromised federal budgets. Nevertheless, under the Roosevelt administration, the Federal Arts Project and wartime media programs served as central methods of imbuing African Americans with a sense of political authority. As the first administration to recognize publicly that African Americans mattered as citizens, New Dealers forwarded a cultural agenda that, despite all of its limitations, marked a significant turning point in the production of black culture. Within the context of a larger cultural apparatus that largely omitted or stereotyped African Americans, the government programs offered creative outlets that were unavailable elsewhere. New Deal cultural development represented a continuous process of negotiation, as both black and white officials championed some symbols, ideas, and media, while discarding others. Therefore, this book recounts a history of creativity, ambition, and unprecedented possibilities; but also a history of limitations, bigotry, and political machinations.

Four major themes illuminate the significance of government-sponsored cultural development in the history of the Roosevelt era and the struggle for African American civil rights. First, programs under the WPA and other wartime agencies served as important locations for black cultural advancement at a time when black minstrel images still predominated commercial culture and popular music, radio, and film industries segregated, demeaned, or excluded African Americans. Second, debates within these cultural projects illustrate the importance of what the FTP Negro Unit director Carlton Moss termed "cultural emancipation" to the civil rights struggle during this period: groups such as the National Association for the Advancement of Colored People (NAACP) deemed cultural autonomy and representational agency vital in the quest for racial equality.[3] Third, government-sponsored cultural development reflected a pattern that would repeat itself during the Depression and World War II and that would provide continuity between the 1930s and 1940s, solidifying the Roosevelt administration's reliance on art and media projects as viable forms of racial policy into the postwar era.

Lastly, my focus on the politics of cultural development serves as an alternative model for examining civil rights. Building on the work of historians such as Glenda Gilmore and Jacquelyn Dowd Hall, who recognize the New Deal era as a critical point in "the long Civil Rights Movement," this book shifts attention to the cultural arena and its place in the African American freedom struggle. As Hall urges, "Finally, we must forgo easy closure and satisfying upward or downward arcs."[4] *Black Culture and the New Deal* provides less obvious signs of success and failure and an equally important framework for understanding how black and white Americans wrestled with the racial issues that most concerned them in addition to the compromises they often made in challenging the status quo. The significance of these interracial negotiations lies in the fact that racial change was subtle, often incremental; what became advantageous for some people was sometimes damaging for others. Due to varying degrees of white liberalism, the heterogeneity of the black artistic community and black civil rights organizations, and the constant political pressures facing all administrators, this history is one of competing interests yet many shared goals. Nevertheless, conversations abounded concerning the persistence of racial stereotypes, the nature of black artistic directorial authority, and the overall employment of African Americans in the culture industry. This dialogue proved to be as central to civil rights history as the racial politics that unfolded on the shop floor, in the armed forces, or within the legal system.

Black Culture and the New Deal chronicles the relationship between two groups. On the one hand, liberal white administrators during the New Deal developed artistic programs to recognize the talents and contributions of African Americans, enveloping black men and women with the mantle of federal programs as no presidential administration had ever considered or attempted. On the other hand, black Americans who participated in this federal enterprise capitalized on the political power of culture in their fight for respect, recognition, and—most significantly—an equal form of American citizenship. Among white officials such as Harold Ickes, Archibald MacLeish, Hallie Flanagan, and Elmer Davis, the production of federally sponsored media projects embodied the New Deal's larger ambition to embrace and promote a multiracial, multiethnic nation. In the

FWP's American Guide Series, the plays of the FTP, and the "Americans All" mantra that resounded in most World War II propaganda, white administrators stressed that Americans of all colors and nationalities not only built the nation, but that America's progress depended on their continued contributions. These officials believed that giving attention and devoting resources to formerly underrepresented groups would better facilitate both economic recovery and wartime mobilization. As government officials reiterated this message in cultural bureaucracies such as the FAP and the OWI, they incorporated "Negro Studies" or "Negro Affairs" into program initiatives. Thus, if cultural programs came to assume a central role in forwarding New Deal racial progressivism, it was because many white men and women believed that the treatment of black Americans was not just important but critical to the nation's future as an inclusive democracy.

The fact that the currents of a larger national agenda often shaped cultural development, which was stewarded under primarily white direction, does not mean that intellectuals, musicians, and artists did not wield authority. It is precisely *because* the New Deal government sponsored these programs that African Americans were offered a unique opportunity. As the historian Nikhil Singh contends, during the New Deal era black activists and intellectuals constructed a "black counter-public sphere," which mobilized against economic and social injustices.[5] During this genesis of black political thought, improvements in the cultural arena featured prominently on the political agenda. For organizations such as the NAACP, struggles for representational agency, the obliteration of racial stereotypes, and the excavation of black history from the margins accompanied the fight against segregation and other forms of discrimination. The Roosevelt era, therefore, represented a significant moment in the history of civil rights because African Americans played an integral role in shaping the course of government-sponsored cultural programs and in negotiating their own representation. As historians have come to explain more recently, the advancement of black cultural politics did not solely occur within isolated developments, such as the Harlem Renaissance or the Black Arts Movement, but rather as an ongoing dialogue in tandem with calls for structural political change.[6]

This notion of the cultural as the political was explicitly promoted in the 1920s, when Harlem Renaissance artists developed a literature and imagery that broke from the Anglo-American literary cannon and championed a "New Negro." Scholars have long evaluated the political character of the Harlem Renaissance and its impact within the larger civil rights movement.[7] For historian David Levering Lewis, the Harlem Renaissance served as a form of "civil rights by copyright"—a hallmark of African American artistic achievement that allowed men and women to explore and condemn America's tortured racial past. Despite the creativity that flourished, both black political organizations and white influence largely compromised the movement's success.[8] Other scholars, however, have challenged Lewis's criticism, urging more precise historicizing and arguing that the cultural arena was the only outlet for black political activity during the 1920s. As scholar Ann Douglas contends, "the most pressing reason for the New Negro's decision to work through culture, not politics, was that this was the closest Harlem could come to so-called real politics."[9] Regardless of the scope of its political impact, the Harlem Renaissance served as a foundation for the artistic developments that emerged during the Roosevelt era. While some scholars mark the death of the Renaissance with the 1935 Harlem riot, the dynamics it generated, and many of its complications, moved into New Deal cultural programs.[10] Historian George Hutchinson argues, "the movement's legacy was amplified throughout the late 1930s and institutionalized in programs such as the Federal Writers', Arts, and Theatre Projects, which incubated the next generation of African American artists."[11]

Similar to the Harlem Renaissance, the FAP and wartime media projects witnessed the kind of interracial cultural exchange that both fueled and circumscribed African American cultural expression. The interracial relationships fostered during the New Deal era, however, were not inherently exploitative. Like those scholars who have recently worked to give a rich description of the complex cultural interworkings of the Renaissance, I argue that the interracial dynamics that undergirded New Deal cultural production was not always to the detriment of African Americans. As Hutchinson attests, "historical dramas have been interpreted in such a way as to fit relatively fixed ideas about interracial relations, and the complexity of these dramas is lost."[12] In addition to continuing the kind of interracial alliances formed during the Renaissance, New Deal programs also carried on the practice of utilizing culture as a political weapon. While white government officials may have understood artistic developments as racialized programming, which could serve in place of "real" racial politics, African American political leaders and program participants considered New Deal cultural projects as tantamount to organized challenges against economic and social inequality. If in the 1920s African Americans in Harlem were "translating politics into cultural terms," then during the New Deal this process was reaffirmed and extended within the programs of the federal government, even in the midst of increasing activism among both formal political organizations and grassroots movements.[13] During the Roosevelt era, black political mobilization did not negate the need for artistic cultivation; on the contrary, activism made positive developments in the cultural arena all the more critical.

For many black leaders, the "cultural self-determination" woven throughout federal art and media projects was a pivotal step in combating discrimination.[14] According to FAP directors such as Sterling Brown and Carlton Moss, if white Americans could understand their black counterparts beyond minstrelsy, perhaps they would deem black men and women worthy of other civil rights. Indeed, as historian Grace Hale forcefully contends, a culture of segregation underpinned both the de jure and de facto structures that institutionalized racial inequality.[15] For black Americans in the 1930s and 1940s, this culture of segregation—minstrel images, exclusion from historical narratives, and other commercialized distortions of blackness—needed eliminating in the same way that discrimination in other areas was under attack. Although African Americans recognized that a more positive racial imagery or black control of cultural representation could not substitute for the political and economic rights which they so ardently sought, black participants understood culture as central in procuring civil rights. Far from Harold Cruise's later charge that African Americans could not understand "the strategic importance of the cultural front in relation to the political and economic fronts," during the New Deal era African Americans involved in federal programs and black political organizations conceptualized culture and politics as inherently intertwined.[16]

In this braided narrative, it is also important to understand the limitations of a methodological framework that separates black and white individuals into two groups with distinct political agendas. First, while white officials most often served as project directors, African Americans exerted varying degrees of power and influence, blurring the line between administrator and artistic participant. The black poet Sterling Brown served as a director for the FWP in his own right, establishing criteria not only for other African Americans but also for white writers in the program to follow. Black performers who worked on the *Jubilee* radio shows disseminated important racial meaning in their delivery of melodies and lyrics, whatever the intent of white producers. In these cases, black intellectu-

6

INTRODUCTION

als and musicians obscured the role of "producer," making racial lines more difficult to demarcate. Second, this book is not a history of generous liberals and eager black participants but rather of negotiations between individuals who shared many of the same interests. Although liberalism always revealed its limits, and African Americans often displayed a more intense personal investment than their white colleagues in the content of artistic productions, the ideas of white and black individuals echoed each other as frequently as they contrasted. Finally, a binary opposition may at times mask the intraracial politics that shaped the contours of programming. Black individuals debated with each other over the structure of the FTP's Negro Units and over the kinds of roles black actors and actresses should assume onscreen. Here, the influence of white officials was one of many competing factors. In response to new artistic outlets, black opinion was never homogeneous, and as they asserted agency at the level of production, black individuals often voiced opposing ideas and disparate aesthetic agendas.

Although I emphasize the significance of new artistic opportunities and representational improvements for African Americans working within the federal apparatus, New Deal programs never reached the potential that black participants and political leaders hoped for. Directors such as Sterling Brown became encumbered with the racism of state directors; Hollywood proved less willing than black leaders expected to create a broad range of films that would accurately depict the lives of African Americans. The FTP's Negro Units could only develop productions approved by a primarily white Play Bureau, and both the *Jubilee* radio show and the nature of Joe Louis's wartime activities were dictated by a military that was not interested in disrupting the racial status quo. While all of these programs were ambitious within the context of the New Deal era, they revealed their limitations and left some black men and women frustrated and disappointed. In addition, the irony of government-supported cultural inclusion in the face of political negligence or outright discrimination was not limited to African Americans; similar cultural initiatives undoubtedly applied to other minority groups during this period, and they warrant further treatment by historians. Yet the obstacles embedded within each project do not negate the importance of New Deal cultural programs; indeed, the ways in which African Americans worked to create artistic expression within tightly confined spaces are a critical part of this history.

This book offers a new interpretation of the New Deal era not only in conceptualizing federal race policy but in recognizing the interconnectedness of culture and politics in the 1930s and 1940s. Historians have long evaluated the transformative character of the New Deal; this study turns to the government's cultural arena, explaining how the Roosevelt administration was the first to implement a wide-scale federal arts program that aimed to acknowledge black Americans publicly as a voting constituency.[17] In addition, the personnel and the cultural motivations behind WPA relief programs such as the FWP and the FTP reemerged during World War II. When it came to matters of race, art projects seemingly endemic to the 1930s quite naturally extended themselves to the exigencies of war and into the more prosperous postwar era. But it was the 1930s and 1940s that witnessed the genesis of government-sponsored cultural development. Thus, I have limited my discussion of the New Deal to this period and use the terms "New Deal era" and "Roosevelt era" interchangeably.[18]

Within the field of American cultural history, the Roosevelt era is one of the most studied periods, as scholars continue to probe subjects such as radicalism within films and literature, the activities and perceptions of working-class audiences, and the permutations of wartime political ideologies.[19] Yet the notion of the government as an important cultural producer—at least in the context of a broader cultural apparatus—remains rather marginalized. Among those who study the federal arts projects of the 1930s, most signal the death knell of these programs by 1939; scholars view plays such as the FTP's *Swing Mikado* or the guidebooks written under the FWP primarily as representations of the Depression era's pluralistic ethos.[20] While this characterization is important to recognize, the FAP marked a government impetus on racial issues that would continue for decades. In addition, although none of the federal projects could compete with commercial industry, neither their financial profitability nor their public reception represents the only means of measuring their significance. These programs were important not because they were the most widely acclaimed by American audiences or because they were deemed the most beloved cultural products of the Roosevelt era (although some that the government sponsored were extremely successful), but because they were part of an explicit policy discourse that has received little attention in this historical context.

While this book builds on the work of cultural and social historians who posit that a "culture of unity"—films, radio programs, and mass-produced items—garnered support for the New Deal among previously disengaged groups, the federal government's cultural arena was not solely a means to an end. Government-sponsored culture engendered a political landscape in which government officials and civil rights leaders probed the nature and meaning of black Americanness. Many cultural historians have examined themes of this period: an embrace of everyday people, a critique of managerial authority, and a turn to new American "roots." This study, however, does not situate racial liberalism under the larger rubric of a working-class agenda or the plight of organized labor. Mobilized workers and preponderantly left-wing organizations frequently displayed sensitivity to the plight of African Americans; yet race was often treated independently from class-based concerns.[21]

Still, the influence of the Left warrants consideration, particularly as Communism in America was at its apogee during the New Deal era. The Communist Left played a critical role in mobilizing both whites and African Americans against racial oppression in the South, expressing the immediacy of granting black men and women full social equality decades long before the 1950s. As Gilmore asserts, "The presence of a radical Left, in this case a Communist Left, redefined the debate over white supremacy and hastened its end." In this book, several participants of government projects supported Communism, some as party members with more peripheral political affiliations and some who embraced particular dimensions of Communist ideology without accepting the doctrine as a whole. As historians have come to explain, in conceptualizing the Popular Front, the structure of the Communist Party (CPUSA) was quite nebulous. Men and women adapted particular philosophies that were not always consistent with a party line emanating from Moscow.[22] Certainly, Communist ideology buttressed an overall concern about racial inequality, but it was only one component of the larger struggle for civil rights. And CP membership or fellow traveler status was not always synonymous with the promotion of racial reform. Conversely, many men and women who did not consider themselves Communists nevertheless worked as strong proponents of black inclusion. More significantly, the cause of anti-Communism served as an effective means for government officials to quash cultural programs and to tarnish individuals they deemed "un-American." The testimonies of cultural participants before the House Un-American Activities Committee explicitly questioned the federal role in cultivating racial imagery and in employing African American as workers. Thus, while some individuals profiled in this book considered themselves Communists and at certain moments the Communist Party did exert influence, it is most useful to question how those who embraced and those who shunned Communist ideologies influenced racial programming, rather than whether they stood with the party line.

The scope and approach of this book differ from other histories of race relations during this period. Many scholars have highlighted the gendered and racialized nature of New Deal policies. Delving into this oppressive atmosphere, others have uncovered the activism of white liberals and African American political organizations, demonstrating that even despite the Roosevelt administration's intransigence, black men and women were able to campaign against racial inequality. Particularly in excavating the grassroots mobilization of black communities, historians have provided a more nuanced analysis of the New Deal era. In addition, scholarship has begun to demonstrate the long-term political consequences of Roosevelt's judicial policies, which perhaps reflected the president's most racially progressive actions. While all of this research has been fundamental, my focus on the cultural arena provides an alternative perspective in examining the quest for racial equality.[23]

Organized opposition to concrete forms of discrimination is not utilized as a yardstick of success or failure; thus, the racial dynamics within this book may often seem muted. New Deal cultural developments, nonetheless, were significant in the lives of participants and within the larger contours of federal civil rights initiatives. Because the arts projects were a form of direct outreach to African American performers, artists, and writers, and because the establishment of "Negro Affairs" divisions entailed sustained debates over both administrative form and aesthetic content, they represent a departure from the negligence of previous administrations and a vast difference from those relief agencies driven solely by economic concerns.

The term "cultural apparatus" apparent throughout the book identifies the nascent bureaucracies and personnel encompassing federal arts and media-based programs. Although the discussion of the cultural apparatus centers on projects operating under government auspices, many individuals in commercial industry were often influential in federal programs. Commercial radio shows and films often overlapped with government developments, particularly during the war years. Scholars have understood the New Deal as a critical moment in the history of the American nation when questions of federal responsibility intensified and the beginnings of a welfare system emerged. Shifting the focus to agencies spawned by the WPA, the OWI, and the armed forces—and the "Negro Affairs" divisions that developed within them—I offer an examination of central sites in the history of state building. Like other histories, this study articulates how bureaucratic growth engendered new conceptions about American citizenship and new narratives of inclusion and entitlement. However, when government officials invited African Americans into the artistic process, it was not merely as recipients of federal largesse but to become influential actors in determining the direction and continuation of American cultural institutions. Through this prism, I locate a unique series of debates concerning the nature and orientation of national cultural development.[24]

This book centers on the process of production. Here, the significance of New Deal cultural programs is not measured by the reception of all African Americans, nor are projects evaluated by their impact in changing white attitudes at large. Rather, I examine the importance of the FAP and wartime media programs through the politics that unfolded between and among participants, administrators, and black political organizations. Yet many of these federal projects were disseminated to broad, interracial audiences, and I have ascertained their reception where sources permitted. While a relatively small number of African Americans were involved in government-sponsored programming, the products of their labor received detailed discussion in the black press and literary organs such as the *Crisis* and *Opportunity*.

Each chapter analyzes an important moment in the cultural formulation of racial policy. All of the chapters feature a similar structure, first focusing on the exchange between administrators and then on a program that officials ultimately selected as a means of disseminating a particular racial agenda. While debates over the content and structure are distinct among different media, the same central questions resonate throughout the book: What is considered "black culture"? Can racial programming develop adequately under white direction? How should cultural administrators reconcile the often conflicting ideas of black political leaders, individual artists, and the African American communities often targeted as audiences? Can culture become truly integrated, or should black political expression be addressed in separate programs and publications? While these projects were not the only ones that addressed such issues, each chapter demonstrates an important component of cultural exchange and offers a different example of how African Americans wrestled with varying aesthetic and political choices.

Chapter 1 provides an overview of the complexities of racial liberalism in the Roosevelt administration, explaining why, even with the endorsement of progressive New Dealers such as Howard Ickes and Eleanor Roosevelt, civil rights legislation could never be passed. The chapter also offers a description of the increasing black commitment to the Democratic Party, explaining why black Americans changed their political allegiance after a long-standing dedication to the party of Lincoln. Finally, it presents a background to the development of the art projects, demonstrating how federal sponsorship of writers, artists, and performers merged neatly with reigning concepts of cultural pluralism.

Chapter 2 examines the federal government's attempt to highlight black talents through the FTP, which established separate "Negro Units" and, in doing so, created several highly popular performances for black and white audiences. After analyzing the kinds of plays officials decided both to endorse and to reject for the Negro Units, the chapter moves to the congressional investigations of the FTP and the ways in which a hostile political climate shaped the content of particular play performances. This political scrutiny led the FTP to focus on seemingly more sanitized productions, such as the *Swing Mikado*, which the Chicago Negro Unit performed to a sold-out house for a sustained period of time. Here, although the production achieved popularity through its classic form as a Gilbert and Sullivan opera, black actors were able to imbue the opera with their own racial meaning.

Chapter 3 examines how noted poet Sterling Brown, as editor of the Negro Affairs section of the FWP, attempted to revise traditional narratives of black history. As his largest task was the incorporation of black history into the FWP's largest undertaking, the American Guide Series, Brown and his editors urged state guide writers to reconsider the past of their own regions and to account for discrimination and racism. The chapter discusses the successes and limitations of Brown's participation in writing the American Guide Series, as well as the way he ultimately turned to separate studies of black life as the most effective means for achieving his goals. Like chapter 2, chapter 3 also shows how congressional conservatism affected the larger intentions of the FWP, defining what should be considered "American" and "un-American" materials. The chapter ends with the termination of the Federal Arts Project and its focus on high culture during the 1930s; federal interests shifted to utilizing the mass media during wartime mobilization.

Chapter 4 investigates how the issue of "low Negro morale" came to plague administrators during World War II and how the government endorsed particular media in an attempt to boost black patriotism. In particular, the OWI and the War Department constructed the symbol and persona of Joe Louis to provide black Americans with a model of heroism, sacrifice, and black inclusion in the war effort. Through Louis, the Roosevelt administration could demonstrate that black Americans were indeed important to American victory, while temporarily skirting the issues of segregation in the armed forces and racism in home front industries. The chapter also demonstrates how Louis held a symbolic political meaning for many black Americans, who understood the "Brown Bomber" as a victor over white opponents as well as one whose celebrity had transcended racial lines.

Drawing on the government's discourse about the use of mass media, chapter 5 analyzes how officials conceptualized radio as an outlet for addressing black Americans during wartime. As the War Department developed a radio broadcast entitled "America's Negro Soldiers," administrators came to adopt the variety show format as preferable for creating racially oriented programs. Taking this idea still further, the newly formed Armed Forces Radio Service developed *Jubilee*, an "All-Negro Variety Show" broadcast to both black and white servicemen. Yet, despite its musical base, *Jubilee* offered a highly charged commentary on American race relations. The chapter demonstrates that as black performers coded racial messages in song, or drew attention to army segregation in their dedications to soldiers, they proved that broadcasting could be an effective medium for political expression.

Chapter 6 examines government officials' reviews of motion pictures and evaluates the government's challenge of visually depicting a multiracial America amid the competing interests of Hollywood, the NAACP, and a larger community of black actors. Acting more as a regulator than as a producer, the OWI confronted Hollywood with a series of directives for creating films that would offer particular portrayals of black Americans. While Hollywood was not always complicit, some motion pictures reflected the most progressive racial imagery in government-sponsored cultural programming by featuring an integrated army. Divisions in the black community widened over those wartime films that maintained standard racial conventions, such as *Cabin in the Sky* and *Stormy Weather*, which different parts of the black press criticized and applauded. Thus, this chapter argues that even if the cinematic fantasy of racial egalitarianism contrasted with the reality of segregation and discrimination, black Americans stressed the centrality of control over cultural imagery and production in the larger struggle for civil rights.

This book outlines a process that is not without contemporary resonance. The cultivation of a cultural policy implemented during the Depression and the Second World War featured prominently in the postwar era, while the passage of widespread civil rights legislation lagged behind until the mid-1960s. Although the focus of this book remains on the prewar period, the development process—sifting and discarding, revising and reinterpreting—laid the groundwork for federal initiatives after World War II, when cultural figures such as Louis Armstrong and Duke Ellington assumed important roles in the State Department's goodwill tours, and when images of American racial democracy spread across the globe. As the modern civil rights movement gained momentum, the cultural arena remained a vital source for promoting liberal integrationism, with some individuals and media employed more frequently than others. Whether the official promotion of black entertainers and athletes continues to deflect larger racial conflicts remains a heated topic; yet our familiarity with the federal and commercial elevation of African American celebrities should not obscure the origins of this policy initiative. However much a pervasive imagery of black inclusion now obscures America's troubled racial history, we must understand the specific historical meaning federal programs held for both white and black Americans in the 1930s and 1940s. How American culture initially addressed the "Negro Problem" is as vital a question as why, fifty years after the civil rights movement, the policy still lingers.

chapter one

AMBIVALENT INCLUSION

During the first week of June 1939, Washington, D.C., avidly followed news of the visit of King George VI and Queen Elizabeth. "A crowd as enthusiastic and large as ever greeted an American President on inauguration day turned out today to watch and take part in the pomp," the *New York Times* reported, chronicling all aspects of the historical occasion, down to the king's and queen's attire.[1] On June 8, President Roosevelt received the royals at a state dinner; before approximately three hundred guests, he joined the king in a pledge to "walk together along the path of friendship in a world of peace."[2] Along with proclamations of international cooperation, the evening also included performances that featured what the White House considered "authentic" representations of American music. Showcasing elements of this "vital and undeniably American" folk culture, the evening's entertainment included cowboy ballads, Appalachian folk songs, and rural-based dancing "handed down through generations."[3]

The central focus, however, was on African Americans. In evaluating the origins of American music, the program notes for the evening stated, "above all, the negro has made the most distinctive contribution." At the musicale's opening, the American hosts and their British guests heard the voices of the North Carolina Spiritual Singers, a "community activity group" directed by the WPA's Federal Music Project. As the program explained, the Spiritual Singers included a "cross section of Negro life in the State, composed of workers from the tobacco plants, clerks, doctors, school teachers . . . and housewives." The program also noted that several of the performed folk songs were of "Negro origin" or derived from black minstrel songs. Last, African American contralto Marian Anderson delivered three compositions, including "Ave Maria" and "My Soul's Been Anchored in the Lord"; only two other solo performers, Kate Smith and Lawrence Tibett, were part of the state dinner production. At this important event, for arguably the most respected of foreign dignitaries, the White House chose to highlight African American culture, not in a demeaning fashion, but as an affirmation of African American citizenship and inclusiveness.[4]

This focus on black performance was integral to the Roosevelt administration's development of federal cultural programs and its larger racial policy by the end of the 1930s. However, understanding why African Americans were so centrally staged in an event such as the royal reception in 1939 requires an explanation of how racial issues became increasingly important to the administration's political agenda. We must also consider why New Dealers advocated for the establishment of a federally sponsored arts program, one that would come to play a central role in the government's recognition of African Americans. Upon Roosevelt's election in 1932, neither culture nor race weighed heavily on the political agenda; in a matter of years, the administration's outlook would change.

Race and Politics in the New Deal Era

For decades, African Americans had shown an unwavering commitment to the Republican Party. Although Democrats had made some inroads among African Americans in the 1928 and 1932 elections, African Americans remained faithful to the party of Lincoln during Franklin Roosevelt's first term in office. Even after previous Republican administrations had ignored African Americans and sanctioned discriminatory policies, African Americans' loyalty to the GOP remained steadfast, largely out of an allegiance to the Great Emancipator. As historian Nancy Weiss contends, "The Lincoln legacy was one of the toughest obstacles to overcome in converting blacks to the Democratic Party."[5] With this in mind, Republican Party officials treated the black membership within the GOP as a given and made few efforts before 1936 to reach out to African American voters. This confidence in black Republicanism, however, was not unshakable, particularly when African Americans had good reason to abandon the party. Disproportionately affected by the Depression, black men and women did not see any indication that President Herbert Hoover would initiate legislation to better their economic or social condition. Hoover's Supreme Court nomination of John Parker, deemed "anti-black" by the NAACP, with a record of discriminatory legislation he supported while serving as the secretary of commerce, left many black voters to question the mission of the GOP.[6]

Yet, frustrations with Hoover did not immediately result in black men and women shifting their political allegiance. In 1932, Democrats offered scant evidence that their party would offer a better alternative for African Americans. Before his presidency, Roosevelt had never been a proponent of black civil rights. As New Deal historian Harvard Sitkoff contends, Roosevelt's political career had been a "model of deference to the white South on racial issues" and during his first term, the president demonstrated few actions that would contradict this description. Highly dependent on southern states for political backing and a self-described "adopted son of Georgia," due to his purchase of a home in Warm Springs, Roosevelt was unwilling to make mention of any racial issues that might alienate his supporters. He did not make a significant attempt to court the black vote during his 1932 election campaign, and unsurprisingly, African Americans backed the Republican candidate, Herbert Hoover, in 1932, by a two-to-one majority. With the landslide election of Roosevelt and the Texan vice president, John Nance Garner, the federal government's disinterest in racial matters confirmed the southern belief that these policies should remain the states' province. Roosevelt's first cabinet bore the conviction that any threats to white supremacy could be politically disastrous.[7]

Even if Roosevelt eschewed explicit overtures to African Americans, many testified that in its early days, the New Deal had dramatically improved their lives. As the black political scientist Earl Brown asserted, "countless Negroes were snatched from a living death by New Deal relief."[8] As African Americans suffered extreme poverty during the Depression, New Deal programs were a clear manifestation of the government's concern, particularly in light of Herbert Hoover's skeletal policies. In January 1933, John Gaddis, an African American mechanic, told Franklin Roosevelt that he believed the president was receptive to offering the "few acts of encouragement" African Americans badly needed.[9] According to Gaddis, who considered himself one of the "many forgotten men," the election of Roosevelt ushered in positive changes for impoverished African Americans, especially as previous presidencies had not rewarded these Republican ballots. The creation of agencies such as the National Recovery Administration, the Agricultural Adjustment Administration, and the Civilian Conservation Corps raised African Americans' expectations of the federal government; as a result of these developments, Howard University dean

Kelly Miller urged black men and women to "trust President Roosevelt" in the early days of the New Deal.[10]

In this context, maintaining loyalty to the Republican Party's legacy was less imperative than supporting an administration that had begun to demonstrate a commitment to improving economic conditions. As the *New York Times* proclaimed, there existed a "deep sense of gratitude among the Negroes for the benefits of the New Deal and the fact that the old traditions handed down to them in rather violent steps from the Civil War and reconstruction days are giving way." Besides appreciating the economic benefits of New Deal programs, African Americans also supported Roosevelt for the "recognition" they received from the federal government.[11] Expressing his faith in the Roosevelt administration, one *Pittsburgh Courier* writer stated, "Perhaps more than any other couple ever occupying the White House, President and Mrs. Roosevelt have demonstrated their friendliness and interest in the problems of colored Americans. . . . The couple . . . is setting an example in tolerance, sympathetic understanding and lack of color bias which all white America should follow."[12]

In addition, black men and women were also encouraged by a few progressive administrators. In the early years of the New Deal, some liberal-minded officials boldly confronted racial issues, most notably Interior Secretary Harold Ickes, former president of the Chicago chapter of the NAACP. Ickes viewed the New Deal as a potential vehicle in the battle against racial discrimination. In a letter to the NAACP assistant secretary, Roy Wilkins, in 1933, he confirmed his faith in interracialism: "I have long been interested in the advancement of the Negro, and I do not see how any fair-minded individual, either white or colored, can expect to advance the interests of the Negro if mutuality of contact is not established through the efforts of both races."[13] In addition, a white Georgian named Clark Foreman, who served under Ickes as "special advisor on the economic status of Negroes," sought to combat racial discrimination in government agencies such as the National Recovery Administration (NRA) and advocated on behalf of southern black farmers and workers. Two black intellectuals, Robert Weaver and William Hastie, who served in the Interior Department, exerted important influence within the small coterie of white liberals; it was Weaver and Hastie who successfully lobbied for the desegregation of the department's restrooms and cafeteria. Thus, while Roosevelt himself did not pronounce a commitment to racial reform during his first term, there were some within his administration who believed that African Americans could not go unrecognized.[14]

Although New Deal programs were a far cry from the kind of policies that African American leaders fought for, they nonetheless represented concrete efforts to bring the nation out of poverty. One black political scientist, Earl Brown, placed full confidence in a black Democratic electorate: "They [African Americans] will vote for Franklin D. Roosevelt in November because they are sick of the Abe Lincoln–Civil War claptrap and because they are still being fed by Roosevelt relief."[15] Well aware of this perception among African Americans, by 1936, Republicans made efforts to retain their previously unwavering constituency by harkening back to Lincoln's achievements and emphasizing the overwhelming influence of racist southern Democrats. These kinds of appeals, however, had come too late; although Republicans attacked the New Deal, they could not offer concrete evidence that they would provide a better alternative. By 1934, the number of registered black voters increased in urban areas, particularly following the continuous northern and midwestern black migration during the Depression. Cities with existing strong black communities, such as Washington, D.C., Chicago, and New York City, all witnessed sizable population increases in the 1930s; states such as Michigan, Missouri, and Pennsylvania witnessed growth in the black population by one-third. Thus, for many Democrats, the black vote became important in securing the party's victory in 1936; prospective candidates often could not avoid the topic of civil rights in their campaigns. As the *New York Times* described, one campaign to court the black vote in September 1936 emphasized an aggressive drive in the "pivotal Northern states, where the disposition of some 2,000,000 Negro votes may spell the difference between victory and defeat for Mr. Roosevelt."[16] For the first time, in 1936, black delegates attended the Democratic National Convention, an overture that Republicans were not willing to make.[17]

The newfound promise of the Democratic Party did not prevent black political organizations and individual men and women from immediately decrying discriminatory practices in New Deal agencies. As these agencies were largely decentralized during Roosevelt's first administration, the distribution of relief remained in the hands of local officials. Therefore, African Americans, who still largely resided in the South, faced widespread discrimination in the Civilian Conservation Corps (CCC), the Tennessee Valley Authority (TVA), and other federal agencies, which reinforced the southern political and racial hierarchy. Julian Harris of the *New York Times* described the damaging effects of the National Recovery Act for African American workers, frequently displaced or forced to accept wage differentials that southern manufacturers had instituted under the NRA codes.[18] In the NAACP's annual report in 1933, Executive Secretary Walter White charged that southern manufacturers "thinly disguised" wage differentials as geographical when they were in fact "placed into effect on a strictly

racial basis."[19] Echoing these sentiments, another *New York Times* writer declared, "the Blue Eagle [symbol of the NRA] may be a predatory bird instead of a feathered messenger of happiness."[20] African Americans also condemned Federal Emergency Relief Administration (FERA) director Harry Hopkins for rescinding the thirty-cent-per-hour minimum wage for work relief projects in Georgia. Claiming that the government "has abandoned the high idealism which marked the inception of the New Deal," one *Opportunity* editorial expressed intense disappointment with the Roosevelt administration's hypocrisy. As the government had originally provided African Americans with an unprecedented chance to attain a standard of living "infinitely better that they had ever dreamed of before," wage reductions within FERA, particularly in southern states, confirmed that the president was not holding true to his word.[21] "We question the wisdom of the administration in setting the seal of its approval on the wages of wretchedness," another *Opportunity* editorial proclaimed.[22]

Black individuals and organizations such as the NAACP also opposed the appointment of Clark Foreman, a white man, to the newly created position of "special advisor on the economic status of Negroes." As this was the first position within the New Deal that explicitly treated racial issues, for African Americans the administration's choice of a director symbolized the future course and tenor of federal race policy. As Alphonzo Harris, an employee in the Office of the Treasury and a pronounced "Roosevelt man," wrote to presidential secretary Louis Howe, "the colored man knows his plight better and more fully than anybody else and, if given the backing and the authority of the great United States Government he could work out his economic conditions to the satisfaction of the entire country."[23] Although Robert Weaver, an African American, held the position of Foreman's assistant and Harold Ickes assured African Americans that Foreman was "devoting his life" to the cause of racial justice, the idea of a white "expert" on racial issues did not sit well with many black Americans.[24] This debate over whether a white man could serve as a "Negro affairs" expert in the Department of the Interior would reemerge in the government's cultural bureaucracies as well. In short, the controversy over the appointment of Clark Foreman foreshadowed one of the major issues confronting officials in the development of federal racial policy for years to come.

The Roosevelt administration was cognizant of black criticism, as the president's colleagues and advisers alerted his staff to specific articles in the black press. Referring to a column (condemning the NRA) written by Kelly Miller in the *New York Amsterdam News*, prominent New York Democrat James Hoey wrote to presidential secretary Louis Howe, "you can see from this article that the negroes are looking to the President to do or say something in their behalf. I trust that this matter have earnest and prompt consideration."[25] One *New York Age* article tried to explain the scarcity of political appointments for African Americans since Roosevelt's election by claiming that black leaders were not accurate in charging that the administration had overlooked African Americans in the distribution of these positions. Making a distinction between black political leaders who "shoot at the moon" in seeking out as many posts for African Americans as possible and those who "feel that judgment should be exercised in making demands," the writer expressed his faith that the president would not exclude black men and women in formulating his agenda.[26] In a memo to Louis Howe, *New York Age* editor Lester Walton sought some reassurance that the president would be satisfied with the article's supportive posture: "I trust the editorial 'The Negro and Federal Jobs' . . . meets with the approval of the President."[27]

While these kinds of memos do not indicate how the president responded to individual appeals, they do reveal that correspondence on racial matters passed between administrators at the highest level. Many of those writing to or about Roosevelt admitted that the president and his administrators had not "made definite promises to Negroes and have been most careful not to"; nevertheless, the opinions of black leaders and editorial writers within the black press were taken into account by Roosevelt's advisers.[28] If the Roosevelt administration was still bound to its bastion of southern white supporters, officials ranging from liberals such as Ickes and Foreman to the more politically cautious Louis Howe nonetheless entertained racial issues brought to the president's attention and engaged in an interracial dialogue. These initial exchanges would inform the government's increasing attention to civil rights by the 1936 election, and by the second Roosevelt administration, officials would partially address the grievances of black political leaders. However, despite the administration's ostensible public focus on some racial issues by the second term, "caution and conservatism" still best characterized official policies concerning African Americans.[29]

By the mid-1930s, the topic of race relations had moved from isolated corridors into the New Deal's larger public discourse, due to the black Democratic electorate and the many white liberals who demonstrated a heightened racial awareness. No individual pronounced the federal commitment to civil rights as publicly and as controversially as Eleanor Roosevelt. Before her husband's presidential election, Eleanor Roosevelt did not harbor strong feelings concerning civil rights and was not particularly aware of the major obstacles confronting black men and women. This detachment would soon change as the first lady formed close friendships with the National Youth Administration's Negro Affairs director Mary McLeod Bethune, NAACP executive secretary Walter White, and other black political leaders who exposed her to pervasive discrimination and successfully lobbied her to pursue the cause of racial justice. In an address at the twenty-fifth anniversary of the National Urban League, Mrs. Roosevelt emphasized the need for African Americans to achieve improved standards of living, better education, and an end to racial violence. "In fact we know that many grave injustices are done throughout the land to people who are citizens and who have an equal right under the laws of our country," the first lady proclaimed, "but who are handicapped because of their race."[30] By 1936, Mrs. Roosevelt had become active in the anti–poll tax campaign and the struggle to procure a federal antilynching bill. Although lambasted by southerners—both in Congress and around the country— she continued to advocate openly on behalf of African Americans. Like other interracialists, such as Ickes and Foreman, Mrs. Roosevelt believed that the New Deal provided the possibility for liberal reform and that the federal government should be responsible for eliminating impediments to black advancement.[31]

Like Mrs. Roosevelt, other New Dealers connected progressive social reform and racial equality. In his 1936 speech before the NAACP, Harold Ickes highlighted the fact that the New Deal's "conception of democracy" would be particularly beneficial for the African American "because he pre-eminently belongs to the class that the new democracy is designed especially to aid."[32] Giving meaning to these words, Ickes implemented legislation within the Public Works Administration (PWA) requiring the employment of both unskilled and skilled black laborers; PWA contracts featured a clause requiring that the percentage of African Americans hired on the project payroll match the percentage of African Americans in the 1930 census. As historian Harvard Sitkoff indicates, this system encouraged more inclusionary policies, most significantly in the housing built by the PWA, where black Americans comprised a third of the occupants.[33]

Like Ickes, wpa director Harry Hopkins also had a background in social reform; as executive head of the New York City Board of Child Welfare and director of New York's Tuberculosis Association, he pressed the president to endorse more inclusionary reform policies, targeting groups that had not traditionally been part of federal relief programs. Although the black press had criticized Hopkins for wage reductions within FERA, in his role as wpa director Hopkins worked to eliminate racial discrimination in relief projects, a view the president publicly endorsed in a 1935 speech to state Works Progress administrators. "We cannot discriminate in any of the work we are conducting," said Roosevelt, "either because of race or religion or politics."[34] Hopkins took this directive to heart; influenced by both Eleanor Roosevelt and Deputy Administrator Aubrey Williams, Hopkins worked to ensure that the wpa abided by antidiscriminatory policies. While African Americans in southern states still encountered obstacles in getting on wpa relief rolls, the wpa did make a significant difference in the economic lives of black men and women; one estimate states that by 1939, the wpa sustained a million black families.[35] The wpa also provided an elaborate education program, where hundreds of thousands of African Americans received basic literacy skills, while many others worked as teachers or received vocational training. Still, as Patricia Sullivan contends, Hopkins's own political aspirations often prevented his involvement in eradicating discriminatory implementation methods in the South; like so many other New Deal politicians, he walked a fine line, promoting those policies that would recognize African Americans but would not exasperate his southern colleagues. In this atmosphere, the wpa arts programs provided Hopkins the space to address racial issues without immediately provoking the southern constituency.[36]

In addition, African Americans came to believe in the progressive capacity of the New Deal due to the work of southern interracialists such as Aubrey Williams, head of the National Youth Administration (NYA), and Will Alexander, director of the Farm Security Administration (FSA). Active in civil rights organizations such as the Commission on Interracial Cooperation, the Southern Commission for Human Welfare, and the Southern Tenant Farmers Union, Williams and Alexander were often the most fervent advocates of civil rights within the New Deal administration. At the NYA, Williams pressed for black involvement in all skilled manpower programs. The NYA forbade wage differentials based on geography or race and provided many African Americans with a college education by extending its student aid program to all-black colleges. Like Williams, Will Alexander worked to ameliorate the economic discrepancy between blacks and whites by providing thousands of black farmers and sharecroppers with loans. One statistic reported that over half of the families on FSA rental cooperatives were black; African Americans also represented 25 percent of the families living on FSA homestead projects. Moreover, under Will Alexander, the FSA employed a higher percentage of black supervisors than any other New Deal agency.[37]

While many African Americans applauded the work of white liberals, they also came to view the New Deal as a welcoming space for African American intellectuals and politicians, due to the presence of a number of black administrators and advisers. By the mid-1930s a "Black Cabinet" formed, including individuals such as William Hastie, Robert Vann, Ralph Bunch, Robert Weaver, Rayford Logan, and Mary McLeod Bethune. In addition, a 1936 report prepared by the National Colored Committee revealed that in addition to more noted black leaders such as Bethune and Weaver, there were also African American advisers in the WPA, the CCC, the Treasury Department, the Department of Commerce, the Farm Credit Administration, and the Department of Labor.[38] This emerging black bureaucracy demonstrated that under the Roosevelt administration, white administrators were less able to implement policy without considering the opinions of civil rights leaders and advisers. And as African American administrators fought for several causes such as the abolition of the poll tax, antilynching legislation, and more elaborate antidiscriminatory measures, they encouraged white leaders to understand that the achievement of racial justice was a critical component of New Deal liberalism.

Undoubtedly, black officials made it clear that demands for racial equality would not vanish; looking to expand opportunities for all African Americans, the Black Cabinet became a unique channel for publicizing the actions of the Roosevelt administration, often in the black press. As with the New Deal's economic programs, a black bureaucracy also existed within state cultural programs; individuals such as Sterling Brown, Carlton Moss, and Truman Gibson wielded the same kind of influence that black leaders such as Mary McLeod Bethune exerted in the National Youth Administration.

All of these factors interacted within a political and ideological climate that prompted the Roosevelt administration's leftward turn. The emergence of a Popular Front against Fascism in 1935 gave credence to the New Deal's democratic ethos, ushering in a new vision of American pluralism by seeking out the voices of workers, African Americans, and

ethnic minorities. Throughout the 1930s, the Communist Party had established its willingness to combat racial injustice, both through the International Labor Defense during the Scottsboro trials, and through attempts to
organize workers and sharecroppers in the black belt. Many Popular Front
organizations also campaigned against lynching and labor discrimination,
emphasizing the formation of a social democratic labor party in America,
aligning farmers and workers. In short, the radical Left promoted a broad
vision of social equality. When the Communist Party famously claimed,
"Communism is Twentieth-Century Americanism," it signaled a shift, not
necessarily in the popular adoption of Marxist ideologies, but rather in
the embrace of a new leftist cultural framework. Here, the federal government's recognition of African Americans became part of a larger political
struggle on behalf of the "forgotten man." As historian Michael Denning
explains, individuals wove in and out of New Deal programs and Popular Front organizations rather seamlessly, fomenting a proletarian-based
cultural renaissance. Thus, the formation of the inclusionary Congress of
Industrial Organizations (CIO), opposition to totalitarianism abroad, and
the ambition of the New Deal all fostered an atmosphere conducive for
civil rights reform.[39]

While over time all of these factors contributed to black Americans'
increasing support for Roosevelt, the president would never support any
far-reaching structural change. The political composition of Congress
posed the most formidable obstacle to the passage of any racial legislation. During both the Roosevelt and Truman administrations, southerners
accounted for no less than 40 percent of Democrats in Congress, chairing
about half of the committees. Although many southern politicians became
increasingly critical of the Roosevelt administration after 1936, particularly
after the enactment of some antidiscriminatory policies in relief agencies,
their consistent presence within the Democratic Party forced the president
to take a more moderate position on civil rights. New Deal political scientists Ira Katznelson, Kim Geiger, and Daniel Kryder assert that, "even at the
height of the New Deal, the Democratic party required the acquiescence of
southern representatives, who as potential coalition partners for Republicans could, if they chose, block the national program."[40]

Although Roosevelt's attention to African Americans became more pronounced by his second term, he never endorsed civil rights as a priority
within his agenda, nor did he exhibit the determination of his wife or liberals such as Alexander and Foreman. This was in part because the president had less sympathy when it came to racial issues. Roosevelt's unwill-

ing posture, however, was also due to southern loyalty. While Roosevelt understood that African Americans formed an important bastion of political support within the Democratic coalition, and thus they necessitated some recognition from his administration, he was never willing to provoke the hostility of southern Democrats by advocating wide-scale racial legislation. As New Deal historian William Leuchtenburg asserts, "If the President assaulted the barriers of Jim Crow, neither southern blacks, few of whom could even go to the polls, nor white liberals in the South, who were a decided minority on racial issues, could have given him the backing he would have needed."[41] Thus, while the Roosevelt administration proved far more racially progressive than any of its predecessors, and while liberals such as Ickes, Williams, and Alexander worked on behalf of African Americans, in the end, New Dealers could not meet the most pressing demands of black political leaders.[42]

Roosevelt's reluctance to support a federal antilynching law illustrates the importance to him of maintaining southern support, as well as his attitude toward some civil rights leaders. Early in 1933, in an address to the Federal Council of Churches of Christ in America, Roosevelt strongly denounced lynching as a "vile form of collective murder . . . which has broken out in our midst anew."[43] Although Roosevelt continued to condemn the practice of lynching in some public settings, he did not intervene when some northern and most southern Democrats filibustered federal antilynching bills, first in 1935 and again in 1938. Roosevelt's support of the antilynching bill would have completely alienated southerners in Congress, splitting the Democratic Party and sounding the death knell for all future New Deal programs. Because many African Americans looked to the president for support of a federal antilynching bill over the course of the 1930s, black politicians and activists, including Oscar DePriest, Charles Houston, and James Weldon Johnson, regarded his unwillingness to oppose a southern filibuster as a sign of hypocrisy. Houston warned Roosevelt that his failure to support the Costigan-Wagner antilynching bill in 1935 might cost him the black vote in the 1936 election; by 1938, when Roosevelt continued to remain silent, NAACP president J. E. Spingarn declared that Roosevelt's indifference would be a "fatal blow to those of us who have accepted your leadership."[44]

The most persistent black politician on the antilynching legislation, however, was Walter White, who flooded the president with letters stressing the importance of this legislation. Presenting the president with Senate polls, reports of recent lynchings, and a large collection of articles featured in southern newspapers that opposed the filibuster, White attempted to present overwhelming evidence that the bill was not only a national priority but that many southerners supported it, disgusted by the "demagogic utterances of a small group of so-called Southern statesmen."[45] While the president, largely under the urging of Mrs. Roosevelt, engaged in frequent correspondence with White and met with him on more than one occasion, Roosevelt and his advisers always believed that he personally could not take a strong stance on this kind of legislation. Presidential assistant William Hassett warned that it would be "entirely too dangerous" for the president to attend an NAACP annual convention to discuss the "problem of lynching" upon the invitation of Walter White; in response, the president wished the NAACP a "most successful meeting" but declined to attend.[46] Furthermore, White's correspondence increasingly irritated the president. Roosevelt adviser Stephen Early related that White had been "bombarding" the president with his letters and that some of his writing was "decidedly insulting." Early targeted White's criticism of the president in relation to the antilynching bill as evidence of his disrespect; in addition, he noted that White "has been one of the worst and most continuous of trouble makers" even before Roosevelt stepped into office.[47] After reading Early's memo, Mrs. Roosevelt revealed a much more sympathetic position towards White, relating that although he "has an obsession on the lynching question," this position was understandable among African Americans who had undergone consistent persecution. However, Mrs. Roosevelt also claimed that White's behavior was part of an "inferiority complex" that fueled overly aggressive behavior, noting, "it is worse with Walter White because he is almost white."[48] Although Mrs. Roosevelt made this statement in 1935, before she engaged in civil rights activism, her correspondence reveals the volatile nature of White's relationship with the administration, even among his staunchest supporters.

The administration's response to calls for antilynching legislation was indicative of the official response to all matters that seemed politically impractical. While Roosevelt and his advisers did not dismiss racial issues, they also did not garner the level of federal commitment that both black leaders and many white liberals expected. Political scientist Kevin McMahon provides evidence that Roosevelt exhibited a great degree of racial progressivism in his Supreme Court appointments and within the Justice Department; however, it would take time before African Americans could perceive the tangible effects of judicial reform.[49] With an immediate need to reach out to African Americans by 1936, New Dealers turned to alternative methods. Balancing the interests of black voters and conservative white southern politicians was a tenuous proposition; to receive and maintain the support of African American voters, New Dealers sought a sustained—but more politically sanitized—treatment of racial issues.

Art and Government

The Federal Arts Project would come to offer an effective form of racial policy that officials had not initially considered. Only after New Dealers began to support a white-collar relief program did they determine the central role that African Americans would play within it. The very notion of a government-sponsored cultural program was progressive in and of itself; in previous decades, art and entertainment had existed solely as private or commercial enterprises. Yet as industrial capitalism exposed its fallibility after the crash of 1929, America would begin a process of national self-exploration, a rethinking of all aspects of society. As radical Michael Gold argued of the Depression, "whatever comes of it, it marks a great turning point in the consciousness of the American nation. . . . We are at the beginning of some new germination whose form is still veiled in the mysteries of the womb."[50] For intellectuals and policy makers alike, a search began for a new sense of authentic American culture—one that championed national values and traditions by celebrating regional and racial diversity. Describing the ideological renaissance that would come to emphasize America's rich communities, cultural visionary Lewis Mumford pronounced, "More public good has come out of the bankruptcy of the economic order than ever came regularly out of its flatulent prosperity."[51]

During the 1930s, cultural programs reflected the larger ambition of the New Deal. Before the development of the FAP, the federal government had supported music and art on a more isolated and sporadic basis. Although Roosevelt was not an art aficionado, his elite background had exposed him to classical music, theater, and art. Thus, throughout his life, Roosevelt had believed that the principle of access to the arts was "as logical as access to the ballot box or schoolhouse."[52] As governor of New York, Roosevelt, with his state relief director Harry Hopkins, had employed needy artists under the supervision of New York's City College Art Associations. Before 1932, more than one hundred artists in New York were part of a state-sponsored program of teaching and painting murals for settlement houses.[53] With the 1932 election, the Roosevelt administration ushered in radically new ideas about the federal role in providing economic aid. By substituting work relief for direct relief under programs such as the Federal Emergency Relief Act of 1933, the Roosevelt administration furthered progressive ideas that valued individual skills and sought community-building enterprises.[54] Particularly significant was the administration's acknowledgement of white-collar unemployment, which had previously gone unnoticed in contrast to the plight of manual workers.

When the president appointed Harry Hopkins as director of the FERA, Hopkins conducted a survey of 180,000 families revealing the unutilized skills of white-collar workers, including artists and writers. With these findings, Hopkins set out to develop a program that would combine the financial needs of white-collar workers with the aesthetic improvement of the country.[55] In the early 1930s, New Dealers such as Hopkins lamented the inaccessibility of fine art venues. Most theaters and art galleries were located in major metropolitan areas; one estimate concludes that only one in ten Americans had seen a famous work of art. Even in urban areas such as New York City, there were only approximately two dozen art galleries. The same applied to dramatic theater and symphonies, which did not frequently tour smaller communities. Thus, most Americans turned to mass entertainment—movies, radio, and magazines. Furthermore, as sound films and recordings lessened the need for live actors and technicians, many faced technological unemployment. In response, Hopkins and his administrators envisioned a federal arts program with a focus on regional art centers and touring companies, which would solve the problem of cultural scarcity while providing jobs to those displaced by the film and recording industries.[56]

Under the New Deal, the first large-scale endeavor of federally sponsored art came in the Public Works of Art Project (PWAP), established as part of the Civil Works Administration (CWA) in 1933. This project hired painters and sculptors to work on government buildings in forty-eight states; in its eighteen-month duration, the PWAP gave jobs to 3,600 artists and created 16,000 pieces of art.[57] Largely the brainchild of artists George Biddle and Edward Bruce, the PWAP was the first national art project, employing artists on the basis of reputation and talent. Biddle, a painter from a prominent Philadelphia family and brother of future attorney general Frances Biddle, had formed a relationship with Roosevelt at Groton and Harvard. Influenced by artists such as Mary Cassatt and Diego Rivera, Biddle expressed the philosophy that art should serve a social purpose. Biddle's experiences with Mexican muralists after the Mexican Revolution also inspired him to press for a program linking art to relief. Edward Bruce, who would administer the PWAP from Washington, served as president of

AMBIVALENT INCLUSION

the Pacific Development Company before turning to painting as a career. Although he exhibited his artwork for ten years, the Treasury Department eventually recruited Bruce to advise international monetary concerns. As an advocate of both art and government patronage, Bruce was a likely partner for Biddle in securing the PWAP.[58]

Bruce, Biddle, and Hopkins represented the ideologies of a host of cultural enthusiasts who would form the backbone of the FAP. When, in 1935, New Dealers confronted the fact that both the CWA and FERA were not extensive enough to address the needs of the millions still unemployed, they devised a new, more ambitious program based entirely on work relief. Authorizing five billion dollars for this purpose, the Emergency Relief Appropriation Act, which established the Works Progress Administration in May 1935, became the largest single appropriation at the time. In August of that same year, the president extended allocations to the WPA for the establishment of the FAP, which had divisions in music, theater, art, and writing. Jacob Baker, who worked in the FERA and was Hopkins's assistant administrator of the CWA, became Hopkins's assistant administrator of the WPA and the director of the FAP.[59]

Officials couched blueprints for the FAP in the language of relief, and 90 percent of all FAP employees were required to come from welfare rolls. Yet, this emphasis on employment should not obscure the aesthetic goals of Roosevelt, Hopkins, and the directors of the federal arts projects. Prominent sculptor Gutzon Borglum described Hopkins's artistic vision: "Mr. Hopkins . . . has opened the door, a crack, but opened to this great field of human interest and thought. The world of creative impulse, without which people perish."[60] Liberal administrators understood art to be a tool of reform, as community theater, concerts in the park, and painting classes could improve living in lower-income regions. As a democratizing force, a federal arts program would create a community of "cultural consumers," whose lives would be enriched by access to music, theater, and visual art. With highbrow/lowbrow distinctions ostensibly muted, more Americans could partake in the kind of culture that New Dealers viewed as socially uplifting.[61]

One of the staunchest proponents for the democratization of the arts was Holger Cahill, the director of the Federal Art Project (the fine arts section within the FAP). Cahill, former director of exhibitions at the New York Museum of Modern Art and a former curator at the Newark Museum under John Cotton Dana, had conducted art classes for immigrants and had developed some of the first exhibits of American folk art. Having been a student at the New School for Social Research and Columbia University, Cahill admired the philosophy of John Dewey, who argued that art derived value from participation rather than observation.[62] Likewise, Hallie Flanagan, director of the Federal Theatre Project, became crucial in advocating the vision of a cultural democracy. After Flanagan took part in the 47 Workshop under famed director George Pierce Baker at Harvard, she became one of the first women to hold a Guggenheim Fellowship. It allowed her to study theater in revolutionary Russia; a devotee of regionalism, she insisted that "only a theatre which springs from or penetrates into city, town, village and farm can be called American theater."[63] In addition, the director of the Federal Writers' Project, Henry Alsberg, expressed an equal faith in producing "art for the millions." After a brief stint in law, Alsberg became a journalist in 1913, first working for the *New York Evening Post* and then abroad as a foreign correspondent to the *Nation* and the *London Daily Herald*. He, like Flanagan, visited Bolshevik Russia several times and later became a director of the American Joint Distribution Committee, which aided famine victims of the Russian Revolution.[64] Federal Music Project director Nikolai Sokoloff, conductor of the Cleveland Symphony, was, however, the least devoted to the popular arts. Committed to employing only the most talented, professionally trained musicians, Sokoloff argued that the masses could only be culturally educated by exposure to "good music." Expressing little interest in folk music or any other nontraditional musical contributions, Sokoloff attempted to conserve the traditional notion of "high culture" more so than directors of other projects did. Certainly, the Federal Music Project was dedicated to providing music for as many communities as possible; however, Sokoloff emphasized musicians' talent and pedigree over the potential benefit for audiences.[65]

As was the case with Flanagan, Alsberg, and Cahill, most individuals involved in the Federal Arts Project were liberal intellectuals committed to social reform. The pluralistic, democratic ideologies of many intellectuals, such as Van Wyck Brooks and Constance Rourke, resonated strongly during the Depression and became central to the content of the arts projects. As historian Alfred Jones describes the search for a new "useable past," "The leveling influence of the Depression encouraged an emphasis upon the classless, inclusive character of the national experience."[66] The fusion of culture and politics took place as intellectuals not only administered state cultural programs but also cultivated a New Deal sensibility based on both a discovery of America's folk roots and celebration of a new national character.

ONCE ADMINISTRATORS BEGAN TO DEVELOP the components of the Federal Arts Project, it became clear that these government-sponsored programs would not only employ African Americans but would represent them in contributory fashion. While theater or writing projects did not address Walter White's pleas for structural legislation, they did address another goal of the NAACP—to eradicate racial stereotypes and to preserve black cultural autonomy. Furthermore, art projects proved to be much less politically threatening—at least initially—in the eyes of southern politicians. For the directors of these projects, particularly Hallie Flanagan and Henry Alsberg, developing the national culture was essential in procuring a racial democracy. However, in their production, federal art projects wavered between promoting progressive materials and containing racially charged content. Facing constant bureaucratic entanglements and the looming threat of congressional opposition, administrators and participants understood cultural development as a consistently complex and often repressive endeavor. What had initially emerged as sites of unbounded possibility quickly revealed tight parameters. Yet, even within this restrictive atmosphere, African Americans seized the opportunity to write their own history, to act in unconventional roles, and to serve as administrators of this new national culture. The struggle for "cultural emancipation" had indeed begun.

chapter two

HOOKED ON CLASSICS

"Drama is culture, and the culture of the race portends its advancement," John Silvera wrote in his foreword to a list of "representative plays" of the Federal Theatre Project's (FTP) Negro Units, "a new era is dawning for the Negro artist." For a black administrator such as Silvera, the Negro Units represented a space for cultivating new talent among black playwrights and performing socially relevant material. Silvera and others struggled to establish criteria for African American drama: "Is the play a competent piece of craftsmanship? Is the theme a possible situation? Would its presentation be acceptable by and for Negro audiences?"[1] Several productions fit this description and indeed transformed the nature of theater in the 1930s, not only in their racially charged content, but also because most Americans had never attended a live production until that period.

Of the Negro Unit productions, the most popular and successful was the *Swing Mikado* (1938), a syncopated version of the classic Gilbert and Sullivan comedic operetta depicting romantic mishaps and political foils in nineteenth-century Japan.[2] On 31 December 1938, the *Chicago Defender* proudly reported that the *Swing Mikado* had captivated Secretary of the Interior Harold Ickes; although Ickes had initially planned to attend only half of the performance, the first number was compelling enough to keep him in his seat for the rest of the evening. For Ickes, the *Swing Mikado* exemplified his own progressive inclinations on racial matters, as he exclaimed: "No people . . . can consistently be suppressed on the basis of race, color or creed, when they persist in making cultural contributions of real importance and benefit."[3]

Ickes's condemnation of widespread inequality would not translate into an executive policy barring institutionalized racism. Still, the FTP's Negro

Units represented an important policy initiative in offering employment to black theatrical workers and in providing them with roles that countered the stereotypes frequently found in commercial theater. Indeed, the motivation for developing separate black units of the FTP and large-scale productions like the *Swing Mikado* was to employ black theatrical workers and bring socially provocative entertainment to both black and white communities. However, as a live, interactive genre, theater proved to be a highly contested vehicle in the construction of government-sponsored culture. While the FTP's Negro Units represented the government's mission to acknowledge and celebrate American diversity, the development of a black theater also engendered debates over the nature of administration as well as competing definitions of a black American aesthetic.

Central to the administration of the Negro Units was the Play Bureau, an editorial unit that selected and developed plays based on a constantly evolving set of criteria. The primarily white playreaders often reevaluated what constituted relevant theater, and they arrived at inconsistent opinions when scrutinizing the structure and content of a "Negro play." When the bureau's reviewers rejected certain plays as "inappropriate" or accepted them as "appropriate," and when directors championed black musicals such as the *Swing Mikado*, they demarcated particular notions of black culture. Whether advocating race-related themes that they believed were most pressing or "blackening" classic productions, theater project administrators privileged particular visions of African Americans as more authentic reflections of black life and more indicative of black artistic talent.

Even while operating within these narrowly proscribed spaces, African American performers promoted a diverse series of racial representations, expanding theatrical roles beyond the confines of conventional racial stereotypes. This is not to say that Negro Unit plays were subtle in their promotion of racial justice: some of the first plays selected drew on themes of unionism, black solidarity, and discrimination. Socially conscious plays such as *Big White Fog* (1938) and *Turpentine* (1936) offered the kind of descriptions of racial inequality that Federal Writers' Project (FWP) administrator Sterling Brown would urge state directors to include in editing the American Guide Series.

From the beginning, federal officials conceived of the Negro Units as separate entities within the FTP. Although black actors sometimes performed in productions that featured mostly white players, FTP administrators viewed the Negro Units as a hallmark for black theater. While other ethnically or nationally based units existed within the FTP, such as a Yiddish vaudeville unit, a German unit, a French theater, an Italian theater, and an Anglo-Jewish theater, the separateness of the Negro Units is particularly significant because it was strongly advocated by black theatrical workers.[4] Unlike the initial goals of Sterling Brown in the FWP, these dramatists did not hope to integrate black theater into the mainstream but instead aimed to build upon earlier black repertories such the Krigwa Players and the Lafayette Players. Like these dramatists, the Negro Units could promote African American playwrights, directors, and actors, providing socially significant material for black audiences. The goals of developing an organic black theater remained particular to the genre and would continue to resonate into the postwar era, particularly in the Black Arts Movement. Yet, within other genres of government-sponsored culture— the writing of the American Guide Series and wartime films—visions of racial separatism were regarded by some black intellectuals and political leaders at least as a shortcoming and, by the 1940s, inimical to a racial democracy.

From their onset, FTP productions were drawing in audiences and garnering enthusiastic reviews; however, by 1937, intense congressional scrutiny into New Deal relief programs targeted the Federal Arts Project. The theater division received the most criticism among the FAPs, largely due to the radicalism of its director, Hallie Flanagan, but also in relation to the "liveness" of the genre. Congressional investigations of the FTP intensified by 1938, and as WPA budget cuts anticipated the eventual demise of the project, administrative opinions shifted on what constituted "suitable" black theater. For some producers, such as the *Swing Mikado*'s Harry Minturn, the classic musical became a preferred performance genre.

Yet it would be a mistake to attribute this support for musical theater solely to anti–New Deal agitation. Even before those involved in the FTP testified before the House Un-American Activities Committee (HUAC), the FTP's Play Bureau considered musical elements as a positive feature of most scripts. Following the success of the New York City Negro Unit's performance of *Macbeth* (1936), FTP administrators looked to other representations of classical theater that could successfully be "blackened." When *The Mikado* ranked at the top of audience preference surveys, directors realized that a performance with an all-black cast might appeal to white audiences, while providing black actors with roles outside of minstrel caricatures.[5]

The *Swing Mikado* did produce the major outcome that directors de-

HOOKED ON CLASSICS

sired—the show was a hit, running for five months as a sold-out venture. Yet the performance was not the more politically sanitized vehicle that administrators hoped for. Even in the absence of direct racial themes evoked in other FTP plays such as *Big White Fog* and *Stevedore* (1934), the *Swing Mikado* had significant political implications for black performers on two levels. First, the show provided black actors with new, unconventional roles that had previously been the sole province of their white counterparts. Second, in its "swingcopation"—an alteration of the traditional music to a swing tempo, some lyrical shifts, and a change of locale—the *Swing Mikado* offered a black American rendering of the Anglo fantasies that Gilbert and Sullivan had so successfully popularized and commodified. The process of cultural development leading up to the *Swing Mikado* and the debates about the show that followed illustrate the multiplicity of interests at stake in the performance of African American identity. In the FTP, as Los Angeles Negro Unit director Clarence Muse would assert, "the whole thing was political . . . this was politics to the ninth degree."[6]

The dynamics within the Negro Units are significant for what they reveal about the larger history of national cultural development. First, understanding the criteria the Play Bureau imposed in selecting Negro Unit performances demonstrates how complex the issue of racial representation had come to be. As questions abounded over what constituted a "Negro play" or "Negro themes," officials advanced particular narratives while discarding others. The development of an African American theater centered on those topics that playreaders stated were relevant and acceptable to both black and white audiences, rather than the sole employment of black playwrights, actors, or technicians. This selection process starkly contrasted with the ideas of an organic black theater offered by artists and intellectuals at the outset of the FTP, which in and of itself reflected varying opinions within the African American community.

Second, the evolution and production of a large-scale performance such as the *Swing Mikado* illustrates how many factors—Play Bureau preferences, the success of other classical productions, and Congress's rising hostility to the FTP—influenced the nature of black theater. Black political leaders and artists offered their opinions and perspectives, which were often taken into account; however no single interest group (and certainly not the Communist Party, as HUAC alleged) was the final arbiter in determining the plays that Negro Units performed. Lastly, the *Swing Mikado* illustrates a theme that will resonate throughout the book: even if the production did not advance the cultural or political themes that many African

Americans had long advocated, it still offered artistic agency to those black men and women involved in the creative process. As the *Swing Mikado* was inspired by African American dance and musical improvisation and performed entirely by black actors in a new setting, the meaning it offered contrasted with its white predecessor.

FTP *Beginnings: A Director Is Born*

Including theater as one of four arts programs was never a question in the mind of WPA director Harry Hopkins. Hopkins, who understood theater to be "part of, and not apart from, everyday existence," set out to create an ambitious theatrical undertaking, by bringing various forms of performance to all American regions.[7] Although the structure of the FTP was unspecified at its inception, Hopkins sought to acknowledge the legitimacy of actors as workers and thus to pay their salaries through federal support. With as many as 25,000 unemployed actors, technicians, craftsmen, and other theatrical workers, the task of creating an employment program that developed productions of quality and breadth seemed daunting.[8] Hopkins, however, expressed his determination: "The Federal Theatre project has not only the purpose of providing employment to unemployed theatre workers, but also the purpose of meeting the great public demand for instruction in amateur dramatic work. . . . The aim is to turn the director's mind toward the environmental and economic problems of the people in his community, to give him new understanding of his position as dramatic spokesman for the community and provide him with a method for dealing with its psychological and emotional needs."[9]

To promote this agenda, Hopkins first had to select a project director. His choice of Hallie Flanagan, a former classmate at Grinnell College, revealed his larger aims for an experimental theater program. Flanagan, who built a theater program at Grinnell in 1919, attracted the interest of George Pierce Baker, conductor of the esteemed 47 Workshop at Harvard. Like other 47 Workshop alumni such as Eugene O'Neill, Van Wyck Brooks, and George Abbott, Flanagan was immersed in playwriting techniques fostered by a "cooperative, self-sustaining, theatrical laboratory." Flanagan became Baker's production assistant and most remarkably demonstrated her talent for writing in a satirical comedy entitled *Incense*.[10] After receiving a master's degree from Radcliffe in 1924, Flanagan became director of an experimental theater program at Vassar College. By 1926, Flanagan's artistic achievements at Vassar had earned her a Guggenheim Fellowship for study of the European theater—the first to be awarded to a woman.[11]

Hallie Flanagan, national director of the Federal Theatre Project. (Library of Congress)

It was during her time abroad that Flanagan's theatrical vision most firmly crystallized. She found great inspiration in post-Bolshevik Russia, where Russian actors, directors, and designers invented new forms of theatrical expression. As the Russian theater served as a forum for social and political opinion, it fulfilled Flanagan's hope that the genre could promote a dialogue between actors and patrons, revealing "inner life and values." While she noted that the theater was frequently a source for disseminating propaganda, Flanagan believed that Russian artists had elevated the stage beyond mere entertainment or luxury to become a vital center for community building. As Russian dramatists performed in schools, prisons, villages, and factories, they broadened the medium to a more democratic enterprise.[12] In 1934, Flanagan returned to Europe, where she marveled at the creativity of Greek and Roman theater and the exhaustiveness of plays that reached into small villages and traveled on open trucks. Most significant, she found that Greek productions were funded by the state. Flanagan commented of one production, "whatever had gone on had evidently been worth paying for out of government money, for this theatre had been erected and the plays put on at the expense of the government."[13]

These observations would inform Flanagan's work as FTP director.

When the Roosevelt administration established the WPA in April 1935, with a provision for unemployed theater workers, Hopkins called on Flanagan. Upon her arrival in Washington, Flanagan was courted by many New Dealers, who suggested she direct the new program. Hopkins asserted his confidence that audiences would attend theater put on by relief workers, and that relief appropriation could meet the needs of those in the industry. Setting aside the framework of expensive Broadway productions, Eleanor Roosevelt suggested that quality performances could exist on the same small budget Flanagan utilized in the Vassar theater. Flanagan embraced the opportunity to be part of the new Federal Arts Program, particularly at the first meeting with the other arts project directors. She reminisced:

> It was one of those evenings in which everything seemed possible. . . . We believed that we would find on relief rolls people with energy, ability, and talent to achieve any program we set up. We thought of old and young artists working together in an apprentice and master relationship. . . . All of us had lives at one time or another in small towns and we believed that such communities would show great interest in concerts, plays, and art exhibits offered at prices people could afford to pay. . . . The art projects were being set up to deal with physical hunger, but was there not another form of hunger with which we would rightly be concerned, the hunger of millions of Americans for plays, pictures, and books?[14]

Flanagan's feeling of exuberance, the sense of possibility that she had witnessed in Europe and created at Vassar, remained with her as she executed the position of FTP director. As FTP deputy national director Robert Schnitzer recalled, "There was a team feeling. This was one of the things that Hallie could develop, an absolutely 'gang feeling' that we were all out for something together. I've never in my life felt that peak of idealism and of accomplishment."[15] Like all the arts project directors, Flanagan understood that the theater program was an unprecedented effort with great national significance. This seemingly limitless sense of ambition is what fueled the most experimental and often controversial productions, offering unique opportunities to both FTP employees and patrons.

As a woman heading a large-scale government operation, Flanagan garnered much press attention. Referring to her as a "Woman Dictator," the *New York News* exclaimed, "her word is absolute and final. She wields autocratic authority. She is the biggest boss of show business the world has ever known."[16] Although other newspapers did not depict Flanagan in such militaristic language, they nonetheless emphasized her deft leadership qualities in highly gendered terms. "Hallie is responsible for everything: hiring, firing, every little detail down to the last vase of flowers," *New York Woman* reported. "She makes drastic changes . . . but she's kept her skirts clean and her reputation intact." Admiring the tenacity and versatility of this "Little Woman with a Big Job," *New York Woman* particularly reveled in Flanagan's ability to maintain romance in her marriage to Vassar professor Philip Davis while undertaking all facets of the FTP.[17] With less attention to Flanagan's physical characteristics and personal life, *New York Times* journalist Brooks Atkinson still revealed the same admiration for Flanagan's vision and managerial capacities: "Although many people in the Federal Theatre succumbed to the emotional frenzy . . . Mrs. Flanagan remained cool and confident. . . . From the beginning she has been the graveyard of all doubts about the project."[18]

Once Flanagan became FTP director, she quickly implemented plans for the structure of the project. Flanagan and others had conceived the idea of setting up five regional centers with both touring and production companies. These flagship offices would train actors and aid playwrights with research and technical services. The goal for each regional office would be to establish relationships with local theaters and universities and develop community dramas based on local history and heritage. Arts project directors would develop major policies in Washington, D.C., that would then be implemented by the regional directors and state officials. Flanagan's ultimate selection of regional directors reflected her own preference for small community theaters—only a few individuals had Broadway backgrounds. Regional, state, and city directors included E. C. Mabie of the University of Iowa Theatre (Midwest region), Thomas Wood Stevens, former director of the Department of Drama at the Carnegie Institute and an alumnus of the Wisconsin School of Players (Chicago region), and John McGhee, director of the Birmingham Little Theatre (South region). The large task of New York City director went to playwright-producer Elmer Rice, president of the nascent Theatre Alliance, who had first assisted Flanagan in the general development and conceptualization of the FTP. Significantly, the selection of these directors was based on their ability to envision the theater beyond a commercial institution. As Hopkins stressed, the foundation of the FTP required individuals who knew "the profits won't be money profits."[19] As the controversy over the *Swing Mikado* would later demonstrate, this initial emphasis on the noncommercial aspect of the project would later lead many in Congress to question the economic purpose of federal relief programs.

Within the FTP, men and women could take artistic risks by utilizing new techniques and tackling nontraditional subject matter. In addition to developing regional units, Flanagan and the other FTP directors also undertook plans for a children's theater, a vaudeville unit, dramatics in Civilian Conservation Corps (CCC) camps, and a separate theater for black stage employees. The program also developed various ethnic divisions, classical theater, radio, and the Living Newspaper—dramatic enactments of contemporary issues. As the majority of WPA funds went to the wages of relief workers, individuals could rely on a stable paycheck that small regional theaters could not provide.[20] One estimate indicates that the FTP employed an average of 10,000 theater workers annually and that productions collectively drew audiences of more than 65 million from forty states.[21] Between 1935 and 1939, the FTP put on 830 major productions and smaller plays; admission to plays was free or minimal.[22]

The possibilities available to both black and white FTP employees were largely due to the progressive nature of Flanagan's vision. "The theatre must become conscious of the implications of the changing social order," Flanagan warned regional directors, "or the changing social order will ignore, and rightly, the implications of the theatre."[23] To achieve these ends, Flanagan first suggested that playwrights eschew literary imitation of bourgeois models and instead address those issues confronting every-day Americans. "We must see the relationship between the men at work on the Boulder Dam and the Greek chorus," she stressed. More than the promotion of any one technique, Flanagan stressed urgency in grasping the project's potential for social impact. As she told officials, "We cannot be too ambitious." Flanagan spoke of a theater that not only reached Americans across the country but that reflected the diversity of the cultural landscape. As she challenged New York directors, "Let us stress the very attributes of FEDERAL THEATRE which make it difficult—its size, its vast extent—and let us make these attributes serve us."[24]

Structure and Ideology for a Black Theater Unit

The Negro Units developed in the program's initial stages served as part of the FTP's larger goals: to acknowledge American diversity and to aid those who had been economically and culturally marginalized. Although Flanagan had little previous experience with black theater, as she had served on the faculty of white institutions, she was a staunch supporter of black artistic endeavors. Flanagan despised all forms of discrimination, and the FTP issued strong policies against segregation or racial discrimination— in a few instances, white project managers who could not work with black actors or who attempted to implement segregation in touring companies were fired. It was not just Flanagan's attitudes that prompted the FTP's racial tolerance; the Emergency Relief Act of 1935, which established the Federal Arts Project, prohibited any form of discrimination based on race, creed, color, political activities, or party affiliation. These conditions buttressed the FTP's reputation as a champion of civil liberties, serving not only to employ hungry dramatists but also to address inequities facing many employees.[25]

As it improved the economic welfare of African American participants, the FTP provided opportunities beyond relief. The program would come to employ men and women and train them in set building, costume design, and other elements of the theater, and it became an outlet for many black individuals to apply their trades in a more creative capacity. As significant as the wages it offered were, perhaps even more important, the FTP provided African Americans with new theatrical opportunities. As the FTP historian Rena Fraden describes the history of black Americans in the theater, "no group in America has been so invidiously represented onstage and so relentlessly prevented from working backstage."[26] One estimate concludes that of the 25,000 unemployed theatrical workers in the winter of 1931, 3,000 were black men and women.[27]

In prior decades, African Americans had few theatrical opportunities outside of minstrelsy, and although there was a growing independent black theater for a while, this attempt was rather short-lived. As the actress Rosetta LeNoire explained, "I worked for years playing every role ever written for a maid. . . . Then I began to get better roles in the Federal Theatre."[28] The minstrel shows that dominated popular theater in the late nineteenth and early twentieth centuries contained a series of demeaning racial stereotypes. Even the pioneering musical comedy *A Trip to Coontown* (1898), produced by African Americans and performed on Broadway, was a derivation of minstrelsy. While vaudevillians George Walker and Bert Williams pushed racial boundaries by running the first black company to perform on Broadway in 1903 with the musical *In Dahomey*, they conformed to the strictures of racial caricature. Scholars have begun to probe the political nature of these productions and the ways in which Walker and Williams were able to subvert the oppressive framework of minstrelsy; still, white expectations always confined them to it.[29]

Other developments in black theater at the turn of the century include *The Shoo-Fly Regiment* (1907), written by black songwriters Bob Cole and J. Rosamond Johnson, which featured male leads that were not stereotypical and love scenes between black men and women. The team of Cole and Johnson followed up the *Shoo-Fly Regiment* with *Red Moon* (1909), depicting the relationship between Native Americans and black Americans.[30] Yet, while these Broadway musicals may have veered from traditional standards, they were always intended for primarily white audiences. Black patrons remained segregated in the balconies, if they were able to afford the price of admission. Indeed, these performances were milestones in the larger history of black theater, with black audiences often finding political meaning that eluded white patrons. Nonetheless, within a commercial culture infused with racial stereotypes and distorted images, the performances were more an aberration than the norm. By the 1920s, plays penned by white playwrights, such as Eugene O'Neill's *All God's Chillun Got Wings* (1924), Paul Green's *In Abraham's Bosom* (1926), and Dubose Heyward's *Porgy* (1927), provided some black actors with parts that veered slightly from demeaning conventions.

During the mid-1910s and the 1920s, there were a few notable black theaters, which nurtured black talent and exemplified the kind of theater that Negro Unit advocates later proposed. Beginning in 1915, the Lafayette Players, which African American playwright and historian Loften Mitchell considers "the outstanding Negro theatre group of their time," offered new interpretations of popular plays as well as original materials.[31] For these performers, the objective was not only to embody roles that white actors had claimed as their own but also to enrich the artistic life of the community. Lasting until 1932, the Lafayette Players were highly successful in performing Broadway plays for a black audience in ways that would offer new artistic opportunities.[32]

During the 1920s, Harlem was also home to the Krigwa Players, founded under the auspices of the NAACP's literary organ, the *Crisis*, dedicated to an organic black theater. The Krigwa Players espoused a mission to produce plays written by, for, and about African Americans—the first theater company to accomplish this goal.[33] As part of the New Negro movement, the Krigwa Players received materials from literary contests in the *Crisis* and *Opportunity*; several plays treated racial injustice and subjects such as lynching. By Krigwa's second season in 1927, W. E. B. Du Bois served as general chair, and a small company had been established; notably, the Krigwa Players went on to win the Samuel French Award for the best unpublished play, "Fool's Errand," in the Fifth Annual National Little Theatre Tournament.[34] Although internal disputes and a lack of quality materials written by black playwrights stunted Krigwa's existence after three years, the players set an important precedent for the kind of black theater that many hoped to establish as a permanent fixture. As director John Houseman would attest, veterans of these organizations, particularly the Lafayette Players, would be central in developing the FTP's Negro Units.[35]

With the creation of the Lafayette Players and other independent black repertories, many black intellectuals engaged in discussion over the benefits of an independent black theater. In the *Crisis* and *Opportunity*, black scholars such as W. E. B. Du Bois, and New Negro intellectual Alain Locke set forth criteria for black drama. Decrying the fact that black actors, relegated to demeaning roles, could only earn a living by solely catering to an "alien group" (white audiences), Du Bois pronounced that "the best of the Negro actor and the most poignant Negro drama have not been called for."[36] He believed that a successful black theater must produce plays by black playwrights, about black life, and in black neighborhoods. Along similar lines, Alain Locke advocated a laboratory where all dramatic and technical skills could be cultivated. "Not that we would confine the dramatic talent to the . . . plant-rooms of race drama," Locke explained, "but the vehicle of all sound art must be native to the group—our actors need their own soil, at least for sprouting."[37] Although Du Bois warned that black art would not be enough to alter the racial status quo, as even the best black dramas remained under the scrutiny of white critics, producers, and theater owners, he urged black artists to expand their creativity and to produce work outside the expectations of a white audience. "We must come to the place where the work of art when it appears is reviewed and acclaimed by our own free and unfettered judgment," he proclaimed.[38]

The success of *Shuffle Along* (1921), written by Eubie Blake and lyricist Noble Sissle, along with writers Flournoy Miller and Aubrey Liles, proved the commercial potential of a musical penned by African Americans with a black cast. Running for 504 Broadway performances, under the direction and production of black Americans, *Shuffle Along* included hits such as "Love Will Find a Way" and "I'm Just Wild about Harry."[39] Most notably, *Shuffle Along* attracted both white and black patrons, and fully integrated audiences became more visible through the show's duration. In giving the black musical legitimacy, *Shuffle Along* not only spawned imitators, making black musicals a fixture on Broadway, but boosted the careers of some then unknowns in the chorus: Florence Mills, Paul Robeson, and Josephine Baker.

Yet as *Shuffle Along* drew its inspiration from vaudeville, with blackface as a mainstay, some New Negro intellectuals charged that the musical upheld minstrel stereotypes.[40] Stock characters remained in most other black productions in the 1920s and early 1930s, and as Broadway held the possibility for fame and fortune, most black actors chose that route over attempting to form smaller, but more racially conscious theater. With the Depression hitting commercial theater and competition from the movies causing a high rate of technological unemployment, the economic crisis deeply affected a large majority of black actors. With theater in an already precarious position, white producers were more likely to feature tried and true performances than to risk placing black actors in an unconventional capacity.[41] Bemoaning these conditions in 1934, *Opportunity* writer John Lyman stated, "it is an exceptional season that brings more than two or three plays of Negro life to the professional stage."[42]

When the FTP was in its infancy, Rose McClendon, a famed actress and activist, first suggested to Hallie Flanagan that African Americans have their own separate units. Holding a certificate from the American Academy of Dramatics, McClendon had not only performed in such plays as *In Abraham's Bosom*, *Porgy*, and Langston Hughes's play *Mulatto* (1935) but had also played a leading role in organizing black theatrical groups in Harlem in the 1920s and 1930s. On the board of the Harlem Experimental Theatre and one of the founders of the Negro People's Theatre in 1935, McClendon was a champion for black playwrights and racially relevant material. Although the first production of the Negro People's Theatre, Clifford Odets's *Waiting for Lefty* (1935), was not based on the work of a black playwright, it did reflect a theme later common in the FTP: "blackened" versions of formerly white productions. As McClendon regarded the Negro People's Theatre as a pivotal moment in building a black theater, theater historian Jay Plum argues that McClendon's vision directly influenced the mission of the FTP's Negro Units. For McClendon, the concept of separate Negro Units was essential to furthering the work she had done in Harlem, and many who had previously worked with McClendon, such as Frank Wilson, Carlton Moss, Harry Edwards, and Edna Thomas, became central to the project.[43]

Yet in the formation of the Negro Units, a debate—between the desire to produce racially progressive, community-based drama and the ultimate need for white recognition and support—first manifested in the selection of the New York City Negro Unit director. Rose McClendon became the leading candidate. Yet the issue of whether black individuals should

necessarily direct Negro Units quickly came to a boil, as various groups in Harlem offered their opinions on the matter. The major conflict was between black performers involved in Harlem's tradition of community theater and the black intelligentsia. While those who had previously performed with independent black companies such as the Lafayette argued that black theater should remain in the hands of local veterans, more established actors, race advisers, and teachers argued that a black director would not have the experience to undertake such a large endeavor "in a White man's world." The latter group posited that it would take time for black artists, who were previously excluded from positions of authority in the theater, to gain the necessary training. Furthermore, they emphasized that the Negro Unit needed a white man with connections to both Broadway and the government for the project to gain respect and recognition across racial lines.[44]

McClendon urged that her friend John Houseman be appointed director because of his experience and professional associations. McClendon had worked with Houseman on a dramatic version of Countee Cullen's *Medea* (published as *The Medea and Some Poems* in 1935), and Houseman had a long history of working with racially themed material. While Houseman eventually ran the New York City Negro Unit, McClendon was given the position of codirector. Unfortunately, McClendon served mostly as a figurehead during these initial stages because she was suffering from an advanced stage of cancer and died within the first month of the project. Houseman remained at the helm of the Negro Unit, working with a team of white advisers that included Orson Welles. Yet he intended for the New York City Negro Unit to come under black direction eventually. "The few non-Negroes who are aiding in its formation," he told the *Amsterdam News*, "are leading their services at the request of Ms. McClendon and her group. Their relegation to the theatre is temporary, it being obviously essential that a Negro theatre should eventually be operated by Negroes."[45]

To ensure this transition, Houseman worked closely with black aides Edward Perry, who had been Houseman's stage manager in a black production of *Four Saints in Three Acts* (1934), and Carlton Moss, a graduate of the Dramatic Department of Morgan College in Baltimore and the first black playwright employed by the National Broadcasting Company. Not all of those involved had a theatrical background: Harry Edwards, a noted West Indian long-distance runner, took on a central administrative position as a way to gain status "in the world of Negro affairs."[46] The Lafayette Theater became the site for the New York City Negro Unit production; in the beginning, there were 750 African Americans on the New York City project alone, with older actors who had worked in Harlem stock companies alongside well-known actors such as Jack Carter and Canada Lee. Of those 750 individuals, only about half had extensive theater experience. Although the official intent of the FTP was to employ theatrical workers, the project was willing to employ African Americans who did not have a stage background, particularly for technical positions.[47] Upon Houseman's departure in the summer of 1936, Edwards, Moss, and actor/director Gus Smith (who coauthored the FTP-performed play *Turpentine*) would become directors of the New York Negro Unit.

Many white employees remarked on the racial progressivism of the FTP. Actor John Randolph described the project as a "great political awakening," because the project aimed to present the problems of social and economic injustice. "It was the first time that workers were put on the stage, Black workers," Randolph described, "and what I loved was the amount of Black people that came to the theatre."[48] Individuals involved in the New York units such as Hallie Jonas commented on the frequency of racially mixed audiences for FTP performances; Augusta Schenker described her friendship with actor and FTP administrator Carlton Moss, the first black person she claimed she ever had "any dealings" with.[49]

The New York City FTP was the center of the project and of the Negro Units, and it featured units for black youth, African dance, and vaudeville.[50] Several other cities developed Negro Units, including Philadelphia, New Orleans, Detroit, Los Angeles, and San Francisco as well as smaller cities such as Newark, Raleigh, and Peoria. By the end of the project in 1939, twenty-two cities had served as headquarters to Negro Units, and many individuals that had never viewed black performance outside commercialized racial stereotypes, or who had never been to the theater at all, were exposed to black theater for the first time.[51] Although it is not entirely clear how integrated the audiences were for all Negro Unit performances, a 1936 *Crisis* article stated that Seattle and Los Angeles witnessed primarily white audiences whereas Newark and Boston hosted racially mixed audiences.[52] Chicago and New York audiences always comprised a large number of black theatergoers, often because of the productions' frequent location in black neighborhoods.

New York City FTP Negro Unit theater and stage workers. (Franklin D. Roosevelt Library, Hyde Park, N.Y.)

While the Negro Units did not initially have black directors, African Americans eventually secured some directorial positions in major cities; in addition to Smith, Edwards, and Moss in New York, Clarence Muse directed in Los Angeles, Ralf Coleman in Boston, and Theodore Brown was the assistant director of the Seattle Negro Unit.[53] The scarcity of black directors, however, should not obscure the integral role of black administrators and participants in both influencing the content of productions and in procuring the artistic and technical talent for quality performances.[54]

As many black FTP participants revealed, the project was a life-altering experience. Black director Clarence Muse, who ran the FTP's Los Angeles unit and produced *Run Little Chillun* (1933), recalled that when he arrived in California, he only found four or five African Americans in the FTP. After he decided to direct *Run Little Chillun*, he found 165 black participants, most of whom had been performing other, more menial jobs such as ditch digging. Pointing out the incredible opportunities the show offered for these men and women, Muse explained that although most of the *Run Little Chillun* cast and crew had never worked in theater before, about 40

Los Angeles FTP *Negro Unit director Clarence Muse.*
(Franklin D. Roosevelt Library, Hyde Park, N.Y.)

percent remained active thereafter. When asked what the FTP could do for people, Muse exclaimed, "Revitalize! That would be a great tonic, a magnificent rebuilder of confidence and faith in America."[55]

Carlton Moss viewed the FTP as pivotal in what he defined as "cultural emancipation" for black Americans. In attempting to "erase the negative effects of the minstrel," the FTP had put forth other options for black theater that in times of economic depression, in Moss's opinion, would advance the struggle for civil rights.[56] Black administrator John Silvera emphasized the FTP's role in furthering the careers of many black participants who went to Hollywood in the 1940s, some of whom went on to high-profile careers as musical directors and scenic designers.[57] Among these were actors Rex Ingram, Canada Lee, and Edna Thomas, who were celebrated in performances such as *Haiti* (1938) and *Macbeth*; some of these individuals played central roles in race-themed Hollywood wartime motion pictures. As the Negro Units offered employment to black directors or stage designers who would have faced discrimination in other venues, they gave many black employees public exposure and connected them to prominent white liberals such as Orson Welles and John Houseman. Writing in 1938, *Opportunity*'s Edward Lawson declared, "the Federal Theatre's very existence has been a godsend to Negro actors in a period when practically no other opportunities for employment were open to them."[58]

The Search for Authentic Black Theater

When the Negro Units were first established, FTP administrators were not certain about what type of plays these divisions should produce. With many of their goals echoing those of Du Bois, to build a black theater based on the talents of black playwrights, the Play Bureau, the central agency for the evaluation of all plays, began sifting through potential material. In listing some plays for recommendation, the Play Bureau underscored the following characteristics for a black theater:

> More and more has the place of the Negro in his community, his efforts to combat repression, racial, economic, and political, become the theme for dramatic representation. Most of the plays herein presented deal with the social and economic phases of this struggle. They are important as representing a definite break with the traditional concept of the Negro as a music-hall, tap-dancing comic figure. It is not to be inferred that the plays are therefore dull and somber. Almost inevitably, the good humor and fun-loving elements enter. They are irrepressible. The dominant theme, however, is seldom lost sight of.[59]

While the Play Bureau attempted to break with racial stereotypes, the traces of racial essentialism in this passage would echo in much of the bureau's play critiques. Comprised of an interracial staff (although the majority were white), the Play Bureau confronted the dilemma of selecting plays that would cater to a wide audience while still evoking important racial themes.

Those who directed the selection and development of plays under the National Service Bureau (which encompassed the Play Bureau) were a group of highly skilled writers and publishers. Having already earned a law degree from Fordham University, Emmet Lavery, director of the National Service Bureau, wrote several plays for the stage before joining the FTP, such as *The First Legion* (1934) and *Monsignor's House* (1936). He later penned several screenplays such as *Hitler's Children* (1943) and *Behind the Rising Sun* (1943).[60] Francis Bosworth, who acted as the first director of the National Play Bureau (before the National Service Bureau was formed), was head of the drama department at Columbia University when Flanagan asked him to join the project.[61] Converse Tyler, who served as chief of the playreading department of the Play Bureau, had taken journalism classes at Columbia University and then served as a drama and movie critic for the *Stamford (Conn.) Sentinel*. Tyler also enjoyed a stint as an actor, appearing in stock plays and on Broadway with such actors as Shirley Booth and Humphrey Bogart.[62] Playreader Harold Berman wrote for the *New York Journal American* and later worked for the Voice of America for two decades.[63] In addition, playreading supervisor Ben Russak, a former student of the New School for Social Research, had an extensive background in publishing, eventually founding and becoming president of the publishing house Crane, Russak, and Company.[64]

Most individuals involved in the Play Bureau were committed to the cause of social justice, sharing the liberal sympathies of many officials involved in the art projects. Like the members of several writers' guilds, with backgrounds in both experimental theater and liberal publications, Play Bureau administrators were sympathetic to the plight of African Americans and often condemned racial inequality. Some were particularly inclined to take a more active role in left-wing politics. Emmet Lavery was chairman of the Hollywood Writers Mobilization and president of the Screen Writers Guild in the 1940s. For years, Harold Berman worked for the Anti-Defamation League of B'nai Brith. And the leftist sympathies of FTP playwright Gene Stone and actor John Randolph were exposed when they were blacklisted during the 1950s and appeared as hostile witnesses before the House Un-American Activities Committee.

As plays poured into the Play Bureau through play brokers, literary agencies, or from the authors themselves, the organization was initially a refuge for many theatrical employees who needed work but could not find jobs in their trades. Harold Berman joined the FTP as an actor, but when there were no roles, he moved to the playwriting department. As Berman stated, initially there were several readers who were "semi-literate," and the work often was shifted onto more skilled readers.[65] Francis Bosworth recalled that in the beginning of the project, 160 unemployed playwrights served as playreaders. These men and women reviewed about five plays a week.[66] Within the Play Bureau, a core of experienced readers handled the bulk of reviews, sometime even after others had already read the plays.[67] The group that Harold Berman identified as a "special Play Reading committee" consisted of those individuals whose names most frequently appeared on reviews for plays considered for the Negro Units.[68] Whether

Converse Tyler gave the racial material to his most experienced readers is unclear, but it appears that the Negro Unit plays did not go out to a random selection of reviewers.

Much of the work submitted to the Play Bureau was written by established, published playwrights. African American women such as Alice Dunbar Nelson, Mary Burrill, and Georgia Douglas Johnson—all of whom had work that was under consideration—featured prominently in the Harlem Renaissance. Dunbar Nelson had published several poems in the *Crisis* and *Opportunity* throughout the 1920s, and her antilynching play, *Mine Eyes Have Seen*, was published in the *Crisis* in 1918.[69] During the Harlem Renaissance, Georgia Douglas Johnson served as host to a number of prominent black writers such as Langston Hughes and Countee Cullen, founding the S Street salon as a forum for literary discussion; many of her plays were published in *Opportunity* and performed by the Krigwa Players.[70] Mary Burrill, who published her play *Aftermath* in the *Liberator* in 1919, taught drama at the Paul Lawrence Dunbar High School; the Krigwa Players also performed *Aftermath*, in 1928.[71] Others who submitted plays to the Play Bureau were equally important in furthering black theater. Randolph Edmonds, who submitted his play *Old Man Pete* (1934), formed the Southern Association of Dramatic Speech Arts in the 1930s with a goal of producing plays penned by African Americans. Over the course of the 1930s and 1940s, Edmonds published several scripts, which were regularly performed at black college festivals.[72] Abram Hill, who submitted "Hell's Half Acre," studied theater at Lincoln University in Pennsylvania while maintaining a job in the CCC's drama division. After graduation in 1938, Hill worked as a playreader in the FTP, and when it was shut down, he became a researcher for the FWP, working with Roi Ottley on the book *New World A-Coming*. In 1939, Hill received a scholarship to the New School for Social Research, where he penned the widely performed play *On Strivers Row* (1939) and came to direct the American Negro Theatre, founded in 1940.[73]

Plays submitted to the bureau also included the work of several established white playwrights. Edward Shelton, who penned the controversial play *The Nigger* (1909), was prolific; after graduating from Harvard University in 1908 he went on to write *The Boss* (1911), *The Garden of Paradise* (1914), and several other socially provocative plays, which were performed around the country.[74] By the late 1920s, Julia Peterkin, whose play *Boy Chillen* (1932) was under review by the bureau, had published two novels that treated racial issues, *Black April* (1927) and *Scarlett Sister Mary*, winner of the Pulitzer prize in 1928.[75] Dion Boucicault, perhaps the most famous white playwright whose work came before the Play Bureau, had written a number of popular, sensational plays during the nineteenth century. Boucicault garnered success with *The Poor of New York* (1857), and his play *The Octoroon* (1859), which was considered by the Play Bureau, was extremely well received by Victorian audiences.[76] Other famous authors whose work came under review included Harriet Beecher Stowe, Langston Hughes, and Countee Cullen. However, not all of the plays under FTP review were published materials; men and women without an established background in theatrical writing penned many of the scripts.

As African American playreader John Silvera explained, the Play Bureau evaluated plays for the Negro Units to determine whether they "would be suitable for production." Although the general criteria for finding plays "acceptable" were vague, supervisors implied that they would not consider topics that were "too militant" or "unproduceable."[77] Yet, Ben Russak declared that the Play Bureau would not censor dramas depicting the "Black problem in this country" and that the agency would make every effort to encourage black writing and eschew racial stereotypes.[78] But, like all liberal administrators who operated within the New Deal cultural apparatus, officials with the Play Bureau held pragmatic concerns that engendered demarcated evaluations. As the democratic goals of the FTP stated that plays be performed to the widest, most diverse audiences, care was taken in selecting and shaping dramatic performances to make the least problematic depiction of race relations. Furthermore, as administrators privileged certain causes for social awareness, they often diminished the importance of topics that, though pertinent to many black communities, were not foremost on the government's agenda. Nonetheless, many of the plays that the Play Bureau initially selected explicitly evoked radical themes that would contrast with plays produced in the last years of the project.

Readers for the bureau revealed certain structural aesthetics that would be necessary for a play's acceptance. Poor writing and a lack of technique often factored into the basis for rejection. "This play tells a garbled, overly complicated story," reader John Rimassa commented on a play entitled "Enchanted Figures." "He [the author] bothers none at all or very little with characterization."[79] Not only did readers often remark that a play's characters should possess more depth but that the central narrative should follow a certain trajectory, with several identifiable climaxes.[80] The status of the author seemed to have relatively little bearing on a play's acceptance. A Langston Hughes poem "The Big Timer" was submitted for consideration as a play, in addition to his published one-act play *Angelo Herndon Jones*

(1936). Although the readers commented on the quality of the poetry in "The Big Timer" and the potential for "good dramatic recitation," the majority agreed that Hughes's work "could not be considered a play, because it is not of dramatic construction."[81] Another even suggested that Hughes's work had "insufficient development of character and incident resulting in confusion."[82] Reader John Silvera, one of the few black Play Bureau employees, reported that the Hughes poem was suitable only as a "vaudeville sketch," having what he considered to be little "dramatic value."[83] Reviewers' particular preconceptions of what constituted the dramatic genre determined the suitability of potential plays, and in these cases, the presentation of racial topics had less relevance than the structural definitions of the Play Bureau.

The Play Bureau, however, was interested in cultivating an open dialogue on racial issues and in offering new kinds of roles to black actors. Thus, it became part of the bureau's policy to reject plays that furthered racial stereotypes, whether in their content or characterizations. Condemning "primitive" dialogue, reader Nathan Spiegel, for example, condemned one play as "tediously told tripe . . . buried in stereotypical detail."[84] Another play, "Laugh Sing and Pray," dramatizing one man's temptations and ultimate salvation through piety and religion, was vehemently declared "just another example of the Negroes-are-basically-happy-children-without-brains school of anthropology."[85] In commenting on the use of stereotypes in these plays as "assumed and unreal," readers sought out material that could provide a fuller portrayal of humanity.[86] Thus, they eschewed Harriet Beecher Stowe's *The Christian Slave* (1855) with its dichotomy of extremely benevolent or uncompromisingly evil characters.[87] In addition, shallow endorsements of stock characters, such as the urbane, educated New Negro, incensed readers. "It has been the writer's pleasure to meet a number of distinguished and sophisticated colored people but none quite so artificial . . . as the puppets in this play," reader Converse Tyler exclaimed in a review of "Heaven's My Home."[88]

In determining what was stereotypical, however, reviewers related their own assumptions on what constituted "authentic" black life. Playreaders exhibited a great deal of scrutiny when reading scripts that dramatized the lynching of black men, such as "Nobody Knows." One reader commented: "An amateurish Harlem-rouser with the old, shopworn story—a white girl is attacked by a Negro, but not harmed, and a white mob lynches the wrong Negro. Only the familiar burning at the stake is missing."[89] Another reviewer complained that "the story itself is neither fresh nor the treatment individual—being the usual Southern lynching of the usual innocent Negro—the author planting a maze of circumstantial evidence to convict him, that is completely incredible. Stale and trite subject and treatment."[90] The latter passage indicates that in dismissing some material as "stale and trite," reviewers often denied the very persistence of racial violence. Thus, charges of inauthenticity sometimes masked painful realities that were deemed too controversial for the stage.

In general, the subject of lynching was precarious for the Play Bureau. Georgia Douglas Johnson's play *Safe* (1929), which depicted a black mother who killed her child after witnessing the lynching of another man, elicited varying responses. Some readers charged that the play lacked passion, asserting that the story was told "casually and factually," reduced to a claim that "the sight of a lynching drove a Negro mother crazy."[91] Another reader, C. C. Lawrence, commented, "I wonder why she [the author] is not brave enough to show the whole truth. . . . I believe she could show the suffering and anxiety of these poor people in a much greater way."[92] Thus, some readers indicated that a full treatment of lynching required that the "true" feelings of black men and women, including the psychological effects of this horrific violence, be shown. Ironically, in claiming to seek out a full range of human emotion, readers sometimes rejected the portrayal of those feelings that seemed less "natural," and perhaps less acceptable, to potential audiences.

Conversely, other readers criticized *Safe* not for its inability to depict human suffering but, as one put it, for the "glaring weakness of utter exaggeration." Claiming that the play "follows from an absurdity—that they lynch Negro boys 'Down South' for defending themselves from thieves," reader Charles Gaskill denied the play's very premise—the possibility that black men who hit their white bosses could be lynched.[93] Again, in claiming the cultural authority to recognize "authentic" black theater, some readers used their power of review to reject the existence of certain racial injustices. Some reviewers in the Play Bureau further dismissed the gruesome, but realistic, depiction of lynching in "Hell's Half Acre." Conveying concern about the sensitivity of the subject, albeit ambiguously defined, the readers rejected a play that portrayed an "old cracker Granny" who had pickled the body parts of lynching victims. Even John Silvera, the black reviewer, agreed that these "gruesome realities . . . have no place in Federal Theatre offerings. There is a much more wholesome job to be done."[94]

These types of comment reflect the Play Bureau's internal conflict over presenting subjects that could potentially offend audiences. Although it aimed to present realistic representations of racial problems in America, it also wanted to avoid exacerbating racial tensions. Thus, most readers rejected plays such as "The Dark Tide," which portrayed a light-skinned black woman who commits suicide when she fears her white husband might discover the truth about her race, and *The Octoroon*, which depicted a slave woman who would rather die than be separated from her white lover. Although readers admitted that the issues of miscegenation and "passing [as white]" were important subjects for discussion, they agreed that these topics could "do much to destroy that friendship that now exist [*sic*] between the whites and colored."[95] Alexander Cutner, who wrote the most positive, yet still tentative, review of "The Dark Tide," recommended it (with several changes in dialogue) for the black theater in Harlem, Jewish organizations, foreign audiences, and those in New York City. Cutner expressed great concern about the play, claiming that its theme of interracial marriage would "disturb audiences creating race antagonisms."[96]

In reviewing *The Octoroon*, readers also placed more emphasis on the negative reactions of black audiences. The play follows the plight of a woman who becomes enslaved to a man she despises and separated from her white lover, the slave owner's enemy. Reviewer Metrah Willie declared that the play was outdated and "would not . . . appeal to colored audiences."[97] The most inflammatory reaction, however, came from a review of *The Nigger*, which details a governor's discovery that he is of black ancestry, forcing him to end his engagement to a white woman and to incite his own lynching. One reader decried the work as "inept and unsuitable for present day production. This play is obviously the 'stuff' that goes toward race hatred. There ought to be a law."[98]

Playreaders often declared what they felt constituted a "Negro play," dismissing material that might disturb both white and black audiences. In an evaluation of "Rich Harlem," reviewer Herbert Hutner wrote, "This is not a Negro play. It deals with no problems which could . . . be said to affect any strata of the Negro people—as Negroes." While "Rich Harlem" focused on a character's belief in Garveyism, professing the need for black business institutions that cater to black consumers, Hutner repudiated the play, stating that the black characters' "problems in no way differ from [those of] whites of the same strata." Hutner's negative reaction primarily stemmed from his disdain for the play's unflattering racial depictions, as well as its "stiff and awkward dialogue."[99] He discredited the portrayal of Garveyism because he believed it was not authentic; he also stated that the play characterized African Americans as ruthless criminals. These same charges surfaced in a review of "Enchanted Figures," which characterized racketeering and interracial conflict in Harlem. As the reviewer complained of the frequent use of stereotypes, "This play cannot [be] said to be a Negro play, since no effort is made to analyze characters."[100] For these Play Bureau reviewers, what constituted a "Negro play" was one that evoked characterizations that they deemed as more accurate, regardless of racially oriented themes or the participation of black actors.

As they preferred to advocate some social causes over others, readers often dismissed plays for their lack of attention to the "Negro Problem." Such was the case with *Boy Chillen*, a play about the connection between a white mistress and her black servant, who work together to protect the servant woman's grandson from violent law enforcement authorities. Claiming that the play was "more concerned with a fancied bond among women despite color differences than it is with any subject of Negro relations," reader Leonard Sacks did not deem *Boy Chillen* a "Negro play."[101] Another reader of *Boy Chillen* agreed that the play did not have a "social viewpoint" and that the interracial bond between women was not relevant to the "Negro Problem."[102] Playreaders made the same comments about *Old Man Pete*, which described the plight of black parents in the South whose children encourage their move to Harlem. As the parents become a burden to the children, they are eventually told to leave; in the last scene, the couple freezes to death after falling asleep on a park bench. In reporting that "the play could be transferred to a white environment," one reader insisted that there was "nothing whatever that is Negro in the theme."[103]

These plays depicting family relationships, despite their being centered on subjects such as migration and interracial cooperation, did not fall under the scope of "Negro plays" due to certain preconceived notions of what Negro Units should produce. Although the FTP fashioned itself as a pioneer in developing black theater, at the forefront in dramatizing the most significant racial themes, it often bypassed subjects that confronted many black Americans. This stagnant view of "Negro plays" prevented the FTP from putting forth a more diverse and nuanced repertoire of plays based on a more sophisticated understanding of racial issues. Here, both potential audience response and the racial biases of Play Bureau reviewers shaped the administrative goals to advance a black theater; the process of determining which plays were suitable for production illustrates the complexity of furthering new, nonstereotypical materials for African American production.

New York Negro Unit production of Walk Together, Chillun.
(Franklin D. Roosevelt Library, Hyde Park, N.Y.)

Yet it is important to recognize the politics of both the FTP and the Negro Units, whose leftist bent often led to the promotion of labor themes. Plays recommended for production, as listed in the National Service Bureau's "List of Negro Plays"—such as *Stevedore*; *Walk Together, Chillun* (1936); and *Brother Mose* (1933)—featured themes of worker resistance and unionization. Commending these plays for their "timely material" and "social significance," Play Bureau reviewers placed the exploitation of black labor and the formation of African American unions as important topics for dramatic evaluation. Likewise, in their praise of the play "They Shall Not Die," a dramatization of the Scottsboro incident, Play Bureau readers further revealed their inclinations toward social realism. Thus, as the bureau advocated themes of racial injustice in both the workplace and the legal system, it narrowed definitions of black authenticity to suit particular audiences and to avoid inciting racial animosity.[104]

The Play Bureau also recommended plays depicting the history of black resistance. Three plays, "The Opener of Doors," *Haiti*, and *Black Em-*

pire (1936), all portrayed the revolt of slaves against the French in Haiti (1791–1804), leading one reviewer to comment that "it is a subject close to the heart of every Negro."[105] Playreaders emphasized that certain dramas would be particularly appealing to black audiences; yet the historical nature of these plays eliminated more controversial contemporary racial issues. In addition, the Play Bureau aimed to reach a general audience by recommending plays with strong musical components. "The spirituals and chorals provide a tremendously moving background," one reader wrote of *The Green Pastures* (1930), while another admired the "unusual musical setting" of *Run Little Chillun*.[106] Suggesting that the play *John Henry* (1936) should be performed based on its dramatization of black courage and persistence, the reviewer also expressed enthusiasm towards the "symbolical musical background."[107] *Run Little Chillun* depicted divisions within the black church, while *John Henry* portrayed the life of a man victimized by slavery and Reconstruction. Here, preconceived notions about the production appeal of black music may have won approval for otherwise controversial plays. Because the FTP promised to democratize theater in America and to satisfy the interests of diverse communities, music that readers considered to be distinctly "Negro" was significant in the evaluation of a production's potential success.

While the Play Bureau often imposed criteria on Negro Unit plays that narrowed the scope of artistic and political expression, the FTP still performed a number of plays that tackled racial inequality in an uncompromising manner. In the context of a commercial theater strongly unwilling to break with conventional roles for black actors, many productions supported in the early stages of the FTP were pathbreaking. Plays such as *Stevedore* and *Hymn to the Rising Sun* (1936) invoked the persistence of white prejudice while depicting poor labor conditions. Plays penned by black Americans included Theodore Ward's drama *Big White Fog*, which depicts intraracial prejudice, the appeal and rejection of Garveyism, and the embrace of Communism and radicalism. Frank Wilson's *Brother Mose* featured the plight of black residents who are moved off their land by white authorities; it proved highly successful, playing in twenty cities. Hughes Allison's *The Trial of Dr. Beck* (1937), examining the prosecution of a light-skinned man who had killed his wealthy, dark-skinned wife (and who harbored the theory that black men should only marry light-skinned women in order to whiten the race), had enough success to be moved to the famed Maxine Elliot Theatre on Broadway. Insofar as all of these productions treated controversial issues, neither white nor black audiences accepted them uncritically. Like reviewers in the Play Bureau, African American communities held their own preconceptions of what constituted authentic black theater, with great diversity of opinion. Fraden suggests, "a people's desire for self-representation seems inevitably to involve a degree of exclusion . . . stereotype, and mystification." Nevertheless, the eventual production of racially provocative material, despite the opposition that surfaced from some FTP officials and audiences, illustrates the FTP's commitment to alternative explorations of black life.[108]

Black political organizations such as the NAACP proved heavily invested in the activities of the FTP, as Walter White served on the advisory board of the Five Arts Project of the WPA. As part of this committee, White solicited potential scripts from friends such as Sherwood Anderson for Negro Unit production, commenting on the "great paucity of good Negro plays."[109] White also participated in FTP discussions concerning discrimination and unfair layoffs within the arts projects. Play Bureau administrator John Silvera appealed to White for assistance in securing greater representation of black Americans throughout the FTP, in the national office, and on the Play Production Board.[110] The black playwright Abram Hill also sought the support of White for the production of his antilynching narrative, "Hell's Half Acre." As Hill indicated, "its successful production would certainly enhance the cause of the Anti-lynching Bill. If you do no more than ask that the play be given careful consideration, it would mean a lot." White's involvement and apparent accessibility on these matters reveals his interest in improving conditions for black dramatists.[111] At this time, while White was vigorously campaigning for the passage of the federal antilynching bill, his activities on behalf of African American artists indicate that improvements in the cultural arena were linked to the larger black political agenda.

The NAACP also did not hesitate to voice opposition to plays that it found unsuitable for production. Upon learning that the Newark Negro Unit planned to put on Octavus Roy Cohen's play *Come Seven* (1920), Roy Wilkins indicated to National Service Bureau director Emmet Lavery that his organization strongly objected to Cohen's plays, which featured "caricatures of the race." Exclaiming that it was not necessary that the cast perform a "so-called Negro play," Wilkins demanded the play's cancellation; he also, however, asserted that white playreaders, "many of them without previous experience or knowledge of Negroes except the information they have received from newspaper headlines," were not fit to be judges for Negro Unit material.[112]

Although Lavery promptly responded to Wilkins with the news that *Come Seven* would not be performed, he was offended by Wilkins's charge of white ignorance, claiming that a black reader always served as a consultant and emphasizing that "diversity of opinion regarding the merits of racial drama" would always exist.[113] Just a day later, Wilkins retreated a bit, admitting that black Americans were "inclined to be supersensitive on many points" due to a history of misrepresentation and praising the FTP for the advances it had made in black theater. Although concerned that the FTP not "fall heir to the errors which have been made repeatedly by Broadway and Hollywood producers," Wilkins acknowledged that Lavery was making an ardent effort to represent black Americans in a positive, accurate manner.[114] Significantly, this exchange not only demonstrates the great investment of high-ranking NAACP officials in the Negro Units, but also the combination of both sensitivity and confidence that FTP directors such as Lavery projected. While Lavery responded to Wilkins's request by canceling the production, he did not merely accept Wilkins's additional critiques of the project without refutation, proclaiming, "but we do make a consistent and thorough effort to understand the particular problems of Negro theatre."[115]

Yet, for some black Americans, the FTP did not reach its potential in securing the foundations for a viable black theater. *Opportunity* writer Edward Lawson exclaimed, "the people of Harlem know what they want, and even a stirring play like 'Haiti' will not draw them into the theatre unless it rings true to Negro life." What made a drama "true to Negro life," for Lawson, was a specific criterion: it had to be written, directed, and performed by African Americans. He stated that classics such as *Androcles and the Lion* were perhaps not the most relevant performances for black audiences, and that the FTP should instead focus on a "typically Negro play about the trials and tribulations black men face today." While the FTP had an enormous impact on altering the kinds of roles black performers were able to take on, the prescriptions made by Lawson were perhaps necessary for black theater to sustain itself long after the FTP's termination.[116]

The Stage under Fire

The willingness of FTP administrators to support contemporary, progressive material was rather short-lived. As all parts of the Federal Arts Project came under increasing scrutiny from conservatives in Congress by 1937, with the FTP as the central target, the nature of "acceptable" performances changed dramatically. Congress had been critical of the FTP since the production of its first plays. In 1936, charges were made against the farmer/ labor cooperation play *Triple-A*, which one congressman described as "pure, unadulterated politics."[117] During the same year, Republican congressman James Davis warned other members of the House that the government allowed spending "by a woman [Flanagan] infatuated both by the Russian theatre and the U.S.S.R."[118]

Congress demonstrated its hostility by cutting relief appropriations for the project. As Roosevelt's Court-packing plan further aroused the ire of New Deal skeptics, who had challenged WPA programs from the outset, Congress reduced the project's funding in June 1937. Anti-WPA animosity ran so high that the House even voted to reduce the salary of director Harry Hopkins. Although various organizations such as the Workers' Alliance and the American Federation of Musicians protested the budget cuts and although Hallie Flanagan made several pleas to key Washington organizations, Congress drastically reduced WPA allotments. For the FTP, one-fourth of its funds were gone, leading to a reduction of the New York project by 30 percent and abolishing the smallest units. Flanagan directed project administrators to cut nonrelief workers first, and then relief workers, depending on their "actual value to the Project."[119] This had a major impact on all FTP endeavors, but it had particular implications for the Negro Units, which, by 1937 had become a vital outlet for black theatrical employees shut out of commercial theater.

By the fall of 1938, charges against the FTP had intensified as Congress undertook a widespread investigation of all "un-American" activities. At the height of anti–New Deal agitation following a recession in the summer of 1937, conservative Democrats increasingly joined Republicans in an effort to thwart New Deal legislation. In the 1938 congressional elections, Republicans regained a significant presence in the House and Senate, and the Roosevelt coalition was slowly dismantling. This conservative atmosphere propelled more formal investigations of Communist activity that Congress had suspected since 1935. The House Un-American Activities Committee (HUAC), headed by Martin Dies of Texas, relentlessly pursued the FTP as a hotbed of Communist activities, scrutinizing all aspects of both productions and employee backgrounds. With Hallie Flanagan accused by former WPA employee Hazel Huffman of having an "active participation and interest in all things communist," the Dies committee questioned several FTP participants on the Communist Party's influence over both the director and the project as a whole.[120] Many individuals admitted to certain connections between Communist organizations and the FTP, while others reported discrimination based on their political beliefs. While the Dies committee had much interest in the background of supposed Communists, it had little interest in the motivations or backgrounds of "helpful" witnesses. Many who testified, such as Huffman and Francis Verdi, had been fired or refused promotions; others may have been urged to testify by persuasive politicians. The accusations of witnesses went unchecked, and the evidence of subversion was primarily what FTP historian Jane DeHart Matthews characterizes as "an amazing mixture of truths, half-truths, and outright untruths."[121]

For the most part, subversion was a subjective matter, based entirely on the beliefs of the committee. In many instances, race was a central factor in determining "un-Americanness." The Dies committee did not openly object to the existence of the Negro Units in furthering black theater, but often it made the connection between the presence of African Americans on the project and "un-American" behavior or theatrical content. When the Dies committee questioned New York stage manager Charles Walton, he admitted to attending an FTP party that was allegedly filled with Communists. He also maintained that many black men were dancing with white women at the party.[122] Subjects of "social equality and race mixing" also arose in the testimony of actress Sallie Saunders, who reported that while she was working for the FTP, a black man had asked her on a date. When she reported this to a superior, Trudy Goodrich, Saunders claimed, Goodrich encouraged interracial dating and "felt sorry" that Saunders would not accept the invitation. Charging that employees of the FTP "hobnob indiscriminately with them [black people]," Saunders provided the committee with another example of behavior that was supposedly common among Communists.[123]

Furthermore, the Dies committee targeted some racially charged plays in their search for "inappropriate material." During the testimony of Hallie Flanagan, Congressman Joseph Starnes cited a passage from the play *Stevedore* as vulgar and profane: "LONNIE: God damn dem, anyhow. What dey think I am? Do I look like some kind of animal? Do I look like somebody who'd jump over a back fence and rape a woman?" Here, Starnes objected to the "use of the Lord's name in a profane way," and more ambiguously, "absolutely vulgar statements"; the subject matter and the frank use of dialogue were particularly unsettling. Whether or not this was "un-American" was not an issue as much as whether American taxpayers should support "profanity." Although the committee did not explicitly state that the topic of lynching was unsuitable for an "American" play, the opposition towards

HOOKED ON CLASSICS

Stevedore's more explicit material, coupled with the committee's outrage towards interracial mixing, indicated how politicians voiced racial anxieties under the rubric of anticommunism. The Dies committee's objections also highlight the ways in which individuals linked Communism and sexuality; more uninhibited sexual behavior or speech, which many white Americans had long stereotyped as "Negro," were also flagged as "Communist" in the committee hearings.[124]

Three Little Maids to the Rescue

Even before the Dies committee began its investigations, appropriation reductions and federal censorship signaled the precariousness of the entire FTP, making the selection of productions a more cautious task by the summer of 1937. Hallie Flanagan described this shifting political climate as demonstrated by the FTP magazine's career: "Its economic, racial, and social point of view, in line with administration and W.P.A. polities in 1935, was considered inimical in 1937."[125] Some regional directors viewed plays with racial themes as more potentially explosive, and the FTP's earlier goals of presenting the economic and social obstacles to racial progress became increasingly marginalized. The Chicago Negro Unit's selection of its next production reflected this official hesitance in considering racially charged material and the need to seek other alternatives.

In the fall of 1937, after appropriation reductions, Harry Minturn, acting assistant director to the national director of the FTP, targeted productions for the Negro Unit that would provoke less controversy. With a background in vaudeville and as a producer and manager of popular shows, Minturn was principally concerned with entertaining large audiences through fairly traditional vehicles.[126] With the positive reception to all-black versions of *Macbeth* and other classic theater such as *Androcles and the Lion*, Minturn believed that an all-black version of Gilbert and Sullivan's beloved *The Mikado* would delight audiences without stirring political debate. Indeed, the casting of black performers in Shakespearean dramas signaled a remarkable moment in American theater history. The "voodoo" *Macbeth*, directed by John Houseman and Orson Welles for the New York Negro Unit, drew rave reviews from both white and black audiences, setting a precedent for other classic productions that would incorporate black actors. As the director of the National Service Bureau, Emmet Lavery, explained, the FTP explored the important question, "why should Shakespeare be reserved for White actors?"[127] Black performances of classical theater such as *Macbeth* and the *Swing Mikado* were eventually the most widely regarded of all FTP productions, often altering white theatrical tastes. "Jack Barrymore said he'd never again be able to see a White *Macbeth*," asserted New York unit director and writer Max Pollock.[128]

As audiences indicated their preferences in one FTP survey, Gilbert and Sullivan productions were the second most requested type of play behind Shakespeare. Of all the Gilbert and Sullivan plays, *The Mikado* received the highest number of requests. With FTP performances of the traditional *The Mikado* achieving acclaim in a variety of cities, a Negro Unit *Mikado* could, in the minds of directors, employ a large number of black participants while satisfying the tastes of white audiences. Moreover, as in *Macbeth*, black actors would be able to perform in roles previously reserved for white actors—black audiences would appreciate a show that did not feature conventional racial stereotypes.[129]

According to Duncan Whiteside, technical director of Chicago's Great Northern Theatre where the *Swing Mikado* was rehearsed and performed, the idea of "swinging" the show came from the improvisations of black actors and actresses. When the Chicago Negro Unit was slated to perform *The Mikado*, rehearsals began, and while the actors were on break, they often started improvising with the rehearsal accompanist, tap dancing and adlibbing the music. When Harry Minturn saw this during one visit to the set, he insisted to the show's then director, Kay Ewing, that the show be performed in swing, exclaiming, "listen to that. That moves; it's got something." The "swingcopation" of *The Mikado* changed the entire conceptualization of the show, with new direction, choreography, and set design. Minturn eventually came to direct the show, and although he may have suggested swinging *The Mikado*, he understood the importance of preserving the play as Gilbert and Sullivan had written it.[130]

Thus, the *Swing Mikado* came to be a hybridization of the classic—staying true to the original lyrics of the operetta, while "swinging" three songs and changing the original Japanese setting. As Minturn related in his director's notes, the locale moved to "an imaginary coral island in the Pacific Ocean." This called for brilliant, multicolored lighting, a set design that would adapt to elaborate dance numbers, and "exotic" costumes that combined African, Southern Pacific, and Japanese elements. Despite these dramatic variations, Minturn was adamant about the *Swing Mikado*'s adherence to the traditional script and score. As he relayed, other than the three songs performed as swing, "the score was sung perfectly legitimate and straight."[131] Furthermore, Minturn stressed that although the Negro Unit was performing the musical, it was not a "Negro play." One publicity report exclaimed, "as Director Harry Minturn points out, this 'Mikado' is not specifically Negro. It is all-American."[132]

Yet, in advocating and producing the *Swing Mikado*, Minturn offered a critical opportunity for black men and women in the Chicago FTP, not only to perform new kinds of roles, but to endow *The Mikado* with their own artistic interpretations. Whether Minturn intended it or not, the African Americanization of *The Mikado* had significant political implications for black performers. Producers such as Minturn supported the show based on the attraction of black performers "swinging" to upbeat tempos; however, they had little understanding that this new convention, the *Swing Mikado*, could also become a vehicle for new forms of black cultural expression.

The 1938 *Swing Mikado* replicated the plot of Gilbert and Sullivan's 1881 opera, with few variations in the script. The play centers on the travails of Nanki-Poo (Maurice Cooper), the Mikado's (Edward Fraction) son, who has secretly disguised himself as a trombone player to escape marrying an older woman, Katisha (Mabel Carter). Nanki-Poo is in love with a young schoolgirl, Yum-Yum (Gladys Bourcee); when he learns that Yum-Yum is to marry Ko-Ko (Herman Greene), the Lord High Executioner, he plans to kill himself. As the Mikado has ordered that an execution take place as soon as possible in the town of Titipu, Nanki-Poo offers himself to Ko-Ko for public execution in return for marriage to Yum Yum for a month. Ko-Ko accepts, knowing that it is he who will be beheaded if he does not find another candidate. As Yum Yum and Nanki-Poo make their plans to marry, they soon learn that the wife of an executed man must be buried alive. Ko-Ko then comes up with a plan to present the Mikado with a death certificate for Nanki-Poo, while he and Yum Yum escape. When the Mikado arrives, he accepts the execution, but of course learns that it is his son who has seemingly been killed. With his own life now in danger, Ko-Ko brings Yum Yum and Nanki Poo back to town, marries the elderly Katisha himself (the woman who Nanki-Poo was originally escaping), and all ends happily.

The actors and actresses who played the lead roles in the *Swing Mikado* reflected diverse performance backgrounds. Gladys Bourcee, Mabel Carter, William Franklin, and Frankie Fambro all had received operatic training, performing with the Verdi Opera Company and giving concerts at noted venues such as the Chicago Civic Opera House. Lewis White and Edward Fraction had both participated in all-black musicals such as *Porgy and Bess*, *Blackbirds of 1936*, and *Shuffle Along*. The most widely applauded *Swing Mikado* performers, Maurice Cooper and Herman Greene,

The cast of Swing Mikado. *(Federal Theatre Project Papers, Performing Arts Reading Room, Library of Congress)*

both came from popular theater. After winning a radio contest sponsored by NBC and the *Chicago Daily News*, Cooper toured thirty-seven states as a concert singer; Greene, a thirty-year vaudeville veteran, had never before performed in comic opera. Many of these actors had been born in the South; Cooper and Bourcee hailed from Kansas City. Cooper and Carter were college graduates, and other actors received musical training at institutes such as the Chicago Conservatory of Music. Although some of these actors had entertained audiences for decades, none had the popular recognition they would receive from both black and white audiences for the *Swing Mikado*.[133]

In the nineteenth century, this simple tale of love and mistaken identity reflected an English fetishization of Japanese culture. Most revealing was the 1885 Japanese Exhibition in Knightsbridge—the Japanese demonstrated the art of serving tea and other customs while geisha women presented themselves as the embodiment of an oriental character. In *The Mikado*, this spectacle translates into familiar Japanese caricatures and images, as the opening players describe their own commodification: "on many a vase and jar / on many a screen and fan / we figure in lively paint."[134] As theater historians argue, the English exoticization of the Japanese in *The Mikado* parallels a similar dynamic in American popular culture—the spectacle of black bodies and music for white amusement. As a form of white entertainment (at least in part), the *Swing Mikado* itself could have only offered another display of black primitivism, with actors scantily clad amidst tropical settings. However, the legitimizing force of the classical operetta prevented this kind of dissipation. Furthermore, the black embodiment of quasi-Japanese stereotypes replaced minstrel stock characters; as black actors became versions of another racialized, commodified group, they could ironically still display new artistic forms of expression.[135]

The swing of the *Mikado* was not a mere musical alteration—it required blackening the performance, altering formerly Japanese symbols and privileging those elements considered "Negro." The makeup of slanted eyes and small puckered lips revealed the orientalist theme, while costumes bearing bold colors, feathers, balls, and African-inspired headdresses separated the *Swing Mikado* from the original *Mikado*. In making this distinction, however, directors paved a new course in the history of black theater. The show was not part of an American tradition of romancing and caricaturing black mannerisms, but rather reflected Gilbert and Sullivan's tradition of satirizing aristocratic mores. Here, the Japanese façade in *The*

Mikado served as the vehicle for British actors to scrutinize Victorian society. The rigidity of law, formality of behavior, and emphasis on public morality pervaded British culture in the late nineteenth century.[136] The use of a façade, or mask, to comment on both individuals and society was not unfamiliar to black men and women, who over the centuries had utilized specific techniques of subverting the dominant power structure. In the *Swing Mikado*, the façade became not only the quasi-orientalist personae but also the classical structure of the opera. By acting in what was promoted as a "straight" *Mikado*, black men and women were validated as "serious" actors, but by swinging it (and thereby blackening it), they were able to endow *The Mikado* with distinct racial meaning. The music and lyrics of Gilbert and Sullivan, like the Japanese façade for British actors, thus became a portal for critiquing dominant cultural paradigms.

Although some traces of Japan remained (most noticeably in the song "My Object All Sublime," where the Mikado speaks of his role as the emperor of Japan), the setting was dramatically different. As one publicity bulletin described: "No Japanese lanterns, no screens, no pagodas. Coconut palms, bamboo and totem poles instead. Sarongs have replaced the ladies' kimonas. The Mikado wears a tophat, and he makes his entrance not, as heretofore, to the mutter of ladies' fans but to the lapping of waves in a South Sea war canoe!"[137] To adapt the show to its new cast and setting, writers altered the first lines of the show. Instead of singing, "If you want to know who we are / we are gentlemen of Japan," *Swing Mikado* actors chimed. "If you want to know who we are / we are High Steppers from afar." The script was further changed to suit the region since the actors no longer claimed to be "on many a screen and fan," but rather "on many a screen and star."[138]

By moving the *Swing Mikado* to a Pacific island, producers infused the production with the exoticism that they believed a swing performance required. Yet in equating blackness with a faster paced musical score and declaring it ill-suited for the original Japanese setting, directors were also reifying the same stereotypes of Japanese men and women that the classic *Mikado* put forth. In the minds of producers, Japanese were not only unable to swing, but the Eastern world of deference, precision, and morality could not adapt to high tempos and sexualized movement. In part, what initially put the swing in the *Swing Mikado* was a series of white assumptions and representations that defined the criteria for marketable and entertaining black theater. In providing the "authenticity" that producers argued the *Swing Mikado* demanded, as Houseman and Welles had attempted with the "voodoo" *Macbeth*, the FTP also hoped to provide black participants with a space more "adaptable" to their particular talents.[139]

The real swing—a shifting definition of theatrical tropes—came from the black performers themselves. Here, the quasi-erasure of orientalism significantly affected the cultural authority of black performers. If indeed the players were "High Steppers from afar," then the *Swing Mikado* inverted into a commentary on power within a black society. Although original *Mikado* lyrics were mostly replicated, this new form bore a different meaning within the context of American race relations. The pure love of Nanki-Poo escaped more conventional depictions of black men as lustful and adulterous; the omnipotent Mikado represented black political stature. As an exploration of relationships within a black community, the *Swing Mikado* bore neither the oppressive characteristics of minstrelsy nor the controversy of more contemporary, racially conscious FTP performances. Furthermore, while the classic *Mikado*'s setting and nationality had been altered, the *Swing Mikado*'s strict adherence to the plot and lyrics pronounced the story as transcending racial lines. Within the context of the play, black men and women experienced the same happiness, pain, and friendship as those white counterparts who had performed in the *Mikado* for almost a half century. Thus, for some white patrons, the black rendition of *The Mikado* perhaps affected their thinking about race even more than socially conscious plays with "Negro" themes, which may have seemed less accessible.

The syncopated music and modern choreography earned the *Swing Mikado* its highest acclaim. Although only three songs were "swung," they had an enormous impact on the performance. "A Wandering Minstrel," "My Object All Sublime," and "The Flowers That Bloom in the Spring" were first sung in the "straight" version intended by Gilbert and Sullivan, and then swung in encores. This technique served to legitimize the artistic capabilities of black actors who performed the classical lyrics, but it also afforded those same black actors the authority of their own interpretation. In swinging each song, which involved dances such as the Jitterbug, the Truck, and the Lindy-Hop, black men and women asserted that this was indeed their *Mikado*—not a mere recitation of white men's words and music. Furthermore, the selection of those songs that were swung reveals much about the cultural motivations of the producers, who prioritized the desires of the audience and the need to keep the original script intact. It is most likely that "A Wandering Minstrel" was swung because it was one of the more recognizable *Mikado* melodies; however, other factors came into

Four Jitterbugs from Swing Mikado. *(Federal Theatre Project Papers, Performing Arts Reading Room, Library of Congress)*

play. The three swung songs were positioned in the beginning, middle, and end of the show, with swing versions neither opening nor closing the production. With "straight" songs as the first and last compositions that the audience heard, directors aimed to envelop the more innovative elements of the show with a traditional framework. The heated politics of the FTP aroused suspicion of any production that could be interpreted as subversive; thus it was important for the producers to promote the show as "authentic" Gilbert and Sullivan.

Yet audiences would not easily forget the swing elements, in part because the "swingcopated" songs brought the audience to their feet, but also because they were integral to the plot of the story. "A Wandering Minstrel"

HOOKED ON CLASSICS

(a fascinating choice, given the double entendre) introduces Nanki-Poo, explaining his sentimental nature as well as his patriotic loyalty. Likewise, "My Object All Sublime" heralds the Mikado, listing his expectations as a leader. As these particular compositions were swung, these central characters, Nanki-Poo and the Mikado, became overtly connected to black artistic authority. Their positions within the performance became elevated as the romantic male lead and the story's patriarch transformed into magical purveyors of modern forms of song and dance. This particular Nanki-Poo and Mikado could transport the sights and sounds of urban nightlife into the folds of a classical operetta. Furthermore, the show's climactic dance number, "The Flowers That Bloom in the Spring," incorporated trucking and cakewalking into several encores, and the song morphed from a trite love song to an elaborate celebration of the power of movement. By replacing the simplicity of the song with a display of physical complexity, *Swing Mikado* actors forcefully shifted a performance of canonized words to a previously unseen articulation of movement.

Swing Mikado: *Received, Reviewed, Duplicated, Radicalized, and Commercialized*

When the *Swing Mikado* opened on 25 September 1938, Chicago audiences had eagerly anticipated its arrival. With a cast of seventy and a forty-piece orchestra, the scale of the production was larger than most FTP performances. Anxious about the public reception, Duncan Whiteside recalled, the producers were thinking, "My God! With a Black cast and swinging, what are the traditionalists going to do? They're going to snatch their hair out by the handful."[140] The fears of Whiteside and others were quickly put to rest, however, when the show began: "The overture started with a straight traditional *Mikado* sound. And then during the process of the overture, the arranger had stepped up the tempo and began to get a little left-hand beat into it. I knew before the curtain went up we had a smash hit because feet were pounding all over the audience. . . . And when they swung into it, why, we were home free and knew it. But it's not often you know before the curtain goes up that you've got a hit."[141]

Glowing reviews flooded in almost overnight, many claiming that the performance would satisfy "even the most exacting patron of the Savoy."[142] Theater critics admired the cast's ability to perform the words of Gilbert and Sullivan and applauded the production's precision and authenticity. "They [the cast] get over words and music better than most Whites who claim to be Gilbert and Sullivan specialists," the *Chicago Daily Times* pronounced.[143] Likewise, the *Chicago Tribune* reviewer exclaimed, "he [Maurice Cooper] is the best Nanki-Poo I have ever heard, bar none."[144] Black newspapers such as the *Chicago Defender* strongly agreed, declaring the production a "supreme achievement" and championing the actors and actresses for bringing forth new "entertainment and appreciation to the American public."[145] Viewing the performance in terms of racial advancement, more so than white newspapers that evaluated the artistic and technical elements of the show, black reporters understood that the show contributed to Carlton Moss's concept of "cultural emancipation."

While many white reviewers would have agreed with *Daily Record* reporter Ben Burns when he urged readers to "truck on down to the Great Northern Theatre-way for the hottest swingeroo to hit town since the King of Jitterbugs, Benny Goodman," they could not avoid depicting the performers in an essentialist manner.[146] The *Chicago Evening American* declared that the performers were a "lusty Negro company" and that the show was a "good colored comic opera—Ethiopera."[147] Although white critics acknowledged that the black cast delivered a highly entertaining and vivid rendition of *The Mikado*, one reporter claimed to have noticed some diminished accuracy in the dialogue, as "wit numbers were lost in the rich thickness of Africa-American [*sic*] speech."[148] In addition, the transformation of the original Japanese was met with some ambivalence among reviewers; Gail Borden of the *Chicago Daily Times* certainly had expectations of a Japanese *Mikado*, which caused some confusion: "It seems silly to dress the members of the chorus like coolies when they are supposed to be very stiff and proper gents."[149] While these reviews undoubtedly reveal the persistence of racist characterizations, they also indicate how difficult it was for some critics to move outside of a minstrel framework. Because commercial theater offered so few roles for African Americans outside of stereotypes, some white critics either internalized the *Swing Mikado* in terms of their own expectations or disregarded it altogether.

However, other reporters admired the costumes and setting that some of their colleagues (mostly white ones) found particularly disconcerting. Katherine Irvin of the *Chicago Sunday Bee* celebrated the show's alternative locale, stating that the "background of ever moving, deep blue Pacific waves . . . put the audience in the mood to fully appreciate the colorful, fantastic and undeniably becoming costumes that combine Japanese, Malay and African ideas in the most artistic manner."[150] For this reviewer the elements that others had declared demeaning to the original *Mikado* were perceived as cross-cultural contributions that only provided it with more

HOOKED ON CLASSICS

texture. Black newspapers revealed a similar appreciation of the performance's foray into an artistic rendering. "The two scenes [backdrops] . . . are lovely . . . one feels that he is really in the locale of Pacific sunshine and moonlight," the *Chicago Defender* reported.[151] The *Associated Negro Press* also commented on the beauty and quality of the set design, describing the show as "colorful, refreshing, and well done."[152] With more comments on the response of the white audience, as well as praise for individual performers, black newspapers remained more focused than white ones on the benefits the show offered to its participants, as well as the precedent it might set for future productions.

Speaking to the power of the swing numbers, Lloyd Lewis of the *Chicago Daily News* commented that after these songs, "your drama delegate was disappointed to find the performance slump back into the orthodox score for an hour."[153] Also requesting more "swingcopation" was Ben Burns of the *Daily Record*, noting, "the audience resented the use of the original script as a ball and chain."[154] For other reviewers, however, the idea of a swing *Mikado* was not as successful, as Gail Borden indicated, "I've seen bigger audiences wowed a lot more by good companies doing it straight." Noting the downsides of trying to "better an original" when the original did not need bettering, Borden praised the singing abilities of the cast, but urged the FTP to pursue "more comic opera" in its traditional form.[155] In a more scathing review, Dorothy Day of the *Herald and Examiner* claimed that the swing arrangements were "trite, and the dancing, instead of being a variation of the original style and the concept of the 'shag' artist . . . is no more or less than the conventional steps you can see any night."[156]

The skepticism expressed by Dorothy Day and other reviewers did not prevent theatergoers from flocking to the Great Northern Theatre. As the most successful program staged by the FTP, the *Swing Mikado* ran for five months in Chicago, selling out at almost every performance. As *Swing Mikado* attendance totaled approximately 250,000 people and cleared $35,000, the *Chicago Tribune* declared the show the "Hit of the Season."[157] "So great is the demand for seats that they are being put on sale four weeks in advance," C. J. Bulliet of the *Chicago Daily News* reported. "I know one woman who has seen the show eight times and she's intelligent."[158] The success of the *Swing Mikado*, however, eventually prompted a larger drama to unfold, causing Congress to question the goals of the WPA. As Hallie Flanagan exclaimed, "if Federal Theatre had ever wanted to produce a cycle of plays epitomizing its own projects . . . Chicago [would have been staged] as melodrama."[159]

In the summer of 1938, Illinois FTP director John McGee had already begun negotiating with New York producer J. J. Shubert to move the *Swing Mikado* to New York under commercial auspices. Because McGee conducted many of these meetings in secret and attempted to persuade some cast members to sign contracts with Shubert, Midwest regional director Howard Miller and Florence Kerr, regional director of the Women's and Professional Program, decided to terminate his employment.[160] McGhee's actions prompted the concern of director Harry Minturn, who made it clear to Hallie Flanagan that he did not want to give up the show to commercial theater. Minturn was concerned that if the show closed in New York, performers would return to FTP without the possibility of a *Swing Mikado* reopening. There were also no guarantees that New York producers would use the same cast. In particular, Minturn was reluctant to give up a show that the Chicago FTP had created and that had proven to be a moneymaker. Although Flanagan and Florence Kerr shared some of Minturn's sentiments regarding the preservation of the show's origin, they nonetheless could not ignore the WPA's central motivation to return people to private industry. In a compromise, the show moved to New York City under WPA auspices, opening on 1 March 1939, at the New Yorker Theatre on 54th Street, where it ran until May.[161]

The New York debut of the *Swing Mikado* was an event of enormous proportions, drawing the attendance of Eleanor Roosevelt, Mayor La Guardia, and Harry Hopkins. Even more so than Chicago reviewers, however, New York critics lamented the lack of swing in this *Mikado*. "They scarcely swing it enough," recalled *New York Times* critic Brooks Atkinson. "It ought to swing from end to end; it ought to get in the groove and stay there," exclaimed *Stage and Screen* reviewer John Anderson.[162] Addressing the artistic opportunities the *Swing Mikado* afforded black performers, *New York Post* writer John Mason Brown criticized the show's reluctance to completely break from tradition. Brown indicated that the show "takes no chances" in offering new lyrical and choreographical interpretations, giving black actors little room for their own artistry.[163] Viewing the *Swing Mikado* as many black newspapers did, the *Daily Worker* evaluated the show in the larger context of economic and social opportunities rather than pure theatrical autonomy. Yet in urging the producers to "gain courage and jazz up the whole show," the *Daily Worker* still envisioned greater artistic freedom as the next step, once the presence and employment of black actors were guaranteed.[164]

Those who had called for more "swingcopation" in the *Swing Mikado*

Eleanor Roosevelt and Colonel Francis Clark Harrington, director of the wpa, attend a Swing Mikado *performance in New York City. (Federal Theatre Project Papers, Performing Arts Reading Room, Library of Congress)*

were soon granted their request by commercial theater. When producer Michael Todd was unable to secure the rights to the *Swing Mikado* before its original Chicago run, he developed his own version in the spring of 1939, the *Hot Mikado*, which swung the entire performance and featured famous black actors such as Bill "Bojangles" Robinson.[165] With more money for costumes and sets than the FTP could ever afford, the *Hot Mikado* became a much slicker version, suiting the tastes of many critics and audiences. Offering a huge cast of dancers, musicians, and elaborate visual effects, the performance contained many attractive elements that the FTP simply could not replicate.

New York's FTP *Swing Mikado*, on the other hand, was facing its own troubles. By 1939, with Congress eager to cut "un-American" WPA programs and the relief budget in general, further actions were taken to abolish the FTP. Over the course of its investigation, the Dies committee received enough ammunition to confirm the project's allegedly subversive activities, quieting many supporters of white-collar relief programs. Yet further hearings conducted by the House Subcommittee on Appropriations, headed by southerner Clifton Woodrum (D-Va.), temporarily eschewed the question of subversion and instead turned to the economic

Jitterbugs dancing in the aisle during a Swing Mikado *performance in New York City.*
(Federal Theatre Project Papers, Performing Arts Reading Room, Library of Congress)

components of federal relief. Here, the *Swing Mikado* became a subject of debate, as anti–New Dealers such as Woodrum hammered into the show's production and employment records. Woodrum interrogated Florence Kerr on every aspect of the *Swing Mikado*: How many of the principals were on relief? What proportion of the cast was theatrically trained? What was the cost of equipment, costumes, and rent? Were the actors who played Nanki-Poo and Yum-Yum "colored"? This line of questioning aimed to support congressional claims that the FTP was not solely concerned with relief and supposedly revealing the same type of boondoggling found in other WPA agencies. Woodrum also asked whether commercial producers had sought out the show; Kerr responded that those producers were only willing to employ part of the company.[166]

All of these questions underscored the issue of whether the FTP was an agency to boost the theater industry as a whole, or whether it was solely a relief project. The hearing also raised the dilemma of whether successful productions, such as the *Swing Mikado*, could exist under FTP auspices without damaging commercial industry. Although Kerr and Colonel F. C. Harrington, Hopkins's successor as WPA director, made several arguments relating to the *Swing Mikado*'s benefit to the theater business, congressional skeptics remained unconvinced that the FTP was not competing with a "languishing and sick" theater industry. For many politicians, productions such as the *Swing Mikado* had gone far beyond providing relief to unemployed theatrical employees.[167]

When members of Congress questioned them about commercial producers who were interested in buying the *Swing Mikado*, FTP administrators felt enormous pressure to sell the show. Thus, when producers Bernard Ulrich and Marvin Ericson made a "bona-fide offer," federal officials begrudgingly accepted.[168] The only change in the production would be new scenery, as federal property could not be used by the private sector. The commercial *Swing Mikado* opened on 1 May, playing at the 44th Street Theater, right across from the Broadhurst, where the *Hot Mikado* ran. The "Mikadization of New York" went even further, as the International Ladies Garment Workers Union did their own version, the *Red Mikado*, satirizing various elements of political conservatism. But the competition of the black *Mikado* productions eventually led to their demise; the commercial *Swing Mikado* ran for only twenty-four performances (along with sixty-two performances under the FTP at the New Yorker) and the *Hot Mikado* left Broadway after eighty-five shows. *Swing Mikado* producers were able to tour their show for a short period, but the show's popularity was compromised by other versions, such as Philadelphia's *Mikado in Swing*, not to mention higher audience expectations brought on by Todd's star-studded version. Thus, by the summer 1939, the "Battle of the Black Mikados" had ended, though leaving an indelible mark on the future of black theater.[169] These many *Mikados* proved that white individuals were willing and eager to view black entertainers in roles outside minstrel stereotypes; yet, they still offered the comfort of a recognizable artistic format where the audience could sing along. The proliferation of *The Mikado*, therefore, resulted from the fusion of one the most beloved musicals with white America's insatiable desire for black performance.

As Congress reviewed another relief bill in June 1939, it became evident that the future of the FTP looked grim. Under this legislation, the Federal Writers', Art, and Music projects could continue only under local

sponsorship—however, the Federal Theatre Project would be abolished. There were some supporters in Congress and many esteemed actors and directors who promoted the FTP's continuation. However, they were not able to sway the majority of politicians who were adamant about its dis-
continuation and who consistently drew their criticism from the findings of the Dies committee. As the termination of the FTP was a sticking point in the relief bill, which also granted relief funds for public works buildings and other WPA projects, neither legislators nor the president—who called the abolition of the FTP "discrimination of the worst kind"—were willing to jeopardize larger relief aims to maintain a controversial theater project. On 30 June 1939, the relief bill was amended to include the payment of three months' salary to all FTP relief workers, and the project was shut down.[170]

MANY ASPECTS OF THE FTP made it seem more radical, and therefore more threatening, than other arts programs. Larger in scope, but also featuring live performances, the theater was an arena that lacked a protective shield against the dissemination of political opinion. Just as the *Swing Mikado* reflected much more than the recitation of Gilbert and Sullivan lyrics—offering a new, racialized interpretation of the play's movements, words, and design—other FTP performances testified to the inherently political nature of culture. Congressmen were less comfortable with the politics of the stage than the narratives embedded in the FWP's American Guide Series, even as the FWP underwent its own scrutiny.

In this politically volatile atmosphere, performances such as the *Swing Mikado* would prove more adaptable to national cultural priorities. With its musical elements, reliance on a familiar narrative, and eventual employment of noted celebrities (such as the commercial production featuring Bill Robinson in the *Hot Mikado*), the *Swing Mikado* foreshadowed the kinds of productions that the government would construct during the war years. Robinson himself would feature centrally in several wartime cultural programs aimed at buttressing "Negro morale," and components of the *Swing Mikado* would become featured in the development of other federal programs centering on black musical performance, such as the *Jubilee* radio show. Certainly *Jubilee* and the *Swing Mikado* were created under very different organizations and with differing intentions; however both featured a talented array of black entertainers who used a conventional musical forum to convey unconventional politics.

The assumption that an independent black theater would be the best forum for the examination of black life reveals a particularity of this form of government-sponsored culture in its endorsement of separatism. Bureaucratic structures such as the Negro Units, devoted to the distinctive contributions of racial and ethnic groups, would starkly contrast with a wartime official culture emphasizing the commonalities of all Americans. In addition, officials within other divisions of the FAP, such as the FWP, did not initially intend to treat black Americans as a separate group, espousing the American Guide Series as a holistic documentation of America's regions. In the development of the American Guide Series, the study of black Americans received a very different bureaucratic and artistic treatment than the FTP's Negro Units, although confronting similar political obstacles. The search for authentic black culture would continue but under new types of authorities with a different set of priorities and motivations. Provided with the means to reconstruct the history of African Americans, FWP administrators such as Sterling Brown aspired to develop a "truthful" written narrative. Yet, revision proved a difficult endeavor. The form and viability of FWP publications would be determined by competing interests within the program and by conservative forces outside of it.

chapter three

THE EDITOR'S DILEMMA

In a speech delivered to the National Negro Congress in October 1937, the renowned writer and poet Sterling Brown, national editor of the Negro Affairs division of the Federal Writers' Project from 1936 to 1939, relayed the many obstacles facing black authors: "The Negro writer is faced by a limited audience: his own group, for various reasons, reads few books and buys less; and white America, in the main, is hardly an audience ready for truthful representation of Negro life. The Negro writer has the job of revising certain stereotypes of Negro life and character, whose growth extends from the beginning of the American novel in Cooper to the latest best seller, 'Gone With the Wind.'"[1] While this outlook reflects Brown's own pessimism, it was shaped, at least in part, by his experience with the FWP's Negro Affairs. FWP director Henry Alsberg appointed Brown to this position in the spring of 1936, recognizing him as a guardian of black history. Overseeing the racial content of the FWP's major undertaking, the American Guide Series, Brown committed himself to the eradication of stereotypes and the extraction of African American history from the margins.

As the development of the American Guide Series was the primary focus within the FWP, its national directors believed that the positive depiction of all minority groups—particularly African Americans—was an important goal for state and national officials. Yet, even at the project's inception, Brown was immediately conscious of potential roadblocks, and as he became more deeply entrenched in the FWP bureaucracy, he faced entanglements with state writers, directors, and white racial attitudes that hindered his ultimate goals for revision. At the beginning of Brown's directorship, questions immediately surfaced: Would white America accept black history as part of the narrative? How would white FWP workers respond to the criticism of a black editor? Was a government-sponsored initiative the most viable means for fulfilling these racial initiatives?

Despite the resonance of these loaded issues, the FWP and the American Guide Series held important political implications for black Americans. Whereas the narrative of white historians dominated major events in black history, such as slavery and Reconstruction, the American Guide Series endowed black FWP employees with cultural authority. Sterling Brown's appointment as the director of Negro Affairs demonstrated liberal administrators' belief that important historical revision should be placed in the hands of a black leader—significantly, without the kind of debate that FTP officials engaged in. Through their comments and editorials, Brown and his assistants provided a powerful counternarrative to traditional racial iconographies, pressing the general reading public to understand black life in what they believed to be a more inclusive, less stereotypical fashion. Here, Brown responded to the call of famed historian and bibliophile Arthur Schomburg, who issued a warning to black writers a decade before the creation of the FWP:

> The American Negro must remake his past in order to make his future. . . . For him, a group tradition must supply compensation for persecution, and pride of race the antidote for prejudice. . . . The Negro has been a man without a history because he has been considered a man without a worthy culture. . . . But there is no doubt that here is a field full of most intriguing and inspiring possibilities. Already the Negro sees himself against a reclaimed background, in a perspective that will give pride and self-respect ample scope, and make history yield for him the same values that the treasured past of any people affords.[2]

Brown's treatment of black men and women in the American Guide Series and his compilation of a massive black history in the "Portrait of the Negro as an American" (PNAM) project served as the most sustained and widespread response to this initiative. Although Brown encountered several obstacles in editing the guide series, and although the PNAM project was never published, his role as a national editor reflected a newfound opportunity for an African American within the federal government's cultural apparatus.

Scholars have recently displayed a great deal of interest in the Federal Writers' Project and in Brown as a significant figure in the African American literary cannon, and they have provided new insight into the New

Deal's racial ethos.[3] Yet in attempting to "shift the focus away from the administrative aspects of the Writers' Projects," the cultural and political context of Brown's federal position becomes less pronounced.[4] Certainly, Brown's tenure as Negro Affairs editor was important because of the progressive materials that he and his editors produced, but also because of his role in shaping the government's larger racial agenda, confirming the increasing federal emphasis on cultural development. Working in the national office with other central FWP editors, Brown held the highest post of any African American in the WPA's four arts programs and was largely responsible for designating how black American culture would be delineated in the national record. Brown was also responsible for designating the kinds of racial imagery the nation's cultural apparatus would advance, setting a model for how the government could best incorporate "Negro affairs" in the future. Furthermore, as state editors had to submit all copy to Brown for review—as an African American expert—they could not easily ignore his comments.

When Brown accepted the position, it became clear that although the FWP was dedicated to illuminating a more pluralistic America, it was not feasible to procure that same diversity among state employees. Negro Affairs editors always encountered limits in adding African Americans to state payrolls and incorporating them into the guidebooks. Although FWP directors did not initially conceive of undertaking separate studies of black culture and history, such as *The Negro in Virginia* (1940), to remedy the deficiencies of the guidebooks, they did eventually serve that purpose, providing black editors with more editorial control. The experiences of African Americans in the FWP came to buttress the notion that perhaps the best method for employing black artists and for examining black culture and history was through racially separate forums.

Brown's biggest obstacles were undoubtedly the bureaucratic composition of the FWP and the bigotry of many state editors; however, he also had to contend with Congressman Martin Dies's committee, which relished delving into any racially suspect behavior or writings that they came across and targeting the FWP as "un-American." Yet, if Brown and his editors wrestled with the complexities of defining the contours of African American history—facing resistance from within and without—they nonetheless documented the heterogeneity of black communities across America and fought for what they believed were more accurate representations. For these editors, representation was a means of empowerment, and they took the reigns with a heightened sense of possibility. Many liberal FWP

THE EDITOR'S DILEMMA

administrators hoped that black history and American history would eventually become synonymous and that through the American Guide Series they could set the record straight.

The conflicts that ensued under a black editor within the FWP were unique among the programs of the Federal Arts Project. In other federal programs, official debates arose over whether black individuals should necessarily take charge of racial issues; yet FWP director Alsberg appointed a black editor in charge of Negro Affairs from the outset, without discernible disagreement on the matter. Tensions existed between state and national officials of the FWP, and Brown's position was volatile due to state sensitivities on racial matters, particularly in the South. The complexities of the editorial process that Brown faced, however, should not undermine the political weight of his directorship. Once Brown assumed the directorship, all state editors had to recognize his authority and submit copy to him, even if they disagreed with his suggestions. Furthermore, this administrative post was a milestone in chronicling black history, inasmuch as the federal administration endorsed the kind of bottom-up history Brown strongly endorsed. As Brown's vision for the PNAM foreshadowed the work of New Social Historians in the 1960s and 1970s, the government became a locus for broadscale historical revision.

Creating the American Guide Series

New Deal officials had pressed for an initiative to research black history even before the creation of the Federal Arts Project. Federal Emergency Relief administrators authorized a small-scale project in Kentucky and Indiana in which twelve black college graduates interviewed ex-slaves under the supervision of Kentucky State College professor Lawrence Reddick. Although they gathered approximately 250 interviews between September 1934 and July 1935, the purpose of the relief project was to employ black college graduates, and most employees had little college training or interviewing experience. FERA workers also attempted to construct a more general folklore study; however, this project and the ex-slave interviews required trained writers and anthropologists that FERA was not able to procure on a national scale. The accounts of ex-slaves and other forms of oral history alerted directors to the need for a larger apparatus for recording these experiences, and significantly, the need for black personnel. Yet, historian Norman Yetman contends, due to the disorganization that manifested when FERA attempted to record slave narratives, FWP director Henry Alsberg was initially reluctant to take on the same endeavor under his program. Although interviews were conducted independently within southern writers' projects, it was not until April 1937 that the Washington office assumed direction of the slave narrative collection.[5]

Officials expressed an interest in documenting American pluralism within other agencies predating the WPA. At the same time as the early ex-slave interviews, the Civil Works Authority authorized states such as Connecticut and New Mexico to begin surveys of historic sites and to preserve records relating to local communities. Although this venture employed at least a thousand writers, it was not enough to meet the larger number of those unemployed. Demanding federal relief for writers on a national scale, left-wing organizations such as the Writers Union, the Unemployed Writers Union, and the Authors Guild conducted pickets in New York City and petitioned Washington officials. Their actions influenced administrators such as Jacob Baker, FERA director of Work Relief and Special Projects, who worked with his assistants to develop broadscale employment programs.[6] With a background in publishing as a manager at Vanguard Press in New York, and with ties to writers and artists in Greenwich Village, Baker was particularly sympathetic to the needs of writers when formulating relief plans.

The impetus for the American Guide Series came from Katherine Kellock, whose writer husband, Harold Kellock, was a close friend of FWP director Henry Alsberg. Katherine Kellock had used the Baedeker guidebooks while pursuing relief work in southern and central Europe after World War I, and upon returning, she had taken on settlement work in New York before attending Columbia University as a history major. Administrative concerns about appropriate methods of providing white-collar relief, coupled with a federal interest in detailing America's regional histories, led Kellock to propose the American Guide Series, based on the famous Baedeker guides. Lobbying at private Washington parties and suggesting the idea to several WPA officials, Kellock's determination eventually paid off. With the success of a guidebook in Connecticut, written under FERA auspices and published in 1935, FERA director Jacob Baker became convinced that a guidebook series would be the most feasible project for unemployed writers. Not only would the guidebooks fill a void in American culture, chronicling previously unexplored communities, but they would also boost tourism by encouraging Americans to explore the country. Furthermore, the American Guide Series could aid a large number of white-collar professionals, extending not only to authors and journalists but also clerks and even some clergymen.[7]

THE EDITOR'S DILEMMA

The viability of the guidebook project under FERA ensured its lifespan once the WPA allocated funds for white-collar programs. The FWP specifically stated that the major undertaking for writers would be to prepare a five-volume guidebook of the United States, divided by region. The FWP also established a project for interviewing ex-slaves and conducting folklore studies that had begun under FERA.[8] To head the FWP, Jacob Baker, now director of WPA white-collar programs by 1935, selected Henry Alsberg, a former New York journalist, theatrical writer, and political activist. Although involved in radical politics during the 1920s, conducting rallies for civil liberties with anarchist Emma Goldman, Alsberg's radicalism had become tempered by the 1930s, when he worked primarily for the government. As supervisor for records and reports issued by FERA, Alsberg worked closely with Jacob Baker who recognized Alsberg's strengths as an editor.[9]

"The directors of the [Federal Writers'] project . . . are endeavoring to make the Guide more than a handbook of tourist information," Alsberg stated, with high hopes in mind. Envisioned as a creative and imaginative project that would focus on all aspects of American life from industry to arts to folklore, the American Guide Series was much more than an improvement of the Baedeker guides (which Alsberg duly noted were published before the widespread use of the automobile); they were a direct representation of the New Deal's pluralistic outlook. Alsberg and the central FWP staff in Washington envisioned a broad readership for the guides who would rely on these books for an understanding of their own communities as well as regions they hoped to visit. For many writers, the project would offer an opportunity to research new aspects of American life, while providing them with time to write novels, poetry, or undertake other types of work outside project hours. Alsberg proclaimed, "The project of the American Guide was inaugurated in order to solve the problem of caring for writers who need government aid and who at the same time must preserve their integrity and independence."[10]

As Alsberg selected (or Baker appointed) the central FWP staff, its composition reflected the progressive sensibility of other WPA agencies. Associate director George Cronyn had published two novels and had taught English at the University of Montana; he also revealed an eclectic background ranging from cowboy to stage manager. The other top administrator, Reed Harris, had served as editor of Columbia University's student newspaper, the *Spectator*, where he broke from campus tradition by charging the university with elitism, labor exploitation, and unscrupulous financial practices. Harris's editorials prompted the university administration to expel him, provoking a massive student protest for free speech, which eventually resulted in Harris's reinstatement. He later used his muckraking talents as a journalist, working for the *New York Times* and the *New York Journal.* Most of Alsberg's major editors were old friends with liberal inclinations. Research editor Lawrence Abbott and literary editor Waldo Browne had written for and edited leftist periodicals such as *Literary Digest*, the *Dial*, and the *Nation.* Field supervisor Joseph Gaer, a Russian immigrant with experience in a California FERA project, had various publications in literary and folklore journals; Lawrence Morris, another field supervisor, formerly acted as assistant editor of the *New Republic.* In addition, although they did not work exclusively on the American Guide Series, FWP folklore editors John Lomax and B. A. Botkin and socioethnic studies director Morton Royse shared the cosmopolitan outlook of other FWP officials. Most FWP administrators had traveled extensively, studied at elite universities, and engaged in social work, and they expressed a similar fervor for celebrating America's folk roots through the study of regional communities. Their pluralistic outlook inspired directors to promote the greatest geographic, racial, and ethnic diversity within the state guides.[11]

Although FWP administrators had originally conceived of the project as a study of five regions, this idea became increasingly problematic, due to both the difficulties in defining particular regions and the great deal of time required to complete these far-ranging studies. Legislators in Congress, already questioning the purpose of the Federal Arts Project, called for fast production. Under these pressures, FWP associate director George Cronyn instead proposed guides on a state-by-state basis. Accepting this idea, Alsberg appointed forty-eight state directors who would oversee the project and would submit all copy to the Washington office for editorial approval. The staff that worked on the American Guide Series reflected a hodgepodge of occupations, exhibiting varying levels of experience as writers. Due to the WPA regulation that 90 percent of project personnel come from public relief rolls, many established writers, who had gained some financial support from the Authors League of America, were not eligible for the project. In addition, employment quotas did not often match the percentage of writers in each state; three-quarters of the states were unable to find professional writers to employ, while cities such as New York required a larger allotment.[12]

As a result, criteria for writers in the states eventually came to describe "almost any other occupation that involved an understanding of the English language and some training and observations in the preparation of records."[13] Many writers in the project, particularly in rural states, were not even trained in spelling and grammar—and often ignored questions of accuracy in presenting information. Although this seriously affected the quality of the guides, shifting the entire burden of editorial responsibilities to state and national directors, the FWP nonetheless achieved one of its objectives: it relieved a number of Americans from poverty. According to FWP coordinating editor Jerre Mangione, in Nebraska, one of the states most dramatically affected by the Depression, starving to death was a real possibility; and for at least one Nebraska couple who were considering suicide, being on the FWP payroll was literally a lifesaver.[14] At the project's height in April 1936, payrolls included 6,471 names; by 1938, when Congress had dramatically reduced relief allocations, the number employed was approximately 3,500.[15] FWP historian Monty Penkower estimates that in its four-year span, an average of 4,500 to 5,200 people worked for the project consistently.[16]

Despite the large number of amateur and inexperienced writers employed on the project, there was a contingent of established authors and poets. States such as Illinois, New York, Massachusetts, and California, all thriving literary centers, contributed some notable writers. These included Saul Bellow, Nelson Algren, Margaret Walker, and Richard Wright in Illinois; James Hopper and Kenneth Rexroth in California; Conrad Aiken in Massachusetts; Claude McKay, Lionel Abel, Maxwell Bodenheim, and Ralph Ellison in New York; and Zora Neale Hurston in Florida. These writers, however, comprised a small minority of FWP employees; one 1938 survey indicated that of the 4,500 workers, only 82 were considered "recognized writers" and 97 had held "important editorial posts."[17]

Several state directors had also achieved prominence as writers and academics. These individuals included Vardis Fischer (Idaho), a Pulitzer prize-winning novelist; Harold Merriam (Montana), chairman of the English Department at the University of Montana; and Harlan Hatcher (Ohio), professor of English at Ohio State University, who had published several books, articles, and short stories. Many of the directors reflected local color in their own work, with attention to the plight of workers, farmers, or other underrepresented groups. Among southerners working on the project, some state directors promoted liberal views in their own work, which encouraged the cooperation of Negro Affairs units in preparing the guidebooks. North Carolina director Edwin Bjorkman, a native of Stockholm, served as editor of the *Asheville Times*, and had published essays and two novels that treated issues such as evolution and psychology. Massachusetts-born Texas editor J. Frank Davis worked as a newspaper correspondent for forty years, penning the historical novel *The Road to San Jacinto* (1936), a depiction of Texas's struggle for independence against Mexico. Davis also wrote two character studies of black life, which writer E. Current-Garcia claimed featured a black hero who was "far removed from the usual slapstick burlesque type common in Southern fiction."[18] Lastly, Lyle Saxon, the Louisiana director, received the O'Henry prize for a collection of his short stories and published four novels chronicling life in the South. Saxon addressed racial themes in his novel *Children of Strangers* (1937), which examined the lives of "Louisiana octoroons, offspring of many generations of black and white miscegenation, who inhabit the Cane River country near Natchitoches."[19] Overall, state directors revealed a diversity of backgrounds, and political factors often influenced their appointments. For example, Pennsylvania director Paul French was the governor's cousin and the vice president of the American Newspaper Guild; one Nebraska director was recommended by the editor of the *Lincoln Star*, the only New Deal newspaper in Nebraska, as well as by Independent senator George Norris, a staunch Roosevelt campaigner.[20]

The Vision of Sterling Brown and the Problems of Administration

For Brown and his editors, representing black Americans in the guide-books required the willingness of staff writers to procure information on black life. At the inception of the program in December 1935, Henry Alsberg had expressed his concerns: "I am sure that there is discrimination in the southern states against employment of negroes on the Writers' Projects. I have raised this point in several jurisdictions and have received assurance that something would be done to ameliorate this situation. I have a field representative going to Georgia tomorrow and he will have definite instructions to see that a few negroes are employed on the Writers' Projects in that state."[21] To counter the undeniable problem of discrimination, Alsberg also proposed the appointment of a black administrator who would be responsible for the sections of the guides that would be "devoted to the negro race." Anxious to receive "special permission" from WPA director Harry Hopkins, Alsberg indicated, "I feel that it would be only just that one able negro writer be given a position here in Washington, so that the American Guide will do justice to negroes."[22] After securing funds for a national editor of Negro Affairs and consulting several black leaders, Alsberg appointed Brown, a Howard University professor, poet, and literary critic, in the spring of 1936.

Born on 1 May 1901, in Washington, D.C., to Adelaide Allen Brown and the Reverend Sterling Nelson Brown, Brown spent much of his youth on the campus of Howard University, where his father taught in the religion department. Surrounded by Howard's black intellectuals such as Kelly Miller and Alain Locke, he quickly developed an interest in black literature and art. Brown attended the distinguished Dunbar High School, where noted African Americans such as Angelina Grimké and Jessie Fauset served as instructors; among the others attending Dunbar at the same time were William Hastie and Charles Drew. In this environment, Brown thrived as a student, achieving an academic scholarship to attend Williams College at the age of seventeen. Although Williams subtly enforced racial separateness, Brown benefited from his relationships with the other black students, including Allison Davis, Carter Marshall, and Mortimer Weaver. Some of these individuals — Davis, for one — would later serve as major contributors to the FWP's Negro Affairs division, working closely with Brown on a number of projects.[23]

Brown's studies at Williams focused on literary criticism, and he also began to write poetry. After graduating, he attended graduate school in literature at Harvard, where he was deeply influenced by the poetry of Robert Frost and Edwin Robinson. While these literary figures centered their writing on the lives and emotions of ordinary people, Brown also became interested in their emphasis on regionalism, admiring how these two poets illuminated the American landscape with a particular honesty. The writers of the Harlem Renaissance also deeply influenced Brown, who came of age as a poet in the 1920s. Although several of Brown's poems appeared in such periodicals as the *Crisis* and *Opportunity* during that decade, as well as in Countee Cullen's anthology, *Caroling Dusk* (1927), literary scholars do not traditionally characterize Brown as one of the major figures of the Harlem Renaissance. Most prolific in the 1930s and 1940s, Brown was nonetheless indebted to writers such as Langston Hughes and Jean Toomer, who spoke to the aesthetic value of folk music and language, drawing attention to the black masses. According to Brown biographer Joanne Gabbin, although Brown lauded the work of Harlem writers like Claude McKay and Countee Cullen, it was the highly experimental nature of the poetry of Toomer and of Hughes that most inspired him.[24]

Like much of the literature of the Harlem Renaissance, Brown's seminal work *Southern Road* (1932) reflected a passion for understanding both humanity and region, portraying southern black folklife with a concern for language and traditions.[25] Through this work, Brown asserted that dialect was not necessarily demeaning and could represent the true emotions of African Americans. Brown's poetry challenged what some literary schol- ars consider a "middle-class exclusivity" that pervaded New Negro literature, providing a vehicle for examining the perspective of ordinary African Americans.[26] After graduating from Harvard in 1923, Brown taught English at Virginia Seminary for three years, where he became enmeshed in the black rural communities in Lynchburg. From his experiences with the folk traditions of these men and women, he came to conclude that "dialect, or the speech of the people, is capable of expressing whatever the people are."[27] Brown's interest in what he considered "authentic" black illustrations and the traditions of local communities would fuel his activities as Negro Affairs editor and would shape the content of several projects.

After holding teaching posts at Lincoln University in Missouri and at Fisk University in Tennessee, Brown joined the faculty of Howard in 1929. At this time, the university was at the center of black education, drawing some of the most distinguished African American intellectuals. Ralph Bunche, E. Franklin Frazier, and Rayford Logan taught at Howard during the 1930s, creating a forum to discuss the problem of racial inequality. When Alsberg selected Brown as editor of Negro Affairs, mainly based on his reputation as an educator at Howard and his extensive publishing record, the FWP director did not view him as a politically controversial figure. In addition, with his elite educational background and interest in American folklore, Brown was similar to FAP officials such as Alsberg and Hallie Flanagan.[28]

In selecting Brown as an administrator, Alsberg did not question whether a black individual should run the Negro Affairs division. This contrasted with the experience of the FTP, where debates proliferated over the choice of a director for the New York Negro Unit, and where black participants eventually decided upon the white John Houseman. Certainly, these genres were very different; for one thing, as some black intellectuals argued, the attraction of a racially mixed audience and the various aspects of theatrical production depended on an industry run by white people. But the choice of Sterling Brown had much to do with Alsberg's own belief that black scholars best understood black history. Alsberg supported the need to eradicate racial stereotypes and to present accurate accounts of black history; Brown's background in attempting both these goals, coupled with his academic connections, ensured that the FWP would attempt to depict African Americans free of stereotypes and include them throughout the text.

Like other black writers in the 1920s and 1930s, Brown believed that cultural representations directly related to the political and economic progress of black Americans. As Brown biographer Joanne Gabbin contends, "the treatment of an oppressed group in literature parallels its treatment in life, and predictably, the greater the incidence of oppression, the greater degree of misrepresentation . . . in the literature."[29] In his criticism of existing black studies, Brown best stated his motivation to correct the "misrepresentation" of black history:

> The Negro in America has been greatly written about, but most frequently as a separate entity, as a problem, not as a participant. Largely neglected in broad historical consideration, or receiving specialized attention from social scientists, the Negro has too seldom been revealed as an integral part of American life. Many Negro historians have attempted to counter the neglect, but the result has been over-emphasis, and "separateness." Where white historians find few or no Negroes and too little important participation, Negro historians find many and too much.[30]

It is worth noting that Brown's criticism of separatism stood in stark contrast to those black individuals, such as Rose McClendon, who were formulating the FTP's Negro Units. For those black men and women in the FTP, a black theater could become a community-building enterprise, advancing black playwrights and performers and enriching black audiences. Sterling Brown, however, did not initially advocate this vision; while he hoped to employ as many black writers as possible, his goal for production was to incorporate black life into the mainstream.

In a letter to Horace Mann Bond, Brown sarcastically commented on standard guidebooks: "You know the thing: Stone Mountain, 'it was here that the Crackers couldn't pay Gutzon Borglum so he left them without torsoes [sic]' . . . cotton fields, 'it is here that darkies want to be born so that they can dance and sing and swing rhythm.'"[31] In procuring black academics such as Bond, Allison Davis, and others to make up an advisory board for Negro Affairs, Brown's dedication to the project was manifest from the onset. As he announced to *Opportunity* editor Elmer Anderson Carter, "I am anxious to do a good job here. You know my anxiety to see the record straight on matters concerning Negro history and life."[32] With two editorial assistants from Howard University, Ulysses Lee and Eugene Holmes, and another editor, Glaucia Roberts, Brown reviewed all copy for the state guides. He also worked on other FWP projects such as the ex-slave narratives and the WPA historical records survey. In addition, he took on the responsibility of attempting to provide African Americans with employment in as many states as possible.

While Brown tirelessly worked to attain equal treatment for black employees within the FWP, the bureaucratic structure of the agency often stymied his efforts. Reliant on central office directors to pressure state directors to hire more black employees, Brown was often unable to exert influence outside the Washington office. Hired in an advisory and editorial capacity, Brown's presence was not immediately felt and his directives as an administrator did not begin to reach field offices until almost a year after he took the position. Moreover, as state FWP workers often used the guides as a rallying cry for state distinctiveness, white supremacy often underpinned state pride. Finally, the administrative disorganization and overly ambitious scope of the FWP made it generally difficult for Brown and other officials to attend to all instances of racial discrimination in state offices or omissions in the guidebooks.[33]

When Henry Alsberg first insisted that state directors record "all material dealing with Negro life" and report on the number of black workers, state directors reported the difficulties in accomplishing these directives.[34] In Nevada, state director David Williamson indicated that there would be little information to provide on black individuals, as they "have fitted unostentatiously in the social framework, taking no part in politics as a race." When Williamson contended that Nevada had "no Negro 'problem,'" he was assuming that any treatment of black life would involve the depiction of antagonistic race relations.[35] For many state directors, however, the difficulty in finding subject matter paled in comparison to the problem of employing black workers. Particularly in the South, racial hostilities presented a significant obstacle. In Alabama, the state director asserted, "it would be unwise to give a Negro this job. . . . There is considerable racial sensitiveness in Tuskegee and vicinity."[36] Along similar lines, North Carolina state director Edwin Bjorkman declared that because segregated accommodations that were "required for such employment" had not been established, black men and women could not work on the state's project.[37]

Bjorkman seemingly upheld the principle of white supremacy in the structural composition of the project. Both Bjorkman and associate state director William Couch resisted Washington's encroachments on their editorial and employment practices, preventing the North Carolina guide from fully reflecting Brown's vision.[38] Still, Bjorkman's ideas about the content of the guidebook reveal a modicum of receptiveness to Brown's revision initiatives. Although he adhered to segregation, Bjorkman admitted, "The problem involved in this matter is one that has troubled me from the very start" and pledged to try to improve conditions.[39] Despite the near absence of black workers on the North Carolina project, Bjorkman did report that writers were devoting attention to black life in Durham, Raleigh, Winston-Salem, and Gastonia. In detailing the history of these cities, the administration had to "deal very carefully" when describing race relations, and Bjorkman admitted that North Carolina "can hardly be said to have given the Negro a fair chance."[40]

While racial tensions on the project often ran high, Brown recalled an incident where his interference tested the rigidity of Jim Crow practices in Oklahoma. He related that white state workers in Oklahoma initially prevented the only black man working on the project from using the drinking fountain—white workers declared that a separate colored fountain would have to be installed. After Brown intervened, attempting to "straighten that out" state editors seemed to relax their boundaries. Brown remembered state officials coming to exclaim, "Hell, stop this foolishness. A drinking fountain is a drinking fountain is a drinking fountain. Everybody drinks out of the drinking fountain." Brown recalled that conflicts such as this one were frequent, and as he monitored the presence and treatment of African Americans on the staff, he was always aware that there was more at stake than the representative inclusion of black men and women in the texts.[41]

Vermont, North Dakota, Montana, Rhode Island, and Maine lacked significant black populations, and the projects in those states encountered difficulty in employing black FWP workers. Utah and Indiana reported that very few black individuals were qualified to write for the project. Nevertheless, Utah director Maurice Hore indicated that he had no opposition to employing black workers in principle.[42] And in Indiana, director William Meyer positively evaluated one qualified black prospective employee, but the individual had instead taken advantage of an opportunity to study in Paris. With the difficulty of hiring "competent colored people from relief rolls," Meyer concluded that this individual had been an exception; most black men and women were engaged in domestic or manual labor.[43] Similarly, in Delaware and Washington State, several "qualified persons" interviewed, but they were not on relief. In Arizona and New Hampshire, there were eligible writers; however, these candidates preferred to work in other fields, such as education.[44]

Finally, government cutbacks in the summer of 1937, which placed quota reductions on nonrelief workers, presented another obstacle to the employment of black workers. In Charleston, South Carolina, directors Laura Middleton and Augustus Ladson criticized this blow to federal relief, which often caused the dismissal of many black workers who did not maintain relief status. Pleading with Harry Hopkins to "see the injustice and make correction . . . by having a continued Negro representative group in Charleston," these state directors were outraged that all four of their black workers were dropped while the white staff remained.[45] Likewise, in Florida these quota reductions forced the staff to reduce the number of black workers from ten to three—an incident that deeply angered directors because the laid-off workers were producing rich studies on black life.[46] Thus, relief cuts, discrimination, and a lack of qualified candidates led to a relatively low number of black employees on the project; of 4,500 FWP workers in 1937, only 106 were African Americans.[47]

While most states faced obstacles in hiring black workers, New York, Illinois, Louisiana, and Virginia employed large numbers of them and produced vibrant studies. Virginia, Louisiana, and Florida were exceptional in having their own separate African American units. The noted black writers Roi Ottley, Claude McKay, and the young Ralph Ellison worked for the New York FWP; Richard Wright and Frank Yerby worked in Chicago. In Virginia, the Hampton Institute aided and headquartered the large staff of writers under the black scholar Roscoe Lewis, who developed the project *The Negro in Virginia*—the first published FWP study to focus solely on black Americans. Similarly, professors Horace Mann Bond and Allison Davis at Dillard University in New Orleans fueled studies of black men and women in Louisiana through institutional support and the employment of a relatively large number of talented black writers. In Atlanta and some other cities, organizations like the Urban League provided additional resources for research and volunteered to reassign workers, such as those employed with the National Youth Administration, who qualified to work as guidebook writers.[48]

Taking on Revision

While racial liberalism undergirded the motivations of most of the New Dealers who conceived the Federal Arts Project, the projects were still primarily a relief effort. The American Guide Series not only offered the possibility of illustrating a new American aesthetic—based on local culture and folklife—but it also served the more tangible purpose of boosting tourism. Here, African Americans and ethnic groups gave depth to each region, which state writers would package to travelers as part of rediscovering America. As one WPA press release indicated, "In some of these State guide books the Negro is treated only incidentally, but is nevertheless found to be a vital part of many interesting incidents in the history of states and localities—far more so than the ordinary reader is aware."[49]

For Negro Affairs editors, however, the excavation of black history was about much more than tokenism. Brown and his assistants insisted that their work in the guidebooks served important political objectives by challenging the central narrative of black history. White historians such as U. B. Phillips buttressed ideas of racial inferiority that had largely dominated the history of black Americans. According to Phillips's influential study, *American Negro Slavery* (1968), African Americans were childlike, faithful servants to benevolent masters under slavery.[50] Although black historians such as Carter Woodson and W. E. B. Du Bois had written accounts that contradicted conventional white narratives, the white reading public largely ignored these studies.[51] Officials intended the guidebooks, on the other hand, for a mass audience that took pride in both state and national history.[52]

For southerners in particular, the appointment of an African American expert was a blow to their sense of regional authority and propriety. With southern identity rooted in particular histories of slavery, the Civil War, and Reconstruction, any claims that contradicted familiar white narratives represented an assault on both the racial status quo and the sense of white historical ownership. While many southerners appreciated the opportunity to write their state histories, they frequently balked at federal directives. Thus, Brown's appointment not only represented an effort to revise traditional white histories of black men and women, but the position itself announced that officials in Washington—not in Alabama, South Carolina, or Mississippi—would be the final arbiters in documenting southern life. That a black man occupied a central role in the federal reconstruction of history was perhaps one of the most radical features of the program, and it left many southerners seething. Still state directors were obligated to recognize administrative procedures involving Brown's review and opinion.

The state guides followed a two-part format, first describing the locale by subject, such as architecture or industry, and then devoting a section to cities and towns. City and town sections included tours of historic sites, landmarks, and parks intended for automobile travel, with highway and mile indications. Although descriptions of black Americans were frequently part of the city and town essays, some guides included separate essays on racial topics. Virginia and North Carolina featured essays on "The Negro," while Pennsylvania, Ohio, and Nebraska provided sections on "Folklore and Ethnic Groups" or "Ethnic Elements" that included black Americans. Other states, such as Michigan and Texas, titled their sections on black Americans "Racial Elements," while Florida, Indiana, and Alabama had no specific subject essays on their black populations. Although Brown expressed the view that African Americans should not be written about as a "separate entity," ostensibly he did not oppose the fact that several guides presented black men and women in separate subject essays within a larger account of a state's history and landscape. Still, the separation of African Americans in the guidebooks represents one of the many concessions that Brown would make in guaranteeing black inclusion.

Like the Play Bureau of the FTP, Brown and his assistants sought to eliminate derogatory racial characterizations. With similar intentions of securing more truthful and authentic depictions, these editors immediately targeted stereotypes. Thus, Negro Affairs ordered state editors to capitalize the word *Negro* and to "avoid use of the word darkie."[53] They also urged writers to avoid "debatable generalization" and "Romantic narrative, not the possession of the folk."[54] Brown also chided state writers for "paternalistic" or "condescending" tones, particularly in drafts for southern guidebooks that exhibited a style that he regarded as careless or "flippant."[55] Along with the eradication of stereotypes, the issue of black visibility was fundamental for editors. Of his encounter with Tennessee writers, Brown exclaimed, "You wouldn't believe this, but at the start they didn't event count Negroes in the population."[56] And this exclusionary practice was not limited to guidebook writers in Nashville. In Pennsylvania, where early drafts neglected the 6,382 black residents of Harrisburg, state writers followed folklore editor Benjamin Botkin's suggestions and mentioned the "6,000 Negroes, many of whom live in the substandard area near the capitol."[57] In some city essays where Brown charged that "the Negro is here disproportionately and inadequately treated," writers incorporated Brown's instructions to describe the black population with more accuracy.[58] After reviewing Brown's suggestions for the East St. Louis

THE EDITOR'S DILEMMA

section of the Illinois guide, writers detailed the "shocking ferocity" of the 1917 riot and the death of more than a hundred black men and women. While Illinois writers did not devote the desired amount of space to African Americans, their guidebook did describe black individuals as "important elements in political and labor struggles" in East St. Louis.[59] Along similar lines in Ohio, state writers revised an essay that had initially failed to mention Toledo's role in the Underground Railroad network.[60]

Some southern editors were also receptive to Brown's insistence that state writers attend to all segments of their states' black population. In comments on a Florence, Alabama, essay, one Negro Affairs editor indicated that black Americans must be described in detail "not only as an integral part of the city's life, but in their own right, if the treatment is to be representative."[61] While the Alabama guide in general left much to be desired and was infused with racial stereotypes, the Florence essay did reflect changes that the editor had suggested. "More than in almost any other section of the State," the guide proclaimed, "the Negroes in the Muscle Shoals district have advanced culturally and financially." Although not as thorough as Brown and his editors would have hoped, the Florence section went on to mention black employment in the TVA and in other professions and highlighted the notable black congressman Oscar DePreist.[62] As Alabama historian Harvey Jackson notes, "to a surprising degree Alabama's *Guide* gave readers a look at black life that was far more positive and candid than one might expect."[63]

In an undated memo, most likely written in the earlier stages of the FWP, Brown expressed confidence that state writers were following his editorial suggestions. As he described, "The response to criticisms sent out from the office has been all that could be desired. Dogmatic generalizations and expressions of prejudice have occurred less and less frequently."[64] Although Brown may have painted a rosy picture of his position for higher-ups in the FWP, it also seems likely that he wrote this memo before becoming fully entrenched in the project. Some writers, in the South and elsewhere, continued to omit discussion of significant black populations from city essays. While Arizona writers took the advice of editors and included some material about the black community in the Tucson essay, the few sentences they provided did not do justice to the second largest black population in the state.[65] State writers ignored the "sizable" black community in the Nogales, Arizona, essay, even after Brown's suggestions.[66] While it is not entirely clear why state writers included black men and women in some city essays and omitted them in others, this kind of exclusion dem-

THE EDITOR'S DILEMMA

onstrates that although Brown and his staff wielded significant influence, they often had limited control over the content of the final product.

FWP director Henry Alsberg was aware of the fact that state editors sometimes ignored Brown's suggestions and issued a directive in June 1937. Condemning state directors for their inconsistency in recognizing black communities, Alsberg related that much of the "state copy" left black Americans "unmentioned or inadequately treated." Urging directors to center their attention on black life in work, school, church, and at home, Alsberg claimed that this information would enrich the guidebooks, "especially if treated with sincere realism."[67] Alsberg was not the only high-ranking administrator to take up the issue of the inclusion and portrayal of black Americans in the guidebooks; as early as 1936, upon the project's inception, Associate Director George Cronyn lashed out at Alabama FWP director Myrtle Miles for her inadequate and distorted portrayal of black Americans. "Alabama History which does not cover Alabama's colored population . . . cannot be considered as fully representative of Alabama," Cronyn concluded, promoting an unwavering stance against this form of bigotry.[68] Miles eventually responded to Cronyn's criticism, giving more weight to African American communities. Thus, while Brown and his assistants were the most vigilant on matters of race, directors such as Alsberg and Cronyn served as a secondary source of enforcement when states did not implement Brown's editorial directives. Although state directors did not implement all of Brown's suggestions, and the intervention of Alsberg and Cronyn was sporadic at best, the willingness of higher-ups to support Brown's objectives demonstrates an unprecedented federal commitment to African American cultural advancement.

However, by November 1938, Negro Affairs editors were feeling the weight of their responsibility, charging that the enormity of their task required more resources from the FWP. Editor Glaucia B. Roberts, who joined the staff of Negro Affairs in 1936 and assumed most editorial responsibilities while Brown held a Guggenheim fellowship from 1937 to 1938, related that writers in various states were disinclined to include "*any* mention of the Negro population constituent in State and city guide copy." In addition, she charged that because the FWP had failed in procuring "capable Negro research workers," the task of writing about black men and women fell solely on the Negro Affairs editors. To remedy some of these issues, Roberts called for additional workers to undertake research, to assist in the editorial process, and to collect and file relevant information; yet, it seems that FWP officials never met these personnel requests. Thus, editors increasingly had the task of supplying more content, and in some states they were solely responsible for representing African Americans in the guidebooks.[69]

Still, in many cases there was significant editorial exchange. After Eugene Holmes derided Pennsylvania writers for their lack of attention to black communities, exclaiming that "one paragraph does not do justice" to the large community of African Americans in Philadelphia, Pennsylvania writers extensively expanded on the experiences of black Americans in sections on ethnic groups, religion, education, and music.[70] The Pennsylvania guide also described early abolitionist activities, black foodways in South Philadelphia, and the formation of the Free African Society led by Absalom Jones and Richard Allen.[71] The Indiana guide, which Brown initially deemed "not adequate at all," also improved dramatically.[72] After a year of editorial exchange, with Glaucia Roberts urging that writers further examine all aspects of Indianapolis's black community, the Indiana guidebook documented the migration of black Americans and addressed factory work, political activities, and leisure pursuits.[73]

Mention of discrimination and segregation was a radical element of the American Guide Series. Brown's task was even more daunting in the case of southern guidebooks, and some state writers were more willing than others to offer evidence of racial inequality. In the Texas guide, where Brown's editors alleged that writers had portrayed black people as a "lazy-good-for-nothing lot" during the period of Reconstruction, the section was later revised, noting that black individuals had been "cast adrift" by an indifferent government.[74] In South Carolina, writers also made significant revisions regarding education, taking the advice of Roberts to overcome "misrepresentation" and portray the state more "accurately and adequately."[75] In accordance with editors' requests, writers described the large discrepancy between white and black public education in the first three decades of the twentieth century, admitting that the annual school term for white Americans was considerably longer than for their black counterparts.[76] These revelations most likely came under the urging of racial liberal Louise Jones Du Bose, who served as assistant director on the project, but received less credit than the more politically conservative director, Mabel Montgomery.[77]

Unfortunately, attention to racial inequality and discrimination was not common within other southern guidebooks. Although Glaucia Roberts suggested that state writers should mention the role of Alexandria, Virginia, as home to the "chief slave-dealing firm in Virginia," the published

THE EDITOR'S DILEMMA

state guide neglected to discuss this fact.[78] In the same vein, writers in Mississippi were reluctant to comment on the lack of public expenditures for black education, even as Brown exclaimed, "there is too much omitted, too much glossed over."[79] Furthermore, Arkansas writers omitted discussion of the poverty, dispossession, and evictions facing more than 150,000 black farmers, and a frustrated Eugene Holmes decried, "No one reading this essay would believe that some of the worst conditions in the country . . . are in Arkansas."[80] Still, Arkansas writers did document that black workers were the lowest paid in the state (bringing down the Arkansas average) and that agricultural workers endured a heavy burden. As the guidebook stated, "The difference between the city Negro and his rural relatives is probably wider than that between town and country white people."[81] Here, Arkansas writers straddled the line between the harsh reality Holmes had hoped for and the more picturesque depictions found in other southern guidebooks.

In implementing some of Brown's suggestions, some southern writers offered interpretations of segregation beyond theories of African American inferiority. While admitting to some instances of racial inequality, South Carolina writers also declared that black Americans encountered a prejudice "which faces all the lower classes in any social order"; here, black and white Americans "of the lowest economic class" were not that different from one another. Certainly, poverty was a central feature of rural life across racial lines in South Carolina, and state writers provided little evaluation of how segregation and discrimination dramatically worsened the plight of black residents. Yet, while admitting that African Americans sometimes met discrimination "in the courts" and that "Jim Crow customs generally prevail," the guidebook also asserted that segregation was ignored "in numerous instances" depending on the locale. The guidebook assured readers that racial discord was limited to certain segments of the population, largely due to economic competition among poor black and white farmers. Among "cultured Negroes" and "socially disposed Whites," an amicable relationship prevailed with "interracial loyalties and friendships that are characteristically Southern in their nature." This evaluation of segregation as a practice predicated by class, rather than race, veered from more conventional descriptions of African Americans as a homogenous group.[82]

Nevertheless, many southern guide writers sought to buttress the racial status quo through stereotypical images. Southerners capitalized on certain cultural perceptions of the region, and cherished traditions, familiar narratives, and conventional images played an important role in state identity and tourist appeal. Here, the efforts of Brown and his editors were most limited, as writers' interest in depicting the plantation romance often trumped the need for authenticity. In the Texas guide, the essay on "folklore and folkways" hailed African Americans for "the racial gift of melody." Depicting the annual Emancipation celebration as a time when jovial black southerners danced and sang to their "heart's content," Texas writers ignored the profound historical and cultural meaning of the celebration, instead invoking cartoonish images.[83] In a section on Florence in the Alabama guide, writers claimed "the Old South touches the new in the Negro quarters," nostalgically professing "mammies in bandanas argue with educated young women in modern dress over the best methods of seasoning 'potlicker' or feeding and training babies."[84]

Paradoxically, even in instances when southern writers admitted to the economic and social progress of black citizens, they could not veer from traditional racial stereotypes. The Montgomery, Alabama, essay described various types of black housing, a few notable schools, and pronounced, "Negroes have played an honorable part in the city's quiet steady growth."[85] However, writers found it difficult to avoid minstrelesque descriptions: "Its [Montgomery] atmosphere of measured dignity tempered by cordiality is matched nowhere else in Alabama. A Negro boy—his face wreathed in smiles—usually accosts the traveler with, 'You don't have to tote that grip, boss man; I'll do it cheap'; and a resident will willingly give directions and accompany the stranger a block or more to set him on the right road."[86] Similarly, the Mississippi guide smacked of racism and condescension, as in one essay that stated, "The Mississippi folk Negro today is a genial mass of remarkable qualities. He seems carefree and shrewd and does not bother himself with the problems the white man has to solve. The tariff and currency do not interest him in the least. He has his standard, silver, and he wants no other kind. As for the so called Negro Question—that, too is just another problem he has left for the white man to cope with. Seated in the white man's wagon, and subtly letting the white man worry with the reins, the Negro assures himself a share of all things good."[87] As writers further asserted, most white Mississippians knew what the average black person was like "well enough to understand something of his psychology, his character . . . and like him well enough to accept his deficiencies."[88] Brown and his editors had made many suggestions for revising this account, which they laced with comments such as "too many broad generalizations" and "absurd"; however, in this case, Brown's comments could not counter the racial ideologies of Mississippi writers.[89]

Southern directors sometimes made their resistance to Brown's comments well-known. In particular, Alabama director Myrtle Miles and South Carolina director Mabel Montgomery both articulated a disdain for Brown's intervention. Montgomery charged that Brown harbored a "Northern slant," and Miles asserted, "Alabamians understand the Alabama Negro and the general Negro situation in Alabama better than a critic whose life has been spent in another section of the country, however studious, however learned he may be."[90] As historians Joanne Gabbin and Jerrold Hirsch contend, these incidents demonstrate a clash between a sense of regional propriety and Brown's aim to eliminate stereotypes and manifestations of white paternalism. Alabama's Myrtle Miles had held stints as a reporter in her home state and as a public relations coordinator for the New York Central Railroad; one Alabama newspaper described her as "a Southerner by birth, a resident of Alabama since an infant, and a journalist by profession."[91] While sensitive to the inclusion of black men and women in the guidebooks, Miles was perhaps more eager to accommodate a white southern readership.

Still, administrative pressure forced the pens of Alabama writers, leading to a more balanced portrayal of black Americans. Associate Director George Cronyn had begun corresponding with Miles early on in the project when Miles failed to note Booker T. Washington's significance within the state; as early as 1936, Henry Alsberg was contacting Miles to provide material relating to black Americans, insisting that they be "well represented."[92] After reviewing Brown's revisions for the Florence essay, Miles made it clear to Cronyn that she did not wish to draw "attention to the Negro to overbalance that of your foreign population in other states, for example, or to seem fantastic or perhaps offensive to Alabamians."[93]

What is particularly interesting here is that although Miles strongly objected to Brown's criteria and intervention, she stressed the importance of including cities that have produced "outstanding men" such as "[Oscar] DePriest and Mitchell, congressmen; Jesse Owens and Joe Louis, athletes."[94] As these figures, particularly Louis, would feature centrally in the state's wartime agenda, Miles provided a fair barometer of which black individuals southerners would likely find acceptable. Nevertheless, it seems that Brown was able to make a dent in the Alabama guidebook; because of his persistence, coupled with Cronyn's and Alsberg's close at-

tention to the matter, state writers implemented many of Brown's suggestions, offering several positive depictions of black Alabamians.

In the case of South Carolina, the debate between Brown and Mabel
Montgomery concerned the Beaufort section, where writers described
African Americans as a "picturesque group." While Montgomery charged
that her South Carolina experts understood the black residents of Beaufort
much better than Brown did, she also noted that South Carolina residents
would appreciate this kind of literature. Brown's condemnations of the
guide's "half truths" led to additional revisions, and although there remained a certain amount of "paternalism and condescension," in Brown's
view, the final guidebook presented a vast improvement over earlier
drafts.[95] Where African Americans were once described by state writers as
"a happy people, primitive, unmoral" the completed guidebook depicted
the occupations and residences of these men and women, commenting
that "Beaufort Negroes have been the focus of numerous social and educational campaigns sponsored by Northern White people."[96]

Although states outside of the South did not prove as tenacious in their
commitment to regional authority, some state guidebooks still invoked
romanticized racial images. The Dover, Delaware, essay revealed that black
residents "whistle melodiously" during work.[97] Even some guidebooks that
contained a wealth of positive contributions, such as Ohio, offered racial
caricatures as a fixture of state distinctiveness. Taking pride in the fact
that Ohio natives Tom Rice and Edwin Forrest ushered in "the beginning
of the American minstrel show," which had become "the most original
music-dramatic form produced in America," writers were seemingly oblivi-
ous to damaging stereotypes.[98] Writers listed several songs made famous
by Ohio minstrel Dan Emmett, such as "Dixie" (the marching song for the
Confederacy), championing this element of Ohio's cultural history. These
pronouncements ignored the psychological effects that distorted representations had on African Americans who, the writers professed, came to
Ohio in a "search for equality and opportunity."[99]

The fact that some state writers continually represented black Americans in a demeaning manner, however, does not diminish Brown's important role as Negro Affairs editor. While the guidebooks were often a far
cry from what Brown, and certainly modern readers, would hope for, his
position as editor was pivotal within black cultural politics. White directors could not publish their guidebooks without sending copy to Brown,
and while they often balked at his comments, the mere fact that they had
to consult a black expert was a transformative feature of the FWP. In most

cases, writers at least followed Brown's suggestions with minimal changes. In segregation-era America the presence of Negro Affairs editors was not an insignificant development, particularly within the only presidential administration to sponsor a broadscale arts project.

The most direct and pronounced statement Brown made during his tenure as a FWP editor was in "The Negro in Washington," a chapter in the Washington, D.C., guidebook. This essay began with the city's central role in the interstate slave trade and included descriptions of political apathy, unemployment, poverty, and other manifestations of racial inequality. In this scathing condemnation of the nation's capital, Brown professed, "The Negro of Washington has no voice in government, is economically proscribed, and segregated nearly as rigidly as in the southern cities he contemns." While Brown devoted much space to black achievements in scholarship, the arts, athletics, and the military, he reiterated the impediments that stalled future progress. Both prescriptive and analytic in his essay, Brown perhaps hoped that it would engender an awakening among white D.C. residents—many of whom were perhaps unaware of the squalid conditions so many black citizens endured.

In addition, as Brown's contribution provided the depth and breadth few other guidebooks would devote to African Americans, the Washington, D.C., guide became a model for the full incorporation of "Negro Studies." This guidebook directly addressed some of the inadequacies of other state guidebooks; for example, Brown described Alexandria's role in the slave trade (a fact that Virginia writers would not include). In addition, it exemplified the type of racial honesty that Brown intended for all of the FWP documents. Although the Washington essay was damning, Brown managed to avoid what he characterized as the "temptation" of depicting "counterstereotypes of villainous Whites and victimized Negroes."[100] In the end, Brown's critique was not of individuals but of segregation, which led to "grave consequences" in all areas of life for both white and black Americans. If Washington was making some advances "in the direction of justice," the persistence of Jim Crow ultimately brought Brown to the following conclusion: "In this border city, southern in so many respects, there is a denial of democracy, at times hypocritical and at times flagrant."[101]

"The Negro in Washington" presented both the most thorough examination of African American life and the most explicit critique of American race relations among any of the guidebooks. This document was exceptional not only in its content but also because Brown undertook it without the kind of editorial exchange that shaped the writing of black history in other state guidebooks. Without the bureaucracy, Brown could more easily advance his own interpretations; however, the objective of the FWP was to be a collaboration among writers and researchers who would excavate the culture and history of all communities. Therefore, "The Negro in Washington" was emblematic of the kind of separate projects Brown would later take on—involving more consensus than debate, and veering away from the integrationist model Brown had initially advocated.

Guidebooks under Review

According to *Publisher's Weekly*, the American Guide Series "sold steadily and have demonstrated their worth as continuing, staple volumes."[102] State guides sold for two to three dollars; publishers issued between 5,000 and 10,000 first editions.[103] While in general reviewers did not characterize guidebook sales as overwhelming, many claimed that they were attracting a wide readership. Published by major commercial presses such as Houghton Mifflin, Viking Press, Oxford University Press, and Hastings House, by 1941 many state guides had gone into second printings and were stocked in bookstores across the country. Smaller bookstores tended to feature selected state guides, while larger retailers would carry the entire series. Libraries, schools, and the chambers of commerce carried copies of the guidebooks, and they were promoted over the radio and through circulars on railways, airlines, and bus companies.[104] The Missouri Guide fared exceptionally well, topping the St. Louis nonfiction bestseller list for many weeks, with a long waiting list in the local library.[105] Likewise, the New Orleans Guide stood among the best of local studies, remaining on the best-seller list for six weeks.[106] Furthermore, some other racially themed FWP projects did well, such as *Cavalcade of the American Negro* (1940), which sold 55,000 copies by 1941; the *Washington: City and Capital* guide (1937) was one of the first to sell out of its first edition of 8,000 copies and was on the recommended list for the Book-of-the-Month Club.[107]

Reviews published in mainstream periodicals such as *Time* and the *New Yorker*, as well as more specialized journals, were less interested in the number of copies that had been purchased than in the guidebooks' larger potential in influencing American culture. For some writers, more impressive than the individual guidebooks was their organization as a series, as *New Republic* reviewer Albert Horlings exclaimed: "I hope the publishers will cooperate to make libraries feel as naked with an incomplete series of the Guides as they would with a dozen volumes of the Encyclopedia Britannica."[108] Likewise, Robert Cantwell noted that if organized and prepared for historians and researchers, the American Guide Series and other FWP projects could "revolutionize the writing of American history and enormously influence the direction and character of our imaginative literature."[109] For these writers, the guidebooks had captured a vision of America than had not been previously documented. Their portrayal of the nation's eccentricities, unexplored communities, and everyday lives led *Saturday Review of Literature* reviewer Frederick Gutheim to declare, "these books are guides to the real America, not the tourist America."[110]

Although most reviewers agreed that the guidebooks were nuanced, their evaluations were not without criticism. Opinions ranged over which guidebooks were the best; and some reviewers underscored the project's limitations, charging that many who worked on the guides were "writers only by aspiration or appointment."[111] While one reviewer commented that the American Guide Series had been unanimously praised by critics, another declared, "They are competent, readable, and well worth having, but they are also uneven in quality. . . . There are errors and deference to local Pierponts."[112] Practicality was a factor for some, who described the Washington, D.C., guide as well-written, yet "too bulky to be carried about by the ordinary traveler"; another reviewer deemed it "the weight-lifter's guide."[113] Furthermore, Jared Putnam of the *Nation* found southern racism exasperating, particularly in the Mississippi guide. Referring to the "anti-Negro passages," Putnam claimed, "If many such passages of arrant non-sense creep into the copy, the usefulness and prestige of the guide series will be seriously impaired."[114] Still, reviews did not always represent liberal largesse, as *Saturday Review of Literature* writer Blair Bolles found the guidebooks too heavy on representations of poverty, working conditions, and other manifestations of social injustice. Bolles commented, "A casual sightseer interested in finding out about the city he is visiting probably doesn't care much about the living habits of the poor or the working conditions of unskilled labor." Bolles's prescriptions for more reader-friendly guidebooks stated that they had "best avoid the overtones of both the social worker and the chamber of commerce."[115]

Most black men and women viewed the FWP as a momentous opportunity. The *Chicago Defender* praised *The Negro in Virginia* and the *New Orleans City Guide* (1938) as pioneering works in uncovering African American culture, folklore, and previously marginalized individuals.[116] Still, some black writers were critical in evaluating the guidebooks. In *Opportunity*, reviewer Henry Jenkins evaluated the North Carolina guidebook, initially charging that state writers "have remained true, on the whole, to the Southern tradition." The basis for this claim was the guidebook's portrayal of Reconstruction under black domination. Yet, Jenkins credited the guidebook with a praiseworthy account of black business achievement and notable figures, while also pointing out that "even the Federal writers are aware that all is not right in North Carolina." While the guidebook posited that North Carolina highlighted interracial goodwill, Jenkins underscored that it also detailed black disenfranchisement, segregation, and the violent realities of the 1898 Wilmington Race Riot. For Jenkins, the North Carolina guide certainly left much to be desired, but it held the promise that America's history could eventually be captured from the perspective of all citizens.[117]

The guidebooks drew international admiration as well, including that of British scholar D. W. Brogan, one of the leading intellectuals on American life and culture. Describing how the guides revealed America to be comprised of "elements in the compound," Brogan indicated, "Yet here they are, Poles, Irish, Germans, Maronites, Jews, Negroes, Welsh . . . striving, and on the whole thriving." For Brogan the "great merit" of these books was that they celebrated "the *real* United States."[118]

The Irony of "Negro Studies"

By the winter of 1937, Brown expressed great anticipation about a series of auxiliary projects, which, among other things, consisted of a "book of narratives by ex-slaves," a study of the Underground Railroad, and a history of black folklore.[119] Requesting the support of NAACP executive secretary Walter White, particularly in light of congressional pressures to terminate the arts projects, Brown emphasized the significance of these books: "We are confident that these works will be of great importance to the study of the Negro in American life. . . . For the first time, we have an opportunity to tell the Negro's story with the direct sponsorship of the Federal Government."[120] It is likely that Brown initiated this research with the intention of countering the inadequacies of the guidebooks; as the government had demonstrated an interest in black history, Brown capitalized on the opportunity to utilize FWP funds to their fullest extent.[121] Unlike the guides, these auxiliary projects focused entirely on black life, including sections devoted to biographical sketches, contemporary culture, folklore, and materials on slavery. Documents included in the "Negro Studies Project" heading in the Library of Congress's FWP finding aid were far more detailed than those in the guide series; topics ranged from the Scottsboro trials to the Boston Female Anti-Slavery Society to the memoirs of individual men and women.[122]

Although much of this material did not appear in the guides, it most likely informed other studies published by the FWP. Successful projects based solely on black experiences included the Chicago Project's *Cavalcade of the American Negro* (1940), and the Georgia Project's *Drums and Shadows: Survival Studies among the Georgia Coastal Negroes* (1940). However, the most widely acclaimed FWP study on black culture and history was *The Negro in Virginia*, an exhaustive account which used ex-slave interviews, previously neglected books and records, and newspapers that dated as far back as 1619. Through its pioneering use of oral history, the book evaluated significant events from the surrender at Appomattox to the Great Depression from a black perspective. Supported by Hampton Institute and supervised by black scholar Roscoe Lewis (who had the backing of the liberal-minded state director, Eudora Ramsay), *The Negro in Virginia* became a model for all the FWP studies that followed.[123]

Writers for these projects relied on black history research compiled for the guidebooks even after the demise of the FWP. Former Illinois FWP writers Arna Bontemps and Jack Conroy used these findings in their work on black folk traditions, titled *They Seek a City* (1945), while Chicago sociologists Horace Cayton and St. Clair Drake used the research for their study *Black Metropolis* (1945). Roi Ottley, former supervisor of the Negro Unit in New York, used the FWP materials in his influential book, *New World A-Coming* (1943); FWP findings were also incorporated into *The Negro in New York*, which was finally published in 1967. Even as recently as 2004, a manuscript entitled "The Negro in Pittsburgh"—a compilation of materials edited by those who worked on the Pennsylvania guide—was published as *The WPA History of the Negro in Pittsburgh* after spending decades unexamined in the Pennsylvania State Library in Harrisburg.[124] In addition, the project fueled the thinking of some established writers; Zora Neale Hurston published two works, including her seminal novel, *Their Eyes Were Watching God* (1937), while working on the Florida project. Arna Bontemps (with the Illinois FWP) and Claude McKay (with the New York FWP) published *Drums at Dusk* (1939) and *Harlem: Negro Metropolis* (1940), respectively.

The need for auxiliary projects raises the question of whether the FWP could create an integrated project that thoroughly incorporated black Americans and fulfilled the expectations of African American intellectuals. Although Brown initially criticized the trend toward separateness in writings by black historians, he eventually directed this kind of scholarship, for lack of a better alternative. Thus, while the FWP did not intend to develop separate black units when it was initiated, administrators such as Brown slowly came to realize that achieving black aesthetic goals eventually might require this separation.

Separatism clearly manifested in Brown's compilation of materials for the "Portrait of the Negro as an American" (PNAM) project. For Brown, the PNAM would compensate for some of the uneven treatment of black Americans in the guidebooks, representing a more ambitious attempt to write black history through the broadest use of resources. As the PNAM was developed between 1937 and 1940, Brown and his colleagues collected materials for understanding black history in its totality.[125] Thus, using ex-slave narratives, diaries, newspaper accounts, and contemporary scholarship, black intellectuals validated the credibility of particular forms of documentation. In privileging certain sources, Brown and his colleagues were making a methodological assumption; like the reviewers in the Play Bureau, the staff of the PNAM selected those voices that shaped the narrative they intended to promote. The sense of possibility exhibited in the PNAM illustrates a vision of government-sponsored culture without limits. Although the PNAM would never reach fruition, its materials would importantly contrast with the increasing confinement of media projects developed during World War II. This kind of historical investigation into racial inequality and discrimination, even at the level of development, would not be possible within federal programs a few short years later when War Department officials discouraged any public acknowledgement of racial antagonism that might contradict the war's democratic ethos.

The PNAM study contained nineteen chapters, beginning with one on slavery and ranging from topics such as the arts, to war, business, and black experiences in the West. Editors included Ulysses Lee and Eugene Holmes, Brown's Howard colleagues and assistants in the administration of the FWP's Negro Affairs. Describing it in one memo as a "cross section of Negro life from the earliest days to the present," Brown hailed the PNAM for its promise of "authenticity," "accuracy," and "readability."[126] Since the study would be of interest to both black and white readers, Brown claimed, the book would not be "an exercise in race glorification"; instead, it would satisfy the "wish to see the truth told."[127] Brown denied that the PNAM offered any "thesis to be proved or cause to be advanced," yet the revisionist content of the study homed in on both the centrality of black men and women within American history and the persistence of discrimination that continued to hinder racial advancement.[128]

Much of the manuscript highlighted black pioneers or exceptional individuals. This emphasis would remain an integral feature of government-sponsored culture in the 1940s; more than any other aspect of the PNAM, its rediscovery and celebration of notable black Americans would later serve wartime administrators as their preferred form of cultural inclusion. The PNAM devoted sections to "Inventions by Negroes," discussing the scientific discoveries of individuals such as astronomer Benjamin Banneker and even a "Short History of Madame C. J. Walker," the successful entrepreneur who famously invented hair-straightening products.[129] A section on "Notable Negroes of Washington, D.C.," presented biographies of politicians such as Oscar DePriest and Blanche K. Bruce, medical professionals such as Simeon Carson and Daniel Wiseman, and educators such as Carter Woodson and John Francis Cook.[130] A chapter on sports listed Jesse Owens and Joe Louis as subjects for discussion; there was also information on less-famous athletes such as William Lewis, who, after playing football for Amherst College and Harvard University, served as a coach for Harvard from 1895 to 1906, becoming the first black man to receive national recognition as a football player.[131] Lewis later went on to become President Taft's assistant attorney general; yet the information about him and others, such as Paul Robeson, who became significant racial activists, was confined to the subject "In Sports."

The project highlighted famed writers and performers, demonstrating that minstrelsy did not completely define the talents of black Americans. Editors included information on the independent producer John William Isham, who developed a production entitled "Oriental America" in 1896, which was described as "the first Negro show to play on Broadway proper and the first to break away from the burlesque type of entertainment."[132] In addition, the PNAM revealed the black origins of particular forms of music, while critiquing the white commodification of black voices and bodies. A section on music relayed the sentiments of composer Will Marion Cook: "'Developed Negro Music has just begun in America. The colored American is finding himself. He has thrown aside puerile imitations of the white man.'"[133] Although Europeans and American expatriates were demonstrating a consciousness and appreciation of black aesthetics in the first decades of the twentieth century, it was not until the mid-1920s that white New Yorkers found value in black music and art outside of a minstrel tradition. Eugene Holmes remarked, "If we peer under the surface of the cabaret life for which Harlem has been so famous, we will find that there is a lot more underneath than the mere entertaining of whites."[134] Thus, Holmes argued that white fetishization of black culture masked the value of African American art within the black community, as cabarets proved an important economic and artistic base for black residents in Harlem.[135]

Keeping in line with Brown's criticism of black writers who too often invoked a black victim/white oppressor paradigm, the PNAM underscored interracial efforts in the arts and in politics. As Brown and some of his colleagues had themselves benefited from strong relationships with white intellectuals and politicians, they understood interracial struggles for racial justice. Thus, a chapter on abolition related the experiences of fugitive slaves such as Anthony Burns, whose arrest in Boston resulted in an attack on the Boston courthouse led by the white abolitionists Theodore Parker and Wendell Phillips. The letters of the abolitionist Lydia Maria Child also illustrated the experiences of several fugitive slaves who were permitted to remain in the North by liberal-minded judges.[136] The PNAM also included descriptions of white scientists and scholars who refuted biological arguments of black inferiority as early as 1787. Significantly, the work mentioned that the Princeton University president, Samuel Stanhope Smith, published *An Essay on the Causes of the Variety of Complexion and Figure in the Human Species* (1787), contending that all of mankind evolved from a single race.[137]

Brown's goals in writing the PNAM predated and anticipated studies of the New Social Historians of the post–civil rights era, such as Eugene Genovese and Lawrence Levine who, using sources such as the FWP's Slave Narrative Collection, sought to revise the traditional white narrative of history and to examine modes of resistance against systems of domination.[138] Within the chapter "Struggle for Freedom," the PNAM chronicled the actions of men and women who remained enslaved, yet achieved a "superiority" or "self-reliant existence" despite the confines of the institution.[139] Like Levine's research, the PNAM documents revealed that music, song, and dance had historically "salved the sores of oppression" for black Americans since slavery. They demonstrated that performance was a mode of subversion, enabling black individuals to channel their hardships into community-building enterprises.[140] Like the African American historians that would follow him, Brown understood that investigating resistance required complete understanding of American racial inequality. This federally funded research into discrimination, violence, and segregation was indeed innovative at the time and would prove a unique aspect of the manuscript materials.

Using the ex-slave narratives that were simultaneously being conducted under the auspices of the FWP, the PNAM writers were able to present varying perceptions of the "peculiar institution." One essay, "Incidents in the Lives of Slaves," used the words of ex-slaves Josiah Henson and John H. Simpson to describe the role of the overseer, the unlimited extent of slave punishment, and the sexual assault of black women.[141] Exposing the fallacies of the proslavery argument that the institution prevented racial "amalgamation," the PNAM writers offered excerpts from historical writings that described the frequency of interracial sex in slaveholding states.[142] In discussions focusing on institutionalized inequality, one excerpt from W. E. B. Du Bois's *Black Reconstruction* emphasized the opposition of white southerners to black schooling: "If the Negro public school system had been sustained, guided and supported, the American Negro today would equal Denmark in literacy."[143]

A chapter entitled "The Negro Has a Hard Time" confronted the most oppressive and violent examples of racial discrimination. A series of articles presented detailed descriptions of race riots, chain gangs, the Ku Klux Klan, and the Scottsboro trials. One essay surveyed newspaper headlines on the days preceding the Washington race riot of 1919, stressing that African Americans were targeted as thieves and rapists, with typical headlines claiming, "White Woman Is Attacked by Negro."[144] Describing more contemporary incidents, another document condemned the effects of the National Recovery Act on black workers in Florida, who were frequently fired once employers were forced to pay minimum wages. As the report charged that black unemployment led to crime, it described an incident where, upon learning that a black man had stolen some canned food, a crowd of white people threw a rope around the man's neck and tied him to a telephone pole. Here, the PNAM not only directed attention to the racial implications of New Deal policy but also to the violence that could ensue.[145]

Perhaps stemming from Brown's encounters with southern guide writers, the PNAM also derided America's romanticization of the South. In one document, the journalist Marta Gruening argued, "the entire country seems, in fact, to be suffering from a bad case of the Old South disease . . . and the infection may be quite as virulent in Southern fans in Augusta, Maine, as those in Augusta, Georgia." Emphasizing the prevalence of racial stereotypes, particularly that of the contented, docile slave, Gruening contended that neither black nor white Americans could develop culturally or socially amidst a nostalgic belief in "the beautiful Southern civilization." Urging readers to recognize the brutality of slavery and to challenge the iconography of a chivalrous, hospitable Old South, Gruening bemoaned the misuse of history for political gain.[146]

Unfortunately, the PNAM never reached publication. Brown resigned from the FWP in the beginning of 1939; FWP historian Monty Penkower claims that at the time, Brown's full-time teaching at Howard University prevented his being able to further direct the project.[147] By that time, Brown was well aware that Congress would eventually abandon the Federal Arts Project, making it impossible for him to achieve his goals for the PNAM under federal auspices. Although Congress did not target the PNAM itself as "un-American," its attack on the arts projects as a whole stifled the publication of this potentially progressive and enlightening manuscript. In August 1939, Brown expressed his interest in completing the PNAM, possibly under the auspices of the Rosenwald Fund, using office space at Howard University, but his correspondence does not explain why this idea never reached fruition.[148]

Politicians and the Pen

When the Dies Committee began its congressional investigation of un-American activities in New Deal relief agencies in 1938, the FWP was almost as suspect as the FTP. Primarily targeting the New York unit, which had the most publicized connections with the Workers' Alliance and other Popular Front organizations, the Dies Committee held hearings to question workers and directors on the charge that the project was an organ for "'class warfare' propaganda."[149] Former Communists such as Edwin Banta and Ralph De Sola alleged that an overwhelming proportion of FWP workers were controlled by the Communist Party, and that hiring practices favored those with radical sympathies. As with the FTP investigations, the words of Banta, a "feeble old man of seventy," and of De Sola, who displayed a certain degree of hostility towards many of his former FWP colleagues, went unquestioned and unchecked.[150] The testimonies of these witnesses, however, were not entirely unfounded. According to FTP historian Monty Penkower, in places such as New York, Los Angeles, and Chicago, Communist Party connections sometimes aided prospective employees. In Massachusetts and Minnesota, the party often expressed grievances on behalf of disgruntled or dismissed workers. Still, Communism seems to have had little bearing on the ideological content of the guidebooks, as Penkower claims: "In most states, they [Communists] constituted only a small number of the project's workers and had little if any influence on its activities." Jerre Mangione contends that although considerable political conflict sometimes arose within project offices, such as the New York City division, even in divisions with a high number of left-wing writers, such as the Illinois office, political affiliation usually did not affect the quality of the work. Because the FWP had rescued many of its employees from the economic depression, most of them stayed focused on the goals of the project and would not think of endangering their livelihood by spending project time on outside activities.[151]

Brown's exchanges with state writers demonstrate that there was a spectrum of political opinion. The presence and accuracy of racial themes in the guidebooks was a product of individual writers' beliefs and inclinations, coupled with Brown's urging. Still, where racial matters were concerned, the presence of Communism was significant in two important ways. First, those who were supporters of Communist ideologies— whether as card-carrying members of the CP or fellow travelers—would have more likely been sympathetic to the plight of black Americans and more dedicated to procuring black employment and representation. Second, racial issues were a lightning rod for anticommunists, who targeted examples of "improprieties" (as was the case with the FTP) as evidence of subversion and thus reason to terminate arts projects. Because of the more politically sanitized nature of the guidebooks, the FWP was under less scrutiny than the FTP, but there were a few incidents where Congress targeted racially charged materials as un-American. While congressional committees seemed to shift the focus away from the authors, who in both cases were black men, they nonetheless made it clear that the connection between Communism and African Americans was tangible and a cause for deep concern.

The Dies Committee was determined to prove that the guides were an outpost for radical politics. The committee particularly questioned director Alsberg about the content of the New Jersey and Montana galley sheets, which allegedly "promoted class hatred." In response to charges that the New Jersey guide presented labor in a particularly partisan manner, Alsberg replied that galley proofs were always revised and that particular attention would be paid to "things which seem offensive, unfair . . . or partisan from a class angle."[152] Primarily concerned that the guidebooks reach publication, Alsberg was much more accommodating to the committee than his colleague Hallie Flanagan. In addition to its charges against some of the guidebooks, the Dies Committee targeted the anthology *American Stuff* for featuring allegedly subversive material. Focusing entirely on Richard Wright's essay "Ethics of Living Jim Crow," which Chairman Dies regarded as "the most filthy thing I have ever seen," the committee asked Jacob Baker's successor as head of white-collar relief, Ellen Woodward, to state her opinion on the piece. Citing passages that contained profanity and spoke explicitly of discrimination, the committee asked Woodward if she found anything "rehabilitating" about the essay. Woodward admitted that Wright's essay was "filthy and disgusting" but contended that this was irrelevant: *American Stuff* was developed outside project hours by creative writers and was not published by the WPA. Still, the Dies Committee persisted in their inquiries, noting that Henry Alsberg had written the foreword and that other witness had testified that the book was written on project time.[153]

A compilation of short stories, poetry, art, and folklore written by various FWP directors and writers, *American Stuff* (1937) portrayed Depression-era America with realism; as one *New York Times* reviewer commented, "There is almost no 'escape literature' here."[154] While Wright's essay was not the only material that treated race—Sterling Brown included poetry and black spirituals, and convict songs were provided by other writers—it was the most explicit condemnation of racial inequality. As this essay would become part of Wright's first book, *Uncle Tom's Children* (1938), it also served as the basis for his autobiography, *Black Boy* (1945). With its candid depiction of Wright's experiences in various types of employment and his everyday encounters with white people, "The Ethics of Living Jim Crow" detailed the violence, cruelty, and exclusion Wright faced in the Jim Crow South.[155] Reviewer William Smith of *New Masses* declared it "the most successful material in the book."[156] Jerre Mangione, who helped to compile the book and was himself a contributor, called the essay "easily the most powerful piece of writing in *American Stuff*."[157]

This praise from left-leaning individuals, however, was strongly countered by the Dies Committee's outrage; the committee dwelled on the profanity in Wright's account, presenting passages of the essay to Ellen Woodward out of context. Seemingly, it was the use of words such as "nigger," "bastard" and "son of a bitch," that perturbed members of the Dies Committee—not necessarily the world of bigotry and pain that Wright so carefully crafted. As an aura of racial liberalism pervaded Washington, D.C., at least superficially, Roosevelt's opponents—particularly southerners—

could not target calls for racial justice as "un-American" in and of themselves. Like its condemnations of the FTP production *Stevedore*, the Dies Committee targeted a racially provocative essay that it considered "profane" as evidence of subversion.

In 1939, the House Subcommittee on Appropriations (the Woodrum Committee) continued its investigation of the FWP where the Dies Committee left off. It was here that Congress most directly challenged the revision of black history. Prefacing his charges with his praise for "the splendid contributions that the Negro race has made . . . to our national life," Representative Frank Keefe (R-Wisc.) proceeded in alleging that certain parts of the guidebooks were written under the influence of "communist agitators." Before describing the material in question, Keefe made it clear that his charges were not a reflection of personal prejudices:

> I say to you, members of Congress, that in this discussion it makes no difference to me what an individual's outward color is if his heart and soul is red, exemplifying the flag of communism. . . . In reading the article referred to in this so-called guide book I was impressed by the very obvious spirit running through it, which indicated, to me at least, an attempt on the part of the writer to portray the oppression of the Negro by the white race and thereby stimulate a feeling of class hatred.[158]

Keefe's example was Brown's essay, "The Negro in Washington," in *Washington: City and Capital*, which included a statement that George Washington Parke Custis, foster son of President George Washington and father-in-law of Robert E. Lee, had left a tract of land in Arlington to a black daughter named Maria Syphax. Keefe chafed at the idea that this manufactured essay had been written by a "young Negro student trained at Howard University" who was not listed as a notable writer in the public catalog of the Library of Congress.[159] Interestingly, in targeting Brown's essay, which was arguably as stinging an indictment as Richard Wright's piece, Congress would single out what it believed was a historical inaccuracy rather than descriptions of discrimination.

Keefe stated that he had attempted to contact Sterling Brown to discuss the validity of these facts but that Brown did not reply. Brown admitted as much, claiming that he did not respond to Keefe's initial correspondence "probably [out] of procrastination due to a heavy schedule." Brown, however, did address Keefe's charges in a letter to Henry Alsberg. In response to charges that the essay "The Negro in Washington" was influenced by Communists and "sought to stir 'class hatred,'" Brown explained that what Keefe considered subversive were honest attempts to portray black life and the "adverse circumstances" facing black Americans. Brown cited the several examples of racial cooperation in the guide, noting that "white humanitarians have protested his [the black man's] enslavement and abuse, and farsighted statesmen have worked toward his integration in the total pattern." Furthermore, responding to allegations that the information on George Washington Parke Custis was false and gathered by a "young Negro student trained in Howard University," Brown asserted his full confidence in the validity of the relationship between Custis and Maria Syphax. "The relationship has long been a matter of common belief among Negroes of Washington and among certain White people," Brown proclaimed. In addition, his research source on the subject, E. Delorus Preston, was not a young Howard student, as Keefe argued, but rather the dean of a black college in Florida with a doctorate in history from Ohio State University, who had been an undergraduate at Howard—some twenty years earlier.[160] Although Keefe's charges further roused the fury against "anti-American" developments within the Federal Arts Project, the "Negro in Washington" remained intact. Yet the incident illustrated how explosive the revision of black history could be.[161]

BY THE TIME THE RELIEF BILL of June 1939 placed the FWP under state sponsorship, the ambition of the project had waned. The turning over of the project to state and local authorities had grave implications for black participants; as the NAACP pointed out in a press release opposing state control of the arts projects, "this would seriously cripple, particularly in southern states, the already small opportunity given Negroes and particularly Negro writers."[162] As stated in the previous chapter, with this bill the FTP was abolished; the focus of the FWP was centered on the completion of the guidebooks, leaving projects in more rudimentary stages by the wayside. Although almost all states secured sponsors to continue the completion of the guidebooks, it became clear that the project was in its final phase. Particularly after Alsberg left the project in August 1939, replaced by Michigan FWP director John Newsom, the project experienced an administrative push to complete the guides as quickly as possible. In 1940, some nearly complete projects such as *The Negro in Virginia* and *Drums and Shadows* reached publication, and the last of the guides came out by the end of 1941. The bombing of Pearl Harbor, however, forced the Writers' Project (its new title as of 1939) to quickly adapt to war mobilization. Renamed the Writers' Unit of the War Services Subdivision of the WPA, the agency devoted itself to writing manuals such as the "Servicemen's Recreational Guides" and Ohio's *Bomb Squad Training Manual*. By this time, the agency diminished to a barebones operation, as the wartime economic boom left only about two thousand people on state relief rolls. Ultimately, the Writers' Unit came to a close in February 1943, ending what one administrator deemed "the biggest literary project in history." When Congress eradicated the entire WPA in June 1943, the remnants of the FAP finally ended.[163]

During the earlier congressional hearings, Alsberg had attempted to save the FWP, proposing that it evolve into a permanent agency within the Department of the Interior and placing much faith in the influence of the project's "godmother," Eleanor Roosevelt. Many black leaders also passionately urged for the continuation of all arts projects in their personal correspondence. Along with appeals to Walter White, Sterling Brown urged Charles Jones of the National Urban League to protest "against the discontinuance of the Federal Writers' Project." Suggesting that the Urban League write to politicians, Brown explained the value of the FWP's projects, which "instead of being subversive and un-American . . . reflect and inspire the finest sort of patriotism."[164] Doris Kravis, executive secretary of the Public Use of Arts Committee, also pleaded with Walter White, claiming, "The Negro people . . . long denied their rights for cultural expression and enjoyment, have found in the arts projects a partial answer to this problem. There can be no question of the need for a continuation and expansion of these activities."[165] In response to these and other letters, Walter White related to President Roosevelt that "the material which has been gathered in this field [the FWP] is, in my opinion, of infinite importance in giving white Americans a more true picture of the part which the Negro has played which . . . is necessary if democracy is to survive."[166] While directors such as the FWP's Alsberg and the FTP's Hallie Flanagan argued against the termination of the arts projects on many different cultural and economic grounds, for black individuals the end of the Federal Arts Project not only signaled the closing of unique employment opportunities but a waning of their representational agency.

THE TERMINATION OF THE FWP stymied the publication of the "Portrait of the Negro as an American" project and other studies that featured untold histories; it also erased many white-collar employment opportunities heretofore unavailable to black Americans. Yet the political forces that undermined the FWP and propelled its demise do not diminish the historical impact of the project. As FWP writer and poet Arna Bontemps proclaimed, "For the first time since the Harlem period of the '20s, Negro writers had a chance."[167] Even with all of the obstacles he faced as Negro

Affairs editor, Sterling Brown still claimed that the FWP had a huge effect on black writers: "I think it taught a lot of them that writing was worthwhile and that writing was a craft. You had to know something to write. It gave them a social background, and it gave them a great sense of regionalism. . . . Yes, I think it had a great aesthetic effect. It was one of the best things that ever happened to our writers. It would be good if we had something like that right now . . . because a lot of our writers really need discipline."[168]

What had initially been conceived of as the most politically viable form of employment for a large number of white-collar workers allowed the unparalleled incorporation of black Americans into the American historical narrative. Within the American Guide Series and auxiliary projects, Sterling Brown and other black writers strove to depict African American life as complex and paradoxical. Although this federal support was short-lived, it had a lasting effect, building the foundations of social history by privileging the experiences of marginalized groups. While African American writers may have not reached an audience beyond academic circles during the 1930s, the interest in the "forgotten man" would become central in the writing of American history and the organization of university curricula and departments by the 1960s.

Brown's involvement with the FWP had a more immediate resonance, however. The celebration of particular African American individuals—from athletes to politicians—was a central feature of the guidebooks that would also become part of wartime racial propaganda. If the guidebooks pronounced African American citizens worthy of documentation, wartime rhetoric would even more boldly celebrate the contributions of black men and women and the significance of their history. Furthermore, cultural administrators would display the pluralistic vision advanced in the guidebooks more visually by the 1940s, as Americans of all racial and ethnic backgrounds were projected together in patriotic unity on the silver screen, morale boosting posters, and army photographs. If the Federal Arts Project had established a cultural framework for expanding the notion of American citizenry in the 1930s, the war years made it imperative that all men and women believe the nation recognized them.

In a forceful letter to Congressman Fredrick Taylor, the chairman of the House Subcommittee on Appropriations, Alain Locke expressed the meaning of the FAP for African Americans during the 1930s:

> I can and would like to testify before your Committee to the fact that the W.P.A. cultural projects have saved an important segment of our most significant progress from being engulfed in the disastrous flood of the economic depression. This is not merely a service to the restricted group itself, but to the whole racial group for whom these talents must furnish the leadership and inspiration. Its continuance, therefore, would have the soundest and most constructive social consequences, and its discontinuance, especially for an already handicapped group, would have the most unfavorable social consequences and political repercussions.[169]

Although these projects were discontinued, their inclusionary impulse would quickly reemerge in radio shows, films, photographs, and other media-based projects. And while many of the African American artists working within the FAP would be employed by war bureaucracies, new talents would also emerge, furnishing various styles of "leadership and inspiration" for black audiences. Yet, as administrators debated the viability of cultural programming, contrasting opinions within the African American community would more publicly evaluate black employment in the culture industry and question the improvement of racial imagery. When cultural programs became a hallmark of domestic propaganda, they continued to exist as limited, often repressive spaces. The barriers that both Sterling Brown and FTP performers had encountered would only prove more formidable during World War II. Thus, as the racial environment became increasingly volatile during the war years, the need for cultural solutions to the "Negro Problem" became even more pronounced. The media may have changed, but the political impulse, and all of its complications, remained consistent. And African Americans continued to fight.

chapter four

CONSTRUCTING G.I. JOE LOUIS

In 1940, Franklin Roosevelt underscored the importance of African American patriotism when democracy was under siege. "The European conflict with its spread of the Nazi and Fascist influence makes a challenging appeal. . . . This is a time for national unity and I am strengthened in my hope for the preservation of peace . . . by the knowledge that the American Negro has maintained a cherished tradition of loyalty and devotion to his country."[1] Even before the bombing of Pearl Harbor, the government's priorities had shifted to the international arena, affecting federal rhetoric and policies concerning black Americans. As federal program administrators had celebrated cultural differences among racial and ethnic groups during the 1930s, War Department and Office of War Information (OWI) officials would continue this policy during the 1940s, while subsuming it under the banner of unity and patriotism.

The war initiated new forms of government-sponsored culture on radio and film, and program administrators became much more wary of the kinds of projects they would develop. Congressional hostility towards the FWP and the FTP had proven how highly contentious and politically controversial images, sounds, and written representations could be. State officials understood that they would have to confront an explosive set of racial tensions while gingerly balancing competing political and social interests; therefore, they treaded much more carefully in the construction of cultural programs. Articulating the precariousness of the situation, the OWI's racial adviser, Milton Starr, declared, "the pure principles of democracy are far from fulfillment in the life of the American Negro. Considering the grave dangers facing the country, it is . . . desirable and necessary to de-emphasize our many long-standing internal dissensions and to close ranks as much as practicable for the duration."[2]

As America entered the war, state program administrators sought to integrate black Americans into the cultural apparatus as they had done in the 1930s. Yet the treatment of racial issues would unfold within much tighter parameters. Unlike the Federal Arts Project, which administrators initially envisioned as an enterprise for creative autonomy and expression, wartime cultural programs were created with explicit goals of boosting morale and propagating the nation's democratic ethos. In this highly charged political context, state administrators grappled with the precarious endeavor of promoting black inclusion while sidestepping the issue of racial equality. Although some officials understood and even sympathized with those African Americans who believed that the war against Fascism abroad exposed the hypocrisy of American racism, cultural program administrators abided by the official line that the war was not a testing ground for social reform. Official rhetoric during the war years slightly differed from the 1930s, when program directors sought to represent African Americans as part of a larger pluralistic ideology. In the 1940s, officials pronounced media-based programs the solution to the "Negro problem"—a means of securing black support when they perceived the possibility of African American dissent. Chandler Owen, former coeditor of the Socialist journal *Messenger* and a strong opponent of U.S. involvement in World War I, described the essential posture of African Americans toward participation in World War II, when he served as a public relations official and authored the morale-boosting pamphlet *Negroes and the War*. Owen told the president in 1941, "In spite of the tendency of the colored people to follow your leadership . . . almost no influence has been exerted over them on the international situation. . . . I think some concerted, dynamic movement to enlist the united support of the largest racial minority in the country should be inaugurated at once."[3]

Owen's call for a "movement" to maintain black loyalty reflected an official concern that African Americans might not continue to support a war for democracy while American discrimination persisted. By the onset of World War II, black expectations ran high, fueled by wartime egalitarian rhetoric and African American political mobilization. As officials were unwilling to implement structural change, discontent became manifest among black politicians and in the black press. As one "Open Letter to President Roosevelt" in the *Crisis* proclaimed, "despite your exhortations to unity, and your acts clearly indicating unity as national policy, the thir-

124

CONSTRUCTING G.I. JOE LOUIS

teen millions of Negro American citizens have not been made an integral part of the nation's war effort. . . . We, who are willing and anxious to fight for the Four Freedoms, are not free."[4] While the establishment of the Fair Employment Practices Committee marked a significant federal attempt to curb racial discrimination in defense industries, this was an isolated initiative during the war years. As the Roosevelt administration was largely unable or unwilling to push for legislation that would disrupt the racial status quo, administrators in the War Department and the OWI professed that the use of black cultural symbols could reconcile the escalating "Negro problem" with official pronouncements of American egalitarianism. The use of culture to reduce wartime racial tensions became a subject of frequent debate, and officials questioned which individuals and which sector of the media could best address African Americans without alarming white southerners.

If government-sponsored cultural programs were an experimental means of shoring up African American electoral support in the 1930s, they were essential to military mobilization by the time of the bombing of Pearl Harbor. Yet the wartime cultural apparatus was not monolithic; those who formulated cultural programs during World War II expressed a variety of opinions on policies and procedures. While the OWI and the War Department did not merely echo one another in their plans for morale building, they did express a similar understanding of the need for depoliticized racial programs and of the effectiveness of mass culture in securing their objectives. Plans to construct more sanitized cultural media led some racial liberals to resign their posts; out of conviction or in response to pressure, others adapted their politics to the larger national agenda.

The political exigencies of the 1940s, however, should not obscure the continuities within cultural development over the course of the New Deal era. Most significantly, many men and women employed with the Federal Arts Project (FAP) served as administrators in wartime agencies or performed in projects sponsored by the OWI or the Armed Forces. Ulric Bell, former director of the Kentucky FWP, served as an OWI overseas administrator; FTP Negro unit director John Houseman worked in development at the Armed Forces Radio Service. Houseman's FTP assistant and successor as New York Negro unit director, Carlton Moss, penned the script for the influential propaganda film *The Negro Soldier*; FTP actors Canada Lee and Rex Ingram performed in wartime films such as *Lifeboat* and *Sahara*. In addition, *Macbeth*'s Edna Thomas was featured in the War Department radio series "America's Negro Soldiers." There were also several white New

Deal liberals whose influence during the 1930s would extend to wartime operations. Lowell Mellett, director of the National Emergency Council, became head of OWI's Motion Pictures Bureau, while former librarian of Congress Archibald MacLeish and Pulitzer prize-winning playwright Robert Sherwood directed OWI predecessor agencies, the Office of Facts and Figures and the Office of Coordinator of Information, respectively.

While these individuals advanced a new political agenda in the 1940s, the wartime programs they coordinated replicated some features of the FAP. Programs like the FWP and FTP, while receiving scrutiny during congressional investigations, had demonstrated the feasibility of focusing on black cultural contributions and entertainers without arousing a great deal of hostility among the larger, racially conservative public. Many of the issues facing cultural administrators in the 1930s, particularly debates over selecting black directors, also arose in wartime agencies. In addition, the question of whether African American programs should be kept separate from mainstream programs was always at the fore among both artists and officials. At times, directors and participants advocated for all-black programs as a communal endeavor, and at other moments they decried separatism and demanded representational integration.

The media, however, had dramatically changed. With the new priorities of war production, projects that had once focused on the dissemination of high art quickly gave way to a propaganda machine based on mass culture.[5] Rather than the symphonies, paintings, and theatrical performances that had dominated official conceptualizations of "art for the millions" in the 1930s, officials now focused on radio and film—the media proven to reach the largest number of Americans. By 1940, 83 percent of Americans, both urban and rural, owned radios and faithfully tuned in to such popular programs as *The Jack Benny Program* and *Amos 'n' Andy* during the 1930s.[6] As America entered the war, film was at its apogee as the most popular form of American leisure entertainment. One 1944 statistic revealed that a full eighty cents of every dollar spent on "spectator amusement" went to motion pictures; during this period, films attracted approximately eight-five to ninety million moviegoers per week.[7] As these media attracted the greatest audiences, cultural administrators naturally perceived them to be the most effective instruments for disseminating wartime ideologies. While Archibald MacLeish, director of the Office of Facts and Figures, dismissed the idea that "writers and other artists have no function in time of war," he did admit that they would have to re-orient their work to emphasize "why America is at war and the nature of the peace that must follow the war."[8]

Radio and motion pictures served to buttress American propaganda, and celebrities that graced the airwaves and the silver screen enlisted in the war effort. While white entertainers such as Bob Hope famously entertained troops, and actress Betty Grable became the most popular pinup girl among servicemen, black celebrities served a similar function. Performers such as Duke Ellington and Louis Armstrong frequently played at war-related functions, and rising star Lena Horne began to rival Grable among both white and black soldiers.[9] Yet, by 1942, no African American was more beloved among both white and black Americans than heavyweight champion Joe Louis. Exemplifying the plight of so many African Americans who migrated to northern and midwestern cities in hope of a better life, Louis's rise to stardom represented the African American dream. Louis, however, was also an icon of American victory. The fighter's triumph over German Max Schmeling in 1938, coupled with his patriotic pronouncements as the war unfolded, rendered him a potent symbol. After a series of debates within government agencies, administrators affirmed Louis's political value as the "Brown Bomber" who stood for heroism, unity, and, as part of the Armed Forces, black military participation. In and through the Louis persona, state managers could advocate an ethos of racial liberalism, while still skirting the issue of discrimination in several areas of American life.

To the chagrin of Walter White and other black leaders, the baptism of this American hero required Louis's muted stance on the most serious problems plaguing black individuals. The official construction of Joe Louis involved a depoliticization of the "Brown Bomber" as he became the quintessential symbol of Americanness; administrators ensured that Louis was overtly disconnected from charged racial issues, instead representing black patriotism and black citizenship. Governmental attempts to demarcate the construction of Joe Louis, however, demonstrated how goals of cultural production often could not anticipate the alternative meanings that images offered. Whether or not constructions of Joe Louis overtly challenged racial discrimination, they were not void of political content. When the government featured Louis in military boxing exhibitions, on film, and on war posters, this iconography furthered the more racially charged symbol of a strong, victorious, and sometimes armed black man. Furthermore, as the most visible black figure of the war era, represented as a moral,

Joe Louis demonstrating boxing technique to soldiers at the Cavalry Replacement Center at Fort Riley, Kansas, where he underwent basic training. Photograph by Press Association, Inc. Courtesy of AP/Wide World Photos. (National Archives, RG 208 PU-120V-13)

patriotic man, Louis countered racial stereotypes that frequented popular culture. Before World War II, the government had not glorified black individuals as war heroes; therefore, Louis's embodiment of this cultural space bore important political implications.

As historian Thomas Holt argues, Joe Louis represented one of a few African American cultural heroes who were able to transcend race in the 1930s and 1940s. Louis's politically sanitized persona allowed both white and black Americans to derive their own meaning from the Brown Bomber, whether as an athlete, a racial icon, or a patriot. As Holt contends, "Race is the medium through which other fundamental conflicts in the social system are 'lived' and 'fought through.'"[10] Yet the multiplicity of meanings that Louis engendered does not diminish the fact that he often countered the racial status quo in both action and iconography. As a black man who had publicly knocked out a glaring symbol of white supremacy, Max Schmeling, Louis could not be divorced from the political implications of that historical bout. If government administrators chose Louis because of his quiet demeanor and acquiescence to patriotic ideals, they also chose him because of the significance he held for the black community. This influence, however, cut both ways; while African Americans may have been more apt to support a war that Joe Louis endorsed, his victories over white men in the ring only fueled black aspirations towards racial equality. Therefore, when it came time to promote Louis vigorously, administrators still questioned and debated which forms of racial programming would be the most effective. Louis's celebrity and propaganda value were unique; yet the kinds of discussions that led to the promotion of the Brown Bomber would also surface in the development of radio programs and motion pictures.

War Agencies Confront the "Race Problem"

Of the agencies that addressed racial policy, the War Department displayed the most conservative posture. Secretary of War Henry Stimson rejected the prospect of an integrated army, claiming that black men did not express the military initiative of their white counterparts. Defining segregation as an "established American custom," the army demonstrated its unyielding adherence to the racial status quo, stonewalling most challenges from black organizations and white liberals. Maintaining segregated training camps and relegating black individuals to labor or service units, the War Department worked to maintain the traditional racial ideology under the guise of military expedience. Military officials spent more time discussing and lamenting the "Negro problem" than they did evaluating black soldiers as a valuable manpower asset. Although neither the War Department nor the officer corps was monolithic, the defense of segregation and many other southern racial norms was a prevalent element of military life throughout the duration of the war.[11]

The OWI, on the other hand, employed New Deal liberals who viewed racial equality as essential for advancing and defending American democracy. Many administrators had already established relationships with black leaders, and they encouraged an interracial dialogue. Composed initially of civilian information organizations, the OWI inherited a staff of intellectuals and journalists who viewed themselves as a central "idea center," disseminating truthful information to the public. Librarian of Congress and poet Archibald MacLeish, popular CBS radio commentator Elmer Davis, and Lowell Mellett, former editor of the *Washington Daily News*, were among the key players in the OWI. Yet, the OWI constantly met opposition, as many program administrators and a majority of the members of Congress were highly suspicious of its purpose as a propaganda agency. For

Elmer Davis, director of the Office of War Information, awaits an "On the Air" signal to begin his weekly broadcast on world news, March 1943. Photo by Office of War Information. (Franklin D. Roosevelt Library, Hyde Park, N.Y.)

Secretary of State Cordell Hull, the OWI threatened the authority of the State Department because it sometimes abided by "a policy widely divergent from the official foreign policy." Thus, the State Department balked at the agency for wanting to "make policy, and not simply use it." Individuals such as Henry Stimson and naval commander Frank Knox also viewed the civilian information agency with skepticism, complaining that it could interfere with military operations and security. Although Director Elmer Davis met regularly with military officials and Secretary Hull, the OWI could only undertake those projects that met with their—often reluctant—approval. In addition, as the elections of 1942 further buttressed the position of conservatives in Congress, the OWI was on shaky ground, perceived by many politicians as another troublesome liberal New Deal institution. Conservatives attacked the OWI as a "New Deal publicity center," and when several OWI publications provoked increasing controversy, the Domestic Branch was eventually abolished.[12]

While liberals in the OWI exhibited a progressive stance on racial issues, the demands of a highly politicized Congress and the administration's official policy on quieting wartime racial tensions consistently compromised liberalism within the agency. The ambivalence of some OWI administrators was revealed during the first crisis concerning the racial management of the war—A. Philip Randolph's proposed march on Washington in June 1941. For Randolph, the march was "in the interest of securing jobs and justice in national defense and fair participation and equal integration into the Nation's military and naval forces."[13] Director MacLeish of the Office of Facts and Figures (OWI's predecessor), who supported many programs excavating black history when he was the librarian of Congress and consistently opposed discrimination in government agencies, expressed his opposition to the march quite explicitly.[14] In correspondence to Attorney General Frances Biddle, MacLeish attached a memo drawing attention to the possibility that "Axis and American fascist forces" would "incite the Negro population" and "foment actual violence on the widest possible scale." To another correspondent MacLeish concluded, "Just what can be done to forestall the projected 'March to Washington,' I don't know. We are watching the situation carefully, however, and will do what we can."[15] Whatever liberal sentiments officials expressed, some were more reticent to support large-scale black political mobilization. Administrative hesitance towards publicly endorsing racial reform would figure greatly in the types of programs that cultural officials developed to improve black morale.[16]

As the organized efforts of Randolph demonstrated, black discontent was undeniable as America entered World War II. To develop programs that would ameliorate these attitudes, administrators first attempted to locate the source of black antipathy towards the war effort. In surveying black residents in Memphis and New York, OWI administrators claimed, "The poor morale they [African Americans] manifest at present does not stem from lack of patriotism, isolationist sentiment or any lack of enthusiasm for democratic values. It is a direct result of the frustrations they experience in their daily lives."[17] Another OWI report, written in the aftermath of the 1943 Detroit riot, found poor housing conditions to be the "arch offender" among conditions in black neighborhoods. Likewise, this report regarded inadequate recreational facilities and poor transportation as "inter-racial irritants," while Adjutant General J. A. Ulio significantly noted the effects of "the advent of warmer weather," a major factor in the recent riots.[18]

CONSTRUCTING G.I. JOE LOUIS

OWI racial adviser Philleo Nash stressed that black expectations bore greatly on morale. "Both now and as the war progresses," Nash stated, "the situation of Negroes will be one which will be highly frustrating, inasmuch as there will always be a wide gap between the extent and conditions of Negro participation in the war and their own desires." Claiming that African Americans had become increasingly cognizant of the demand for their labor and military service, Nash reported that African Americans could use their manpower to bargain for "participation on equal economic terms." Given the increase in the black electoral presence, Nash insisted, now more than ever, the government had to assure black Americans that they would benefit from supporting the war. Insisting that "Negroes are agitating for, demand, and expect, much fuller participation than at present in industry, the armed forces, and civilian defense," Nash urged program administrators to recall the dim aftermath of World War I, when black political expectations had been quickly dashed.[19]

Blacks' ambivalence towards the war was equally troubling to individuals outside the government, where explanations for black discontent proliferated. In a letter to the Office of Facts and Figures, prominent black attorney John Levirt Kelly stated that most African Americans had "no ties to the European continent, not even far distant ones." In his opinion, it was therefore likely that black Americans considered the war a "white man's war."[20] Caroline Blake, a white member of the National Urban League, indicated she had learned that African Americans were "unconvinced that they have, in fact, a stake in this country." Pleading to Director MacLeish to help black people through "these troubled times," liberals like Blake reminded government officials of the similarities between German and American racism.[21] John Hammond, a prominent white jazz critic and talent agent for the Columbia Broadcasting System angrily recalled his visit to a black army training camp in Muskogee, Oklahoma. After entering a dance hall in the "colored area of town" to recruit musicians for camp shows, Hammond was immediately escorted out by four white MPs who warned him to stay away from "knife wielding Niggers." Describing this visit in a letter to the *Washington Post*, Hammond expressed his shock and anger over the rigidity of segregation, regarding it as "complete as anything one might find in fascist countries."[22]

Southern author Lillian Smith offered one of the most scathing condemnations of the racial status quo, denouncing the hollowness of democratic propaganda in her piercing, highly ironic parody, "Portrait of the Deep South: Speaking to Negroes on Morale":

Don't you know defeatist talk about Jim Crow
is exactly the kind of talk that pulls morale down low?
And for god's sake, stop asking us to call you mister
(You think I'd want a nigger to marry my sister?)
Listen, colored folks,
you ought to be thankful you have a claim
to be called American (even in name) . . .

Come on darkies, time to start a song
Time to open your mouths now and bellow out strong
and show the whole world you're as good
an American
as we are
and you'll fight to the last drop
of your blood
for us (but stop that fool complaining
about Red Cross separating it
you know they can't mix white and nigger blood)

Yeah, we'll fight, you'll fight
and we'll fight
to the last Jim Crow drop
to rid the world of Hitlerism
and Nazism
and all them OTHER ISMS
and save the American Way
so that things can go on forever
and ever
and
ever
just as they are
down here
today.[23]

The critiques made by both government officials and public cultural figures furnished black leaders with a fertile ground for demanding better conditions in the military and on the home front. Criticizing businesses and restaurants declared "off limits" to black troops in Walla Walla, Washington, NAACP assistant secretary Roy Wilkins wrote Director MacLeish, "These are the policies which make it difficult, if not impossible, for Negro leaders, or anyone else, to lift the morale of Negro Americans in the war effort."[24] In a report to the attorney general, the Fraternal Council of Negro Churches in America demanded investigations of several racially motivated murders, some involving severe police brutality and others with possible links to the Ku Klux Klan. Fraternal Council chairman W. H. Jernagin used the issue of morale as an incentive for criminal investigations, asserting that "in every type of injustice the working of evil forces . . . undermine[s] our country's whole victory program. . . . We are sure that you do not want any obstacle to prevent the Negro people from giving their full, united strength to the winning of this war of survival."[25]

Some black organizations, however, believed that the government was actively formulating policies to better race relations in response to their grievances. After visiting ten government agencies to discuss an end to "un-American discrimination in all phases of the war effort," members of the Southern Negro Youth Congress (SNYC) formed the impression that state officials seriously considered their proposals. "Our government is fully committed to a policy of the most resolute prosecution of the war," SNYC's report states. "The dominant attitude among the officials . . . is one of sympathy with the need of allowing the Negro people to serve . . . with dignity and in posts of responsibility."[26] In spite of these positive reactions, many black leaders found themselves excluded from the official dialogue. When denied an invitation to the Women's Interest Section of the Bureau of Public Relations meeting, Mary McLeod Bethune angrily informed Secretary of War Stimson, "We are anxious for you to know that we want to be and insist upon being considered a part of our American democracy, not something apart from it."[27]

Cultural Solutions and Their Problems

In conceiving remedies to the "Negro problem," white administration officials set the parameters of potential programs. While MacLeish asserted that no government agency should accept any tenets or principles of racial segregation, public condemnations of discrimination were another matter.[28] Although Milton Starr related that the OWI's plans would not "recommend policy for the correction of many injustices . . . from which the American Negro suffers," he did concede that "obviously improvement in the morale of the Negro would automatically follow any real social, political or economic gains."[29] Whatever their own progressive leanings, government administrators made it clear that programs to boost black patriotism would not directly challenge the racial status quo. As Philleo Nash proclaimed, "granting small concessions [to black Americans] . . . does not imply any intent on the part of the Federal Government to make the largest concession of all . . . to break down the pattern of social segregation."[30] Thus, the administration focused on endowing African Americans with a sense of purpose while carefully stressing that racial animosity weighed heavily on the national rhetoric of democratic unity. War officials agreed that the major goal of federal programs would be to underscore black American citizenship; however, administrators expressed differences in regard to the types of methods they would pursue. Theodore Berry, a black lawyer from Cincinnati and president of that city's NAACP from 1932 to 1938, served as liaison officer to the Office of Facts and Figures (OFF). He articulated one approach:

> A program of morale building can be conceived in two general phases which might roughly be termed as "superficial" and "fundamental." The superficial phase would include the use of all techniques designed to stimulate and arouse patriotic fervor, such as parades, rallies, glorified heroes, posters, radio and motion picture appeals. The fundamental phase would include the utilization of all psychological techniques for molding public opinion in the basic ideas and thought involved in the purposes of the War and [be] designed to eliminate divisive interests and unite all people in the prosecution of the War.[31]

For Berry, the more extensive use of radio and film to "indicate the participation of the Negro in the war effort and American life" went part and parcel with more overt political measures such as the investigation and prosecution of the "mistreatment of Negro civilians and soldiers." And like Walter White, who at approximately the same time was campaigning to convince Hollywood film executives to develop more positive roles for African Americans, Berry understood that cultural advancement accompanied structural change. Yet, in his push for more concrete steps toward racial reform, Berry also suggested that the OWI should press for a presidential repudiation of "the statements of any persons . . . who seek to incite racial feeling and prejudice."[32]

At the time, federal officials were not prepared to issue politically charged protestations of racial inequality; however, they embraced the concept of media-based programs to promote black inclusion. Berry warned of the limitations of these tactics, claiming, "a postage stamp with a picture of a Negro author or parades and music will not be enough to improve morale."[33] These kinds of pronouncements differ from those made by an administrator such as Sterling Brown, who in the 1930s undoubtedly pressed for structural change, yet articulated the principle that imagery could serve as an important site of racial progress. Such statements indicate how the war revealed a more explicit discourse among some African Americans serving within state cultural agencies, as the political environment demanded urgent attention be given to democratic practices.

Once administrators adopted a policy of formulating cultural programs, heated debates arose over who was best qualified to handle racial issues. Tensions came to a boil when Milton Starr, a white southerner, became a dollar-per-year adviser to the OWI on matters pertaining to African Americans. Starr owned a chain of southern movie theaters in black neighborhoods, and his sponsorship of the *All-American Newsreel* was highly criticized by Walter White and William Hastie, former dean of Howard Law School and the first civilian aide on Negro affairs to the secretary of war. As the *All-American Newsreel* featured black participation in the war but was only shown to black audiences, White and Hastie charged that these films would only diminish the amount of material on black soldiers in regular newsreels, leaving the white public uninformed. Furthermore, White claimed that Starr had a background as an "exploiter of Negroes" because the *All-American Newsreel* was sold at a higher rate than other newsreel services to segregated theaters.[34]

With this arsenal of information on Starr, an infuriated Walter White bemoaned the white southerner's position as a racial adviser, announcing to OWI director Elmer Davis, "I know of no scholastic qualifications he possesses nor of any study he has made of the problems involved, nor even of his being acquainted . . . with responsible Negro or white students of the Negro such as educators, editors, churchmen, and the like."[35] Echoing these sentiments, Theodore Berry became increasingly frustrated by the influence of Starr on racial policies within the OWI, charging that he had not been copied on Starr's memoranda. Starr's prescriptions for improving "Negro morale" were in opposition to Berry's calls for more systematic racial reforms, as Starr blamed black leaders and the black press for stirring up protest that was "consciously or unconsciously assisting the enemy."[36] Due to the divergent opinions between himself and Starr, as well as the "reluctance in the Office to frontally attack white racial prejudice through propaganda," Berry resigned his post in the OWI, with little hope that the agency would promote racial betterment under Starr's advisement.[37] Although Elmer Davis insisted that Starr was genuinely "devoted to the betterment of the Negro," the gradual replacement of Berry by Starr indicated that administrators were committed to making use of more sanitized cultural programming and avoiding tactics that would further incite existing racial conflicts.[38]

Likewise, William Hastie, as the civilian aide to the secretary of war, found that his appeals to directly confront racial issues fell on deaf ears. A student of Felix Frankfurter at Harvard Law School, Hastie entered the War Department with high expectations of initiating racial changes. Yet, these hopes were soon dashed as Hastie's objectives, such as the desegregation of army mess halls, motion picture theaters, and post exchange facilities, along with the appointment of black officers, were stymied. Hastie claimed that Undersecretary of War Robert Patterson ignored his reports and that policies relating to African Americans were often evaluated by another War Department committee without his knowledge.[39] When Hastie accused the War Department of misleading the public—for example, questioning Patterson's official statement that black aviation squadrons at Tuskegee were performing similar tasks as their white counterparts—the Air Force no longer consulted him on racial matters. As Hastie's more confrontational tactics became more difficult for the War Department to contain, he, like Theodore Berry, was excluded from official meetings and left ignorant of several departmental proposals. In 1943, Hastie resigned his post out of disgust with the War Department's unyielding position on segregation and discrimination in the military.[40]

The tensions arising from the more radical viewpoints of several black administrators led to discussions concerning the racial composition of war information bureaucracies. Administrators in OWI proposed the idea of a "Negro deputy" or an agency to handle all aspects of the "Negro problem" that concerned the government. Eventually, they rejected the idea of a separate "Negro ministry" on the basis that it would "itself be segregation of a kind to which Negroes would object."[41] Instead, officials proposed an agency or individual that would handle the problems of all minority groups, because others such as "the Spanish-American, the Jew, the alien and many first generation citizens" confronted "the same disabilities against which Negroes justly complain."[42] Furthermore, when considering whether a deputy handling minority problems should be white or black, administrators insisted that the deputy should be white: "If a Negro were selected his selection would advertise the individual as a Negro specialist—which would produce criticism from both Negroes and conservative whites."[43]

Here, the landscape of war had dramatically altered the notions of black expertise and black separatism that had permeated the FAP. Although FTP administrators struggled over whether the Negro Unit director should be white or black, the decision to appoint John Houseman had been based on his connections within the industry, rather than whether black or white communities would object to a black director as a form of racial essentialism. Nor was the establishment of Negro Units criticized as a kind of segregation. Furthermore, the appointment of Sterling Brown drew no controversy, as Henry Alsberg had taken the position that a black scholar was best suited to write black history. Black opposition to the appointment of Clark Foreman as "special advisor on the economic status of Negroes" in the 1930s could have served as an important reminder that African Americans preferred a black "expert" on issues affecting their community over a white one.

However, the heightened racial climate produced by war meant that the process of building a racial bureaucracy in the 1940s would indeed be precarious. Thus, with domestic discord threatening, black leadership positions—even within the cultural apparatus—were less frequent during the war years than they had been in the 1930s. Although administrators initially criticized the idea of a separate bureau for Negro affairs, they eventually came to target African Americans as a separate minority group in media-based public relations campaigns. Truman Gibson Jr., Hastie's more moderate replacement as civilian aide on Negro affairs to the secretary of war, made the distinction that although the army had "avoided propagandizing particular groups" in the past, by 1943 it had become necessary to provide "factual information" for individual minority groups who "come from clearly defined communities . . . with an affinity of blood and ideas."[44] Thus, when the OWI stipulated that every "radio, motion picture, poster, pamphlet . . . must have its Negro counter-part," plans to raise morale quickly circulated to other government agencies and cultural industries.[45] Officials particularly targeted radio as an area excluding black Americans: "One of the most glaring errors has been the utter failure to use radio as a vehicle for reaching the Negroes. Negro people do not respond to 'White programs' and 'White' speeches. The only 'White' person they listen to and believe is the president, in whom they still have faith. . . . With the wealth of recognized Negro talent available for cooperation in such government operated radio shows, this fact seems most deplorable—especially when it could be remedied so simply."[46]

Discussions of the use of motion pictures mimicked these attitudes; for instance, one OWI official claimed, "recent surveys show that Government propaganda pictures have been leaving the Negro people cold and unimpressed."[47] Officials scurried to find alternatives to this cultural void. They advocated radio programs featuring black soldiers, human-interest stories in black magazines such as the *Crisis*, newsreels showing black military activity, and favorable articles about black experiences in the white press. Program administrators intended for these ideas and images to feature black Americans without reference to inequality. Thus, the very presence of black bodies and voices could demonstrate American racial liberalism, concentrating discussion on black achievements and steering the dialogue away from discrimination.

To implement specific visions of black inclusion, administration officials first proposed new policies for the press—purportedly one of the biggest threats to black morale. Officials in the Office of Facts and Figures suggested that because white newspapers rarely published any news about black individuals, the black reader had to "turn to his own newspapers" such as the *Pittsburgh Courier* and the *Chicago Defender*, which often left him "isolated in his thoughts and actions."[48] Writing to Director MacLeish, assistant OFF director R. Keith Kane asserted, "Among the Negroes, it must be demonstrated that this is not a race war and that other people allied with us have colored skins."[49] Therefore, government agencies warned against press reports that could stir public outrage towards racial inequality; yet they also issued a series of guidelines to avoid racial stereotypes and to preserve "dignity" among African Americans. In one instance, *New York Age* editor Fred Moore alerted the Army Information Service that photos were being taken of black soldiers who were "forced to pose eating watermelon." In response, the War Department's Bureau of Public Relations (BPR) issued a report stating, "no group within the Army should be singled out for stories or pictures emphasizing racial or religious characteristics."[50] The BPR demanded that all photos have explanatory captions, identifying all individuals in the photos, and prohibiting the quotation of black soldiers in dialect. Furthermore, the BPR issued a directive, based on a suggestion from NAACP assistant secretary Roy Wilkins, stating that all writers should capitalize the word *Negro* and use it consistently when describing black Americans. Stressing the need to respect certain requests of the black community, BPR administrator D. P. Page indicated that the secretary of war "prefers to use the designation 'colored.' It is our wish . . . to conform to the practice of leading Negro writers and publications."[51]

While administrators in the OWI and the War Department had spoken of incorporating black individuals into war publications, this idea went unfulfilled. Out of the hundreds of war posters produced by the OWI, Treasury Department, all branches of the armed forces, and private industry, only a handful featured African Americans.[52] While there were many photos taken of black soldiers published in mainstream periodicals such as *Life* magazine, the government frequently censored them. Picturing black men in uniform could serve a positive function in the black press, but in the white press it could arouse anger, particularly among white southerners, who believed that black military service could potentially weaken the white racial hierarchy.[53] As several white southerners ironically charged that excessive coverage of black soldiers could damage the "promotion of unity," war officials walked a thin line in formulating a multiracial narrative.[54]

As war propaganda managers attempted to balance this divergent range of interests, the promotion of popular entertainers, athletes, and military heroes came to feature prominently in plans for raising black morale. OWI racial adviser Milton Starr suggested the use of popular bands, such as Cab Calloway and Jimmie Lunceford, and stage and screen entertainers, such as Ethel Waters, Bill Robinson, Eddie Rochester, and Paul Robeson, all of whom "would have great value in any propaganda program." Starr also advised that black military heroes such as Brigadier General Benjamin Davis Sr. and Dorie Miller appear in pamphlets and make public appearances. The OWI's major emphasis was the need to focus solely on "prominent Negro *names*," which it felt would have the greatest impact on black civilian and military audiences. Of course, these "prominent Negro names" did not include political activists such as A. Philip Randolph or NAACP secretary Walter White. The distinction between popular and political black figures was made quite explicit, as Milton Starr stated: "It might be well to ask the question as to who would draw the biggest audience, Joe Louis or Walter White. The answer is obvious."[55]

War Department Officials Salute Private Joe Louis

Indeed, no project or individual played a greater role in war morale and propaganda than heavyweight boxer Joe Louis. As arguably the most famous black celebrity, Louis had come to embody the values of patriotism, humility, and sacrifice by the early 1940s. This was due in large part to his soft-spoken, polite demeanor, which whites viewed favorably in contrast to the more controversial Jack Johnson, the first and last black heavyweight champion until Louis. Johnson, who held the championship from 1908 to

1915, offended most whites and many blacks with his ostentatious living, confrontational manner, and affinity for white women. Antagonizing both his opponents and the press, Johnson threatened the racial status quo by challenging white expectations of black deference. While many African Americans viewed Johnson's actions as heroic, others saw him as an embarrassment. Generally, white people used him as proof of black savagery and incivility.[56]

To avoid the negative publicity that plagued Johnson's career, Louis's boxing managers told him that he must not only exhibit strength in the ring but also good behavior outside of it. When Louis was only nineteen, black manager John Roxborough brought him into his home, instructing him in proper dress, manners, and nutrition. Roxborough also created a set of commandments that Louis had to abide by; these circulated in many newspapers once Louis had begun his professional career:

1. He was never to have his picture taken along with a white woman.
2. He would never go into a nightclub alone.
3. There would be no soft fights.
4. There would be no fixed fights.
5. He was never to gloat over a fallen opponent.
6. He was to keep a "dead pan" in front of the cameras.
7. He was to live and fight clean.[57]

Louis's adherence to these "rules" shaped his public image during his professional career. Whites' praise of his athletic abilities, largely stemming from his "good behavior," assured Louis of unprecedented credibility as a black boxer. His sportsmanship and nonconfrontational demeanor led the white press to accept and eventually to applaud his career as a boxing champion.[58]

On 25 June 1935, Joe Louis prepared to fight the "Italian Giant," Primo Carnera. In light of Mussolini's threats to invade Ethiopia, the bout was politically symbolic; as one of the few independent, predominantly black countries, the fate of Ethiopia became increasingly important to African Americans, who viewed its colonization as "the final victory of the white man over the Negro."[59] Louis's knockout of Carnera in the sixth round signaled the beginning of his career as a boxing superstar, and African Americans understood the victory as one of the most significant racial achievements of all times. As Maya Angelou indicated, a loss for Louis would represent "our people falling. It was another lynching, yet another Black man hanging from a tree. One more woman ambushed and raped."[60] Describing the feelings of black men and women who listened to the fight on the radio in a general store, Angelou articulated how although Louis had not ever made any pronouncements about the racial implications of his boxing, African Americans still understood his victory in racial terms:

"Champion of the world. A Black Boy. Some Black mother's son. He was the Strongest man in the world. . . . Those who lived too far had made arrangements to stay in town. It wouldn't do for a Black man and his family to be caught on a lonely road on a night when Joe Louis had proved we were the strongest people in the world."[61]

Likewise, in his article "Joe Louis Uncovers Dynamite," Richard Wright illustrated the incredible jubilation brought on by Louis, not just by his refutation of white supremacy, but by the feelings that he stirred in black men and women everywhere: "From the symbol of Joe's strength they took strength, and in that moment all fear, all obstacles were wiped out, drowned. . . . Here's that something, that pent-up folk consciousness . . . here's a fleeting glimpse . . . of that heart that beats and suffers and hopes — for freedom."[62] Unlike some white reporters, who described the fight in terms of Louis's rise to boxing superstardom, many black individuals saw themselves and their futures in the "Brown Bomber." From the pens of black authors such as Wright and Angelou, to the streetcorner games of black children, to the songs of musicians such as Count Basie and Cab Calloway, Joe Louis occupied an unparalleled symbolic space within black culture. Louis had demonstrated to all Americans that a black man could indeed triumph over a white opponent.[63]

Americans on both sides of the color line were optimistic about a Louis victory in 1936, anticipating a historic moment when the Brown Bomber would knock out German Max Schmeling for the World Heavyweight Championship.[64] There was no doubt that Louis would defeat Schmeling, as confident headlines declared, "Schmeling Is Due for Sure Beating in Battle Tonite," "Louis in Perfect Trim for Big Bout," "Joe in Tip-Top Condition."[65] Playing down American racial animosities, reporters focused on the international implications of the fight at a time when white supremacy took a backseat to American supremacy. In light of these high expectations and Louis's stellar boxing record, Schmeling's victory over Louis stunned America. Furious, the *Washington Post* immediately resorted to racist remarks in its declaration: "Dar Schlager had completely dismantled Joe . . . who had entered the ring a fresh strong athlete [and turned] into a grotesque type of a tired Negro."[66] The black press sought explanations for

Louis's defeat. As one reporter stated in the *Amsterdam News*, Schmeling's win was "like a nightmare [that] reached out through space, and ripped out the heart of the country."[67] Speculation loomed over the possibility of Nazi poisoning, Louis being "doped," and other types of German sabotage. A columnist for the *Pittsburgh Courier* assured readers that Louis had to have been doped due to the fact that "his (Louis's) hair was disheveled . . . he had a funny stare in his eyes . . . his whole facial expression did not show the calmness characteristic of the man, and his color was terrible."[68]

Many African Americans could not forgive Louis. As one "former Louis fan" wrote to the *Amsterdam News*, "I think Joe Louis has lost his nerve since Max Schmeling connected with his jaw."[69] The popular song "Don't Be a Joe Louis" resonated within black communities whose morale has been shattered.[70] With the diminishing faith in Joe Louis came a disillusionment about race progress in general, as one black writer declared: "We ain't no Ethiopia, no Haile Selassie, and now, no Joe Louis—white folks are in the lead . . . the blues are on everyone's lip."[71] What had been lost was partly an African American's chance to prove his superiority, but also the sense that a symbol of progress has been shattered. As one columnist in the black press concluded, "we sincerely wanted Joe to win, because it does something to the Nation's view toward Negroes. . . . the masses put stock in champions. . . . the Negro is no less inferior because Louis loses . . . but the average white will respect a champion."[72]

After many hopes had been dashed, it was with great delight that both black and white Americans witnessed Louis's victory over Schmeling in a rematch on 22 June 1938. The Brown Bomber demolished Schmeling in the first round, elevating the fight into one of the most famous events in boxing history. The *New York Times* described the manner in which Louis "polished off the Black Uhlan from the Rhine," also stressing the "truly representative" racial makeup of the crowd.[73] The black press discussed improving race relations, but pronounced Louis's victory an even more significant win for America. The *Pittsburgh Courier* portrayed Louis as first "son of America, son of Alabama, Black American." Even former heavyweight Jack Johnson, in a special column in the *Pittsburgh Courier*, declared that white reactions to the fight displayed a way of thinking about race "differently and more sanely" than twenty years ago.[74] Yet, some were questioning this type of proxy politics. While he characterized Louis as a "living refutation of the hatred spewed forth daily" and had always applauded Louis's impact on the black community, Richard Wright indicated the need for more direct political action by 1938. "Negroes would have preferred that that refutation [of racial inferiority] could have been made in some form other than pugilism," he asserted.[75]

In celebrating Louis's win, some white newspapers could still not avoid minstrelesque depictions of the boxing champion. One *Washington Post* columnist stated, "Joe Louis, the lethargic chicken eating young colored boy reverted to his dreaded role of the 'brown bomber.'"[76] The *Chicago Tribune* championed Louis's remarkable victory; however, it insisted that Schmeling was the more "cunning" of the two fighters, even though Louis had "greater physical weapons."[77] Other articles written in the following years continued to demean Louis's intellectual capacities. A 1940 *Life* magazine article emphasized Louis's uncultured manner, claiming, "far from being ferocious, Louis is bored by fighting. He does it because he has been told to and does not know how to do anything else."[78] Echoing similar sentiments, a 1941 *Time* magazine article also stressed Louis's ignorance, decrying his limitations as a race leader. In the opinion of the *Time* journalist, whites viewed Louis only as a "lugubrious fellow" and a "mischievous child."[79]

It would take a central war-linked event, the celebrated Navy Relief Society benefit fight in 1942, for white journalists to eschew racial stereotyping and for the government to realize Louis's incredible potential as a wartime symbol. After the bombing of Pearl Harbor, which killed or wounded more than three thousand Americans, the Navy Relief Society sought a high-profile charity event to aid the families of those who died in the destruction. Despite the fact that the navy was notorious among the armed forces for its racial caste order onshore and off, Louis eagerly agreed to the fight as a patriotic gesture, stating, "Ain't fighting for nothing, I'm fighting for my country."[80] NAACP secretary Walter White viewed the forthcoming fight with a certain equivocation, asserting, "one wonders what will be in Joe Louis's mind . . . knowing that neither he nor any other of his 13 million American Negro fellow-citizens can serve in the Navy except as menials."[81] Others in the black press expressed outright opposition to Louis's decision to fight. A writer for the *Amsterdam News* claimed that Louis was the "sacrificial goat" in white propaganda, having much more to lose than his opponent.[82] Furthermore, an article in the *Baltimore Afro-American* reported that many black individuals refused to attend the fight in protest of the navy's oppressive policies.[83] Yet, as always, black opinion was not uniform. Many in the *Pittsburgh Courier* and the *Baltimore Afro-American* supported the fight, deeming Louis a "most unselfish patriot" and suggesting that the event might "shame the U.S. Navy into somewhat lowering the color bars."[84]

On 9 January 1942, almost 17,000 fans sat on the edges of their seats in Madison Square Garden. American flags hung from the rafters and were plastered on every square inch of wall space.[85] Joe Louis would challenge the formidable, 250-pound Buddy Baer, risking his title, and donate his earnings of approximately $100,000 to the victims of the Pearl Harbor bombing. Louis's very participation in the Navy Relief Society benefit fight exalted his patriotism, but as he smashed Baer in the first three minutes of round one, the fight catapulted his status as a powerful cultural icon. Hailed as the best fighter ever by the *New York Post* and the "real champion" by the *Washington Post*, the white press regarded Louis not only as a genuine patriot but also as a credit to the boxing profession.[86] In a speech about Louis, former presidential candidate Wendell Willkie exclaimed that Louis's performance made it impossible for him "to see how any American can think of discrimination in terms of race, creed, or color."[87] Some white reporters, such as Paul Gallico, revealed a significant change in their portrayals of Louis. Gallico's frequently derogatory characterizations included one description of Louis as a "calmly savage Ethiopian" in 1935; yet in 1942, Gallico claimed that Louis had finally "found his soul" and had sacrificed as a "simple good American." For Gallico, "Citizen [Joe Louis] Barrow" now was an emblem of honesty, simplicity, and decency—someone whom both whites and blacks should admire.[88]

Regardless of whether some had questioned Louis's decision to participate in the fight, the black press emphasized the positive impact Louis's victory had on white racial attitudes. The *Pittsburgh Courier* provided the reactions of the Boxing Writer's Association, who professed to Louis, "you are entitled to the highest title known to the American people. . . . Joe, you are an American gentleman."[89] The *Baltimore Afro-American* articulated the enthusiasm of former New York mayor James Walker, who described Louis's patriotism as the equivalent of "laying a red rose on Abe Lincoln's grave."[90] Likewise, the *Amsterdam News* published the words of a Michigan senator who asserted, "[Louis's] sportsmanship, unequaled physical endowments, retained and increased by clean living are now crowned with extreme generosity. Joe Louis is a citizen of whom Michigan and the nation are proud."[91]

These reactions to Louis resonated deeply among state administrators who were evaluating his role as a wartime symbol. Officials in the War Department's Morale Branch, the NAACP, and Eleanor Roosevelt had discussed Louis's military service as early as September 1941, yet as plans developed in December for the Navy Relief Society benefit fight, it became evident that a postfight army induction would buttress public opinion.[92]

Thus, two days after the Navy Relief Society fight, Louis volunteered for the army, reporting for duty at Camp Upton on Long Island. Regarding the nature of Louis's training, F. H. Osborn, chief of the Morale Branch, asserted that like "Martin of the Stock Exchange and Winthrop Rockefeller" Joe Louis underwent a thirteen-week training course without special privileges.[93] After this training, Louis was to receive a first lieutenant commission, but he declined it, stating that he did not have the training for an officer position and asking to be around other men with backgrounds that were similar to his own.[94] Although this gesture commanded further public praise for Louis's generosity, the army did not want Louis to serve as an ordinary private and thus ordered him to serve with the Morale Branch. Black and white leaders agreed that Louis's "fine character" represented "what a clean athlete stands for, irrespective of race." In addition, unlike renowned fighter Jack Dempsey, who avoided service in World War I, Louis would prove that his celebrity status did not preclude his duties as an American citizen.[95]

Once Louis joined the army, Morale Branch officials held numerous meetings concerning his activities. Chief F. H. Osborn was a scholar in eugenics who believed that "social engineering" through film and other media could "teach liberal reaffirmations of American social beliefs."[96] To further these democratic goals, War Department officials consistently emphasized Louis's cultural significance, asserting, "The Army has a tremendous propaganda asset in Joe Louis. To the rank and file of colored people he appears almost as a god. The possibilities for using him are almost unlimited."[97] Even Mary McLeod Bethune, a race leader for decades, commented along similar lines: "There is no one person in the world that men would rather see in action than Joe Louis. He is the greatest single drawing attraction that there is, and he is everybody's favorite."[98] Likewise, Walter White recognized Louis's prominence as a national figure, asking Louis for a photo of himself to place "along with the pictures . . . of other distinguished Americans who are my friends."[99] Memos circulated describing various presentations of Joe Louis on posters, pamphlets, radio shows, and movies. Yet, as his appearances and images illustrated, Louis did not publicly advocate racial equality, or even denounce racial discrimination. Louis was to promote patriotism and racial goodwill while symbolizing black potential and black American citizenship.

Joe Louis and his fellow soldiers at the Cavalry Replacement Center at Fort Riley, Kansas. Photograph by Press Association, Inc. Courtesy of AP/Wide World Photos. (National Archives, RG 208 PU-120V-5)

In September 1943, Joe Louis, George C. Nicholson, Walker Smith (Sugar Ray Robinson), and George J. Wilson formed a boxing troupe under the Army's Special Services Division to tour army camps in the United States and abroad. The boxing tour served the purpose of both entertainment and athletic training; yet, it also could diminish racism by exposing white troops to black men who not only promoted sportsmanship and teamwork but also demonstrated incredible athleticism. In her proposal for this boxing troupe, Mary McLeod Bethune envisioned it: "Can you picture the reaction a soldier would have to see Joe Louis and other great fighters fly across thousands of miles of enemy infested lands and waters, just to put on a show for them? Just picture the feeling it would give a man to see Joe Louis in action anywhere or under any conditions . . . That will create a fine reaction and make a soldier glad to be fighting for a country so thoughtful of him."[100]

This boxing tour fit larger ideas about improving race relations through athletic activities. In a letter to William Hastie, Edwin Henderson, head of the Department of Health and Physical Education in the District of Columbia public schools, outlined the benefits of recreational activities among

CONSTRUCTING G.I. JOE LOUIS

all units in training camps, regardless of race. To ameliorate the existing hostile and "non-communicative attitudes" between black and white soldiers, Henderson proposed a series of individual and team events that could both improve morale and emphasize democratic values through healthy competition. Here, athletics could both invalidate "the myth of race inferiority" and provide soldiers with "a better understanding of what we are fighting for." Yet, nowhere in Henderson's report was there the prospect that these interracial recreational activities could promote the eventual integration of the armed forces. Thus, athletic activities could serve as a rehearsal for black and white soldiers who would soon have to cooperate in war. Competitions from Ping-Pong to football were arranged as "safe" forms of interracial contact that neatly dodged the issue of racial discrimination in the military.[101]

In Louis's forty-six months of army duty, he fought in ninety-six exhibitions in the United States, England, France, and Italy. The tour gave Louis the opportunity to witness the racism and poor conditions within black army camps. His most public challenge to racial discrimination was his refusal to fight or speak in front of segregated audiences, insisting that the boxing tour was "not for any one race group."[102] Yet Louis was not immune to segregation. After using a telephone and sitting on a bench in a "White" waiting room in an Alabama bus depot, police confronted him and Sugar Ray Robinson; when the fighters protested, police took them away to a nearby military post. This incident, publicized in both white and black presses, embarrassed the army, which reissued an existing directive against segregated buses in army camps. In England, Louis was told to sit in a "special section" of a theater with other black GIs; Louis confronted the manager, who recognized him and apologized, claiming that he had received orders from an American military commander.[103]

Despite these unfortunate circumstances, the tour was extremely successful and well-received. Officer Carroll Fitzgerald, who was in charge of the tour in 1943, indicated that Louis's inspiring words to soldiers described the values of "physical fitness and Americanism."[104] After the troupe's visit to a New Orleans base, Major Harrie Pearson commented, "Sgt. Barrow exert[s] a most beneficial effect on both white and colored enlisted personnel. Sgt. Barrow warrants commendation for the friendly and interesting manner with which he conducted his personal appearances."[105] Yet, not all officers had such glowing reports. Major Robert Lough complained that the troupe had missed the train and arrived late, disturbing the plans of officers and servicemen. Confirming Lough's opinion that the tour was

Both civilians and soldiers watch Joe Louis fight Elza Thompson in an open-air exhibition boxing match in Britain, 1 June 1944. Photograph by Wide World Photo. Courtesy of AP/Wide World Photos. (National Archives, RG 208 PU-120V-54)

a "waste and [the] operation unbecoming the military," Lough scolded the Special Service Division for giving Louis and his fellow boxers special privileges.[106] In response, Theodore Bank of the Special Service Division assured Lough that the boxers would be subject to the same military discipline as any other soldiers. Yet he also made sure to emphasize that the tour was "hoisted" upon the Special Service Division by the BPR, not initiated internally.[107]

Other forms of criticism came from journalists who argued that Louis's role as a "money raiser" and "morale builder" would contradict his "conduct and remarks to date."[108] Scolding the army for preventing Louis from encountering the "realities . . . and normal risks of war" as a soldier, one columnist concluded that American morale would indeed be weakened if the army prevented Louis from participating in combat.[109] Yet, these opinions were in the minority; official correspondence indicated an overwhelming support for Louis's activities. The flow of positive reports led administrators to believe that they were successfully boosting morale and curbing racial animosities.

The black press echoed this support, as it documented all of Louis's events during his army service. When Louis was first inducted, black newspapers provided the details of his uniform size, physical examination, and training schedule, particularly emphasizing that Louis was like any other soldier. In reporting that Louis was "asking no favors and getting none," marching in the rain and performing squad drills, papers such as the *Baltimore Afro-American* maintained that Louis could easily shed his sense of celebrity. Articles also described Louis's eagerness to help his fellow soldiers with daily chores, building a sense of camaraderie among his "buddies."[110] Throughout Louis's army tenure, the black press praised charitable actions he undertook on behalf of the war effort. As Louis auctioned off the boxing gloves he wore during a famed fight with Billy Conn, in order to promote war bonds, the *Pittsburgh Courier* claimed that Louis "once again is making a personal sacrifice for which he is fighting."[111] And it was not just the black press that heralded Louis's patriotism throughout the war; the *New York Times*, *Life*, and the *Daily Worker* all reported on the boxing exhibition tour, stressing Louis's efforts to build "racial good will."[112] As Louis and the other boxers visited hospitals and camps, spending countless hours with both black and white soldiers, the emphasis on Louis's public persona shifted to his relationship with servicemen rather than his individuality as an athlete.

While newspaper reports did not mention Louis's feelings concerning racial inequality, his autobiography attests to his dedication to eliminating racial barriers in the military. Although he did refrain from addressing controversial racial issues in public, he waged a more private campaign against discrimination. When the military prohibited fellow soldier Jackie Robinson from playing football and baseball on the camp's team at Fort Riley, Kansas, Louis demanded of Brigadier General Donald Robinson that such restrictions be lifted. As a result, Robinson and other African Americans played on the previously all-white baseball and football teams, which led to the integration of many sports at other army camps, even in southern states such as Georgia and Virginia. Louis also spoke on behalf of Robinson and other black enlistees denied admission to Officer's Candidate school. After much persistence and going through several military channels, Louis persuaded Truman Gibson to investigate the matter—as a result, fifteen black men were eventually admitted. In addition, Louis gave financial aid to many black soldiers he met during his service, so that they could provide loved ones with hospital care or funerals.[113]

For many black servicemen, Louis's altruism and patriotic duties made him an important race leader, even in the absence of a more overt stance against racial oppression. During the war, Louis demonstrated to many African Americans that he had overcome discrimination and could act as a mediator between the races. As word of mouth spread about the boxing troupe, soldiers requested Louis's attendance. Private F. K. Wint declared that having Louis make an appearance at his air force base in Greensboro, North Carolina, would be significant, because his post was "undergoing a great change from White personnel to colored."[114] Private Jimmy Bivens described his elation when he heard that the boxing tour was in effect, stating that morale activities offered black soldiers greater opportunities than the "common labor" at training camps. Bivens, a black fighter himself, pleaded with Truman Gibson to allow him to be part of his own boxing troupe. Although government officials denied both these requests, the letters indicate that black soldiers viewed Louis as a symbol that racial conditions could improve.[115]

While pleased with the positive response to Louis's military tour, administrators in the War Department still reviewed Louis's appearance at certain events with the utmost scrutiny. Truman Gibson consistently denied requests for Louis to attend more politically charged functions. Rejecting the possibility of Louis's appearance at a rally in Baltimore in response to the 1943 Detroit riot, Gibson wrote, "because of the large number of such requests they will all be unfavorably considered."[116] Morale Branch chief F. H. Osborn reacted to such proposals with hostility, such as one for Louis to speak at a "giant demonstration and rally of racial unity" in New York City.[117] It is possible that administrators prevented Louis from attending some of these functions due to the sheer number of requests and scheduling conflicts. Yet, undoubtedly, officials feared those situations where Louis might appear as an advocate for racial reform. The correspondence between political organizations that viewed Louis as a racially charged symbol and those who aimed to protect Louis's depoliticized image presents both the struggle to circumscribe iconography and the difficulty of controlling cultural interpretation.

The War Department also attempted to preserve Louis's image as a moral and upstanding man. In one instance, Lieutenant Mildred Osby, a black member of the Women's Army Corps, requested to act as a secretarial assistant for the boxing tour, listing references such as A. Philip

Randolph, and professing her "courteous" demeanor and her ability to act "under military discipline and control."[118] Yet Truman Gibson denied her request, indicating that male officers would be accompanying the Louis tour. Gibson assured Osby, "I am afraid that even your resistance, built up over years of battling life on your own, would be melted away by the Sergeant's charm with the ladies. You would be even more disturbed emotionally by such an exposure."[119] While the press did not publicize Louis's philandering, his indiscretions were widely known among his managers and friends like Gibson, who tried to maintain Louis's public image as a faithful husband to wife Marva Trotter. Although Gibson purported to protect Osby, in keeping her away from Louis's allegedly irresistible "charm," he was primarily curbing any potential behavior that could tarnish Louis's heroic stature.

At a dinner for the Navy Relief Society on 10 May 1942, Joe Louis, in his army uniform, made a speech in which he stated, "We gonna do our part, and we will win, because we are on God's side."[120] This quickly became a widely circulating propaganda slogan, appearing on one of the most famous posters of the war era. In this poster Private Joe Louis, a gun in his hands and bayonet under his arm, threatens an invisible enemy with a piercing glare. Whether or not Louis would ever use that gun or bayonet in combat was irrelevant to war officials. They predicted that Americans would both recognize the stolid expression that Louis had once given his opponents in the ring (which he would now give to a new enemy) and would identify with the sentimental, religious rhetoric printed at the bottom of the page. A Madison Avenue advertiser named Carl Byoir, however, interpreted the "God's side" phrase quite differently. In his poem, "Joe Louis Named the War," which appeared in the wide-circulation magazine *Collier's*, Byoir wrote:

Maybe those words were stamped
On your great grandfather's heart,
And maybe they were burned into his soul,
And maybe he came to love America
And to cherish its freedoms
More than some people who just inherited them.
And so, maybe you just felt what he felt
And so you named the war
This is God's War . . .[121]

Despite the state's effort to commodify Louis, Byoir's words illuminated the multiple meanings of Louis's famed patriotism. For Byoir, Louis was in some ways reconciling W. E. B. Du Bois's notion of double consciousness—the tension of both black and American identity. Byoir recognized that the war exposed the inconsistency of blackness and Americanness, as well as the legitimacy of black ancestry; his poem elevated Louis above propaganda. Whether or not Byoir's interpretation of Louis's statement resonated in the minds of most white Americans, he nonetheless exposed the fluidity of Louis's symbolic character. As the poem opens, "Joe, you named the war / I don't think you knew / That you were naming the war, / But you named it," it testifies to the porousness of culture, infusing Louis with political substance, even as he is allegedly not attuned to it. Thus, although Joe Louis encouraged black patriotism, his words urged some white Americans, such as Byoir to question the orthodoxy of white nationalism.

The poster itself also signaled a significant departure from wartime racial imagery. As scholar George Roeder argues in his evaluation of censored wartime photos (which were recently made public), the "God's side" poster was a rare depiction of a black man in an aggressive pose. Many photographs of black soldiers, even those who had been wounded, were censored by the government, largely due to southern accusations that the black press was trying to overemphasize the role of black units in the war. Posters featuring black workers, which were few and far between, stressed racial harmony and sacrifice, downplaying any notions of racial militancy. Louis, on the other hand, as an established war hero, with no public opposition to the racial status quo, transcended "acceptable" imagery of black men. The idea of armed black men, long detested by many white Americans, was softened by Louis's established record of deracialized patriotism. Embodying one of the strongest symbols of American masculinity— a soldier prepared for combat—Louis was able to subvert embedded racial ideology. And as the government propagated this image, circulating the poster to hundreds of cities, it blurred the color line by featuring Joe Louis—detached from racial politics—in one of the most politically suggestive stances.[122]

Like the "God's side" poster, the 1944 film *The Negro Soldier* endowed the image of Joe Louis with political meaning. The film, used as a mandatory orientation film for almost all black and white army trainees by the spring 1944, displayed the countless achievements of black soldiers and

CONSTRUCTING G.I. JOE LOUIS

"We're going to do our part
... and we'll win because
we're on God's side"

*Enlistment poster
featuring Joe Louis—
one of the few, and
consequently one of the
most famous, images of
a black man in World
War II propaganda.
(National Archives,
Photo No. 44-PA-87)*

civilians. Carlton Moss, the prolific black writer, producer, and actor wrote the film script and played the title role of a preacher. The film begins in a black church as the preacher speaks to a well-dressed middle-class congregation, praising the efforts of black soldiers in the military. In the midst of commending individual servicemen, some of whom are seated in the congregation, the preacher pauses to recall his experience witnessing the Louis-Schmeling fight at Yankee Stadium in 1938. As the solemn church setting shifts to jarring footage of the fight, the preacher proudly exclaims, "an American first won a victory," but then warns that the boxing match would not be the "final victory." Louis and Schmeling would be matched again, in a "far greater arena and for much greater stakes." The preacher describes the war as a fight "not between man and man, but between nation and nation. . . . A fight for the real championship of the world, to determine which way of life shall survive—their way or our way."[123]

Both black audiences and black political organizations praised the film.

Kansas City Urban League executive secretary Thomas Webster exclaimed, "every citizen, white and black, should see this picture, for embodied in it are all the principles for which we are now fighting."[124] Writing for the *Chicago Defender*, Langston Hughes stated, "it is the most important film of Negro activities yet brought to the screen," adding, "It portrays, without the customary Hollywood stereotypes, the heroic role of the Negro throughout."[125] Although the film veered from the slightest hint of racial inequality, omitting any mention of discrimination in the armed forces (the Civil War sequence did not mention slavery), the film still advanced a powerful portrayal of black history. White and especially black audiences did not need a film to alert them to the existence of segregation, but perhaps they did need to celebrate the extensiveness of black progress, in spite of persistent racism. Certainly, a realistic depiction of black life in America would have more effectively addressed black grievances in the military and on the home front; yet, given the War Department's precarious task of racial management, the film managed to hold blacks in high esteem without disrupting the racial status quo.

Yet, it was the Louis-Schmeling fight, which sets the framework for the entire film, that most directly politicized *The Negro Soldier*. The preacher directs his black congregation to equate Max Schmeling with German savagery; reading from *Mein Kampf*, he warns his congregation of German plans to exterminate "inferior" peoples. Black military audiences, however, were more familiar with American racial ideology, particularly those servicemen in southern training camps. Although the preacher refers to Joe Louis as an American, rather than a black man, the footage of the fight clearly demonstrates that African Americans can obliterate even the most bigoted white opponent. Perhaps a subtle call for black mobilization on Carlton Moss's part, this opening scene emphasizes black superiority, if only in the athletic arena. Furthermore, footage of Jesse Owens in the 1936 Berlin Olympics indicates that the War Department did not hesitate to emphasize black triumph over white competitors in sporting events with international significance.

In September 1945, Joe Louis received the Legion of Merit award in honor of his contributions to the army. Praising Louis for going far beyond the duties "that were reasonably expected or demanded of him," Fred Maloy, officer in charge of the Joe Louis tour, hailed the success of Louis's boxing exhibitions, reporting that attendance at fights had exceeded existing records of attendance at the cinematic events, theater, or other appearances by sport personalities. Maloy further asserted that Louis's presence had ameliorated race relations, causing white soldiers to evaluate their black counterparts more fairly.[126] Truman Gibson expedited the presentation of the award, making Louis's discharge possible at a time when the demobilization process occurred slowly for many soldiers. The Legion of Merit signaled the apogee of Louis's role as an American icon, which, although unstable at the beginning of his boxing career in the 1930s, was fulfilled by his wartime actions. Louis was now, unquestionably, a model American citizen.[127]

THE SYMBOL OF LOUIS did not directly address discrimination or segregation. Nor did Joe Louis himself become a spokesman for racial equality. The issue of low black morale unified liberal and conservative bureaucracies to develop a common racial agenda, and the precarious endeavor of constructing official culture left little space for dissent. Subject to the demands of a highly politicized governmental apparatus, managers attempted to circumscribe the political nature of Louis's iconography, yet wrestled with the tensions of cultural administration and production. Louis, however, was not merely a pawn of white administrators, as he used the tactics he had honed throughout his boxing career to speak on behalf of other black Americans and to lift the morale of all American soldiers. Louis easily incorporated himself into the government's racial strategy because he understood the possibilities of race advancement through incremental white acceptance. Although on a larger scale he advocated black advancement more symbolically, Louis nonetheless made material gains toward racial equality as he aided individual black soldiers and later promoted black entrepreneurship, education, youth clubs, and neighborhood revitalization.

Administrators such as Theodore Berry may not have succeeded in initiating the breakdown of segregation and racial inequality, but the programs developed by the OWI and the War Department did have significant political implications. Certainly, the construction of Joe Louis as an American hero was an effort to propagate particular notions of blackness. Yet as white officials facilitated an interracial dialogue over cultural development, as they had in the 1930s, they incorporated both black opinion and black participation in their morale-boosting campaign.

This solution to the "Negro problem" illustrated how political expediency shaped the definition of racial liberalism, producing a narrative both sanitized and racially charged. The portrayals and actions of Joe Louis indeed offered a subtly politicized commentary on racial issues, despite the intentions of war managers. State officials may have manufactured portrayals of black inclusion in contradiction to the reality of American discrimination, yet they could not always control the meanings that symbols conveyed. This would become even more evident when the army developed the *Jubilee* radio show, a variety program intended to focus solely upon music. As black performers used the show to critique discrimination and to form a cultural community, they further exposed the paradox of government-sponsored culture.

chapter five

VARIETY FOR THE SERVICEMEN

In 1944, Truman Gibson, civilian aide to the secretary of war, and Brigadier General Benjamin O. Davis Sr. expressed great excitement over the activities of the Armed Forces Radio Service (AFRS). Two of the most influential black Americans involved in the war effort, Gibson and Davis indicated that the AFRS was making a "great contribution" and that the program was "easily the best from an administrative point of view."[1] This high praise is not surprising, given the AFRS's achievements in featuring black Americans on the radio. As part of its innovative program schedule to meet the entertainment needs of American soldiers, the AFRS developed *Jubilee*, an all-black variety show employing famous and talented musicians and comedians. Acknowledging the interests of black troops and the morale-boosting potential of individuals such as Duke Ellington and Lena Horne, the AFRS asserted that racialized programming was important to radio's wartime function. Thus, *Jubilee* became part of the larger mission of the AFRS, as stated by the commanding officer, Tom Lewis: "Radio, by holding to the ideal of its charter—by faithfully serving public interest, convenience and necessity—can be the democratic voice of free America speaking to its *own people* . . . and to the *freedom-loving people of the world*."[2]

Like the promotion of Joe Louis, the creation of *Jubilee* was part of the government's wartime agenda to recognize black Americans through cultural programs. Particularly in the War Department, administrators agreed that the best way to feature black individuals on the radio was to develop shows based mostly on music. After experimenting with the variety format in the program "America's Negro Soldiers," officials believed that popular black comedians, actors, and musicians could neutralize the subject of racial inequality. When the AFRS staff developed *Jubilee*, they could rest easy, believing in the benign effects of popular entertainment. Employing luminaries such as Louis Armstrong, Ethel Waters, Bill "Bojangles" Robinson, and Lena Horne, the program's administrators attempted to cool down the heated subject of racial inequality with familiar black voices.

Jubilee represents a unique model in wartime government-sponsored culture as a show that would exclusively feature African Americans. Neither its creators, military audiences, nor black political leaders objected to the show's racial separatism. In part, this seeming acceptance may be a result of the auditory nature of radio—that *Jubilee* audiences never actually saw the African American cast. Whereas all-black films such as *Cabin in the Sky* and *Stormy Weather*, both musical spectacles featuring famed jazz performers, received a great deal of criticism from both the NAACP and government officials, administrators did not regard *Jubilee* as anathema to America's democratic propaganda. Furthermore, the lack of controversy surrounding *Jubilee* may also have stemmed from African Americans' role in creating jazz and whites' expectations for an "authentic" listening experience. If government officials hoped to boost military morale by offering the most celebrated African American performers, it seemed natural that the format of the show would adapt to existing radio practices, which largely segregated the airwaves.

In spite of producers' goals to ensure politically sanitized programming, radio paradoxically provided many black artists with the opportunity to relate political messages. Here, officials could not separate politics and entertainment so clearly, as musical and comedic performances featured on *Jubilee* made both subtle and overt references to American racial tensions.[3] Broadcast to both white and black servicemen, the show legitimated music by black performers that white artists had "cleaned up" and covered in other settings. Furthermore, as music occupied a central position in the political consciousness of many African Americans, *Jubilee*'s popularization of jazz bands and vocalists endowed the show with special meaning for black servicemen. Ralph Ellison described the symbolic position of jazz performers:

> Looking back, one might say that the jazzmen, some of whom we idolized, were in their own way better examples for youth to follow than were most judges and ministers, legislators and governors. . . . For as we viewed these pillars of society from the confines of our segregated community we almost always saw crooks, clowns or hypocrites. Even the best were revealed by their attitudes toward us as lacking the re-

spectable qualities to which they pretended . . . while despite the out-law nature of their art, the jazzmen were less torn and damaged by the moral compromises and insincerities which have so sickened the life of our country.[4]

While offering a rather romantic portrayal, Ellison nevertheless taps into the political power of cultural figures whose music spoke more directly and uncompromisingly about the most serious issues concerning African Americans. For black servicemen fighting in segregated units, undoubtedly sharing some of Ellison's mistrust of politicians, the words of black musicians offered an alternative to the army's hypocritical, standard line on the sanctity of American democracy. Yet, despite the opportunities it offered, *Jubilee* still revealed the same confines as other government-sponsored programs. "America's Negro Soldiers" proved far from the political vehicle some African Americans had hoped for, and operating under the same parameters, *Jubilee* performers were never free from the military's unyielding stance on racial issues. The limited nature of the program, however, does not diminish the ways in which *Jubilee* challenged the perpetuation of racial stereotypes in favor of a more honest discussion of race relations.

The Army Turns to Radio

The consolidation of radio as a mass medium in the 1920s was an important benchmark in the history of American popular culture. From the experimental amateur radio of the early 1910s to the emergence of the National Broadcasting Company (1926) and the Columbia Broadcasting System (1927), Americans had undergone a dramatic transformation in the way they conceptualized entertainment. Statistics reveal that in 1926 one in six families owned radios. By 1940, the majority of American households in both rural and urban areas owned radios. This medium based on listening constituted an important addition to a largely visual culture based on magazines, billboards, and feature films.[5] As media scholar Susan Douglas suggests, radio listening enabled Americans to consider themselves part of a national audience, connecting individuals across regions through a sense of simultaneous aural participation.[6]

During the 1920s, local radio outlets featured a number of black artists. Particularly in major cities with large black communities and a strong base of black musical talent, radio was particularly welcoming to popular African American performers such as Fletcher Henderson, Duke Ellington, and Bert Williams. In Chicago, local stations WBBM and WEDC broadcast a number of black jazz bands, such as Jimmie Wade's Moulin Rouge Orchestra and the Earl "Fatha" Hines Orchestra. Furthermore, the 1920s witnessed the creation of some programs and institutions run by African Americans. Black actor (and New York FTP Negro Unit director) Carlton Moss created *The Negro Hour*, a New York–based weekly drama series; in 1929, the Harlem Broadcasting Company emerged as the first independent black radio enterprise.[7]

The Depression stunted the progress of smaller endeavors such as the Harlem Broadcasting Company and forced many independent commercial stations out of business. By 1934, network broadcasting had eclipsed local programming, largely excluding black entertainers from the airwaves. The networks of NBC and CBS not only circumscribed the employment of black performers but also limited black access to technical work. Radio historian William Barlow explains: "As they rose to the pinnacle of power in the radio industry, both NBC and CBS followed what amounted to a Jim Crow policy with respect to the employment and portrayal of African Americans."[8]

The popularity of *Amos 'n' Andy*, which launched in 1929, revealed that minstrelsy was a highly effective and entertaining broadcasting format. The show—a white caricature of the life of black migrants—exemplified the narrow space for black performers on the airwaves. Radio's absence of visual imagery left more room for interpretation; blackness could be heard, but not viewed, allowing for various forms of racial ventriloquism. As radio reduced black bodies and identities to prescribed "black" aural markers, white performers could portray black experiences just as listeners willingly expected. Whatever the extent to which *Amos 'n' Andy* may have provided some alternatives to the minstrel characters embedded in American culture, the employment and success of the show's white performers allowed for the marginalization of black individuals on the radio and for the industry's discriminatory policies to continue.[9]

Although black musicians had created much of the popular jazz that pervaded most radio programming, white musicians such as Paul Whiteman and Tommy Dorsey often performed the music. Yet black writer and musician Sy Oliver took pride in arranging songs for Dorsey, and black artists did not always consider white performers as cultural appropriators.[10] Often, white and black performers shared and collaborated on materials. Despite these interracial connections, the radio industry segregated much of its programming. Network radio featured black entertainers only as guest performers in white shows, often singing in dialect or assuming demeaning roles. When NBC and CBS ventured to produce a few black shows such as *The Ethel Waters Show* and the *Louis Armstrong Show* in the late 1930s, they were extremely short-lived because southern network affiliates refused to broadcast the programs.[11]

World War II, however, was a watershed in radio broadcasting, providing black Americans with new levels of national radio exposure. Characterized by some historians as a "radio war," it proved the extensiveness of radio not only in broadcasting the outcome of battles but also in home front campaigns for war bonds and food conservation. The medium buttressed wartime unity by connecting those on the home front with those in the military through the shared experience of broadcast personalities and entertainment programs and in the urgency of news updates. The creation of national listening audiences could sometimes transcend the barriers created by segregation, as programs were broadcast to both black and white Americans who could envision themselves as a community rather than as divided individuals. Despite the confining and often exclusionary nature of radio for black performers and technicians, black Americans as an audience (whose access to radio listening was not directed to segregated spaces, as was the case in southern movie theaters) had the opportunity to experience programming in the same manner as their white counterparts.

As they became committed to pronouncing egalitarian rhetoric in the face of Nazi aggression, wartime cultural program managers untangled some of the constraints that had previously prevented black individuals from securing a network radio presence. In developing their "Negro morale" agendas, administrators were quick to notice the lack of black individuals on the airwaves, citing this as a cause for black disillusionment. The Office of War Information (OWI) condemned the neglect of black talent on the radio as "deplorable"; officials denounced attempts to reach out to the black community as "few and pitiable."[12] The black press echoed these sentiments, claiming, "since radio has become big business they have hung out the jim crow sign."[13] Responding to some of this criticism, administrators conceived of morale-boosting programs specifically for black audiences that would be interspersed with war bond plugs and other patriotic pronouncements.

This task of creating racialized programming became even more daunting when the army decided to create its own radio network in 1942. Although there were a few army-owned broadcasting stations before the de-

Staff of the Armed Forces Radio Service, c. 1942. Photo by Jerry Hausner.
(National Archives, RG 330, Box 12, E 1007)

velopment of the AFRS, they did not have the personnel or the technology to reach a large number of servicemen. Once the military founded the AFRS in May 1942, the Navy, Marines, Coast Guard, and Air Corps assigned talent to be part of the AFRS staff headquartered in Los Angeles. The first AFRS radio station in Casablanca broadcast to American troops in North Africa; by 1945, there were 160 AFRS radio stations extending throughout Europe and the South Pacific. At the peak of its World War II operation, AFRS broadcast fifty hours of programming a week, with news, sports, and about forty-three weekly programs that had been stripped of their advertisements. Although the question of commercialization was originally a subject of debate, reports from Bataan indicated that hungry servicemen did not want to hear about the "rich, creamy goodness of some ice cream," and thus commercial spots were eliminated from AFRS programming.[14]

The army also tended to the entertainment needs of servicemen through the creation of V-Discs, a series of phonograph records for the personal use of GIs, in 1943. Some artists recorded directly for V-Discs, but the records also contained material, such as performances from *Jubilee*, recorded in other settings. Illustrating the importance of music, one pamphlet reported that even in isolated areas with no phonographs, the army would ship records and "portable hand-wound machines." Claiming that V-Discs "help bridge the gap from Broadway to the barracks," this pam-

Tom Lewis, commander of the AFRS. Photo by Jerry Hausner. (National Archives, RG 330, Box 12, E 1007)

phlet estimated that V-Disc production reached 300,000 records a month by early 1945.[15]

Although the AFRS was an organ of the armed forces, its principal staff was comprised of civilian personnel—writers, producers, and actors— like other wartime agencies such as the OWI. AFRS commanding officer Tom Lewis had been vice president of the prominent New York advertising agency Young and Rubicam, where he developed and produced radio programs such as *The Kate Smith Show*, *Abbott and Costello*, and *The Aldrich Family*. In 1938, Lewis created Audience Research, Inc., with pollster George Gallup, which was the first agency to measure the box-office draw of motion picture stars and plot lines. As a member of the Hollywood Victory Committee, Lewis was connected to most major film and radio celebrities; in addition to his knowledge of research methods, these relationships made him an ideal leader for troop broadcasting activities.[16]

Other key players in the AFRS shared a background in radio, film, or theater, having worked on some of the most popular prewar productions. AFRS development officials included John Houseman, the first director of the FTP's Negro Units, three-time Pulitzer prize-winning playwright and Roosevelt speechwriter Robert Sherwood, noted playwrights and radio scriptwriters Robert Lee and Jerome Lawrence, Mann Holiner, producer of the all-black musical *Blackbird* reviews on Broadway, and Charles Vanda, CBS West Coast programming chief. These and other white executives from the advertising and radio industries composed the AFRS staff and

developed all of its programs. Ideologically, the key officers in the AFRS shared more in common with liberals in the OWI than they did with military personnel in the War Department. Yet, as much as the AFRS staff may have wished to develop more racially advanced programming, as was the initial instinct for *Jubilee*, the conservatism of the armed forces always constrained them.[17]

The primary mission of the AFRS was, like other information agencies, to build soldier morale. As one pamphlet asked, "Why shouldn't G.I. Joe in the jungle or the Arctic hear his favorite radio shows?"[18] Yet the AFRS asserted that soldiers should not only hear familiar shows but be treated as a new radio audience with special needs. As one officer indicated, "[the audience's] tastes, reactions, and emotional needs are conditioned by a new, different life . . . by constant focus on the task of war." Servicemen should have "education, information and orientation," and the AFRS was never to be used as a propaganda medium. Although officials admitted that radio could never "reconcile a boy from Grand Rapids to a life in Persia," they believed that the right type of programming might assist in the adjustment process.[19]

With research methods previously utilized by Tom Lewis at Young and Rubicam, the Army Special Services Division (ASSD) conducted a study of soldiers' listening habits. In order to develop programs that would appeal to the largest number of servicemen, the ASSD gathered information on "radio likes and dislikes," most frequent listening time based on the hour and the day of the week, and the location of radio listening within camps. After surveying a cross-section of 3,286 white servicemen from fifteen training camps, ranging from New York to California, the ASSD was able to draw some general conclusions for future program development. The most popular types of radio programs (scoring 80 percent or higher) were popular music ("sweet or dance music"), news, and comedy programs; the least popular shows (39 percent or lower) were special events, classical music, and serial dramas. More men reported listening to the radio after 5:30 P.M. (46 percent) than before 9:30 A.M. (21 percent) or during midday (24 percent). The listening peak in the evening was between 7:00 and 8:30. In addition, men responded that they listened on Thursday more than other weekdays, although not by a significant amount (49 percent on Tuesday night as compared to 52 percent on Thursday night). Furthermore, one out of six men owned a radio, making the barracks the most popular place where servicemen could listen as a group. Using these data on listening habits, the AFRS would develop many successful programs, most significantly *Jubilee*, the first long-standing all-black variety program.[20]

Race and the Variety Show

Although *Jubilee* was a product of AFRS radio analysis, it also took cues from other shows that relied on a variety show format to present racial issues. For example, in 1941 the National Urban League developed a program broadcast by CBS entitled "The Negro and National Defense." The program condemned racial discrimination in defense industries and included a strong diatribe against inequality by *Opportunity* editor Elmer Carter. Yet, other show elements included comedy skits featuring Eddie Green and Eddie "Rochester" Anderson, a tap routine by Bill Robinson, and songs by Ethel Waters, Louis Armstrong, and Marian Anderson. While some of the entertainment in "The Negro and National Defense" diverted attention from the issue of racial inequality, many of the comedic skits relayed strong opinions on the subject. In a typical monologue, Eddie Anderson would argue that black people were as skilled as their white counterparts in any profession, but that their white employers constantly overlooked them. During his appearance on the show, Joe Louis expressed pride in the factory job he once held and joked about ignorant white employers who believed in the inferiority of black workers. Although the political concerns of CBS prevented the National Urban League from articulating a more stinging condemnation of racial discrimination in many other areas of American life, the league was still able to direct audiences to influence enforcement of antidiscriminatory policies in the workplace. With its combination of musical elements and direct commentary, this initial variety format presented itself as a viable medium for addressing racial inequality in a less threatening manner.[21]

Creators of *Jubilee* also followed the strategy of the War Department, which undertook its first major attempt to discuss racial issues on the radio in August 1941. War Department officials understood that the material in one of its productions would receive a high degree of scrutiny; much more so than the National Urban League, the government faced numerous political obstacles, particularly the objections of politically influential southerners. Civilian aide to the secretary of war William Hastie initially conceived the idea for a "nation-wide radio broadcast developing

Black infantrymen in training at Fort Belvoir in Virginia.
(Franklin D. Roosevelt Library, Hyde Park, N.Y.)

the role of the Negro in the Army," which was promoted by Hastie's assistant, Truman Gibson. Declaring that a radio show to be broadcast on NBC would clear up existing "inaccuracies and doubts" regarding black interest and motivation to participate in the army, Gibson outlined a program which he hoped could help reduce friction in southern army camps. Show features included a history of black military participation and civilian contributions. To lend official authority to the subject, William Hastie, Under Secretary of War Patterson, and General Robert Richardson would narrate this history. Although Hastie would be the one to speak specifically about black accomplishments, Patterson and Richardson would stress both black loyalty and the benefits of racial unity.[22]

Upon receiving Hastie and Gibson's proposal, the Bureau of Public Relations (BPR), a division of the War Department that handled most matters relating to morale, agreed on the program's production. However, officials at the BPR expressed their own ideas about the nature and tenor of the program. Like Truman Gibson, J. Brechner, a BPR administrator, stated that the program should include a narrative of black loyalty and speeches by government officials such as Patterson. Brechner's outline included interviews with enlisted men, a news summary of recent black accomplishments in the army, and comments by the armed forces' only black general, Benjamin O. Davis Sr. Brechner's recommendations, however, also highlighted the importance of a "high entertainment appeal." He mentioned the need for "good music" and a "light interview" with a "'famous' Negro name" like Joe Louis. Brechner agreed that William Hastie should speak, but his proposal stated that Hastie speak "briefly," emphasizing the encouraging state of racial conditions in the army. Furthermore, Brechner noted the value of bandleader Noble Sissle, namely for his ability to procure other "big name entertainers" as president of the Negro Actors Guild.[23]

Gibson and Hastie considered the BPR's suggestions. In a responding memo, Hastie concluded that the show would include music by "leading Negro artists," a sketch of black participation in the nation's wars, interviews with black air corps trainees, and "short talks" by Patterson and Hastie. He also indicated that a studio audience of more than a thousand was expected.[24] Although the BPR had originally placed most of its emphasis on the entertainment value of the show, this final format continued to highlight official declarations of black military contributions. Intended for "as large a listening audience as possible" and therefore scripted to "combine the lighter element with a heavy dramatic script," the show aimed to satisfy a diverse range of interests on the largest possible number of network stations.[25]

Arranging for Noble Sissle to act as master of ceremonies was not difficult. An influential figure in promoting "Negro morale" by the summer 1941, Sissle had secured a position within the BPR through a number of glowing recommendations from both white and black officials.[26] As one of two black members of the Citizens Committee for the Army and Navy, Sissle worked alongside white entertainers such as Irving Berlin, Bette Davis, and Paul Whiteman. College-educated, Sissle had served as a second lieutenant in World War I and worked with James Reese Europe's famed 369th Infantry Regiment Band in providing troop entertainment. Sissle had established himself as a major entertainer by the 1920s, most notably for the musical comedy *Shuffle Along*, which he cowrote and starred in. Sissle also broke down several racial barriers; his orchestra was the first to perform at one of New York's "most exclusive restaurants, the Princess" in 1931, and then at the Park Central Hotel, which he considered "another precedent for a colored orchestra." Sissle directed both white and black charity affairs for war relief work and was currently serving on a local draft board appointed by Mayor La Guardia.[27]

Gibson encountered more difficulty in securing other performers. The show was scheduled for broadcast on 12 August, and since Gibson was sending requests only two weeks before the event, a number of entertainers declined because they had prior commitments. In attempting to attract Marian Anderson, Gibson pitched the show's lineup, telling her that Dean Dixon, the young black conductor of NBC's Summer Symphony Orchestra, would be participating and that Hastie and Patterson would be speaking. Gibson contended that Anderson's performance was crucial to the show's approval, even changing the date of the program to accommodate Anderson's schedule.[28] Correspondence does not reveal why Anderson did not take part in the production; nevertheless, officials were still able to secure other African American entertainers. With the help of Edna Thomas, executive secretary of the Negro Actors Guild (NAG), Gibson was able to arrange for prominent black actors Canada Lee, Juan Hernandez, Lionel Monages, Eddie Green, Frank Wilson, and Maurice Ellis to perform on the show.[29] African American actors had established the NAG in 1937 to provide financial and emotional support to black performers, attacking demeaning roles and running fundraisers to support independent black theater. Thomas, best known for her role as Lady Macbeth in Orson Welles's FTP production, also agreed to participate.[30]

In addition to seeking out established "Negro talent," Gibson also gathered materials for the show's portrayal of life at black training camps. On 3 July 1941, he sent a letter to public relations officers at black camps requesting "material that might be included in one of the broadcasts together with any anecdotes or unusual items of interest."[31] Although many reports highlighted black military skills, a large majority of the responses to Gibson focused on the musical talents of soldiers. Describing the talents of regimental choirs and orchestras, officers also discussed singing in the mess hall, in the washrooms, and while hiking.[32] One memo of suggestions "offered by the two larger colored organizations" talked mostly about the instrumental and vocal capabilities of particular military choirs and glee clubs. In the same memo, Lieutenant Colonel M. R. Cox indicated that some of these African American servicemen also recommended an "old-type minstrel show," although they recognized that "this may be regarded as 'corny' by today's radio listeners."[33]

Such frequent remarks on the musical abilities of black servicemen

VARIETY FOR THE SERVICEMEN

could be construed as an attempt by white officers to belittle the combat readiness of black troops. While Gibson's requests for information were mediated by white officers, none of these officers suggested that black troops were inferior to their white counterparts (a point that Henry Stimson had often made), nor did any indicate that a radio show focusing on "the role of the Negro soldier" was not an important topic for a national broadcast. Officers who listed the number of professional musicians in their camps may have made the quick association between radio and music, without allowing for the possibility that the show would serve as a documentary about black army life. Their responses are all the more significant because they highlight the assumed relationship between musical entertainment and radio as well as between African Americans and musical talent—and *Jubilee* performers would later politicize these listener expectations in ways that white producers had not anticipated.

The repeated comments about singing in black army camps, however, also reveal a process of community building among soldiers. As several historians have noted, singing and making music was a form of resistance for black slaves who endured repressive conditions. In army camps, subject to white impositions of segregation, black soldiers used song to further a collective identity. Songs ranged from traditional army melodies to black spirituals; in recommending these army songs as a focus for national radio programming, white officers legitimated black culture. At the same time, however, black singing may have been more acceptable to white officers who resisted the idea of black military prowess. By providing military authorities with more traditional evidence of "natural black talents," these officers may have directed attention away from blacks' capabilities as servicemen.

As the War Department's program development escalated, securing African American participants, officials quickly replaced several initial ideas. Despite Gibson's original intentions to create an educational program about black military service, the content weighed more heavily on popular entertainment. In one draft of the show, initially titled "Negroes in the Army," the program included a skit, a vocal performance, a reading of a memo sent by General Pershing, and a speech by Truman Gibson. In contrast, the final draft added a tap dance performance by Bill "Bojangles" Robinson, another, more lighthearted skit featuring black comedian Eddie Green, and the replacement of Gibson with a white official, William Patterson.[34] Through these choices, the War Department revealed its hesitancy to place too much emphasis on black accomplishments without providing listeners with the music and laughs they expected from black entertainers. The AFRS would soon express the same sentiments.

Black Americans had high hopes for "America's Negro Soldiers," anticipating its broadcast on NBC on 12 August. Commenting that NBC "has shown far less prejudice towards the race than most of the other outlets combined," Isadora Smith of the *Pittsburgh Courier* indicated that the show included military dignitaries such as General George Marshall and "other high army and government officials." Despite the fact that Marian Anderson had declined to participate, Smith excitedly reported that Anderson, Paul Robeson, Joe Louis, and "others of like talent" were still in negotiation with NBC to perform. Since these entertainers were not scheduled to appear on the show, it is possible that the *Courier* had been given misinformation regarding the content and participants of the show in order to keep the public interested. As she compared "America's Negro Soldiers" to "The Negro and National Defense," which she considered pioneering, Smith hoped that the upcoming program would "depict the progress of the race, its loyalty and great love for America."[35]

When the show was broadcast, its first skit aimed to calm white fears of black subversion. The skit featured black servicemen in World War I who receive a message from German soldiers containing anti-American propaganda, urging them to desert their posts in the American military. In response, the black soldiers refuse to leave their station and laughingly criticize German ideas of democracy. After this theatrical enactment of black fidelity, Undersecretary of War Robert Patterson declared, "No one dare question the Negro citizen's loyalty, and none dare question his courage." Yet any attempt Patterson made to give credibility to black military performance was contradicted in the skit that followed. Here, comedian Eddie Green played the part of a soldier while actress Edna Thomas served as an army hostess. Unlike the black soldiers in the German skit, Green spoke in dialect, talked about avoiding work, and made several sexual overtures to Thomas's character. Green's clumsy soldier stood starkly against Thomas's responsible, knowledgeable hostess; however, Green's soldier undermined the hostess's pride in her station, as his sexual references not only contributed to stereotypes surrounding both black men and women, but also denigrated the work of women in the military.[36]

Directly after this skit, "America's Negro Soldiers" shifted to Chanute Field, Illinois, where 400 black soldiers were training as ground crew specialists in the Army Air Corps. In interviews, these servicemen discussed the skills they were acquiring in the Air Corps as aircraft mechanics, radio operators, weather forecasters, and parachute riggers. Despite the positive messages relayed by these servicemen, many of whom were educated at universities such as Morehouse, Tuskegee, and the University of California, the program's denial of racial discrimination angered some listeners. In particular, the *Pittsburgh Courier* charged that "America's Negro Soldiers" "amounted to a praise of a jim crow system." Although the *Courier* had expressed high expectations for the show's potential, it asserted that black listeners "knew . . . that they were being compelled to defend a democracy almost nonexistent for them and they did not need Under Secretary of War Patterson to tell them so." Angered that the War Department did not explain how it would "practice the democracy the Administration is preaching," the *Courier* dismissed the program as an empty gesture, offering little for those heroic black soldiers it celebrated. As many black newspapers consistently commented on the paradox of American democracy in their columns, the need for a direct political dialogue overshadowed the presence of a "brilliant galaxy of stars" or an official reaffirmation of black American citizenship.[37]

Given the political affiliations of many of the show's performers, however, the dynamics of "America's Negro Soldiers" may be more complex than a mere acceptance of the racial status quo. Although the show did not directly attack racial inequality, several of the program's black performers had a history of political action. Almost all of the black performers who appeared were members of the Negro Actors Guild—Noble Sissle was president and Edna Thomas executive secretary. Most performers on the show had also been part of FTP productions. Canada Lee and Edna Thomas starred in the controversial *Stevedore*; Lee also starred in *Haiti* and *Big White Fog*, plays with Garveyite and Communist themes. Maurice Ellis, Lee, and Thomas all performed in Orson Welles's "voodoo" *Macbeth*, which made a bold statement about black dramatic abilities, extending the boundaries for other black actors. With few black actors and musicians who had not directly combated race and class inequality during the leftist-oriented productions of the 1930s, the War Department faced the challenge of attempting to sanitize entertainers with overt political connections.[38] Nevertheless, the scripted nature of the program prevented the more racially charged messages from being delivered, as they would be later, by *Jubilee* performers.

After the production of "America's Negro Soldiers," the War Department did broadcast one more program concerning race in September 1942. Entitled *Judgment Day*, the show continued the emphasis on black military history devised by "America's Negro Soldiers." Although the show received positive acclaim, it was the last show on race broadcast directly by the War Department. In attempting to balance increasing black demands of equality with white resistance to racial reforms, War Department officials eschewed a heavy reliance on radio and instead turned to other, less-direct approaches, such as the Joe Louis boxing exhibitions, in tackling the "Negro problem." Due to radio's unique ability to convey powerful spoken messages to a wide audience, it became too dangerous a tool for the already precarious task of confronting racial issues. As historian Barbara Savage observes, "The medium could only be as powerful as the message, and in the case of African Americans, no message was considered politically acceptable to the national, mass audience that radio reached with such speed and ease."[39]

Despite the War Department's resignation, other official agencies and liberal groups proposed more discussions of racial tensions on the radio, without the popular entertainment. For example, *Freedom's People*, created by Ambrose Caliver in the Office of Education, employed the talents of such black intellectuals as W. E. B. Du Bois, Alain Locke, and Carter G. Woodson, who served as advisers. Presenting black achievements in the arts, sciences, and literature, as well as in education and the military, *Freedom's People* sought to instill racial pride while calling attention to discrimination. After hearing the program, many secondary and university teachers requested more information on African Americans that they could use in the classroom, particularly in schools with large numbers of black pupils. The volatile racial atmosphere during war, however, circumscribed the political tenor of *Freedom's People*, and despite its positive reception, the show only ran from September 1941 to April 1942. Likewise, the *University of Chicago Round Table*, broadcast by NBC, was forced to include a representative from the South for its episode on the "Negro question," as southern stations threatened not to carry the program. Although the program offered the opinions of southern racial moderate Howard Odum in a July 1943 program, it was not able to forcefully critique racial inequality without arousing southern protest. Meanwhile, the political program *Town Meeting* provoked intense fury from both white northerners and southerners in May 1945, after program participant Richard Wright called for black agitation and protested laws against intermarriage. With this type of white reaction, the government shied away from programs solely devoted to the "Negro question."[40]

In the midst of these attempts, program managers continued to focus on the variety show format, emphasizing the use of "all prominent Negro stars of stage, screen, radio, and concert."[41] OWI officials indicated that one of the purposes of these shows always would be to "glorify the Negro soldier," and they suggested that programs begin with military celebrities such as Joe Louis or General Davis.[42] While individual black soldiers could discuss army life on the radio, administrators stressed that servicemen should also perform in some musical capacity. Yet, although entertainment-based content only became more popular in the development of AFRS programs, shows like *Jubilee* demonstrated that the variety genre could become much more politicized than the programming offered in "America's Negro Soldiers"—indeed much more than officials envisioned.

Airing Jubilee

When AFRS producers developed *Jubilee* in July 1942, they relied on a diverse roster of shows to meet the tastes of servicemen. An initial AFRS program listed shows such as *Mail Call*, a weekly variety program; *Your Broadway and Mine*, tape-recordings of full Broadway shows; *The Sports Parade*, a summary of major sporting events; and *G.I. Jive*, a daily guest disc jockey show. Almost all of these program proposals responded to soldier preferences for popular music, news, and comedy. Yet, with the high number of soldiers favoring musical variety shows, the AFRS staff asserted that the program needed an addition to *Mail Call*. Thus, the initial program schedule also included a show temporarily titled "Freedom's People," which was "aimed directly for . . . the large number of colored troops in the Army." "Freedom's People" would use recorded programs of black music compiled by the WPA and the Office of Education and would highlight a host of black entertainers. These programs were most likely various *Freedom's People* broadcasts that Ambrose Caliver created in 1941–42.[43]

AFRS officials selected Mann Holiner, who had developed a popular civilian variety show, *Jubilee*, to produce "Freedom's People." Holiner, however, disagreed that the show should be directed towards a black audience. For one thing, that could serve as an implicit acknowledgement of racial tensions within the army; furthermore, an all-black variety show could have great entertainment and morale-boosting value for all troops, regardless of race. Due to the more racially charged implications of the name "Freedom's People," the show was renamed *Jubilee* (capitalizing on the success of Holiner's civilian show of the same name) and was first recorded on 9 October 1942.[44] While Holiner initially planned for the development and production of the *Jubilee* show, the first five episodes were

*Major Mann Holiner,
producer of the AFRS
radio program* Jubilee *in
Hollywood, California.
Photo by Jerry Hausner.
(National Archives,
RG 330, Box 12, E 1007)*

recorded in New York and produced by Charles Vanda, who had worked
as a West Coast CBS programming chief before joining the AFRS. After
January, the program moved to Los Angeles, where Holiner produced it.
According to Ted DeLay, who has written the only substantive history of
the AFRS, the creation of *Jubilee* set the AFRS policy on racial matters. The
agency would not develop programs directed towards the problem of "low
Negro morale," nor would it specifically target any other minority group.
The program would mimic the format of white variety shows such as *Mail
Call* and *Command Performance*, with no mention of the racial policies or
issues that affected both black soldiers and entertainers.[45]

In that sense *Jubilee* contrasted with "America's Negro Soldiers," which
did target black audiences and drew attention to black military contributions. Yet, after the careful balancing act the War Department and the National Urban League had to maintain in presenting black experiences in
the army and in industry, the AFRS concluded that a show based solely
around music and comedy would be the safest route to achieving success on the air. Liberal producers within the AFRS such as Mann Holi-

ner undoubtedly followed the directives of F. H. Osborn, chief of morale, and other higher ups within the Special Services Division. And it was the entertainment-based content of the show that allowed producers to reassure their superiors that racially charged material would be avoided. The AFRS staff did not ignore politically vocal musicians such as Leadbelly and Josh White, whom they booked to perform on *Jubilee*; in fact they appreciated a diversity of musical acts and the range of listener expectations. As *Jubilee* producer Holiner had developed shows for black entertainers in the past, the program became more of an exchange between directors and performers, with more opportunities for improvisation and nuance.

Despite its proclivity to abide by the army's conservatism, the AFRS exhibited concern with its internal treatment of racial matters. One black serviceman reported to the AFRS that the program titled *The Golden Hillbilly Vocalist* made "slurring, low remarks" about black Americans. In response, the AFRS not only vehemently denied that they sponsored the program (they said it was an original program on the American Forces Network) but also indicated that the broadcasters of the program had failed to honor "existing directives."[46] A 1948 memo stating AFRS editorial policy proclaimed that no racial group would be referred to disparagingly, and that "no color differentiation will be made in any manner." Lieutenant Colonel Robert Kearney indicated that the AFRS would not feature dialect stories, nor would it allow "unacceptable" songs such as "Carry Me Back to Old Virginia," "Old Man River," and "Darktown Strutters Ball." Listing these imperatives as central to presenting "good taste" and "good morals," the AFRS exhibited a sensitivity to racial stereotypes that was uncharacteristic of many commercial broadcasters. Although this AFRS policy was presented after the war, the flexibility given to black entertainers on *Jubilee* and the respect given to them by white performers indicate that the AFRS attempted to uphold these principles from the beginning of the show's establishment.[47]

The AFRS regarded *Jubilee* as one of its greatest assets. The AFRS staff selected the show as its fourth most popular, noting that it was a "top favorite with colored troops."[48] These managers, however, did not characterize *Jubilee* as a "Negro show," but instead focused on its function of showcasing "the latest in 'jive and jump' with such artists as Duke Ellington, Lena Horne, Rochester, Art Tatum, etc." While this description indicates that black performers were central, for officials it was important that all servicemen of all races could enjoy the show. Unlike wartime programming such as *Freedom's People*, "The Negro and National Defense," and "America's Negro Soldiers," *Jubilee*'s ostensible detachment from any racial politics engendered its full promotion to an interracial audience. In addition, the show's description may have reflected the liberal ideological background of producers such as Holiner, who did not draw the essentialist distinction of "Negro talent." As a result, the AFRS's characterization of *Jubilee* was no different than its descriptions of white variety programs such as *At Ease* and *Command Performance*.

Fan mail to the AFRS revealed *Jubilee*'s popularity with servicemen. Sergeant Vardy Sponsor reported, "Tonight we and the fellows were sent for the umpteenth time by Jubilee. . . . If you only knew how much Jubilee rates with us."[49] Sergeant John Carter declared, "Your Jubilee program is absolutely tops and the GI's really eat it up."[50] From October 1943 to March 1944, more fan letters were addressed to the *Jubilee* program than any other AFRS show except the highly popular *Command Performance*.[51] Soldiers gushed about the talent of Lena Horne or made requests for performers such as Ida James and Savannah Churchill. This correspondence did not mention *Jubilee* as a "Negro show," nor did it report that *Jubilee* was popular only among black troops. Although some *Jubilee* performers, such as Duke Ellington, had reached white audiences over the radio before the war, for many black entertainers the show provided a larger access to white listeners. With the creation of the V-Disc program, many *Jubilee* performances were captured on record, for servicemen to hear at any time of the day, more than once if they desired.

The AFRS responded to *Jubilee*'s ongoing popularity by establishing the show's position during peak listening hours. Although the hour of broadcast did occasionally change over time, differing across regions, *Jubilee* maintained prime airtime slots. Schedules indicate that *Jubilee* was broadcast on Thursday, Friday, and Saturday evenings; one report listed 72 percent of AFRS stations scheduling *Jubilee* on weekdays after 5:00 P.M.[52] On one schedule, *Jubilee* also aired at noon on Monday, the same time the highly popular *Tommy Dorsey Show* and *Mail Call* aired on other weekdays.[53] When programmed in the evening, *Jubilee* was often the only original AFRS entertainment show, with news or sports preceding and following.

As a show containing many of the era's most popular swing bands, *Jubilee* contributed to what historian David Stowe characterizes as "a larger discourse of Americanism." Swing not only embodied ideas of cultural pluralism forged during the 1930s but also reflected the democratic goals of the war effort. With both artists and music journalists articulating the swing ideology as a reverence for "liberty, democracy, tolerance, and equality," swing became the soundtrack for World War II, replacing patriotic melodies such as "Over There." What Stowe describes as the "militarization of swing" escalated in the creation of V-disks, the rapid distribution of phonographs, the creation of several overseas broadcast systems, and the employment of prominent swing bands for USO tours. In propagating this culture, officials demonstrated their faith in swing's ability to lift morale as well as to promote a distinct American aesthetic.[54]

However, the contradiction of swing's egalitarian promise and its frequent adherence to racial segregation would plague the genre's potential as the war years unfolded. Many black musicians were restricted from performing in service bands and therefore disrupted their musical careers by joining combat units. With black servicemen banned from many big band shows, even those that welcomed Nazi POWs, entertainers such as Lena Horne often cancelled or cut their performances short. Furthermore, black swing bands were subject to segregation when traveling in the South and denied basic accommodations during USO tours. A 1944 report in the *Baltimore Afro-American* declared that of all entertainers performing for troops since 1941, only 39 out of 2,066 were black artists.[55]

Under these conditions, the *Jubilee* show provided a safe haven from the discrimination associated with live performances. Recording in the studio did not involve the humiliation of riding on shabby segregated tour buses, or receiving inferior treatment compared to white entertainers during USO performances. *Jubilee* allowed black performers a high level of respect, equal to that of white entertainers such as Frank Sinatra and Bing Crosby. Furthermore, as a military broadcast, *Jubilee* had a special significance for black artists, because it was exempt from the national ban on recording from 1942 to 1944 and 1948 imposed by the American Federation of Musicians. *Jubilee* discographers Rainer Lotz and Ulrich Neuert contend, "for many bands and soloists the *Jubilee* transcriptions are the only recorded examples of the period, as commercial recording activities had come to a virtual standstill."[56] Although performers were not paid for *Jubilee* appearances, it was the major, and for some the only, outlet for their music to be heard during those years.

Despite *Jubilee*'s tendency to eschew direct political dialogues, many of its performers had a history of political action, most closely associated with Popular Front activities in the 1930s. Several swing performers maintained close ties to the Communist Party, as swing proponents heralded the connection between Communist ideology and the "folk" content of the music. Duke Ellington performed in "A Day of Unemployment" sponsored by black and white Communists in Harlem in 1930 and played during election campaigns for Harlem's Ben Davis, a Communist who ran for councilman in 1934. Meade Lux Lewis and Count Basie participated in "From Spirituals to Swing," a celebration of "authentic Negro music" sponsored by the Communist Party literary organ *New Masses* and the prominent leftist jazz producer John Hammond. Black musicians such as Cab Calloway, Teddy Wilson, Leadbelly, Jimmie Lunceford, and Maxine Sullivan ardently supported Loyalist Spain during the Spanish Civil War, running benefits such as the Harlem Musical Committee for Spanish Democracy, the Spanish Children's Milk Fund, and the Spanish Children's Relief Fund. Furthermore, Duke Ellington's 1941 musical comedy *Jump for Joy* openly challenged minstrel images and condemned the South for its treatment of black Americans. The actions of these and several other *Jubilee* performers demonstrated not only the political significance of swing but also the eagerness of black musicians to use their music to combat social injustice. When they performed on *Jubilee*, these musicians maintained the political consciousness they more openly exhibited in other forums but conveyed their opinions much less directly.[57]

Form, Content, and Political Expression

The producers' first motivation in creating *Jubilee*, like all other AFRS programs, was to entertain the troops. Although MC Ernest ("Ernie") Whitman addressed Americans "from the River Rhine to the River Rouge" in one show, *Jubilee* was only broadcast to U.S. military bases.[58] The show's format clearly responded to troop preferences expressed in War Department surveys. Beginning with performances by celebrity orchestras such as Duke Ellington or Count Basie, *Jubilee* opened with popular big band songs such as "Take the 'A' Train" or "One O'Clock Jump." The program then turned to well-known ballads sung by both male and female vocalists. Before the show's last big band number, which always closed the program, *Jubilee* would feature a comedy skit. Thus, almost without exception, the programs featured a large orchestra, a sextet or quartet (with a male vocalist), and a female vocalist. Musicians were often incorporated into comedy skits, while comedians such as Eddie Green and Eddie "Rochester" Anderson were sometimes brought in to perform exclusively. In addition,

Ernest Whitman, Lena Horne, and Eddie Green perform on the radio program Jubilee, *c. 1943. Photo by Jerry Hausner. (National Archives, RG 330, Box 12, E 1007)*

dedications to soldiers and encouragement for personal requests were a permanent feature of the program. Besides the more famous performers, *Jubilee* also included a number of servicemen who performed in military bands, glee clubs, or jazz combos.

Jubilee's upbeat, vivacious tenor was in part due to MC Ernie Whitman, who established a strong rapport with guests, the live audience, and the listening audience. Although black actors Mantan Moreland, Rex Ingram, and Dooley Wilson served as the master of ceremonies for the first few programs, by the tenth *Jubilee* recording, Whitman had established himself as the program's host.[59] During his career as a comedian, Whitman played more traditional roles as a butler on the radio serial *The Gibson Family* from 1934 to 1935, and as a housekeeper's boyfriend on the popular radio show *Beulah* during the 1940s. He also acted in race-related films such as *The Green Pastures*, *Cabin in the Sky*, and *Stormy Weather*. On *Jubilee*, Whitman took on greater opportunities for self-expression than the stereotypical characters offered to black actors in network programming. With his deep chuckle and his inviting, bellowing voice, he complemented the talents of performers through a catchy jive vernacular. As a self-effacing, overweight man, he was at the center of many comic exchanges when talking about his bottomless appetite. Exclaiming, "everybody loves a fat man," Whitman constructed an endearing persona—up-to-date with all the hottest musicians, while flexible with the dynamics of audience response.

Like Whitman's demeanor, the popular songs played by big band orchestras established familiarity with *Jubilee*'s audience while paying tribute to the most celebrated black swing musicians. Band leaders such as Count Basie and Duke Ellington often played their theme songs "Basie Boogie" and "Take the 'A' Train" with clear melodies and frequent repetition. Likewise, as the first performances of each show, songs such as "Leave Us Linda" played by Cee Pee Johnson or "Sweet Georgia Brown" played by Benny Carter featured recognizable arrangements. Various artists regularly performed "Tuxedo Junction," "Shoo Shoo Baby," and "O Lady Be Good," offering a range of musical interpretations but demonstrating the program's dedication to the tastes of its audience. For many white servicemen, it was the first time they heard black artists play popular songs such as "Blue Skies."

Yet *Jubilee* allowed for a wide range of musical styles, leading many artists to record new music. Singer/comedian Timmie Rogers performed his new song "Scrub, Sweep, and Mop" in 1944; during the same year Ivie Anderson sang "Play the Blues," a song not yet released on record.[60] While it featured more popular swing music, *Jubilee* also highlighted other types of arrangements. During its first appearance, the Teddy Wilson Sextet played an original composition, "The B-Flat Swing," a highly improvisational piece shifting to the unpredictable tempos of Wilson on piano. Wilson's explosive playing bore little resemblance to a big band theme song, avoiding repetition or lingering melody.[61] Instead, the pianist inserted individuality, aggression, and piercing commentary into each musical phrase, reminiscent of Wilson's own political outspokenness during the heyday of the Popular Front.[62] Similarly, the gravitating pulse of Cee Pee Johnson's "Slew Foot," an elaborate percussion jam laced with vocal and trumpet calls, lacked the catchy lyrics or instrumental combinations of popular swing.[63] The absence of a familiar tune countered comforting wartime melodies, often replaced by a call-and-response dialogue. While performers sometimes presented new music, they often teased the familiar into the unrecognizable. Although responding to a flurry of fan mail, Erskine Hawkins's rendition of "I Got Rhythm" blurred an easily identifiable melody into a dizzying array of commentaries be-

VARIETY FOR THE SERVICEMEN

tween instruments.[64] As black orchestras such as Hawkins's improvised the songs that Americans held dear, they endowed popular music with racial meaning.

Most songs on *Jubilee* did not make direct reference to racial and social inequality; however, there were a few exceptions. Timmie Rogers's song "Scrub, Sweep, and Mop" described the menial tasks of black soldiers who were restricted from more highly skilled positions. Warning "they'll put you in the guardhouse" if soldiers didn't clean the barracks or sweep the mess hall, Rogers illustrated both the lack of options for black soldiers and the army's resistance to utilizing black manpower. The song, however, was not a call for black soldiers to accept their station; Rogers urged soldiers not to salute their captain who "has no job in a GI suit." The song further summoned black resistance, asserting, "if you're tired of peeling potatoes and want to go, don't wait for furlough, just go." Listing the work that black soldiers should undertake, such as driving tanks, shooting guns, and digging ditches, Rogers decried the degradation of black labor. As he formulated a powerful critique of black army life, he also employed many popular satires of officer authority often formulated by white servicemen in army periodicals. Mocking the commanding officer had become a feature of World War II comic strips, providing soldiers with a lighter perspective on the military hierarchy. In utilizing this popular trope, Rogers drew attention to some similarities between black and white military experiences, even while condemning their differences.[65]

Josh White's blues ballad "One Meatball" described financial hardship, yet softened the gravity of poverty by portraying it comically. For his first performance on the show, White sang of a man going to a restaurant with only fifteen cents for food. When he ordered one meatball, the only thing he could afford on the menu, the waiter and other restaurant patrons became offended. Asking for bread with his dinner, the waiter replied, "you get no bread with one meatball." White's repetition of the waiter's response received laughter from *Jubilee*'s live audience. In his comic delivery of this tale, with its chorus repeating "one meatball" several times, White averted any charged political rhetoric. Yet, in emphasizing the man's humiliation in the restaurant, not to mention his lasting anguish over the incident ("in my dreams I hear the call, you get no bread with one meatball"), White condemned the gravity of black poverty by offering the most seemingly trivial incident. "One meatball" was not only the one meal the man could afford but also a symbol of the pain and social ostracism he would suffer as a consequence.[66] "One Meatball" was not as directly political as

White's critique of racism in Popular Front songs such as "Chain Gang" and "Southern Exposure." It did, however, reflect the class-consciousness of blues singers from the Piedmont region, such as White, who witnessed high levels of black labor activism during the 1930s.[67]

Relationships between men and women were the most frequent topic of *Jubilee* performances. White programs featured several of these songs, and many of the gender issues that *Jubilee* confronted extended to white and black people alike. Yet, the black experience during the war often changed the meaning of familiar melodies, as the confines of segregation and discrimination, coupled with rapid urban migration, affected interactions between men and women. In this context, the meaning of songs about missing a GI or about a lover's infidelity were embedded within the larger socioeconomic conditions defining black Americans' wartime roles. Additionally, as *Jubilee* often provided its musicians with opportunities that challenged both gender and racial stereotypes, the politics of performance became more loaded. Here, the show was not entirely depoliticized, as black men and women critiqued and redefined ideas about relationships, sexuality, and leisure space.

Songs such as "I'm Going to See My Baby" and "I'll Get By as Long as I Have You," both sung by the ubiquitous Ida James, reflected the patriotic sentimentality of traditional female longing.[68] Similarly, Dolores Williams's performance of "Happiness Is a Thing Called Joe" (a song from the film *Cabin in the Sky*) reveled in one man's ability to make angels sigh, crops grow, and skies clear.[69] Lyrically, "Happiness Is a Thing Called Joe" invoked images of a helpless, weeping woman. However, Williams's improvised spoken sequences (using a call-and-response format) and her shift to Gershwin's "Bess You Is My Woman" in the middle of the ballad separated "Happiness Is a Thing Called Joe" from conventional renditions. Songs such as "Play the Blues," sung by Ivie Anderson, recalled the blues tradition of black women such as Bessie Smith and Ma Rainey who used music to decry social injustice. As Anderson bellowed that the blues "help to ease the pain," she revisited conventional lamentations of a woman longing for her GI; yet in suggesting the blues as the only remedy for heartache, she invited listeners to excavate the racial origins of popular music.[70] Finding solace in songs without "too many melodies," Anderson openly questioned the saccharine tenor of popular swing and instead turned to a form rooted in the black experience.

Sexual candor was often a central part of performances. When asked by Ernie Whitman to say something to the troops, Thelma Carpenter suggestively replied that she couldn't think of anything "appropriate." Under the advice of Whitman, Carpenter let out a lingering sigh, something that would quickly arouse servicemen. Carpenter's delivery of "Do Nothing till You Hear from Me," sung with a deep sultriness, related the idea that a little female infidelity should hardly matter in a relationship where there was real love. Directed towards servicemen apart from their loved ones, the song reflected male anxieties while excusing women's adulterous behavior. Although the song's protagonist admits that she "has been with someone new," she claims her man "will never hear it from me."[71] Similarly suggestive was the song "Knock Me a Kiss," sung by Ida James, that included the lines "I want action" and "let's get lost."[72]

This type of sexual candor illustrates the complexity of performance faced by many women who appeared with a more provocative persona. As their appearances on *Jubilee* were geared towards the entertainment of lonely servicemen, many black women were urged to fulfill male fantasies of female sexuality. Circumscribed by the stereotype of black lasciviousness, many black women may have felt a need to sing demurely about relationships, while others flaunted demeaning stereotypes by exhibiting sexual aggression. Regardless of the degree that female performers displayed their sexuality, *Jubilee*, unlike most radio programs and films, gave these women a certain flexibility. Without scripted characters depicting racial conventions, the variety show provided black women with a space to explore and test the boundaries of their public personalities. As a community of black entertainers, *Jubilee* provided many black women with a degree of comfort in exhibiting sexual candor, not solely for the purpose of entertaining white individuals, but as part of their own self-expression.

In contrast, Lena Horne never exhibited an overt sexual suggestiveness, maintaining a personality of effortless charm and grace. A pinup girl for both black and white soldiers, Horne had become one of the most popular black celebrities during the 1940s, combining beauty with a maternal concern for the servicemen. On *Jubilee*, Horne's luminary status was carefully maintained; MC Ernie Whitman characterized her as "the most famous filly in the armed forces." Horne's performance of "Between the Devil and the Deep Blue Sea" presented the many dilemmas of loving the wrong man, while her rendition of "Just One of Those Things" offered a woman's perspective on why some relationships end.[73] Through these ballads, Horne revealed a certain savvy on the subject of human emotions, lacking the frustration articulated by other women. Horne furthered her expert status in a comic exchange with Butterfly McQueen:

LH: Hello there Butterfly, what seems to be the trouble this time?

BMQ: Same thing, Miss Horne.

LH: You mean men?

BMQ: Yes, the obstinate sex.

LH: Oh Butterfly, you mean the opposite sex, don't you?

BMQ: They sure are. Whenever I come from one direction, they go in the opposite. Gee Miss Horne, I wish I could be like you, whenever I see you you've got a man on each arm.

LH: Maybe so Butterfly, but for every man on my arm, you've got ten on your mind. There must be some way to get men off your mind completely.

BMQ: Oh, don't say that, I'm too young to die. Besides, I think I've finally found the answer to my fondest dreams. He's a PFC named Benny.

LH: Really? What's he like?

BMQ: Neat, nutty, and nearsighted—As soon as I saw him, I gave him that real GI look.

LH: GI?

BMQ: Yes, give in brother, give in.[74]

Here, McQueen's desperation is juxtaposed with Horne's cool confidence. Claiming that she repels men, McQueen lacks Horne's magnetism and ends up suggesting that sex may be the only way to attract male attention. Despite Horne's celebrated status on the program, other women appeared just as frequently as she did, being provided the same artistic freedom. Horne's popularity among servicemen may actually have inhibited her from experimenting with other kinds of expression on *Jubilee*; less famous performers could present various sides of themselves without offending audience expectations.

Male vocalists on *Jubilee* echoed many of the themes of their female counterparts, giving their own interpretation of sounds and stories traditionally vocalized by white musicians. Jimmy Rushing's "Baby Won't You Please Come Home" depicted the ails of a broken heart, while Earle Warren's "Don't Believe Everything You Dream" urged women on the home front to ignore rumors and innuendoes about the sexual activities of servicemen.[75] Like Thelma Carpenter's "Do Nothing till You Hear from Me," Warren's ballad professed the sanctity of true love, which could not be torn apart by wartime diversions. Like the female performers, male vocalists referred to the uplifting power of music. The Charioteers' version of

Lena Horne in Stormy Weather *(1943). (Twentieth Century Fox Film Corporation/Photofest)*

"The Music Master" narrated the story of a musician enlightened by a boy who told the man to "play faster." The ability to "swing boogie woogie and jive" would put the music master at the top of his profession, updating the slower tunes of previous decades.[76]

Songs such as "The Music Master" invoked an urban cosmopolitanism that permeated many male vocals. "Why Don't You Do Right," sung by Maurice Rocco, portrayed a life of drinking, gambling, and womanizing; in between his passionate extended piano improvisations, Rocco urged listeners to "do right" by avoiding vice.[77] The highly sexualized world of nightclubs and dance halls was also depicted in the King Cole Trio's "Slender, Tender and Tall" and "Fuzzy Wuzzy."[78] Asserting that fat women "can't jive" while "the thin ones know how to swing," "Slender, Tender and Tall" brought servicemen back to easier days at the expense of belittling women. Likewise, "Fuzzy Wuzzy" sounded the theme of glamorous dancing girls—"little devils" who undoubtedly were sexually active. While these songs focused on the availability of sexually aggressive women, they also depicted the leisure spaces that were central for all jazz musicians. By oversexualizing women who could "swing," black musicians may have been critiquing the white audiences they performed for at the exclusive dance halls such as the Cotton Club. With their popularity and success heavily dependent on a willingness to play for all white audiences, many musicians appropriated white fascination with a "primitive," "exotic" black urban life to subtly condemn the racial restrictions within the music industry.

Whether or not women performed with the highly sexualized delivery described by some male entertainers, *Jubilee* allowed female artists untraditional positions on the radio. Hattie McDaniel, Lena Horne, and Ida James all served as guest MCs on *Jubilee*, bringing with them attitudes and monologues that echoed Ernie Whitman. Although James claimed not to know very much about being a mistress of ceremonies, her use of language (one band was "ready as a ham on rye") and her sassy rapport with a New York audience during a special Broadway show demonstrated her command of the position.[79] As commercial radio rarely featured black women exclusively, let alone as a program host, this was a unique opportunity for women to exert influence outside traditional gender conventions. Furthermore, *Jubilee* provided some women with a space to express their musical talents in unconventional areas. As most black singers performed with orchestras such as Duke Ellington's or Count Basie's, Dorothy Donegan's delivery of her own piano compositions stood as a departure. Playing her complex piece "Dorothy's Boogie" after a flattering introduction by guest MC Ida James, Donegan's identity as an artist transcended her gender.[80]

As *Jubilee*'s popularity grew, by 1944 white performers expressed great interest in appearing on the show. An exchange between Bing Crosby and Ernie Whitman demonstrates the enthusiasm white musicians displayed towards the program:

EW: On what fleecy cloud did you float in?

BC: Well, Ernie, I happen to pass your solid door every week, I've been knocked out.

EW: I'll admit that once in a while someone hits a riff that's pretty potent.

BC: Just a moment ago I paused in the hall and one of your trombone players apparently inhaled during the two bar tacit, well here I am, suction did the trick, whipped me in here.

EW: Well I must thank that boy for buttering his lips.

BC: I would like to pay tribute to the swell job you guys here in hot horn hall are doing for the cats overseas.

In praising *Jubilee* for its musical talents as well as its success in boosting soldier morale, Crosby celebrated the show for presenting a diversity of music to the servicemen. Performing the popular hit "Shoo Shoo Baby" with the Charioteers, Crosby sang in a jazzy jive vernacular much like *Jubilee*'s black performers.[81] In stark contrast to more famous ballads such as "White Christmas," Crosby's rendition of "Shoo Shoo Baby" demonstrated his ease in adapting to the program's tenor. Among other white performers, Frank Sinatra made three appearances on *Jubilee*, largely to sing with Louis Armstrong and other jazz greats. As most swing bands were segregated, particularly when appearing in major concert halls or dance clubs, many white musicians did not have the opportunity, or were criticized for even attempting, to include their black counterparts.[82] As *Jubilee* allowed white and black entertainers to combine their talents, the program undermined another restriction that the music industry imposed.

By the war's end, white performers such as Jack Benny, George Burns and Gracie Allen, Bing and Bob Crosby, and Harry James all made *Jubilee* appearances. Even screen siren Ava Gardner held a stint as guest MC for two programs in 1947. Introducing popular black musician Jack McVae and building the audience's anticipation for his smash hit "Open the Door,

Guest star Bing Crosby greeted by Eddie Green on Jubilee, *c. 1943.*
Photo by Jerry Hausner. (National Archives, RG 330, Box 12, E 1007)

Richard," Gardner eagerly placed McVae in the spotlight, deferring to his talent. At a time when many Americans considered relations between black men and white women as the ultimate taboo, this public dialogue between McVae and Gardner, and Gardner's pronouncement of McVae's celebrity, made *Jubilee* all the more progressive.[83] The integrated composition of most programs in the postwar years attests to *Jubilee*'s open, inviting atmosphere at a time when American racial tensions remained tumultuous.

Yet the show's format slowly changed as all of the original AFRS staff left their posts by 1946, and in that same year Ernie Whitman left his role as the show's host.[84] Still, black musicians such as Duke Ellington, Count Basie, and Dizzy Gillespie continued to appear frequently on the show, with Ellington serving as MC for the month of March 1949. Although the show maintained a star-studded roster until the end of that year, black artists no longer predominated as they had during the war years. Whitman's replacements included Gene Norman, a prominent white producer of jazz recordings and radio programs in Los Angeles, and white AFRS announcer Leonard "Bud" Widom, who later served as chief of radio programming in

Japan. At the end of 1949, when the AFRS was unable to meet rising technical costs, *Jubilee* was discontinued.[85] When the AFRS produced the show again between 1952 and 1953 during the Korean War, it enforced a strict policy of only using the AFRS orchestra for musical background and only featuring one or two celebrities. The appeal of being included in a musical community with vocalists such as Lena Horne and the bands of Jimmie Lunceford and Duke Ellington had lured many black performers onto the program; this incentive vanished when the AFRS altered its policies. As a result, the last *Jubilee* shows, recorded in the summer of 1953, were composed of white performers such as Merv Griffin, the Andrews Sisters, and Lawrence Welk with white radio and television personality Johnny Grant serving as the primary MC. The specific racial imperatives of World War II had passed, and so did the show's function as a program that could ease racial animosity by celebrating America's most talented black entertainers. The waning number of black performers on *Jubilee* signaled the end of the community-building process that the show had fostered among hundreds of black artists.[86]

AS RADIO OWNERSHIP SKYROCKETED in the 1940s, wartime cultural program administrators internalized the promise of the medium for recognizing black Americans without exacerbating racial tensions. Yet, as they confronted the implications of a large listening audience, the interests of southern radio affiliates, and the competing concerns within state bureaucracies, government officials expressed ambivalence about addressing racial issues over the airwaves. When the War Department accepted the variety format as a viable method for neutralizing politically charged topics in creating "America's Negro Soldiers," the nascent AFRS soon followed. In featuring *Jubilee* as a depoliticized entertainment program, the AFRS allowed for the show's dissemination to a geographically diverse, interracial audience of servicemen.

Yet the *Jubilee* program contained political meaning from its inception, serving as an important outlet for public expression at a time when black Americans were largely restricted from major radio networks. Its broadcasts to all servicemen meant that some Americans who had never heard the swing of Count Basie, let alone the blues of Leadbelly, could gain unique exposure to various forms of black music. Furthermore, because *Jubilee*'s numerous performances stand as some of the only recorded examples of black music during two recording bans of the 1940s, the program has become a significant archive of black cultural expression.

VARIETY FOR THE SERVICEMEN

Although officials intended for the variety format to eliminate political discourse, it allowed black performers to defy the racial stereotyping of commercial programs, to collaborate with white artists, and to offer their own experiences and viewpoints. As black entertainers both subtly and directly critiqued discrimination, gender roles, and white expectations of black performance, *Jubilee* became a potent space for artistic freedom, cloaked in a military uniform. Yet as with all government-sponsored programs, African American empowerment on the *Jubilee* program was never unfettered. The contours of white production determined the extent of personal expression, and although the program touched on some issues significant to African American performers and servicemen, it remained first and foremost an entertainment vehicle.

In creating the AFRS, War Department officials were able to direct programs largely under their own control. This would not be the case with wartime motion pictures. As the domain of Hollywood producers, films underwent government review but were not a direct product of government cultural development. The federal government's more limited role in the construction of official films would unevenly affect the production of imagery. In some films, the motion picture industry would revise unflattering racial depictions, while others revealed an adherence to standard stereotypes. Yet, as film fueled black politicization far more than any other genre, black organizations and the black press would have a much larger role in the development of this official culture. In contrast to the artistic community that the *Jubilee* show buttressed, the construction of official films only exacerbated existing divisions among black entertainers and black political leaders. As government officials attempted to address the politics of the film industry, a vocal black community, and the goals of national unity, their role in mediating culture was most firmly challenged.

chapter six

PROJECTING UNITY

In 1943, a number of prominent black film actors including Hattie Mc-Daniel, Mantan Moreland, and Ben Carter participated in a roundtable discussion on the role of black Americans in the motion picture industry. The *Baltimore Afro-American* sponsored the event, declaring that these men and women had an enormous impact in promoting social change. "You [black actors] are challenged because the motion picture is the greatest propagandizing force for good and evil in the world today," the *Afro-American* editorialist insisted. "The motion picture, more than either the press or radio . . . has a more indelible effect upon the consciousness of people . . . than any other medium of expression."[1] By the time the public read these words, the struggle for more positive representations of black Americans in film was being waged in full force, facilitated by interests in the government, black political organizations, and Hollywood. While racial stereotypes would not be eradicated, their existence would be firmly and very publicly challenged. Important questions would unfold: How did these calls for more positive cultural representations interact with escalating black demands for civil rights? How would both black and white audiences reconcile cultural depictions of military integration and interracial goodwill amid the reality of segregation and race riots?

The issue of black characterizations in motion pictures became critical during the 1940s because government administrators understood that film was central to any propagation of American democracy. In the summer 1942, the Office of War Information's (OWI) Bureau of Motion Pictures (BMP) warned Hollywood, "Unless the public adequately understands the war program, a few military reverses can shatter the high morale of the American people."[2] During the war years, the BMP read approximately 1,652 film scripts before Harry Truman abolished the OWI in 1945. Although officials within the BMP acted more like regulators than cultural producers, they nonetheless shaped the nature of Hollywood productions through the promotion of certain principles. Among those principles considered critical to the national "war program," the inclusion of black Americans stood front and center. Receptive to many of the Roosevelt administration's liberal ideals, progressive Hollywood producers transformed the OWI's articulations of racial policy into a diverse visual spectacle. Motion pictures, like other wartime media, would produce racial imagery that offered some alternatives to traditional racial stereotypes, often celebrating black contributions to the nation. A few wartime films even offered a visual representation, not seen in other forms of government-sponsored cultural programming, of an integrated military effort.[3]

Although the federal government was not the primary producer of motion pictures, Hollywood films were a central component of its cultural programming because they could address its interest in promoting a multiracial nation. Enveloped by the federal cultural apparatus, Hollywood was, like the Armed Forces Radio Service, part of a cultural militarization that required foremost the industry's acquiescence to the ideals of sacrifice, cooperation, and loyalty. As an entity in its own right, however, Hollywood pushed institutional boundaries, aligning itself with administrative officials on some issues, while disregarding their suggestions on other matters. The film genre exhibited the same limitations as other federalized cultural developments; yet it also illuminated how the OWI and Hollywood, both invested in improving racial imagery, often approached the subject in a very different manner.

Due to the liberal sympathies of many in the industry, Hollywood expressed an interest in producing positive depictions of black Americans. Yet, as with administrators in the OWI, these progressive inclinations were constantly tempered by a conservative Congress, southern censors, and many studio heads who were unwilling to challenge racial mores. While considering Hollywood's role as a locus for leftist writers, producers, and actors during the New Deal era, I will examine the limited cultural manifestation of liberal politics, particularly when it came to race. The few, stereotypical roles for African Americans before World War II did not change very dramatically during the war years, as only a handful of films represented African Americans unconventionally. Even within more nuanced motion pictures such as *Bataan*, *Sahara*, *Cabin in the Sky*, and *Stormy Weather*, the relics of minstrelsy often lingered. Thus, while Hollywood was able to produce some examples of nontraditional racial imagery, these efforts were rather sporadic.

Still, it is important to underscore that in contrast to the decades preceding World War II, during the war Hollywood expressed a more concerted interest in improving its depictions of African Americans. While the productions did not often live up to official rhetoric, they nonetheless signaled the beginning of what would be a longer promotion of racial liberalism on behalf of the motion picture industry. As film historian Thomas Cripps describes, "a liberal Hollywood-black alliance that arose from these wartime circumstances not only defined a new black presence in the nation's propaganda (if not always its behavior) but extended its ideology into postwar America in ways that anticipated the modern civil rights movement."[4] Thus, while the racial imagery in war genre films such as *Bataan* and *Sahara*, as well as musicals such as *Stormy Weather* and *Cabin in the Sky*, was not a complete departure from the kind that could be seen in previous films, it did hint at the promise of Hollywood's more progressive racial attitude.

Furthermore, as these films opened amid African Americans' increasing political activism, the general excitement they brought about in the black press indicates that they had significant meaning for the larger freedom struggle. Within the broader trajectory of government-sponsored programs, film therefore became central not only because federal and state administrators heralded motion pictures as the key medium for addressing the "Negro problem," but also because black men and women understood film as an important vehicle in advancing representational politics. The black press frequently noted that film held a privileged place within the war era's cultural hierarchy. As African Americans' reactions to motion pictures demonstrated, improvements in the realm of representation were appreciated on their own terms. The African American press and the NAACP hailed new opportunities for black actors, even in roles that starkly ignored the existence of segregation and discrimination. Although the black community revealed diverse strategies for the use of motion pictures to improve racial attitudes, all agreed that film held a unique position within black cultural politics.

While other cultural historians have examined the films in this chapter, my purpose is to draw attention to how these films were situated within the larger context of New Deal cultural programs and how motion pictures engendered a particular discourse on the politics of African American representation. Debates during film production reflected a particular "conscience liberalism," which Thomas Cripps describes; as other historians demonstrate, the contours of this liberalism affected the types of imagery that studios could put forward. Rather than exploring these films within the history of black cinema, or solely within the context of Hollywood activities during World War II, this chapter examines how film both altered the course of government-sponsored cultural programming and, compared to other genres, provoked the most heated reactions from the black community. Furthermore, I aim to demonstrate why some motion pictures provoked charged responses from audiences while others did not, depending on variables such as gender, racial separatism, and realism.[5]

Hollywood films featured many of the same developmental dynamics as federal wartime programs. Officials debated over which actors, themes, and formats would be most compatible with the government's larger war aims. But because the administration had less control over Hollywood films than it did its own productions, there were many instances where the interests of federal officials within the BMP lost out to other priorities— whether those of studio heads or the black community in the industry. In addition, the racial separatism reflected in films such as *Cabin in the Sky* and *Stormy Weather* received a chilly reception from both the NAACP and the BMP, starkly contrasting with the government's endorsement of other black productions such as the *Swing Mikado* and *Jubilee*. In championing visual spectacles of integration as models for racially oriented filmmaking, the BMP and the NAACP denied the need for realistic portrayals of segregated life; however, in doing so, they evaluated cinematic integration as a milestone within African American representational politics. Ironically, while federal officials espoused the need for racially forward-looking themes, in the end Hollywood's own productions made a more progressive statement than government films such as *The Negro Soldier*.

The integrationist fantasy featured in films such as *Bataan* and *Sahara* would not only represent interracial liberalism at its wartime apogee but also became a hallmark of postwar film culture, when the stakes were raised dramatically. Nevertheless, if some films advanced ideas about racial pluralism, the majority still largely reinforced the notion that American identity was synonymous with whiteness. For African American political leaders and some in the film industry, the war's liberal ethos influenced Hollywood to move beyond the limits it had previously imposed on black performers. Black Americans, however, always couched progress within the context of an oppressive representational history rather than sweeping advances, which could have affected the nation's racial perceptions at large.

The OWI and the Blackening of the Silver Screen

Even more than the employment of celebrities such as Joe Louis and radio programs such as *Jubilee*, film was an extremely potent genre for the promotion of a multiracial nation. As liberal-minded Hollywood producer Walter Wanger claimed, "the American film is our most important weapon. . . . The problem of enlightenment of the masses is a major problem and admittedly the film is the greatest visual educational factor accepted by the masses. . . . [Other media, like] the radio and the press, are more limited."[6] Even though Theodore Berry, liaison officer to the OFF, did not endorse the sole use of this medium to address racial matters, he still believed in the need for a "more extensive use of motion pictures to indicate the participation of the Negro in the war effort and American life."[7] Thus, the OWI pressed for a greater communication with Hollywood to encourage the motion picture industry to use "Negro characters in their feature scripts, with such characters displaying unusual acts of patriotism and loyalty to the armed forces."[8]

By the 1940s, moviegoing was at its apogee as the most popular American leisure activity. As film historian Thomas Doherty explains, the experience of viewing motion pictures typically included a combination of full-length features, newsreels, cartoons, shorter serials, and previews. Before the advent of television, the movie house was the only venue for viewing moving pictures. Seeing a film in one of the more elaborate and ornate theaters was a luxury enjoyed more frequently by white Americans; black individuals normally viewed films from the balcony or rear of segregated theaters or in run-down buildings in black neighborhoods. During World War II, films often reflected experiences on the home front and in the military, providing a certain solace to audiences who sought some reassurance of consistency in a chaotic world. Yet motion pictures also became a vehicle for the government to disseminate American ideology to the widest possible audience, proving that film was useful for much more than mere entertainment. As film could fulfill a social function by enlightening the public, it became another weapon in the battle against Fascism.[9]

Thus, government officials naturally incorporated motion pictures into propaganda agencies. When Executive Order 9182 established the Office of War Information in the summer of 1942, it created a Bureau of Motion Pictures, with a chief who would "serve as the central point of contact between the motion picture industry and Federal officials to the end that the motion picture industry . . . may make the maximum contribution to keeping the American public fully informed on vital aspects of the war."[10] The chief of the BMP, Lowell Mellett, had previously worked as an editor for the *Washington Daily News* and headed the propaganda agency, the Office of Government Reports (which later merged into the OWI), in late 1939. In December 1941, Roosevelt appointed Mellett to the position of coordinator of government films, and in this capacity, Mellett set up a Hollywood office to deal more directly with the motion picture industry. His friend Nelson Poynter, "an interventionist New Dealer" and publisher of the *St. Petersburg Times*, became the director of that office. Both Mellett and Poynter were ardent Roosevelt supporters with little connection to Hollywood. Mellett's and Poynter's paper-thin backgrounds in motion pictures irked many in Hollywood who would have preferred choices closer to the industry; nevertheless, when the BMP was created as a component of the OWI's Domestic Branch, chief Mellett worked in the Washington office along with assistant chief Poynter, who remained in Hollywood.[11]

Within the Hollywood office, script review and analysis fell under the direction of Dorothy Jones, who had worked with prominent film analyst Harold Lowell; she served as the OWI's chief film analyst. Scripts that came into the Hollywood office were sent to bureau staff reviewers who had experience analyzing scripts through formal work in major motion picture studios. Once reviewers had evaluated the scripts, Mellett received copies of their reports in Washington.[12] While the BMP offered suggestions that Hollywood was by no means required to implement, the agency still viewed itself as necessary for ensuring that motion pictures reflected the government's larger wartime goals; its mission for the motion picture industry was articulated most clearly in a manual written in the summer of 1942. Defining the critical issues that would provide the American public with "the weapon of truth," Poynter and Mellett listed key themes for consideration in film production. According to the BMP manual, considering the kind of material that filmmakers usually brought to life on the screen, "It is a challenge to the ingenuity of Hollywood to make equally real the democratic values which we take for granted."[13] Yet the goals of Hollywood did not always align with these directives, nor were studios always receptive to the OWI's input. Taking aim at escapist films such as *Palm Beach Story* and *Princess O'Rourke*, the BMP argued that films should not be making light of war sacrifices or deflecting attention from the most pressing issues of the time. As Poynter proclaimed, "We want to encourage the studios to make films with real guts, films that can cause complaint from pro-Fascist minorities."[14]

Hollywood's seeming disregard for these concerns led directors such as Mellett and Poynter to press for stricter censorship codes and a more intense review process. In December 1942, Mellett informed the studios that henceforth the BMP should receive finished scripts, synopses of proposed productions, and the opportunity to screen pictures in their final stage. Hollywood balked at these instructions, charging the government with infringing on the creative process. In general, the OWI lost much of its support from the motion picture community, and although the process of review continued with many of the changes Mellett had suggested, the relationship between the OWI and Hollywood remained strained. Many conservative studios resented the liberal sympathies of the OWI and viewed it as a propaganda agency unnecessarily invading Hollywood's turf. Yet over the course of the OWI's tenure, Hollywood still implemented many of the agency's suggestions and edited out material perceived as "harmful to the war effort." Yet it was clear that Hollywood had the upper hand in film production, because major motion picture studios developed films regardless of the OWI's concerns.[15]

Such was the case with *Tennessee Johnson* (MGM, 1943), a film that provoked controversy from all angles. In Hollywood's treatment of racial issues, the BMP hoped that it would abide by government directives. As the BMP's manual for Hollywood stated in the second section, entitled "We Are Fighting for Freedom and against Slavery," racial cooperation was a wartime imperative. The manual asserted that as an "oppressed minority," black Americans should view images suggesting a "real . . . legal . . . permanent chance" for "improvement of their status." Thus, films should not only emphasize the horrific implications of life under a dictatorship but also the increasing gains in the economic lives of minorities in a democratic society.[16] When conservatives at MGM wrote the script for *Tennessee Johnson*, its theme contrasted with many of these projected aims. The film centered on the career of former president Andrew Johnson, who had opposed black suffrage and enforced the oppressive black codes during the Reconstruction period. As the film attempted to celebrate this president, largely by condemning the practices of radical Republican Thaddeus Stevens, *Tennessee Johnson* relied upon traditional southern interpretations of the "dark period" in which freedmen and carpetbaggers drove the South into political and social ruin. The film depicted African Americans with the most degrading racial stereotypes, and Stevens, a proponent of civil rights, appeared as a drunken "demonic figure."[17]

The NAACP was appalled upon learning of the script. Writing to Lowell Mellett, Walter White stated, "I strongly believe that the making of this picture at this time would do enormous injury to morale. . . . I believe that MGM could find infinitely more pertinent and valuable films to make."[18] With complaints coming in from many African Americans, the OWI attempted to persuade executives at MGM to change the picture or to withhold it until the war ended. Yet, when the studio refused these suggestions, the OWI eventually caved in, as the need to preserve a civil relationship with the motion picture industry took priority over black opinion. MGM vice president E. J. Mannix assured Mellett, "there is nothing in this picture that you or anyone else need worry about. The best we are doing, or the worst, is the glorification of one of our Presidents."[19] Although the studio agreed to some revisions—the character of Stevens became more sincere—the controversial portrayal of black Americans was resolved by eliminating black people from the film. As film historians Clayton Koppes and Gregory Black explain, "the finished product was an early instance of what later became a frequent tactic when Hollywood faced OWI's racial strictures: writing out." For the OWI, *Tennessee Johnson* raised larger questions about the priority of racial issues; as much as the agency hoped to promote a greater racial tolerance, it would frequently eschew or abandon this goal in order to balance a number of competing political interests.[20]

The position of the OWI was tenuous from its beginning, increasingly provoking congressional hostility as the war unfolded. By the spring of 1943, the OWI was rife with internal dissension, as business-oriented executives challenged the authority of intellectuals and journalists who resigned their employment as writers within the agency. At the same time, a conservative Congress, skeptical of the OWI's intentions and ideology from its inception, mounted a full-scale attack to reduce the agency's appropriations for 1944. OWI pamphlets such as *Negroes and the War* had raised the ire of Republicans and southern Democrats alike, and when Congressman John Taber (R-N.Y.) declared the organization to be "a haven of refuge for the derelicts," other politicians followed suit in lambasting the agency's liberal staff. With other priorities on the mind of the president at the time, and hostility toward the agency in Hollywood, the OWI found itself with few defenders when Congress eventually voted to abolish the agency's domestic branch in the summer of 1943. Although Congress provided the organization with funding to keep some small operations going, such as the production of information shorts, the OWI could no longer function as the major domestic propaganda agency. As OWI historian Allan Winkler contends, "OWI's fate was but one more example of the war's devastating impact on the whole liberal cause."[21]

When Congress crippled the OWI, the BMP's domestic branch ceased to exist as a regulator of motion pictures. As historians Koppes and Black explain, however, the demise of the domestic branch of the BMP only buttressed the relationship between the government and Hollywood, as the reviewing staff of the overseas branch picked up where the domestic branch left off. Both Mellett and Poynter severed ties with the OWI, and the evaluation of Hollywood films was now headed by overseas director Ulric Bell. A former Washington bureau chief of the *Louisville Courier Journal* and state director of the FWP in Kentucky, Bell directed the agency's attention to materials that might be appropriate for foreign consumption, with little objection from Hollywood. As Hollywood could only conceive of the enormous additional profits to be made once markets became liberated by the Allies, the government's role in the production of films was not only viewed as suitable but necessary. Certainly Hollywood studios believed they knew American audiences better than the government did, but determining the likes and dislikes of foreign viewers—that fell under the province of federal officials.[22]

Although the assault on the OWI signaled a pronounced effort to stifle New Deal liberalism, with racial egalitarianism as a major concern of Roosevelt's adversaries, the BMP continued to advocate improved representations of black Americans, even after the domestic branch was eliminated. Whether audiences were domestic or foreign was less pressing than the need for producers to reconsider some of the unflattering racial depictions. In suggesting particular changes for black characters to reflect idealized American values to consumers overseas, government reviewers understood that these improvements would also affect American viewers. Thus, although conservatives had sounded the death knell for the OWI as a liberal propaganda agency, some of its racial objectives came to fruition even after the institution's demise.

Walter White, Hollywood, and the Representational Divide

Scholars have long analyzed the history of black Americans in motion pictures, advancing a multiplicity of interpretations regarding the nature of racial representation. Building onto Donald Bogle's seminal study, *Toms, Coons, Mulattoes, Mammies, and Bucks*, historians and film critics have mapped the historical contours that produced racialized motion pictures, exploring the political function of genre and characterization. While scholars may debate the degree to which particular films reified or diverged from existing stereotypes, there is a consensus that World War II altered the way that major Hollywood studios undertook the treatment of African Americans. Wartime motion pictures may have fallen short of the goals the OWI and the NAACP espoused; nevertheless, they ushered in new forms of imagery and heightened audience expectations.[23]

Since mounting their protests of *Birth of a Nation* in 1915, African Americans had understood that film was a vital medium in the larger struggle for representational agency. Although pioneers such as the Lincoln Motion Picture Company and independent filmmaker Oscar Micheaux had created films during the 1920s and 1930s that presented complex renderings of black life for black audiences, their efforts were isolated endeavors. Major Hollywood productions confined black actors to servile roles or exotic fantasies that satisfied white desires for primitivism. Featuring African Americans on the plantation or in the jungle, Hollywood visually affirmed the racial hierarchy, diminishing the complexity of black communities and obscuring racial conflict. While stock characters may have become more nuanced over time, they nevertheless remained the province of white studios who found little reason or incentive to alter racial norms. Still, as historian Cedric Robinson maintains, black actors such as Mantan Moreland and Stepin Fetchit often improvised within stereotypical roles, providing a "comedic space which paralleled, ornamented, and on occasion threatened the principal plot of the films."[24] Offering alternative meanings within racial caricatures and critiquing demeaning roles through the black press, African Americans were never complacent towards the repressive nature of the studio system.

In addition to marginalizing and stereotyping African Americans, racial imagery in prewar motion pictures also performed the function of shoring up a white national identity. Blackface minstrelsy, more regularly performed by white actors in film before the advent of sound, not only allowed some ethnic actors to more readily assimilate but also provided a racialized counterpoint for not-yet-whitened ethnic groups to stand against. As historian Michael Rogin notes, during the 1920s and 1930s blackface in motion pictures promoted an ethnic homogenization that elided cultural differences while casting African Americans as definitively nonwhite. As Rogin argues, "Blackface operates as vehicle for sexual as for ethnic mobility by offering freedom for whites at the price of fixedness for blacks."[25]

PROJECTING UNITY

Thus, the whitening of Jews and other groups was at the expense of black Americans; although blackface minstrelsy was fading out by World War II, the pervasiveness of the form had relegated African Americans to an inferior status within the landscape of popular culture. While the government's conceptualization of whiteness revealed a more liberal caste, and multiethnic propaganda films and posters revealed celebrated differences among soldiers and citizens on the home front, they could not offer the same kind of inclusiveness for African Americans that motion pictures had afforded to other ethnic groups over decades.

Still, wartime rhetoric underscored the disparity between democracy and racial discrimination, and here, the employment and representation of African Americans in Hollywood films took on a different definition than it had in the prewar years. First, Hollywood studio heads could not ignore government directives, which, although far from radical, demanded less demeaning depictions of African Americans. In addition, Hollywood could no longer disengage the black press or black political organizations, which targeted motion pictures as central to legitimizing America's democratic goals. As early as December 1941, Walter White told Lowell Mellett, at the time newly employed as "Coordinator of Government Films," that "continuing to depict the Negro only as a buffoon or as a menial . . . is a source of constant irritation to American Negroes."[26] While White was an instrumental figure in championing constructive representations on the silver screen, his correspondence with government administrators figured into already existing plans for improving black morale. Thus, unsurprisingly, upon hearing of White's plans to lobby Hollywood industry heads in February 1942, Lowell Mellett described these efforts as "very timely" given his own agency's cultural intentions.[27] The government's suggestions for using film to address the "Negro problem" developed from a series of concerns about an increasingly politicized black public; ideas percolating in the OWI and the War Department provided a welcoming space for White's pleas to the Hollywood community, but in many ways they existed independent of White's efforts.

Perhaps at face value the OWI's aim to reduce black "doubts and confusion concerning our war aims" was not so different from Walter White's hope that films could "raise the morale of the Negroes of the country and throughout the world."[28] Yet, as the OWI and all wartime agencies made clear, the improvement of racial imagery would not accompany any public pronouncements for racial reform. For Walter White, however, the relationship between rights and representation was much more intertwined.

PROJECTING UNITY

As White explained to Hollywood producers: "Restriction of Negroes to roles with rolling eyes, chattering teeth . . . or to portrayals of non-too-bright servants . . . perpetuates a stereotype which is doing the Negro infinite harm. And showing him always as a mentally inferior creature, lacking in ambition, is one of the reasons for the denial to the Negro of opportunity and for the low morale not only of Negroes but of colored peoples throughout the world as it constantly holds the Negro up to ridicule and disparagement."[29] Speeches such as this one as well as his correspondence make clear that White's desire that Hollywood present African Americans more accurately was connected to his larger hopes for the improvement of America's racial psyche. As White argued to Hollywood moguls, racial stereotypes not only affected white attitudes but demeaning caricatures also affected black "opportunity." Albeit making a subtle reference to more concrete economic or political gains, White hinted towards social reform rather gingerly for producers to consider.

As a political pragmatist, White clearly knew the limits of Hollywood liberalism as well as the weight of influential southerners who balked at any images of racial equality onscreen. In 1940, White sent a query to prominent southern newspapers asking if southern audiences would accept films featuring black actors in roles that were not stereotypes. White's letters suggested a film storyline featuring the plight of three generations of black men—one an African chief, one his son under slavery in America, and one his grandson who comes to be a "concert artist at Carnegie Hall." Citing the support of producers such as David Selznick and Walter Wanger, White professed that he did not intend to make a "propaganda" film but rather sought to create new roles for black individuals that would be neither "buffoon nor . . . humble servant." He stressed the South's impact in the development of motion pictures, claiming that "even the most liberal of Hollywood producers" would not create new roles for black people because "the entire South would be cut off so far as distinction is concerned." White asked these southern journalists, do you believe this?[30]

White received a series of responses to this inquiry, all emphasizing the delicacy of the matter. Declaring that White's proposed story should contain a variety of racial depictions, Jonathan Daniels, editor of the *Raleigh News and Observer*, suggested that villains should be "both black and white"; in addition, both black and white southerners should be depicted as "humble as mud" and "shrewdly comic." Daniels stated such a film could be "both possible and popular" among southern audiences, although producers should not label the film a "Negro picture," and any NAACP influence should go unmentioned.[31] Another racial moderate, J. E. Chappell of the *Birmingham News* argued that many southerners would view White's proposed film with little objection, based on the warm reception Marian Anderson garnered when she sang to a mixed audience in 1938. On the other hand, as Chappell explained, racial attitudes always remained potentially explosive and unpredictable. He still urged White to make the film and to test it in front of southern audiences, claiming that it could be "of real service . . . in the cause of race relations."[32]

Expressing less hesitation towards the promotion of new racial imagery, Grover Hall of the liberal-oriented *Montgomery Advertiser* declared, "I think Mr. Selznick and Mr. Wagner are seeing ghosts when they plead that the south would boycott the type of film which you have envisioned." Citing a degree of racial tolerance in Selma, Alabama, Hall told White about his own speech to a group of white high school students on "The American Negro." Hall explained that his purpose was to give "tribute to the character and genius of the American Negro," and to eschew any racial stereotypes or indications of racial shortcomings. Pleased with the positive reaction of both parents and students, Hall indicated that this type of openness was more characteristic of the Selma region. "I assure you that the day of the coon song is dead in the south," Hall asserted, dismissing the "ticky minority" of racist southerners as a small faction. Citing the southern acceptance of films such as *The Green Pastures* and *Grapes of Wrath* that managed to avoid stereotypes, Hall attested to the prevalence of "responsible, enlightened public opinion."[33]

The correspondence of these southern editors illustrates their belief that while racial prejudice would continue to affect the types of films that Hollywood could develop, film could be a powerful force in improving white racial attitudes. Certainly Grover Hall's naïveté about the predominance of racism would be revealed in later boycotts and censorship of certain films; nevertheless, these southern editors hoped that new forms of racial imagery would be tolerated and even appreciated by audiences. These reactions did not make Walter White any less conscious or concerned about the position of the South during his campaign for better screen roles, but they provided him with pockets of support, particularly when lobbying to studio heads. That these more liberal southern journalists expressed confidence in their fellow southerners' willingness to accept new racial representations demonstrates that they did not believe that the mass media would seriously threaten the racial status quo. Yet had White asked these editors to assess public opinion on the eradication of segregation, their reactions would most definitely not have been so favorable.[34]

With the opinions of these southerners and many others in mind, White held the NAACP's annual convention in Los Angeles in July 1942. This meeting followed several visits to Hollywood during that year when Wendell Willkie accompanied White. At the time, Willkie held posts both as special counsel to the NAACP and as Twentieth Century Fox chairman of the board. The location of the NAACP meeting underscores the priority of motion pictures on the organization's agenda—with access to industry heads, the NAACP could reassert its position while many wartime films were still in the development stage. Speaking to studio moguls such as Darryl Zanuck, Walter Wanger, David Selznick, and Hal Wallis at a luncheon on 18 July, White described the NAACP's ultimate aim: to incorporate black Americans "naturally and easily in a script in parts which are not stereotyped."[35]

Given the leftist leanings of several industry figures, Hollywood gave serious attention to the NAACP's concerns. During the 1930s and 1940s, major Hollywood producers, writers, and actors participated in radical politics, some as members of the Communist Party. Actors and actresses such as James Cagney, Carole Lombard, and Bette Davis all supported New Deal programs; studio heads such as Darryl Zanuck and Walter Wanger were ardent racial progressives. Actor Melvyn Douglas demonstrated a particular interest in aiding black children, while producer David Selznick had brought Walter White to a meeting of the Hollywood Anti-Nazi League. Screenwriters most known for their liberal-leftist politics, such as John Howard Lawson, were particularly sympathetic to the pursuit of racial justice. While this political atmosphere seemed most amenable to White's cause, liberals in Hollywood, like those in the OWI, were significantly circumscribed by conservative politics during these precarious war years. Whether written by leftist scribes or produced by racially progressive studio heads, radicalism was often stymied in the making of motion pictures.[36]

After all, Hollywood was particularly sensitive when it came to films that southerners could censor or that could incite racial tensions. Film historian Thomas Cripps acknowledges that White's accomplishments were "ambiguous," given Hollywood's ambivalence towards racial issues and White's status as an outsider.[37] Yet many did express the positive impact of White's presence and suggestions. Screenwriter Sidney Buchman reported, "I have never known a luncheon meeting more inspiring and productive," while a representative from MGM assured, "I am thoroughly in accord with the efforts being made for the Negroes. I will do my utmost in whatever way I can in helping this cause."[38] Universal's Cliff Work made it clear that "we [Universal] have been derelict in our duties by not more clearly recognizing the problem. . . . You may be assured of our personal cooperation."[39] Nevertheless, there were some who viewed White's proposal as superfluous, as Buddy DeSylva of Paramount stated that he indeed "used negro characters," but only when the roles fit "naturally" within the plot. Although DeSylva did not attend the meeting, he was quick to assume that White's political position echoed "negro spokesmen who said that the negro shouldn't be sent to war unless he could receive equal benefits with the white man." "I think it a bad time for the negro to 'try to make a deal'" DeSylva argued, hesitant to encourage cultural integration that might suggest larger social changes.[40]

Most major black newspapers reported White's meeting with industry heads, declaring that Hollywood was central in improving American racial attitudes.[41] *Pittsburgh Courier* columnist Billy Rowe underscored the impact of studios such as Twentieth Century Fox, which had provided actors such as Bill Robinson with lasting roles. Newspapers particularly praised Twentieth Century Fox chair Darryl Zanuck, as he encouraged other studio heads to consider Walter White's suggestions seriously. Because of White's visit, reported the *Courier*, "the industry has taken heed and much is expected from it towards a full integration of democracy into the lives of all races in America."[42] Many columnists had their own strategies for improving conditions for African Americans in motion pictures. *Courier* writer Alice Key pressed for "full screen integration," which included more technical jobs and greater opportunities for black screenwriters.[43] On this point, former FTP Los Angeles director and actor Clarence Muse sounded the need for the employment of black writers, because there was a "bottleneck in material" for talented black actors, making it more difficult to tell important stories about the black experience in America.[44]

Some writers stated more blatantly that the attainment of civil rights was wedded to the position of African Americans in the motion picture industry. As one *Chicago Defender* columnist indicated, "If we are to be successful in our struggle for the complete integration of the Negro into every phase of American life we must militantly demand fair play for Negroes in Hollywood."[45] The belief in Hollywood as a source of racial betterment relied on the expectation of support from white actors such as Henry Fonda,

Humphrey Bogart, and John Wayne. Wayne suggested, "Stories should be created for the Negro that would mean something to both him and America," while Fonda more generally decried the practices of any industry that would "deny a person of ability the right to a place among the forces that made America the land of the free." Like Fonda, Red Skelton spoke less directly to racist practices in Hollywood and more to the possibility of black Americans taking their place in the American "scene," "be it either on the screen or in some other phase."[46] While racial liberalism was certainly a component of political thought among many in Hollywood, racial essentialism often followed. Although claiming, "the color of a man's skin should have nothing to do with his rights," Humphrey Bogart insisted that black entertainers had more options because "the Negro race is blessed with many fine dramatic and musical qualities." Similarly, Lloyd Bacon concluded, "The Negro race is highly dramatic, it has a fire and the color that always blends well in the conducting of entertainment."[47] While the *Courier* included these interviews to underscore the extent of white outrage against Hollywood's discriminatory practices, its readers nonetheless had to endure the reality that in many cases support for black actors was based on stereotypes regarding "natural" black talent.

While some articles in the press praised the NAACP's campaign for more positive racial representations, the organization's efforts incensed many black actors in Hollywood, particularly those performers who had built profitable careers playing maids and servants. In an exclusive article for the *Courier*, former FTP director Clarence Muse criticized White for ignoring the opinion of the Screen Actors Guild, particularly those black performers affected by calls for "better roles." Without the inclusion of the "actors' view," Muse claimed, the meeting between White and Hollywood producers was "a confused one, with nobody knowing just what is wanted as it was more or less a closed meeting." Scrutinizing White's alleged "formula," Muse concluded that the "white-washing" of Hollywood—the employment of more light-skinned black actors playing lawyers and doctors—would not improve the careers of black people in the motion picture industry nor general attitudes on race. Urging that acting should be evaluated on its quality rather than content, Muse championed the cause of those actors who had endured "sacrifice and suffering" to establish themselves.[48]

In defending the rights of actors such as Hattie McDaniel, some columnists described the contributions of black individuals during production. Harry Levette of the *Baltimore Afro-American* contended that McDaniel often rewrote or ad-libbed her lines; Clarence Muse was given authority to rewrite a sequence in *So Red the Rose* when he objected to a particular stereotypical characterization.[49] While participating in the *Baltimore Afro-American*'s roundtable discussion in 1943, several prominent black actors not only confirmed their own agency in the development of films but also attested to the industry's opposition to discrimination. Actor Ben Carter stated that his manager refused to allow a cast to stay in a segregated hotel; comedian Mantan Mooreland reported that he and other actors would not perform in front of segregated military audiences. Proclaiming, "there is less discrimination in the motion picture industry than in any other profession," Carter criticized Walter White for failing to ask actors "what discrimination, if any, we suffer."[50]

In their critique of White's neglect, roundtable participants largely emphasized their own importance as pioneers in black film history. McDaniel recalled her own struggles: "[A] little over a decade ago a colored actor in any form was unheard of on the screen and today many get very good parts." While McDaniel and others opposed the use of dialect outside of period roles and objected to overtly racist caricatures, they challenged the NAACP's alleged pronouncement that Hollywood should eliminate servant roles. For these actors, film roles not only had a financial significance but also engendered greater black visibility onscreen and promoted stature within the industry. "I have a stand-in and hair dresser and other attendants fuss over me as they do any other star," McDaniel exclaimed, asserting that actors who played servants did not receive inferior treatment on the set. As they objected to the pressure brought on by outsiders, these actors did not dismiss the struggle for greater opportunities within the motion picture industry, but rather offered alternative options for how to fight.[51] Although White was well aware of these charges against him, he made little attempt to incorporate these actors' opinions into his strategy.[52]

The division between the NAACP and West Coast actors revealed that views on culture were not monolithic among black Americans and helped wartime program administrators to understand competing visions of racial imagery in their review of films. This is not to say that White and his West Coast critics did not share similar goals; certainly both pressed for better opportunities for African Americans in Hollywood and for an eradication of racist practices. The different perspectives, however, based on class, region, and profession, illuminate why film became such a vibrant, although contested, genre in the discussion of racial politics. Thus, the multiplicity of racial symbols that permeated wartime films resulted from the diverse

Hattie McDaniel, actress and major general of the Women's Auxiliary Defense Corps, with Mary McLeod Bethune, National Youth Administration's Negro Affairs director, at the launching of the S.S. Booker T. Washington, *9 September 1942. (Franklin D. Roosevelt Library, Hyde Park, N.Y.)*

interests of Hollywood and the OWI, as well as the varying opinions within the black community. The expansion of government-sponsored cultural programming did not create an equal allotment of power within the OWI/ Hollywood/NAACP axis; issues that one group supported others often ignored. Nevertheless, as release dates approached, cultural producers anxiously anticipated how both black and white Americans would respond to racialized films and whether new forms of representation would lead to further considerations of civil rights.

The Separate World of Black Musicals

The black community's differing perspectives on racial representation were most explicit in the creation of two all-black musical films, *Cabin in the Sky* and *Stormy Weather*. More in line with the requests of the West Coast actors than those of Walter White, the musicals proved that Hollywood producers had internalized the grievances of various black interest groups and would attempt to address them onscreen. The two most anticipated films in the black press, and the most frequently regarded black "war films" by both contemporaries and scholars alike, *Cabin in the Sky* and *Stormy Weather* were significant financial investments in black talent, comprising the largest employment of black actors, dancers, and musicians to date. Although these films did not speak to issues such as military integration or racial violence, like some of the other films I later discuss, they represent another method Hollywood used to acknowledge the black community. When the OWI critiqued these films for invoking a type of separatism incompatible with the larger war aims, Hollywood's greater influence won out, demonstrating not only its control over the medium but also an understanding of a particular kind of representational politics that escaped reviewers in the BMP.

The all-black musicals are also important because they contained the major—and ultimately most influential—representations of black women in film during the war years. In contrast to some combat films, where black men's intelligence, morality, and dignity were represented in their characters, black women held more traditional female roles in *Cabin in the Sky* and *Stormy Weather*. Nevertheless, within these conventional roles, women such as Ethel Waters and Lena Horne suggested a range of possibilities for black women, outside of the Mammy/Jezebel paradigm. These critiques of the circumscribed representations of black women that had long been featured on both the stage and the screen implied that black women had command of both their voices and their movement, even if that wasn't what was shown onscreen. The liberal atmosphere at both MGM and Fox fueled not only the incentive to produce all-black musicals but a desire that the cast provide their own artistic interpretations. Much like the *Jubilee* radio show, *Cabin in the Sky* and *Stormy Weather* provided traditional frameworks, which allowed African Americans to push the boundaries of their own representations.

As the Hollywood directorial debut of theatrical director Vincente Minnelli, *Cabin in the Sky* (MGM, 1943) started out as an experimental venture during the heyday of MGM's musical unit headed by producer Arthur Freed. Originally opening on the Broadway stage in 1940, *Cabin in the Sky* was choreographed by Katherine Dunham and George Balanchine; its main actors included Ethel Waters (who would also play in the film version), Dooley Wilson, and Dunham as Georgia Brown. Those who conceived the music and script all had left-leaning inclinations, most with backgrounds in black theater. Vernon Duke and lyricist John Latouche, composer of the popular song "Ballad for Americans," wrote the original Broadway music. Prolific screenwriter Joseph Schrank adapted the Broadway script for the screen, and lyricist Harold Arlen, who had worked on productions for the Cotton Club, conceived several new songs for the film, such as the hit "Happiness Is a Thing Called Joe."[53]

A dreamlike musical of love and fidelity, *Cabin in the Sky* features the plight of faithful Petunia (Ethel Waters), whose husband Little Joe (Eddie Anderson) is torn between a life of gambling and a life of piety. Tempted by siren Georgia Brown (Lena Horne) and a sizable lottery winning, Little Joe seems bound for hell until Petunia's prayers save him. Although Joe does end up in a cabin in the sky in heaven with Petunia (although it is later revealed that the whole story has just been a dream), it is only because both Petunia and Georgia Brown have done the good deeds to take him there. Little Joe is little changed; however, Petunia and Georgia control the direction of the film and undergo significant personal reexaminations. Thus, *Cabin in the Sky* largely becomes a commentary on the agency of black women, who are much more dimensional than the men onscreen. The men remain largely buffoons and criminals; the nuances in the female roles are often achieved at the expense of their male counterparts.

Ethel Waters as Petunia may initially appear to embody the Mammy role—donning the requisite bandana—however, she makes it clear from the onset that while she is in love with Little Joe, she is no fool. She realizes that gamblers have been cheating her husband with loaded dice before Joe ever does, and she is quick to throw Joe out of the house when she believes he is involved with Georgia Brown. Yet, even more than her character's acts of strength, Waters's musical narration of this film is what ultimately makes it a story about her own predicament in love and her ability to use faith in coping with hardships. Having directed Waters previously, in the Broadway musical *At Home Abroad*, Minnelli considered Waters his "talisman" in ensuring the success of the film. In particular, Minnelli credited Waters's "very expressive face and eyes" in her smooth transition from stage to screen; it is the individuality that Waters imbues in Petunia that separates her from a stock character.[54]

However pious she may be, when Petunia enters Club Paradise, she lets the town know that she can sing and seduce as well as any siren. It is in her rendition of Georgia Brown's signature song "Honey in the Honeysuckle" that Petunia inverts the mammy figure, demonstrating that even a faithful housewife can exhibit an unadulterated sexuality. Attracting the attention of playboy Domino, who had initially come to Jim Henry's club to see Georgia Brown, Petunia takes on the highly sexualized role, but not without claiming her financial entitlement as Little Joe's wife to his good fortune

Tensions arise between Petunia (Ethel Waters) and Georgia Brown (Lena Horne) at Jim Henry's club in Cabin in the Sky *(1943). (Metro-Goldwyn-Mayer/Photofest)*

(since he won the lottery), despite his having taken up with Georgia Brown. Although the film presents the message that Petunia might not get into to heaven due to this seductive new behavior, it nonetheless shows that Petunia, not her husband, is ultimately in control of her destiny.

In addition to its portrayals of women, film scholar James Naremore notes, *Cabin in the Sky* provides a critical, biting commentary on black urban life. This is most explicit in Club Paradise, the center of gambling, violence, and overt displays of sexuality, which contrast with the serenity of the countryside.[55] Film historian Paula Massood contends that the film represents much of the "antebellum idyll" central to prewar all-black musicals such as *Hallelujah* and *The Green Pastures*, countering the pastoral countryside with the sinful, demoralizing city. For Massood, *Cabin in the Sky* is one of several cinematic fantasies that serve the purpose of both diminishing and castigating African American migration to urban centers in the twentieth century.[56] However, the film moves beyond merely presenting urban space as a center of vice. Although it seemingly advocates a return to rural roots, best illustrated in Joe's life with Petunia, it nonetheless demonstrates that the city is where the most daring artistic expressions occur. Not only do famed performers such as Duke Ellington play at Club Paradise, but the explosive dancing (undoubtedly influenced by Dunham's stage choreography) provides a display of individual interpretation and physical freedom. In addition, the film further challenges racial stereotypes by calling attention to urban life as an antidote to the previously romanticized, rural images of black men and women down on the farm or the plantation. As Naremore contends, *Cabin in the Sky* becomes part of "the breakdown of a pastoral, the death of a bogus authenticity, and the growing urbanization of black images in Hollywood."[57] From the movements inspired by Dunham and the voices of Horne and Waters that demonstrate how black female creativity and talent can extend meaning beyond racial conventions, *Cabin in the Sky* delivers a message about women's choices. While the film ends with Little Joe's self-discovery, it is the stories, songs, and actions of Georgia and Petunia that provide texture to the film's trajectory.

Well aware of the potential protestations of some in both the black press and the liberal white press, Minnelli nonetheless proceeded with his plan for *Cabin in the Sky*, particularly upon the urging of Lena Horne. Although Horne portrays a sexy siren in the film, her involvement in the film's production—which led to her first major role in a feature film—illustrates her significance in the future of racial representations in film. Her Georgia Brown was not a complete departure from the Jezebel stereotype; however, it was a more complex version of black female sexuality, particularly when upstaged by the bravado of Ethel Waters. While Horne stayed true to the pinup girl iconography that boosted her stardom throughout the 1940s, she nonetheless also demonstrated an important artistic agency by influencing directors such as Minnelli and in pushing for the constant inclusion of black Americans in popular culture. Although Horne would come to represent a certain sophistication and dignity that separated her from her portrayal of Georgia Brown (and was much more consistent in her *Jubilee* appearances), she nonetheless understood the sexually charged Georgia Brown as a critical role in her own career.[58]

Like *Cabin in the Sky*, *Stormy Weather* (Fox, 1943) began as a product of white liberal interests who sought to improve upon racial imagery, yet their vision was perhaps too ambitious for wartime Hollywood. Broadway playwright and producer Hy Kraft wrote the film; Kraft had previously worked with black performers and denounced all forms of racial inequality. In his autobiography, Kraft claimed that the film was not very "significant" as it "successfully skirted the real issues of racism"; still, he asserted that the film was progressive in relative terms with "none of the phony Uncle Tom clichés or the pseudo-religious hoopla of the usual Hollywood minstrel-type musicals."[59] Others working on the film slowly encountered obstacles from executives at Fox, who, despite the good intentions of producer Zanuck, eliminated the more "original" material. Black composer William Grant Still quit the project after disputes with music directors. Still charged that *Stormy Weather*'s music was "degrading to colored people" and refused to participate in a production that would "aid white tradition."[60] Furthermore, as Thomas Cripps contends, middle-ranking producers did not have the patience or financial willingness to develop a more innovative film that would have required several revisions and an extended production schedule. Thus, although Kraft, Zanuck, and other liberals at Fox may have hoped that the film would please Walter White and the NAACP, in the end this racial progressivism did not "trickle downhill" to most of the production's directors.[61]

Still, the cultural impact of *Stormy Weather*, particularly the ways in which it furthered positive representations of black men and women onscreen, is important. *Stormy Weather* dramatizes the stage career of dancer Bill Williamson (Bill Robinson) and his relationship with performer Selena (Lena Horne). Although Selena is not a complete departure from conventional depictions of woman—with the major emphasis on her beauty and talent as a singer—she is, nonetheless an independent woman who makes her own career choices. While fulfilling the male gaze, Selena simultaneously aids the career of Bill Williamson; her connections give Bill his first professional opportunities. As a departure from minstrel caricatures, *Stormy Weather* offers a more sympathetic portrayal of the trials black performers must face: the meager pay, the scheming of opportunists who attempt to exploit them, and the reality that even the most talented must start at the bottom. In Selena's second encounter with Williamson, she finds him busing tables and sweeping floors at a nightclub. When Williamson does get his first break, he must defy the production script by performing an impromptu solo dance to get noticed. In essence, these scenes illustrate the complicated trajectory of personal artistic development, a message that not only transcends race but represents an inversion of gender conventions. For it is Bill Williamson, not Selena, who must fight to become a star.

This is not to say the film completely advocates female independence. Although Selena initially refuses to give up her career to become a wife and mother when her relationship with Bill becomes more serious, that defiance quickly fades when she later changes her priorities. Selena, like *Cabin in the Sky*'s Petunia, does not challenge expectations of the domestic roles that women should carry out; Selena is also far from the savvy, quick-witted journalist played by Tallulah Bankhead in *Lifeboat*. However, in the context of cinematic representations of black women, Selena exerts an agency uncommon in other roles of the period. Much of this is due to the actual participation of Lena Horne in the making of both *Cabin in the Sky* and *Stormy Weather* and her indelible influence in the larger wartime iconography. While Selena's world of show business depends on her physical appearance and the generosity of men, *Stormy Weather* posits that a black woman not only can determine the course of her career but can become the central attraction in the larger scope of commercial entertainment.

As the producers of the film attempted to recognize the contributions of black Americans in the military, *Stormy Weather* also pays tribute to black cultural achievements that are equally patriotic. Initially, the film applauds Bill for his service in World War I, but it is his dancing that ultimately represents true service, exemplified in a scene where he performs a solo instead of dancing a primitive tom-tom dance with the rest of the cast. Moving about the stage, leaping from drum to drum, Bill not only illustrates creativity and personal interpretation, but in defying his boss, Chic Bailey, who embodies the snobbish black bourgeois, Bill demonstrates the benefit of own individuality. In essence, Bill sends the message to refute common conventions—his solo is his ticket to a future in the entertainment industry.

This notion of individual artistic agency resonates throughout the film, as major performers such as Fats Waller, Cab Calloway, and the Katherine Dunham dancers all offer different glimpses of black performance styles. Like *Cabin in the Sky*, *Stormy Weather* highlights black leisure sites as important arenas of personal expression and community. Although *Stormy Weather* provides a cavalcade of stars performing some of their most famous music, it is not only for the enjoyment of the film's audiences; it attests to the centrality of song, dance, and other forms of expression for the black patrons within *Stormy Weather*'s nightclubs and ballrooms. Although a film about Bill and Selena, *Stormy Weather* also concerns black men and women who lend important meaning to these performances. The film does not treat the issues of segregation or discrimination; how-

Lena Horne (as Selena) and Bill Robinson (as Bill Williamson) in the musical
Stormy Weather *(1943). (Twentieth Century Fox Film Corporation/Photofest)*

ever, when it comes to entertainment, leisure sites, and matters of artistic choice, politics come to the fore.

As depictions of black culture, *Cabin in the Sky* and *Stormy Weather* are most notable because they provided employment for a large number of black actors and had bigger budgets than their prewar predecessors. As Massood explains, "[*Cabin in the Sky*] indicates a shift away from the production values of earlier black-cast musicals toward the look and feel of a Hollywood studio production."[62] Significantly, far more black actors performed in these films than in more racially conscious war films, demonstrating not only the willingness of Hollywood to bank on the profitability of all-black films, but also its interest in giving more black men and women visibility. Although the films might not have urged American audiences to think very differently about race relations, they undoubtedly propelled the careers of many artists, including Lena Horne, while introducing the choreography of Katherine Dunham to a mass audience. Thus, these motion pictures produced less immediate, though important, gains for black actors, opening up more opportunities for individuals in the future.

While the government did not sponsor these films, the response of the BMP is quite telling, as all-black musicals were more reminiscent of existing cultural programs based on black separation, such as the *Swing Mikado*. As the cultural context of these productions had changed since the 1930s, and as the wartime impetus for the obliteration of racial stereotypes had become all the more pronounced by both the NAACP and the BMP, these films resonated quite differently within the federal agency. The BMP expressed its distaste for both pictures, indicating that neither fulfilled its established war aims. Balking at the amoral nature of many characters in *Cabin in the Sky* and describing Little Joe as "the embodiment of shiftlessness and illiteracy," the BMP criticized the film's promotion of racial stereotypes. "The fact that the film is an all-Negro one also contributes to the feeling of segregation of Negroes," wrote reviewer Peg Fenwick. "This type of presentation . . . not only sets them apart from other Americans but portrays them . . . as unfit for the responsibilities of citizenship."[63] Although the BMP was able to make some small changes in the script of *Stormy Weather*, mainly giving more authenticity to Bill's return from World War I, it still claimed that the film did not "illustrate constructively the stake of the Negro in the war, or his proper place in the American way of life." As with *Cabin in the Sky*, the BMP cautioned against the danger of an "exclusively Negro picture," declaring that the visual presentation of separation could foster racial disunity.[64] Along with many staffers, the BMP's overseas administrator, Ulric Bell, revealed extreme hesitance in distributing these films to allied nations as "any material presenting the Negro in a menial or ridiculous light is bad medicine for overseas consumption."[65] As American segregation was already fodder for the enemy, these films that enforced racial separation could not help in propagating the cause of democracy.

Making its bourgeois sensibilities evident, the NAACP stated outright hostility towards *Cabin in the Sky*, charging that it stymied their cultural goals. "Lena Horne, who is a talented actress and a very charming and ladylike person, is required . . . to do vulgar things that they would not think of having a white actress do," Walter White exclaimed in his evaluation of the film.[66] Objections to the film from both white and black individuals poured into White's office, including a note from *Cabin in the Sky* screenwriter Marc Connelly, who reported that the film did not correspond to his treatment, and that he had instructed MGM not to connect his name to the film.[67] When NAACP executive board member A. P. Tureaud asked White about the possibility of boycotting *Cabin in the Sky*, he responded that the NAACP was not endorsing such action.[68] Tureaud agreed, noting the financial damages a boycott would have on the Lincoln and Circle Theaters in New Orleans, which were members of the NAACP and "constant contributors to our programs."[69]

Yet Walter White revealed less opposition towards *Stormy Weather* than he did towards *Cabin in the Sky*. Commending his friend Fox executive Darryl F. Zanuck on the studio's willingness to release the film during the race riots in Detroit, Harlem, and Los Angeles in the summer of 1943, White emphasized the film's political function rather than its questionable content. "In times of tension affirmative presentation particularly where persons of different races and creeds are shown on screen as getting along together is more important even than in times of peace," White told Zanuck.[70] Why White characterized the all-black musical as an interracial picture is unclear; however, it seems that his concerns lay mainly with the cinematic promotion of black actors during a time of racial strife. Perhaps White mischaracterized the film for Zanuck's sake, in order to underscore the importance of liberal studios such as Fox, which would not let racial antagonism prevent their showing race-related films.

Many others opposed these all-black musicals, such as *Hollywood Correspondent* reporter Peter Furst, who told Walter White that *Stormy Weather* supported the idea that "colored people are all right if you keep them in their place."[71] In the *Pittsburgh Courier*, Porter Roberts told the producers of "all-colored motion pictures," "Yes, gentlemen, the Negro of these United States has come of age. . . . So why not start now to concentrate on more suitable themes for modern colored America."[72] One article in the *Baltimore Afro-American* charged that *Cabin in the Sky* illustrated the "misguided" efforts of Hollywood, citing the film as the dramatization of the "Hollywood black man," a "frightened, cringing creature who is either cheaply, naively sanctimonious or a shootin', killin', drinkin', gamblin', sexin' man."[73] Furthermore, the *Afro-American* drew attention to the protestations of *Stormy Weather*'s music supervisor, classical composer William Grant Still, who refused to follow directions to make "Negro music" crude and "Negro dancing" erotic.[74]

Despite much criticism, positive acclaim also abounded. Black newspapers highly anticipated the release of these films, with much discussion of the music, casting developments, and premiere dates. Reporting that MGM spent $1.5 million on *Cabin in the Sky* and that it was the first all-black film that Hollywood had produced in several years, the black press tended to emphasize the major recognition of black talent in the two films. Giving no criticism of the type of music or racial depictions offered in *Cabin in the Sky*, one article in the *Baltimore Afro-American* called MGM a "pioneer in the field of the all-colored production."[75] The *Pittsburgh Courier*'s Billy Rowe praised *Cabin in the Sky* for having an "eloquence and dignity that is by all odds the most stirring offering that had been yet seen with an all-colored cast."[76] Likewise, *Stormy Weather* was elevated above "run of the mill musicals," becoming the "hottest thing in town," according to the *Courier*.[77]

Yet many of these positive reviews, particularly concerning *Cabin in the Sky*, acknowledged that not all black audiences would appreciate these films. Billy Rowe cautioned that *Cabin in the Sky* would "not please the intelligent Negro, for in it the dice game is prominent, along with ignorance and the zoot suit." Rowe was, however, able to dismiss these more degrading elements, stating that they were given "such a fine touch and so filled with meaning."[78] Another reviewer recommended the movie but made sure to qualify the recommendation: "If you can forget the opening scene, including Miss Waters's condescending to 'crap-shooting' . . . the dis' dat' and Is yo' of Rex Ingram, then you can enjoy the superb acting and musical background of the film."[79]

Some theater owners indicated that many were less than eager to see these films. In Barbourville, Kentucky, Paul Mitchell reported a disappointment in his "colored crowd," whose attendance was not high for *Stormy Weather*.[80] In Chicago, one theater owner wanted to discourage the studios from making any more "all Negro cast pictures," like *Cabin in the Sky*, because some patrons resented the show.[81] Canadian W. R. Pyle described *Stormy Weather* as only playing well to "those who appreciate Negro talent . . . but those are in the minority in small towns."[82] Others, however, provided the opposite reactions. "Good for any small town," one Oklahoma theater owner claimed, stating that *Cabin in the Sky* could "certainly get the folks out."[83] In Louisiana, the film drew "both White and Negro patrons," leading theater owner J. D. Leger to assert that the film could "please the public anywhere."[84] Charles Richlieu of Florida indicated that his initial skepticism was put to rest when "the very best people in town" turned up at a showing of *Cabin in the Sky*.[85] As the large majority of the theaters reporting successful attendance were located in southern towns, the films' use of familiar racial stereotypes undoubtedly attracted those most comfortable with such depictions. These positive reports of southern theater owners indicated that for their patrons, all-black musicals were an acceptable genre at a time when race relations were particularly explosive.

In contrast to the broad acceptance of the FTP's Negro Units and performances such as the *Swing Mikado* in the 1930s, significantly, many individuals opposed the idea of an all-black musical in 1943. In the 1940s, no black-cast motion pictures were under black direction (or government sponsorship); Hollywood never expressed the same kind of racial, political, and aesthetic goals that W. E. B. Du Bois and other black intellectuals long professed. Their aim was for black theater to develop out of an organic community, and they understood that some types of separatism could be beneficial rather than detrimental.

At the same time there were differing perceptions of the entertainment genres by World War II. In the 1930s, theater's highbrow status affected public expectations; because it was "art," audiences could appreciate the blackening of classics such as the plays of Shakespeare, or even original performances featuring black casts as an acceptable experimental venture. Theatrical audiences were self-selecting, and as much as FTP project directors advocated a theater for the masses, theater's cosmopolitan patronage remained constant; certainly the appeal of the *Swing Mikado* was primarily due to its turn on a familiar classic. However, insofar as the theater was a manifestation of "high" culture, the audiences that it drew in could be open to all-black performances in part because they never anticipated the potential for mass appeal endemic to the film genre.

As commercial entertainment, films bore the burden of popular audience expectations—a definition of "popular" that had not applied to the theater since before the Civil War.[86] In addition, the scale and profitability of film, coupled with its status within the cultural hierarchy by the 1940s, made it primarily a vehicle for interracial understanding in the eyes of black leaders. Of course, the changing racial priorities that the war commanded shifted ideas about the cultural promotion of racial separatism. While there had been films controlled by black directors and producers, most famously Oscar Micheaux, by World War II the idea of "race pictures" for black audiences was decidedly out of vogue. For one thing, the war had only increased black expectations that White America would come to recognize their role as citizens, emphasized in combat films and others with liberal themes. Furthermore, the support of white activists in the labor movement and in left-wing political organizations in the 1930s and 1940s led many black leaders to espouse the idea that equality could come through interracial efforts. Thus, if audiences appreciated the *Swing*

Mikado as a "Negro play" in 1938, by 1942 these ideas were no longer compatible either with the cultural politics of war or the developing civil rights movement.

They're in the Army Now

All-black musicals exposed varying opinions on black cultural priorities and representations of separatism. Yet, in advancing the OWI's mission to convey a "people's war," Hollywood also produced several films that heightened the status of black Americans through the symbol of a multiethnic platoon. The OWI manual for Hollywood expressed that the American production worker was "one of us . . . he is a Chinaman, a Negro, a Greek, a Pole"; following this sentiment, the combat film genre underscored racial heterogeneity.[87]

Revealing the greatest departure from racial stereotypes and offering the most direct pronouncements of racial equality, combat films such as *Bataan* (MGM, 1943) conveyed a world absent of racial discrimination. Scripted by future MGM producer-turned-liberal activist Dore Schary and prolific screenwriter Robert Hardy Andrews, this film starkly differed from products of government-sponsored culture in depicting racial integration as an unquestioned reality. Dramatizing the experience of a multiethnic platoon that attempts to prevent Japanese military advancement in the Philippines, *Bataan* depicts both the height of American sacrifice and the brutality of the Japanese enemy. Illustrating the friendship and respect among naïve privates and veteran soldiers, *Bataan*'s platoon features two Filipinos, a Mexican American, and a black American as equal in fighting for the same cause. As each man performs a task critical to their military objective as well as the platoon's protection, the film condemns those who seek individual pursuits and applauds the value of teamwork.

Essential to the platoon's survival is Wesley Epps, played by black actor Kenneth Spencer. When Sergeant Bill Dane (George Murphy) first encounters his regiment, he immediately learns that Private Epps is an expert in demolition. Epps not only participates in the more dangerous and skilled tasks, such as rigging a bridge for explosion, but he is often solely responsible for the lookout post when it is known that the Japanese are encroaching. Epps never questions the commands of the white sergeant, as some of his comrades do, and he reflects a dignity and experience that distinguishes him from some of the more overzealous men. During combat, Epps displays skill in various forms of weaponry, separating him from some white soldiers who have never before used a gun. Epps's deftness as

Multiethnic platoon in Bataan *(1943). (MGM/Photofest)*

a soldier even manifests in his death; he is unavoidably stabbed from behind while killing another man. Epps does not die because he is careless
or overeager to attack the enemy, as is the case with many of the soldiers in
Bataan (and everyone in the platoon dies). Rather, he becomes a casualty
of war because he is outnumbered by the enemy—a fact of war that is out
of his control.

The OWI immediately commended the role of Epps. In his review of the
Bataan script, BMP reader Robert Andrews praised the film for its dramatization of "the part of the Negro race in the war." For Andrews, Private Epps
came across as "efficient, brave, and intelligent"; Andrews expressed his
assurance that the film would alter racial attitudes, "inasmuch as there is
still prejudice in some quarters."[88] This enormous understatement, ignoring the strict policy of segregation in the army, revealed that on many levels
the OWI did not find the disparity between image and reality to be problematic. In characterizing the film as a depiction of a "cross-section of America

... as a people's army fighting the people's war," OWI officials were able to invent a nation where patriotic duties erased racial inequalities. Receiving the official stamp—"This picture makes an important contribution to the Government's War Information Program"—*Bataan* exemplified a film that not only suited the OWI's wartime democratic rhetoric, but which also addressed the NAACP's interest in creating positive roles for black actors.[89] In response, Walter White issued a laudatory public statement: "The National Association for the Advancement of Colored People Thanks and Congratulates Metro-Goldwyn-Mayer Pictures on *Bataan* which give those at home a needed brutal picture of what war really is; and shows how superfluous racial and religious prejudice are when common danger is faced."[90]

Sahara (Columbia, 1943), written by radical screenwriter John Howard Lawson and based on a prewar Russian film, also demonstrated the critical role of blacks in American military endeavors, placing a Sudanese soldier at the center of an Allied military strategy. During the North African campaign, a motley crew of soldiers, led by Sergeant Gunn (Humphrey Bogart) struggle to keep a tank moving through the desert while searching for water. Along the way they encounter Tamboul (Rex Ingram, who had performed with the FTP), a Sudanese corporal who leads them to the nearest well. Tamboul not only displays a great deal of knowledge of the local geography but also defends the rights of an Italian soldier who pleads with Sergeant Gunn not to leave him stranded in the desert. Tamboul's presence in the platoon also serves to emphasize American antiracism; when a captured German soldier objects to being searched by Tamboul, claiming the Sudanese soldier is part of an "inferior race," Sergeant Gunn sarcastically tells the German to rest assured that Tamboul's black skin "won't come off on your pretty uniform." When the men reach the well, Tamboul refrains from drinking water before filling canteens for the other men (he merely licks his hands in between canteens) and refuses the help of a fellow soldier who offers to relieve him from his duty. The exchange between these two men is particularly telling, as the white soldier relays some misconceptions about Africa. Asked if he has two hundred wives, like other men in Sudan, Tamboul replies that men are only permitted to have four wives. He, however, only has one wife. To this, the white soldier comments, "you sure learn things in the army," to which Tamboul asserts, "yes, we both have much to learn from one another."[91]

This discussion not only presents a black man as moral and restrained, but also raises the larger issue of integration. As the men agree that they share common experiences and enjoy each other's company, *Sahara* re-

Scene from Sahara *(1943), starring Humphrey Bogart (second from left) and featuring Rex Ingram (second from right) as Tamboul, a Sudanese corporal who provides vital assistance to a mixed-race Allied squad in the desert. (Columbia Pictures/Photofest)*

lates the potential productivity of a racially mixed army. Of course, Tamboul is not an American, and he represents African support of the Allied cause; nevertheless, he illuminates the possible gains through interracial cooperation. And as he resiliently battles a German soldier who escapes the Allied fort, ultimately saving the lives of some of his comrades while losing his own, the black soldier demonstrates a willingness to fight for democracy at any cost. Like Wesley Epps in *Bataan*, Tamboul exhibits a skill and courage equal to his white counterparts; his white colleagues view him as vital in fulfilling their military mission.

Upon reading the final *Sahara* script, one BPR reviewer had some criticisms of the Tamboul character. Exclaiming that this role demonstrated the military abilities of "the native African soldier and by implication, the American Negro," the reviewer expressed concern that Tamboul might come off as "unnecessarily heroic." Because he directed the troupe to the well in a sandstorm and did not drink the water when rationing it for others, the reviewer described Tamboul as a "sort of Gunga Din," setting him apart from the other soldiers.[92] Ultimately, these suggestions received consideration; in guiding the tank through the sandstorm, Tamboul wears the same goggles as the other soldiers, and when he collects the water from the well, he licks his hands in between filling canteens. With these changes, the reviewer was satisfied that Tamboul became "a convincing brother-in-arms."[93] These types of comments illustrate the sense of balance that producers struggled to maintain; overly emphatic representations of black patriotism might render some depictions invalid, while portraying black soldiers as less heroic than their white counterparts would raise the ire of many audiences.

Most notably, the OWI reviewers praised the film for "driving home the United Nations idea" articulated in the previously discussed Government Information Manual.[94] Citing the film as "one of the best," Ulric Bell, director of the BMP's overseas bureau, urged that *Sahara* be shown in liberated areas.[95] As *Sahara* extended the idea of a "people's war," it buttressed ideas about foreign alliances with a visual projection. The Government Information Manual advised that "We must understand and know more about our Allies . . . our hope for a decent future world lies in this understanding."[96] Constructing Africa (via Tamboul) as one of these allies spoke to the need for racial understanding, not only among Americans but also with the people of other nations. As with *Bataan*, the NAACP praised the producers of *Sahara*, saying that it proved the success of White's Hollywood campaign. "Since July 1942 several companies have made films in which they state that an attempt has been made to improve the role of the Negro," an NAACP press bulletin reported, "but in the opinion of this Association, Columbia Pictures Corporation in 'Sahara' has made the outstanding contribution toward the objective stated by Mr. White."[97]

As revealed in the exhibitor trade journal, the *Motion Picture Herald*, visions of an integrated army or of a strong Sudanese soldier did not seem to raise objections from American audiences, many in small towns and rural areas. Charles Brooks from Marshfield, Missouri, stated that *Bataan* did extra business for his theater; F. R. Christ of Loveland, Oklahoma, regarded *Bataan* as a "nice war picture . . . everyone liked it."[98] Some theater owners stated the film discouraged the attendance of women and children, due to its often "gruesome" nature; Arthur Dame of Penacock, New Hampshire, attributed lower audience turnout to a general "clamor against war pictures."[99] According to these exhibitors, Americans were becoming rather tired of combat films, but as war films went, *Bataan* was "excellent and well liked."[100] *Sahara* received similar reviews from theater owners, albeit suffering the same fate of other war pictures, which one owner charged were "pushing off the business slowly but surely."[101] There were many, however, who reported high attendance at the film. "This picture brought out people that I had never seen in the theatre," D. L. Craddock of Leaksville, North Carolina, wrote.[102] Other southern theater owners such as Benton Roy of Mansura, Louisiana, indicated that the film was widely applauded, playing to a "packed house."[103]

The fact that certain southern and rural audiences seemingly did not object to these particular depictions of racial equality suggests that these white audiences accepted these films as fictional worlds. It is also likely that American audiences in general were swept up into the larger narrative of sacrifice and heroism, these included, and were therefore able to overlook the racial intermixing that in other contexts may have been more troubling. After all, *Bataan* and *Sahara* advocated a solely masculine form of integration, based on a fraternity of soldiers in the absence of women. Without the taboo of white women and black men, military integration was possibly more acceptable in the realm of representation, although many white theatergoers would have strongly objected to it in reality.

Bataan and *Sahara* also did not provoke any charges from the black press, which could have understandably become angry at the films' blatant misrepresentation of segregation in the military. Instead, newspapers such as the *Pittsburgh Courier* hailed *Bataan* as "another great war film," for its "presentation of a stalwart Negro hero," and for opening new roles to actors such as Kenneth Spencer.[104] The black press often referenced the great opportunities given to actors such as Spencer and Ingram, regardless of the fact that they were contributing to a false portrayal of American race relations. These newspapers and the NAACP evaluated the struggle for representation within the history of racial imagery and found the roles of Ingram and Spencer to be groundbreaking. Of course, the issue of structural reforms was not far from view—many in the black community saw better roles as a path to improving racial attitudes, which could eventually eradicate discriminatory barriers. Yet, in the black press, the connection between broader civil rights and cultural representation was not made explicit in discussions of these films, even when the pages preceding the film reviews spoke directly to the need for racial reform.

For instance, the same issue of the *Baltimore Afro-American* that championed *Bataan* for its depiction of Wesley Epps as part of an integrated platoon also condemned segregation in public accommodations.[105] In one article entitled "Take Segregation and Like It," the *Baltimore Afro-American* quoted John Kerr, Speaker of the North Carolina House of Representatives: "Unless colored are willing to recognize certain fundamental principles . . . such as segregation and control of affairs, it seems that your people have an unhappy future in front of them."[106] While the entertainment sections glorified *Bataan* and *Sahara*, other sections simultaneously derided the military for discrimination. For instance, the *Baltimore Afro-American* described quota restrictions affecting the employment of black nurses, stating, "The plan to limit the number of colored nurses in this war also represents an extension of the army's policy of race segregation."[107] Another article in the *Pittsburgh Courier* exposed discrimination against black Americans in aviation, quoting the president of American Airlines as stating that "the Negro would have to become more cultured before he could expect to enjoy the fullness of American life."[108] Furthermore, while one *Baltimore Afro-American* article could overlook the more stereotypical aspects of *Cabin in the Sky* to laud it as a "production of real worth," the same issue of the paper could not ignore other barriers to racial equality. Describing the "color prejudice which is shared by both management and unions" in Baltimore's industrial plants, the article flatly critiqued the practices stifling black advancement.[109]

That the black press was less likely to condemn cultural representations of black individuals as unrealistic illustrates a major difference in the struggle for civil rights versus that for cultural emancipation. As black journalists viewed racial depictions in film within the larger history of representation, they did not necessarily ignore discriminatory practices in industry and the military, but they may have realized that those practices did not affect popular perceptions of an improving racial imagery. And because critics such as the *Courier*'s Billy Rowe understood that the advancement of black Americans was being sought on several fronts—that of politics, employment, education, and cultural representation—it was possible for many journalists to separate images such as fictionalized integration from the reality of segregation. Within the struggle for cultural emancipation, black individuals employed a distinct set of criteria to determine progress; while they praised many films that may have contradicted larger aims for structural equality, African Americans evaluated this imagery on its own terms.

The film *Lifeboat* (Twentieth Century Fox, 1943) illustrated a strong contrast with combat films such as *Bataan* and *Sahara*. Depicting the plight of passengers on an Allied freighter that is torpedoed by a German U-boat, *Lifeboat* traces the obstacles these men and women encounter while trying to navigate to the nearest post. The cast comprises Americans with a

Cast of Lifeboat *(1943), featuring Canada Lee (far right) in a controversial role as the lone black man on a lifeboat adrift at sea. (Twentieth Century Fox/Photofest)*

variety of backgrounds, ranging from Connie Porter (Tallulah Bankhead), an aristocratic journalist, to Kovac (William Bendix), a mechanic in civilian life, to Joe (Canada Lee), a black steward. The role of Joe is very different from the black roles in *Sahara* and *Bataan*: Joe is deferential to the white passengers; his past employment as a pickpocket is revealed and utilized in the plot; and he remains visually separated from the others. As some OWI reviewers themselves remarked, Joe's presence in the movie was less necessary and vital than that of Tamboul or Private Epps, making the role seem merely tokenistic. John Steinbeck penned the short story the film was based on, and it was directed by Alfred Hitchcock. The screenplay was written by Jo Swerling, who was simultaneously advising the War Department on *The Negro Soldier*. All things considered, *Lifeboat* seemed a promising outlet for new racial representations. However, much of Steinbeck's original storyline was lost as Swerling altered the script and as there developed "a slippage of everything they [Steinbeck, Hitchcock, and Swerling] agreed upon." When he saw the film, Steinbeck asked his agent to remove his name from the credits.[110]

There are, however, several moments in the film that underscore Joe's morality and rationality. When the passengers discover that a German has climbed aboard the boat, the other survivors take a vote on whether or not to let him stay. When asked how he would vote, Joe, taken by surprise, asks, "I get a vote?" "Why certainly" replies one of the white passengers. Joe declines this opportunity, stating, "Guess I'd rather stay out of this." Joe's initial reluctance to denounce the German as a traitor strongly contrasts with the other passengers. While passengers decide to allow the German to remain on board because they are dependent on his maritime skills, upon discovering that the German has been hiding his own flask of fresh water, they decide to physically attack him and throw him overboard. Joe, however, refrains from the brutal mob violence, exhibiting a calm restraint, and he demonstrates his compassion for humanity in a recitation of the Twenty-third Psalm upon the suicide of another crewmate, speaking the words that others are unable to remember. Joe, however, does not hesitate to confront aggressors when real danger is imminent. When another victim of submarine warfare swims up to the boat and is revealed as a German, the passengers take him aboard on account of his injuries. Without hesitating, the German pulls a gun on the group, which Joe deftly knocks out of his hand before the trigger can be pulled.[111]

Lifeboat affords Joe the same dependable status as the other black men in combat films. What he lacks is social equality, illustrated through his rank as steward and his visual separation from other characters, even within the confined space of a lifeboat. When the camera pans to Joe, who mostly speaks only when spoken to, the frame often singles him out, moving the white passengers to separate visual spaces. This cinematic segregation may be because, unlike the combat films, *Lifeboat* depicts an arena integrated also by gender. Joe is never on the same side of the boat as the white women—his only close physical contact with them comes when they are all thrown about during a storm. As contact between black men and white women was a predicable hot button for southern audiences, the producers of *Lifeboat* may have been more wary when interracial sex could be inferred in any way. Joe's deference and essentialistic traits effectively restrict him from the white women (who are quickly paired romantically with the white men). Had the lifeboat been occupied entirely by men, it is possible that Joe's character would have received a different treatment.

Although the BMP expressed several concerns in its readings of the *Lifeboat* script, particularly in regard to the character of Joe, Twentieth Century Fox did not incorporate most of the suggestions for revision. In many script and production reviews over the course of the summer and fall of 1943, BMP reviewers indicated that Joe was not only "treated patroniz-

230

ingly" by some of the white characters, but that in presenting a racial separation, the film "follows Nazi propaganda lines which attempt to divide the United Nations by strengthening racial barriers."[112] In the last evaluation of the production, the BMP reviewer continued to criticize the character of Joe, claiming, "it is unfortunate that the only member of a minority race aboard should be characterized as a former pick-pocket."[113] For these and other reasons, namely that the German character seemed superior to his "weak, decadent and materialistic" American counterparts, the overseas bureau of the BMP recommended against *Lifeboat*'s distribution to nations abroad.[114]

Equally displeased with the completed film, the NAACP condemned Twentieth Century Fox for its demeaning characterization. As NAACP reviewer Donald Jones remarked, "Joe Spencer (Canada Lee) . . . sat glooming in 'his' corner of the boat . . . behaving generally after the manner of a steerage passenger rather than an equally beset participant in a grim struggle for survival."[115] Jones insisted that actor Canada Lee had made the most of the part by acting with "great reserve and dignity," while trying to downplay the more stereotypical aspects of the character. NAACP acting secretary Roy Wilkins wrote directly to Twentieth Century Fox vice president William Goetz, expressing extreme dissatisfaction with the studio's treatment of black Americans. "The results thus far have been disappointing," Wilkins charged, regarding Fox's failure to carry out its initial promise to improve roles for black individuals. "Our disappointment has been keenest in connection with your feature 'Lifeboat.'"[116]

Like reviewer Donald Jones, Harry Levette of the *Baltimore Afro-American* commended Lee for his performance, noting that Lee had fought to omit the more demeaning material. According to Levette, Lee was responsible for the elimination of several of the "Yessirs" and "Nosirs" that dotted his character's dialogue in the script, which were not fitting for a black sailor "in such a democratic locality as the lifeboat of a torpedoed ship."[117] Unlike the NAACP, however, Levette cited the role of Joe as "Best Yet for Colored." Levette stated that some of Joe's scenes would have a great impact on the film industry, because they had "never been written before into a film plot."[118] It is possible that Levette reviewed the film favorably in the fall of 1943, because at the time, he had only heard of it. By January 1944, after the film's release to the public, the *Baltimore Afro-American* described the more negative aspects of the character, although with some explanation for the film's treatment. The paper took issue with the fact that Joe was first called "charcoal" by another passenger and was shown separate from other characters. It reported that although Lee objected to being called charcoal, he was informed that reshooting would be too expensive; on the issue of his perpetual isolation, the film's scenarist told Lee that his character was a loner who did not opt to take part in group activities. The *Afro-American* did not question the credibility of these explanations, perhaps because it had endorsed the film months earlier, but also because it still sought to appreciate newer types of roles for black actors, regardless of their shortcomings.[119]

While *Sahara*, *Bataan*, and *Lifeboat* commented directly on American race relations under the conditions of war, *The Ox-Bow Incident* (Fox, 1943) dramatized a historical incident to invoke issues relevant to wartime democratic aims. Depicting the actions of a lynch mob in Ox-Bow, Nevada, in 1885, the film utilized the ever-popular Western genre to provide a stinging representation of unjustified violence. In the film, word has spread that cattle thieves have murdered a local rancher named Kincaid. In a fury, the townsmen (and one Calamity Jane–type woman) organize to lynch the men responsible for Kincaid's death, led by Major Tetley, a bloodthirsty Civil War veteran who still wears his Confederate uniform. Some townspeople discourage unlawfulness and urge the men to wait for the sheriff; in the end, however, the will of the mob triumphs. When the mob finds three men with cattle that bear Kincaid's brand, they are condemned to die. Professing their innocence, claiming that they bought the cattle from Kincaid, these men beg for a fair trial. Yet the mob is relentless in their desire to avenge the death of Kincaid, so they lynch the men, only to find out afterwards that Kincaid is not dead after all.

While the horrific injustice in *The Ox-Bow Incident* surrounds the fate of white men, it undoubtedly made larger reference to contemporary lynchings directed mainly towards black Americans. During the film, a black preacher named Starks (Leigh Whipper) is one of the few who attempt to stop the lynching and wait for the sheriff's intervention. Indicating that his brother was lynched by a mob without proof of guilt, Starks testifies to the effects of lawlessness while demonstrating a morality that others clearly lack. When Major Tetley asks the crowd to vote on whether to proceed with the lynching or wait for the sheriff, Starks is the first to vote against violent action. Ultimately, he and the seven others who oppose the lynching are outweighed, and their protestations have little recourse. Although Starks had accompanied the mob in his capacity as a minister, he takes a very personal stand against lynching, alluding to violence that many black people faced in the 1940s.

PROJECTING UNITY

The BMP applauded *The Ox-Bow Incident* for its powerful message, heralding it as an exemplary vehicle for addressing contemporary concerns. Relating the film to its war aims, the BMP viewed the evils of Fascism through Major Tetley, who needed to "satisfy his craving for power over his fellow man." Illustrating how easily an enemy could manipulate the rhetoric of democracy and testifying to the powerlessness of the few in the face of a law-rejecting mob, the film would only serve to heighten American vigilance against "forces of violence and injustice." Staying true to its wartime goals, the BMP particularly appreciated the depiction of the "forces of democracy," which were "several men of various occupations and race." With particular support for the character of Sparks, who "steps out alone to uphold the way of justice," the BMP endorsed this racial representation as "an excellent illustration of the fact that the Negro people have always been closely linked to our democratic heritage and fight courageously to preserve it."[120]

With less attention to the film's internationalist metaphor and more discussion over the issue of lynching, the NAACP promoted the film as an honest portrayal of mob violence. Studio heads at Fox clearly sought the reaction of key figures such as Walter White and Roy Wilkins, inviting them to a private screening of the film. The film thrilled White, who commended Fox for a "magnificent job . . . in presenting the story of lynching so courageously." Relating an increase in racial violence, White informed Fox vice president William Goetz of a particular lynching in Shubuta, Mississippi, in which there was "no foundation at all for the charge which was made." Stating that *The Ox-Bow Incident* could only heighten public consciousness about this horrific act, White declared that the film was "most opportune."[121] Marguerite Cartwright, Walter White's friend and neighbor, who also attended the private screening, expressed her relief that Hollywood did not obscure the issue of lynching by adding a love story or plot twist that saved the men from being hanged. Cartwright also praised Fox for its willingness to confront more controversial issues that might not reflect an immediate box office draw. Yet, Cartwright also critiqued the film for stereotyping Starks as a "soul-saving religious Negro"; in addition, she questioned the remorse of the lynchers after they discovered that their victims were innocent (citing the frequency of a "carnival spirit" after many lynchings). Thus, even as Fox produced a film that black leaders such as White viewed as highly effective in the pursuit of racial justice, some black individuals still argued that a more realistic dramatization could have been achieved.[122]

Whether American audiences received *The Ox-Bow Incident*'s message is dubious. Mayme Musselman of Lincoln, Kansas, reported that the movie "didn't make us any friends," while an Oklahoma theater owner stated that many of his patrons complained or walked out because they could not understand the film.[123] In Penacock, New Hampshire, theater owner Arthur Dame hesitantly recommended the film as "an interesting picture if you go for lynchings." As perhaps the only one who commented on the film's message, stating it was "something or other against them [lynchings] as a form of punishment," Dame's reaction illustrated that the interpretations of the BMP and NAACP may have not been echoed in public reception.[124] With the film's historical framework and more symbolic references, *The Ox-Bow Incident*'s antilynching politics and their relation to democratic rhetoric were perhaps less clear to audiences. As the topic of lynching was a sensitive issue, particularly in rural and southern areas, theatergoers may have preferred escapist fare or combat films to those that tackled issues close to home. The poor reception to *The Ox-Bow Incident* may partly explain why Fox, led by racial progressive Zanuck, did not more aggressively challenge the racial status quo in its later film, *Lifeboat*; however, *The Ox-Bow Incident*'s production indicates that Fox made a serious attempt initially to satisfy the suggestions of both government administrators and the NAACP.

What sets *Bataan, Sahara, Lifeboat,* and *The Ox Bow Incident* apart from government-sponsored culture, in genres such as theater or radio, is that they not only offer the visual scenario of racial integration but also focus selectively on black men. Although *Lifeboat* featured both men and women, the only black person included in this group was a man, reinforcing the assumption that the black member of the group should represent heroism, sacrifice, and other traits wedded to conventions of masculinity. Indeed, the most progressive racial imagery in wartime films was the province of men, with official support only furthering these representations. Of the black men who played roles in multiracial war films, most had performed in the FTP. Canada Lee, Rex Ingram, and Dooley Wilson (of *Casablanca*) had all been part of the New York Negro Unit, playing lead roles in performances such as *Stevedore, Haiti,* and *Androcles and the Lion*. It also offered them earlier opportunities to perform in nonstereotypical roles and to experiment with their craft. For these men, the FTP also had allowed them to continue working during the Depression years and had led to careers in film.[125]

Other films, such as *Since You Went Away* and *Stage Door Canteen* fulfilled some of the NAACP's requests in providing secondary roles for black actors and presenting racially mixed crowds. Yet the government's most direct acknowledgement of black contributions to American life was the documentary *The Negro Soldier*, discussed in chapter 4. Although the 1944 film was a widespread promotion of black military achievements, it lacked the racial suggestiveness of some Hollywood motion pictures. Eschewing mention of any controversial subjects, such as slavery or segregation, the film applauded the history of black soldiers without giving attention to any racial strife. In its presentation of black accomplishments, *The Negro Soldier* was more reminiscent of the FWP's historically oriented American Guide Series than some of the more forward-oriented images within the film genre.

Thus, with its virtual laundry list of black involvement in American wars, the film stood in contrast to motion pictures such as *Bataan* and *Sahara*, which offered a promising glimpse into an integrated army. While the purpose of *The Negro Soldier* was indeed to inform white Americans that black individuals comprised a large part of American military history, it focused more on intraracial cooperation, glossing over the segregation that made such a film necessary. But as was evidenced in the Joe Louis programs and the *Jubilee* radio show, by 1944 more sanitized celebrations of black accomplishments had become an effective tool within government-sponsored culture. Thus, *The Negro Soldier* functioned as traditional propaganda, supporting a multiracial nation while simultaneously crediting the military institutions that ironically enforced racial inequality.

Most black critics did not complain about the film's omission of more controversial issues. Langston Hughes called it "the most remarkable Negro film ever flashed on an American screen."[126] Others, such as Kansas City's Sumner School principal F. Leslie Clark declared that the film "dispels any idea that the American Negro is a non-entity in the contributing factors which have made the United States a great nation."[127] Yet the *Chicago Defender* also incorporated the views of the film's detractors, quoting one reviewer in *Time* magazine: "'The makers of the film have not included any of the dynamite implicit in a truly forthright treatment of the subject. There is no mention of segregation, of friction between Negro soldiers and White soldiers and civilians.'" Yet, even as it expressed skepticism, the *Time* article assured readers that the picture would still "'mean more to Negroes than most white men could imagine.'"[128] And indeed, the film had an enormous impact, playing to most soldiers who went through the army's Information and Education training programs. In the midst of a segregated army, the film announced to white servicemen that their black counterparts had been a vital part of the American military experience, making it more difficult for white soldiers to deny that African Americans performed the duties of any American citizen.

Once again, the black community supported a film that masked any sign of racial inequality. As with other films, most blacks were willing to overlook the disparity between image and reality although, unlike the Hollywood motion pictures, *The Negro Soldier* was not fictional. Black people could praise a "real" film that glossed over the harsher aspects of life because it still undergirded important representational politics. Inasmuch as the War Department portrayed black men and women with honor because they advanced the cause of democracy, *The Negro Soldier* provided a national challenge to racial stereotypes. Whether it also challenged segregation was seemingly a nonissue to someone like Langston Hughes, who most emphatically stressed the "quality of dignity throughout."[129] Therefore, government-sponsored cultural programming might not address the need for political and economic reform, but for black individuals like Hughes, this was not always necessary—calls for "cultural self-determination" were occurring on a separate, albeit related, front.[130]

The Negro Soldier advanced the potential of more honest films depicting black life. For Carlton Moss, former director of the FTP's New York Negro Unit and screenwriter for *The Negro Soldier*, the film promised to "go a long way to break down the taboo against Negro pictures in Hollywood." Moss was a major driving force in the film's development and promotion; he asserted that the film had shown Hollywood that white audiences would accept a "full length serious Negro film," leading him to pursue the production of another full-length documentary film covering black troops.[131] This follow-up film, *Teamwork*, produced for the War Department, documented the Red Ball Express, which supplied the Allied fighting forces following the invasion at Normandy. *Teamwork* confirmed the critical role of the convoy's primarily black drivers who cooperated with white servicemen to defeat the enemy. Yet because the film was completed after the German surrender, it received little government promotion as officials turned their attention to the occupation of defeated nations. While civilian audiences viewed *Teamwork* in 1945 as a "sort of liberal moral victory," it did not gain the recognition of *The Negro Soldier* due to its lack of immediacy.[132]

While military audiences warmly received *The Negro Soldier*, its presentation in commercial theaters was another matter, particularly in the South. In Memphis, the notoriously scissor-happy Motion Picture Board of Censors prohibited the showing of the film; in parts of Arkansas, Mississippi, and Kentucky, the film was also restricted. As an article in the *Pittsburgh Courier* explained, a bloc of southern politicians had relayed the idea that the film would not sell because of its "'controversial' nature."[133] Although some exhibitors did not show the film, others were persuaded by black leaders such as Truman Gibson and Carlton Moss that the film was a good investment. By May 1944, the film had played in approximately two thousand theaters as a forty-minute feature; when it was released in a shorter version, it played to about five thousand houses, with 80 percent of them catering to white theatergoers.[134]

The censorship of *The Negro Soldier* in some southern cities may seem surprising, given the ostensible acceptance of *Bataan* and *Sahara*. In fact, a 1943 article in the *Baltimore Afro-American* had predicted some degree of censorship, or at least southern distaste, for *Sahara* and *Bataan*; reports from the exhibitor journal *Motion Picture Herald*, however, did not indicate significant opposition to these films.[135] Yet southerners frequently cut African American scenes, or banned the films altogether. In Memphis, censors cut Cab Calloway from the film *Sensations of 1945* and Lena Horne from *Broadway Rhythm*; the *Pittsburgh Courier* charged that southerners refused to accept any films that "place the Negro on a basis of social equality with the whites."[136] But it was not just that these films presented black people as respectable, middle-class citizens; much of the censorship of Horne in *Broadway Rhythm* and particular scenes in *Stage Door Canteen* involved interracial contact between men and women or featured black women as too sexually provocative for a white audience. Interestingly, neither the black press nor exhibitor reviews mentioned southern objections to *Stormy Weather*, which featured many black actors as dignified, well-dressed characters. Yet as an all-black musical, the film did not threaten the racial status quo by offering "inappropriate" interracial contact.[137]

While *The Negro Soldier* did not threaten southern racial or gender conventions, it nonetheless touched on an equally explosive issue. *The Negro Soldier* was not a Hollywood motion picture, but rather a War Department documentary testifying to the equal status of black servicemen. If the film did not portray the reality of segregation, southerners may have taken this omission as a sign of the government's confidence in the institution's eventual demise. Many southerners viewed black military participation with intense hostility, as racial violence in southern training camps illustrated. As the film could only have heightened blacks' expectation and favorable attitude towards securing equality, southerners revealed their anxieties. The worlds of *Bataan* and *Sahara* were fictional, brought to life by actors such as Humphrey Bogart. *The Negro Soldier*, on the other hand, dramatized the plight of armed black men and pronounced them honorable American citizens. Thus, for many in the South, this cultural embodiment of racial advancement could be a potent catalyst for civil rights legislation and activism.

THE BMP UNDOUBTEDLY contributed to the production of wartime motion pictures; one statistic states that from September 1943 to August 1944 alone, the BMP reviewed approximately 390 screenplays, with their changes implemented in 71 percent of the films.[138] However, of these screenplays, many of which were never produced, few included racial themes. Although World War II ushered in some new racial representations in film, movies such as *Bataan* and *Sahara* were rare. Only about a dozen films addressed racial issues in some context, and though more films featured black people on screen, they were mostly performing in secondary roles or as extras. Thus, whatever radical ferment may have existed within Hollywood and the OWI, it was largely contained by political conservatives, southern censors, and a racially sensitive white public. Still, Hollywood films of the 1940s were not irrelevant to the nascent civil rights movement; their development represented not only Hollywood's receptiveness to the needs of the black community but also the willingness of some American audiences to accept new forms of racial imagery.

By 1944, Hollywood producers were acknowledging that black moviegoers constituted a significant segment of consumers, and in the "highly competitive post-war period" it would be more than necessary to maintain a positive relationship with black audiences. Aware that black patrons contributed approximately 10 percent of box office receipts and that demands for black entertainers such as Fats Waller and Dorothy Donegan had increased, Hollywood producers understood that cinematic reforms would not be limited to the war years.[139] By the summer of 1944, several groups, such as the Writers' War Board, the Entertainment Industry Emergency Committee, and the American Guild Artists were demanding that the motion picture industry obliterate racial stereotypes and ensure that no one was "alienated" in the industry based on their "race or religion."[140] Insisting that the public should "see the colored man in his true light," the Writers' War Board, composed of prominent authors, playwrights, and radio scriptmen, urged that Hollywood take a cue from *The Negro Soldier* and immediately feature black individuals as an "essential part of the armed forces."[141] Responsive to this and other requests, several studios vowed that they would endow "race characterizations" with "dignity and propriety," while avoiding racial slurs.[142]

The dialogical relationship between the black community and the motion picture industry persisted after the war. Racial issues would always be a thorny subject for the motion picture industry, and as the black struggle for civil rights gained momentum in the postwar era, Hollywood would confront the challenge of representing black Americans amid dramatically heightened political expectations. By utilizing the most popular cultural medium of film, the government strongly asserted that black Americans made critical contributions to the existence of a democratic nation. Yet, the federal government had less control over officially sponsored films than it did in other cultural genres, and Hollywood motion pictures sometimes promoted more progressive imagery than federal productions. Films such as *Bataan* and *Sahara* demonstrated how, as an outside agency, Hollywood at times had more autonomy to disseminate more provocative messages, even under conservative scrutiny. Indeed, it was the undeniable official- ness of *The Negro Soldier*, as well as its sense of realism—something that was blurred in the imaginary world of Hollywood motion pictures—that drew southern protest.

After the war, the legacy of a liberal ethos proliferated in message films such as *Home of the Brave* (1949), *Pinky* (1949), and *Intruder in the Dust* (1949). Racially conscious motion pictures and the celebration of black actors such as Sidney Poitier mirrored the larger political changes in the postwar period. The desegregation of the armed forces and the legal and social challenges to southern segregation endowed antiracist films with a sense of urgency, bringing image and reality closer to one another. Yet, like the New Deal era, when the mass media softened the official reticence towards racial reform, in the postwar period cultural projects still served the government's interest on matters of race. The cultural apparatus that developed during the New Deal era continued to project America's demo- cratic ethos during the Cold War; integrationist messages resonated over the radio and in motion pictures. In the midst of racial strife, however, pressures for structural change were rising from within and without. Even as African Americans ultimately obtained the kind of civil rights legislation that the government had always been reluctant to endorse, the postwar era continued to witness the contested cultural politics that had shaped black freedom struggles since Emancipation.

EPILOGUE

After he received the seminal civil rights report, *To Secure These Rights* (1947), President Harry Truman expressed outrage towards the prevalence of racial violence and discrimination in America. After discovering that African American veterans had been murdered in several southern states, he declared, "I can't approve of such goings on and . . . I am going to try to remedy it and if that ends up in my failure to be reelected, that failure will be in a good cause."[1] This statement reveals a larger executive commitment to civil rights than Franklin Roosevelt was ever willing to advocate. In creating a Presidential Commission on Civil Rights and issuing his 1948 executive order to ensure "equality of treatment and opportunity for all persons in the armed services, without regard to race," Truman demonstrated an unprecedented presidential interest in the rights of African Americans.[2] If the New Deal era provided the foundation for the civil rights movement, political divisions that had plagued the passage of racial legislation since Roosevelt's first term still remained. Viewing Truman as the ultimate "scalawag," southern legislators remained devoted to the cause of white supremacy, opposing the elimination of the poll tax and the creation of a permanent Fair Employment Practices Commission. After the 1948 election, an alliance of southern Democrats and Republicans in Congress blocked Truman's proposed civil rights measures. While this coalition temporarily stalled federal action, Truman's promotion of racial justice had a profound influence on politics in the postwar period. As historian William Leuchtenburg argues, Truman "had placed civil rights irrevocably on the national agenda, had reconfigured America's election maps, and had set in motion a chain of events that made the greater achievements of the 1960s possible."[3]

If the Truman presidency offered hope for federal intervention, Dwight Eisenhower advocated a more conservative commitment to civil rights. Milestones such as *Brown v. Board of Education* and the Montgomery bus boycott demonstrated the growing success of black activism; however, these seminal events did not prompt a wide-scale executive campaign to end racial injustice. Eisenhower's sympathetic stance towards southerners, coupled with his belief in states' rights, led him to enforce desegregation sporadically, feeling legally bound to defend the integrity of the courts. As Eisenhower's attorney general, Herbert Brownell, later recalled, "I knew that he [Eisenhower] was a strong supporter of states' rights, and although certainly not opposed to the cause of civil rights, he did not intend to be a crusader on its behalf."[4] While many white liberals and African Americans criticized Eisenhower's tardy response to the Little Rock crisis, claiming it demonstrated the president's general disinterest in racial issues, the Eisenhower administration did bring about legislation that would anticipate the federal policies of the 1960s. Developed largely by civil rights advocate Brownell, the 1957 Civil Rights Act established a bipartisan commission on civil rights and provided federal protection for black voting rights and other civil liberties. The Eisenhower administration also initiated antidiscriminatory policies in Washington, D.C., as well as promoting greater racial diversity within government positions. Still, the president's commitment to civil rights was always confined to federal sectors, as he had no interest in using the executive branch to promote desegregation in the South. Therefore, while the administration's racial policies served to reflect "an official image of racial democracy," the president's "pattern of hesitancy and extreme political caution" largely protected white Southerners.[5] Yet, with rising criticism from the international community, the Eisenhower administration would actively promote culturally based programs to buttress America's Cold War democratic rhetoric.

As historian Mary Dudziak argues, American segregation and discrimination provided fodder for the Soviets, who charged that America's racial practices were inimical to the nation's espousal of democratic values. For countries in Latin America and Africa, where the fight against American racial discrimination was seen as part of a larger global struggle against anticolonialism, progress in American civil rights initiatives became increasingly imperative to preserve important international alliances. During the Cold War, global politics forced American policy makers to consider the nation's racial practices in a very different context than they had in previous decades. While both Roosevelt and Truman may have initiated some forms of antidiscriminatory legislation to maintain black loyalty and to sustain the African American presence within the Democratic Party, by the 1950s federal neglect of civil rights potentially threatened to disrupt vital diplomatic ties. Furthermore, increasing media coverage of the southern civil rights movement ensured that images of American racial violence would reach the international community.[6]

A sustained federal initiative in promoting America's democratic values took shape in State Department tours featuring prominent jazz musicians. From the mid-1950s to the late 1970s, several prominent jazz artists including Louis Armstrong, Duke Ellington, and Dizzy Gillespie spanned the globe delivering America's "authentic" culture—jazz—to vital diplomatic regions. As the celebration of performers in integrated jazz bands could potentially counter charges of American racism, the tours offered an alternative to representations of violence and brutality pervading the global media. Although the State Department tours differed from the cultural programs of the 1930s and 1940s in their international focus, the tours were an extension of the government's impulse to rely on cultural programs as a political tactic. In initially endorsing what they believed to be less politically threatening artists such as Ellington and Armstrong, while attempting to bar more critical and outspoken figures such as Paul Robeson and Josephine Baker from performing for foreign audiences, government officials continued to highlight those black culture heroes most compatible with Cold War aims. Yet, like the *Jubilee* shows, the performances of African American musicians could not always be contained, nor could State Department officials anticipate the political opinions that artists would deliver. As historian Penny Von Eschen explains, even though the government designated some black performers as ideal "jambassadors" at the onset of the State Department tours, their increasing criticism of the federal government by the 1960s further complicated the execution of this cultural policy. In particular, Louis Armstrong had publicly condemned Eisenhower's reaction to the Little Rock crisis, voicing solidarity with black Southerners. Due to the government's ineptitude in enforcing racial equality in 1957, Armstrong refused to continue touring for the State Department over the next three years. In this case, government officials had to weigh the potential harm from performers' criticism against the positive impact musicians could bring about (and the international reputations they had already established) in maintaining amicable ties between the United States and those nations susceptible to the influence of the Soviet Union.[7]

The State Department tours continued over the course of three decades, even after the passage of the Civil Rights Act of 1964. While the federal government had finally endorsed the kind of legislation that African Americans had long struggled for, officials still believed that the tours were necessary in promoting America's democratic ideology and in providing other countries with jazz as a "race-neutral expression of American freedom." By the mid-1960s, when race riots pervaded American cities and hostility to the Vietnam War escalated, the priority of maintaining international goodwill remained imperative. Yet, as more and more African Americans embraced Black Nationalism, black performers internalized their music as part of the African Diaspora rather than as an American construction, as State Department officials believed. Von Eschen argues that it was the complexity of meaning within performances that led to their transnational appeal. If the American government intended for artists to project American racial harmony, for some international audiences, performers often served as symbols of resistance to an oppressive racial hierarchy. Like the black men and women who attended the *Swing Mikado* or servicemen who listened to *Jubilee*, some audiences in Africa and Asia did not take these cultural forms merely as indications of black inclusion into white America but as pronouncements of black politics that transcended national boundaries.[8]

While the government's reliance on cultural programs was still resonant in the State Department tours, a broader integrationist vision began to permeate the larger cultural landscape, even in the absence of real integration. Much of the iconography and narratives that the federal government had adopted in the 1930s and 1940s was reutilized in postwar commercial culture, in a way that would symbolically compensate for federal unwillingness to aggressively pursue civil rights. By the end of World War II, many white Americans began to associate racism with the horrors of genocide, and benign interracial cooperation became much more compatible with anticommunism. If anticommunist films warned of the loss of individuality within the totalitarian machine, tolerance of racial and ethnic diversity posed as a form of resistance against the Communist menace. Admittedly, anticommunists frequently charged African Americans and Jews with being agitators, fueling racism and anti-Semitism during the period; however, the larger message of racial liberalism acquired a resonance that would have been unimaginable before World War II. Particularly within the film industry, where traditional minstrel images were becoming less visible, presentations of an integrated society were a frequent invention. The multiethnic platoon featured in war films such as *Bataan* became a staple in postwar motion pictures featuring domestic issues. Integrationist films such as *Blackboard Jungle* demonstrated how African Americans (particularly black men) were able to better white society by becoming part of it. As film historian Thomas Cripps explains, however, liberal "message movies" often did not feature more than one major black character—the "lone black figure who lends dignity and color to the proceedings."[9] Therefore, films created in the McCarthy era espoused the incompatibility of racism and democracy, while still staying within the confines of the period's consensus ideology.[10]

In the music industry, particularly amid the increasing popularity of rock and roll, integration became a fixture of the genre, not only in the collaboration of black and white artists, but as black voices made their way into white American homes over the airwaves. Artists such as Chuck Berry and Little Richard delighted middle-class white teenagers who sought alternatives to the more saccharine tastes of their parents, and many black musicians offered a style, talk, and movement that their white counterparts frequently emulated. While the popularity of black R&B artists often reified white assumptions about black sexuality and promiscuity, rock and roll music nevertheless facilitated an imagined integration, at least for the younger generation. In addition, the relationships between white and black musicians who collaborated in the early development of rock and roll demonstrated a significant cultural interchange. "Oh we're Negroes too," Buddy Holly declared when asked if there had been conflict between white and black performers during a recent rock and roll tour. "We get to feeling like that's what we are."[11] These sentiments were not unique; whether in the racial ventriloquism of Elvis Presley, or the promotion of black musicians by white producers such as Sam Phillips, rock and roll was rooted in a vibrant interracial dialogue.

Yet the creation of rock and roll did not represent an even process of exchange with equal rights and cultural authority provided to artists of both races. More sanitized white performers continued to cover the work of black artists, and African Americans faced inferior treatment on tours and during performances. Even as television phenomenon *American Bandstand* promoted countless black artists onstage, the program still relegated African Americans to less frequent, tokenistic roles as dancers and members of the studio audience. Although *Bandstand* host Dick Clark credited the influence of black musicians in rock and roll's development, integrating the program in 1957, African Americans offstage did not reap the benefits of the music's popularization.[12] Yet rock and roll music was not a total manifestation of white cultural appropriation; it became a metaphor for real possibilities of integration, and the very public connections between white and black performers largely contributed to the ideology of postwar racial liberalism. This progressive cultural arena, however, did not translate to concrete forms of social and political change. As Pete Daniel explains of rock and roll's unfulfilled promise, "In their desire to gain musical insight, musicians created a blueprint for racial cooperation that was lost on both political leaders and most whites."[13]

By the mid-1960s, however, neither the federal government nor the white American public could ignore black civil rights, with the movement in full force and all of its violence and brutality captured on television. Yet, if African American activism reached an apogee in the 1960s, the period also witnessed a new kind of separation of politics and culture in the black political agenda. As Brian Ward explains, some of the most famous black musicians disengaged themselves from the movement, particularly in the early years of the decade. Discouraged by producers such as Motown's Berry Gordy and fearful of alienating white fans, many prominent R&B artists such as James Brown and Sam Cooke did not associate themselves as directly with political causes as black artists had done during the New Deal era.[14] While groups such as the Student Nonviolent Coordinating Committee (SNCC) utilized particular cultural media to reinforce their politics — particularly through the dissemination and popularization of protest music — SNCC and the Southern Christian Leadership Conference (SCLC) did not emphasize the need for cultural autonomy as a pressing political goal. Certainly civil rights leaders understood the significance of utilizing various forms of popular culture, particularly television coverage, to garner public support; however, this focus was vastly different than the political conceptualization the NAACP had been advocating for decades. In the agenda of the organized political movement there was a fissure between the struggle for voting rights, integrated facilities, and antidiscriminatory legislation, on the one hand, and the need for representational agency and cultural self-determination, on the other.

This would not be the case for long. As the tactics and objectives of black activists transformed into the promotion of Black Nationalism by the mid-1960s, the relationship between culture and politics was most pronounced. If Black Nationalism, and more specifically the Black Arts Movement, represented disillusionment with mainstream civil rights strategies, it revealed a more explicit recognition that the cultural realm must refashion African American identity and self-preservation. Like Sterling Brown, Carlton Moss, Langston Hughes, and so many other seminal cultural figures of the 1930s and 1940s, black nationalists sought out what they believed to be more authentic representations of African Americans, advocating for control over the promotion of racial imagery, and aspiring to create self-defined notions of blackness independent of white influence. Viewing the voice of the folk as the center of "real" art, divorcing itself from white artists concerned with formal literary or dramatic standards, the Black Arts Movement reflected the passions of many African Americans in the Harlem Renaissance and later through such federal programs as the FWP and FTP. Yet, while an older generation of African American writers and artists deeply influenced the cultural nationalism manifest in the Black Arts Movement, there was also a historical distinctiveness to the movement. As cultural activist Larry Neal, a critical figure in developing the Black Arts Movement, critiqued the Harlem Renaissance: "It failed to take root, to link itself concretely to the struggles of that community, to become its voice and spirit. Implicit in the black arts movement is the idea that black people, however dispersed, constitute a *nation* within the belly of white America."[15] More avowedly explicit in its social and political purpose, and more forceful in its abandon of white cultural expectations, the Black Arts Movement built upon the rhythms of bebop artists while embracing Africa as a source of aesthetic liberation. Furthermore, as scholar James Smethurst explains, the Black Arts Movement bore regional variations in the 1960s and 1970s, and the nature and content of African American art depended on the contours of local black political organizations, black colleges and universities, cultural institutions, and publishing venues.[16]

By the late 1960s, Black Nationalism demonstrated a far-ranging influence on American culture. Popular music reflected black pride, as artists such as Aretha Franklin and James Brown called for black assertiveness; the development of so-called blaxploitation films provided a new kind of black cultural hero who refused to cater to the demands of white America. Yet, if Black Power provided African Americans with defiant political figures, this ideology also provided white Americans with new ways to proscribe black bodies and sounds. Particularly in athletics, the aggressive, outspoken black man who had been threatening in previous decades—the persona embodied by Jack Johnson at the beginning of the century—became quickly commodified and embraced by white spectators by the 1970s. Discussions concerning black superiority in athletics swirled in national periodicals, viewing aggression and brawn as attributes, rather than cause for white concern. As cultural critic Michael Dyson contends, "the physical prowess of the black body would be acknowledged and exploited as a supremely fertile ground of profit as mainstream athletic society literally cashed in on the symbolic danger of black sports excellence."[17]

By the 1970s, black heroes existed as a permanent fixture in the cultural landscape, as actors, musicians, and athletes. The most damaging impediments to the African American community—segregation and disenfranchisement—were eliminated by law, with the guarantee of federal enforcement against discrimination. Yet, if the civil rights movement succeeded in securing an end to legalized discrimination, it failed to fully reform longstanding economic, political, and social structures of inequality. Neither widespread black political mobilization nor national interest continued in the decades following the movement. As racial inequality in employment, housing, and education persisted, the cultural investment in African Americans only escalated. For African Americans, this has become a double-edged sword. On the one hand, there are an increasing number of cultural role models—individuals who represent black achievement and possibility, often in the face of overwhelming obstacles. These celebrities often contribute substantially to African American education, neighborhood improvement, and political organizations, serving as figureheads, but also drawing national attention to the needs of black communities. On the other hand, however, the prominence of African Americans in entertainment and athletics, and their underrepresentation in politics, major corporations, and other areas has circumscribed racial advancement, as African Americans have fewer avenues to traditional spheres of power. By the end of the twentieth century, corporate investment in black athletes and entertainers had proven itself unimaginably profitable, with seemingly unlimited resources for promotion. Financial capital and public attention remain fixed in the cultural arena.

The proliferation of black culture heroes remains highly dependent on the desire of whites to view African American bodies and to take in the sounds and symbols associated with blackness. While white fetishization of African Americans has always been a central component of American history, the cultural construction of athletes and entertainers at the end of the twentieth century was not solely an updated minstrel show. For one thing, minstrel shows of the nineteenth and early twentieth centuries served to reinforce white identity by representing African Americans only as stereotyped, degraded individuals; however, after 1970, African American performance began to facilitate an erasure of blackness. This is most explicit in Spike Lee's provocative racial critique, *Do the Right Thing* (1989), in an exchange between Pino (John Turturro), the son of an Italian American pizza shop owner, and Mookie (Spike Lee), a black delivery boy. As he tells his father, Sal (Danny Aiello), time and time again, Pino resents catering to a black community, which, he avows, is decidedly inferior; yet after one of Pino's long rants against African Americans, loaded with racial epithets, Mookie confronts him on the hypocrisy of his views. When Mookie asks him to name his favorite athlete, Pino replies it is Magic Johnson. His favorite movie star? Eddie Murphy. His favorite rock star? Prince. To all this, Mookie exclaims, "Sounds funny to me. As much as you say 'nigger this' and 'nigger that,' all your favorite people are niggers." For Pino, however, this is not a contradiction at all: "It's different. Magic, Eddie, Prince, I mean, are not black. I mean, they're black, but not really black. They're more than black. It's different."[18]

The ability for athletes and entertainers to become "more than black" has important political ramifications, as the popular acceptance of these individuals across the color line contributes to the public perception that racial inequality is a part of history rather than a present concern. Those individuals in the culture industry more frequently achieve racial transcendence, in contrast to many African American politicians who often become racialized and therefore seemingly less accessible to white Americans. National attention to the persistence of black poverty, unemployment, and discrimination is sporadic at best, often requiring publicity from influential black celebrities. The contemporary complexities of African American cultural achievement, however, should not obscure the origins of what was historically a positive development for black men and women. Before the 1930s, African Americans only appeared in a popular iconography that reduced them to minstrel tropes. Not until the Roosevelt administration aspired to maintain black political support and loyalty by promoting racially inclusive cultural programs did the federal recognition of black contributions, artistic talents, and heroic potential become a part of American culture. Even as officials shied away from structural legislation, government-sponsored programs still represented a pivotal moment in the struggle for black civil rights. From the African American communities represented in the FWP's state guidebooks to the black soldiers featured on screen alongside white servicemen, American culture increasingly offered more ways for audiences to envision African Americans. Cultural emancipation was finally within reach.

Here lies the irony of this book. In the Roosevelt era, the process of cultural exchange and the progress of black cultural advancement significantly affected both African American participants and America's broader racial iconography. Yet, in the postwar era, the national impulse to continue promoting black culture never paralleled a sustained federal commitment to eliminating racial inequality. Even with the achievements of the civil rights movement and the passage of federal antidiscriminatory legislation, the American tendency to solve political problems with cultural solutions has never quite waned.

In 1993, the newly elected William Jefferson Clinton chose distinguished black author Maya Angelou to deliver a poem at his inauguration. As only the second poet ever selected to read at an American presidential inauguration—the other was Robert Frost in 1961—Angelou reached an unparalleled level of recognition, not only as an African American but also as a woman. For Clinton, Angelou embodied the message of racial tolerance and diversity he hoped to project to the people of color who had elected him into office. For Angelou, however, her poem "On the Pulse of Morning" offered an opportunity to reflect on the nation's blighted history and to call for political change:

> You, the Turk, the Arab, the Swede, the German, the Eskimo, the Scot,
> You the Ashanti, the Yoruba, the Kru, bought,
> Sold, stolen, arriving on the nightmare
> Praying for a dream.
> Here, root yourselves beside me . . .
>
> I am yours—your passages have been paid.
> Lift up your faces, you have a piercing need
> For this bright morning dawning for you.
> History, despite its wrenching pain
> Cannot be unlived, but if faced
> With courage, need not be lived again.[19]

Here, Angelou seeks a national reexamination, arguing that a confrontation with racial injustice can move the country forward. Like Sterling Brown, Duke Ellington, Richard Wright, and many others who, under federal auspices, narrated the painful realities of the black experience in America, Angelou maintains that history proves a most reliable witness. Whether contemporary presidential administrations will respond to Angelou's call and pursue the kind of politics that could truly ensure equal opportunities for all American citizens is uncertain. Undoubtedly, however, whether as culture heroes, political figures, or community activists, black men and women will continue to press for change. The paradox of African American cultural advancement may temporarily obscure the prevalence of American racial inequality, but there will always be voices that testify to its plaguing endurance. With hope, we will eventually hear them.

NOTES

Abbreviations

DRSNA   Division of Recorded Sound, National Archives
FDRL   Franklin D. Roosevelt Presidential Library, Hyde Park, N.Y.
FTP-LC   Records of the Federal Theatre Project, Library of Congress
FWP-LC   Records of the Federal Writers' Project, Library of Congress
FWP-PNAM   "Portrait of the Negro as an American," Outlines Folder,
             Special Studies and Projects, Records of the Federal Writers'
             Project, Library of Congress
GMUSC   George Mason University Special Collections and Archives,
             Fairfax, Va.
LC   Library of Congress
MPBRS-LC   Division of Motion Picture, Broadcasting, and Recorded Sound,
             Library of Congress
MSRC   Moorland-Spingarn Research Center, Howard University,
             Washington, D.C.
NA   National Archives and Records Administration, Washington, D.C.
NAACP-LC   Papers of the National Association for the Advancement of
             Colored People, Library of Congress (and microfilm)

Introduction

1. Eleanor Roosevelt, *This I Remember*, 162.

2. For an examination of southern influence on state policy, see Kryder's *Divided Arsenal: Race and the American State during World War II* (2000). Also see Katznelson, Geiger, and Kryder's 1993 *Political Science Quarterly* article, "Limiting Liberalism: The Southern Veto in Congress, 1933–1950."

3. Interview with Carlton Moss by Lorraine Brown, 6 Aug. 1976, Hollywood, Calif., in GMUSC.

4. Hall, "Long Civil Rights Movement," 1263; Gilmore, *Defying Dixie: The Radical Roots of Civil Rights, 1919–1950* (2008).

5. Singh, *Black Is a Country*, 69.

6. This study is indebted to Barbara Savage's brilliant book, *Broadcasting Freedom: Radio, War, and the Politics of Race, 1938–1948* (1999). Other recent investigations of black cultural politics include Robinson, *Forgeries of Memory and Meaning: Blacks and the Regimes of Race in American Theater and Film before World War II* (2007); Sotiropoulos, *Staging Race: Black Performers in Turn of the Century America* (2006); Erenberg, *The Greatest Fight of Our Generation: Louis vs. Schmeling* (2006); Martin, *No Coward Soldiers: Black Cultural Politics in Postwar America* (2005). Additional titles that analyze cultural expression as part of the civil rights agenda include, but are not limited to, Cripps, *Making Movies Black: The Hollywood*

Message Movie from World War II to the Civil Rights Era (1993); Ward, *Just My Soul Respond-*
ing: Rhythm and Blues, Black Consciousness, and Race Relations (1998); Ely, *The Adventures*
of Amos 'n' Andy: A Social History of an American Phenomenon (1991); Kelley, *Race Rebels:*
Culture, Politics, and the Black Working Class (1996); Rose, *Black Noise: Rap Music and Black*
Culture in Contemporary America (1994); Von Eschen, *Satchmo Blows Up the World: Jazz Am-*
bassadors Play the Cold War (2004); and Feldstein's 2005 *Journal of American History* article,
"'I Don't Trust You Anymore': Nina Simone, Culture, and Black Activism in the 1960s." Of
course, this study is also indebted to Levine, *Black Culture and Black Consciousness: Afro-*
American Folk Thought from Slavery to Freedom (1977).

7. Major titles in this debate include Huggins, *Harlem Renaissance* (2007); Lewis, *When*
Harlem Was in Vogue (1997); Ann Douglas, *Terrible Honesty: Mongrel Manhattan in the 1920s*
(1995); Hutchinson, *The Harlem Renaissance in Black and White* (1995); and Maxwell, *New*
Negro, Old Left: African American Writing and Communism between the Wars (1999).

8. Lewis, *When Harlem Was in Vogue*, xxvii.

9. Ann Douglas, *Terrible Honesty*, 323.

10. This is Lewis's chronology, which signals the moment when African Americans in
Harlem decided to "lay their scissors and pens aside" and to take up traditional forms of
protest. Lewis, *When Harlem Was in Vogue*, 306–7.

11. Hutchinson, *Harlem Renaissance*, 22. While Lewis also highlights this connection,
he still argues that the failure of the Renaissance existed on its own terms, rather than the
legacy it provided in the next decade. Lewis, *When Harlem Was in Vogue*, 292.

12. Hutchinson, *Harlem Renaissance*, 13.

13. Ann Douglas, *Terrible Honesty*, 324; Hutchinson, *Harlem Renaissance*, 22.

14. I credit Grace Hale with this phrase. Hale, "Everyone Is a Negro: Racial Rebellion
from the Blues to the Folk Music Revival," lecture given at the University of South Carolina,
14 Sept. 2006.

15. Hale, *Making Whiteness*. Other studies of racial stereotyping and the formation of
white identity include Lott, *Love and Theft: Blackface Minstrelsy and the American Working
Class* (1993); Roediger, *The Wages of Whiteness: Race and the Making of the American Work-*
ing Class (1991); Rogin, *Blackface, White Noise: Jewish Immigrants in the Hollywood Melting
Pot* (1996); Jacobson, *Whiteness of a Different Color: European Immigrants and the Alchemy
of Race* (1998). For the history of minstrelsy, see Toll, *Blacking Up: The Minstrel Show in
Nineteenth-Century America* (1974); Lhamon, *Raising Cain: Blackface Performance from Jim
Crow to Hip Hop* (1998). For an overall estimation of racial stereotypes across media, see
Dates and Barlow, *Split Image: African Americans in the Mass Media* (1990).

16. Cruse, *Crisis of the Negro Intellectual*, 92.

17. General evaluations of the New Deal include Leuchtenburg, *Franklin D. Roosevelt
and the New Deal, 1932–1940* (1963); and Badger, *The New Deal: The Depression Years, 1933–
1940* (1989). On New Deal liberalism see Brinkley, *The End of Reform: New Deal Liberalism in
Recession and War* (1995); for a study of New Deal political economy, see Colin Gordon, *New
Deals: Business, Labor, and Politics in America, 1920–1935* (1994); for the New Deal's international import, see Borgwardt, *A New Deal for the World: America's Vision for Human Rights*
(2005); for varying perspectives on the character of the New Deal see Gerstle and Fraser,
The Rise and Fall of the New Deal Order, 1930–1980 (1989). Among those who have analyzed
broader connections between mass culture and the New Deal, although not necessarily
in the context of state-sponsored programs, are Lizbeth Cohen, *Making a New Deal: Indus-*
trial Workers in Chicago, 1919–1939 (1990); and Denning, *The Cultural Front: The Laboring*

of American Culture in the Twentieth Century (1997). Barbara Savage is among the few to analyze cultural programs sponsored by the state within the context of New Deal racial ideology. See Savage, *Broadcasting Freedom: Radio, War, and the Politics of Race, 1938–1948* (1999).

18. For various interpretations of the New Deal's chronology, see Gerstle and Fraser, *The Rise and Fall of the New Deal Order, 1930–1980* (1989). Others who evaluate the New Deal as a continuing ethos over the course of the 1930s and 1940s include Denning, *The Cultural Front: The Laboring of American Culture in the Twentieth Century* (1997); Brinkley, *The End of Reform: New Deal Liberalism in Recession and War* (1995); and Gerstle, *American Crucible: Race and Nation in the Twentieth Century* (2001).

19. Some influential titles include Levine, *The Unpredictable Past: Explorations in American Cultural History* (1993); Susman, *Culture as History: The Transformation of American Society in the Twentieth Century* (2003); Denning, *The Cultural Front: The Laboring of American Culture in the Twentieth Century* (1997); Wald, *The New York Intellectuals: The Rise and Decline of the Anti-Stalinist Left from the 1930s to the 1980s* (1987); Stott, *Documentary Expression and Thirties America* (1973); Pells, *Radical Visions and American Dreams: Culture and Social Thought in the Depression Years* (1974); Linda Gordon's 2006 *Journal of American History* article, "Dorothea Lange: Photographer as Agricultural Sociologist"; May, *The Big Tomorrow: Hollywood and the Politics of the American Way* (2000); Buhle and Wagner, *Radical Hollywood: The Untold Story behind America's Favorite Movies* (2002); Erenberg, *Swingin' the Dream: Big Band Jazz and the Rebirth of American Culture* (1998); Stowe, *Swing Changes: Big Band Jazz in New Deal America* (1994); Hilmes, *Radio Voices: American Broadcasting, 1922–1952* (1997); McFadden's 1993 *Journal of American History* article, "'America's Boyfriend Who Can't Get a Date': Gender, Race, and the Cultural Work of the Jack Benny Program, 1932–1946"; and Judith Smith, "Radio's 'Cultural Front': 1938–1948" (2002).

20. Matthews, *Federal Theatre*; O'Connor and Brown, *Free, Adult, Uncensored*; Fraden, *Blueprints for a Black Federal Theatre*; Penkower, *The Federal Writers' Project*; Hirsch, *Portrait of America*.

21. Gilmore, *Defying Dixie*; Denning, *Cultural Front*; Lizbeth Cohen, *Making a New Deal*.

22. Gilmore, *Defying Dixie*, 6; Isserman, *Which Side Were You On?*; Naison, *Communists in Harlem*; Robert Cohen, *When the Old Left Was Young*; Denning, *Cultural Front*, 5–6.

23. For the exclusionary nature of the New Deal, see Graham, *The Civil Rights Era: Origins and Development of National Policy, 1960–1972* (1990); Hall's 2005 *Journal of American History* article, "The Long Civil Rights Movement and the Political Uses of the Past"; and Kessler-Harris, *In Pursuit of Equity: Women, Men, and the Quest for Economic Citizenship in Twentieth Century America* (2001). Accounts of the government's racial policies and black civil rights struggles during the Roosevelt era include Sitkoff, *A New Deal for Blacks: The Emergence of Civil Rights as a National Issue* (1978); Kirby, *Black Americans in the Roosevelt Era: Liberalism and Race* (1980); Korstad and Lichtenstein's 1988 *Journal of American History* article, "Opportunities Found and Lost: Labor, Radicals, and the Early Civil Rights Movement"; Kelley, *Hammer and Hoe: Alabama Communists during the Great Depression* (1990); Sullivan, *Days of Hope: Race and Democracy in the New Deal Era* (1996); Savage, *Broadcasting Freedom* (1999); Leuchtenberg, *The White House Looks South: Franklin D. Roosevelt, Harry S. Truman, Lyndon B. Johnson* (2005); and Gilmore, *Defying Dixie*. For more exclusive focus on the war years, see Sitkoff's 1971 *Journal of American History* article, "Racial Militancy and Interracial Violence in the Second World War"; Dalfiume, *Desegregation of the U.S. Armed*

Forces: Fighting on Two Fronts, 1939–1953 (1969); Dalfiume's 1968 *Journal of American History* article, "The 'Forgotten Years' of the Negro Revolution"; Wynn, *The Afro-American and The Second World War* (1979); Kryder, *Divided Arsenal: Race and the American State during World War II* (2000); and Chen's 2006 *Journal of American History* article, "'The Hitlerian Rule of Quotas': Racial Conservatism and the Politics of Fair Employment Legislation in New York State, 1941–1945." For Roosevelt's judicial policies see McMahon, *Reconsidering Roosevelt on Race* (2004).

24. Skowronek, *Building a New American State*; Gerstle, "Protean Character of American Liberalism"; Heclo, "In-and-Outer System"; Balogh, *Chain Reaction*. Those who focus more exclusively on the relationship between citizenship and the welfare state include Skocpol, *Protecting Soldiers and Mothers: The Political Origins of Social Policy in the United States* (1992); Amenta and Skocpol, "Redefining the New Deal: World War II and the Development of Social Provision in the United States," in Weir, Orloff, and Skocpol, *The Politics of Social Policy in the United States* (1988); Linda Gordon, *Pitied but Not Entitled: Single Mothers and the History of Welfare, 1890–1935* (1994); Kessler-Harris's 1999 *Journal of American History* article, "In the Nation's Image: The Gendered Limits of Social Citizenship in the Depression Era"; Kessler-Harris, *In Pursuit of Equity* (2001); and Canaday's 2003 *Journal of American History* article, "Building a Straight State: Sexuality and Social Citizenship under the 1944 G.I. Bill."

Chapter 1

1. "Crowds Line Route," *New York Times*, 9 June 1939, 1.

2. "King Toasts Peace," *New York Times*, 9 June 1939, 1.

3. "A Program of American Music," 8 June 1939, in White House Office of Social Entertainment, Box 77, FDRL.

4. Ibid.

5. Weiss, *Farewell to the Party of Lincoln*, 28.

6. Ibid., 15–18.

7. Sitkoff, *New Deal for Blacks*, 40–43. On the influence of the South also see Leuchtenburg, *The White House Looks South: Franklin D. Roosevelt, Harry S. Truman, Lyndon B. Johnson* (2005).

8. Earl Brown, "Negroes for Roosevelt," unidentified newspaper clipping, in FDR Papers, President's Personal File, No. 1820, "Negroes," Box 13, FDRL.

9. John T. Gaddis to Franklin Roosevelt, 5 Jan. 1933, in FDR Papers, President's Official File, Group 93, Box 1, FDRL.

10. Kelly Miller, "Trust President Roosevelt," *New York Amsterdam News*, undated clipping in ibid.

11. "Democrats Count on Midwest Negro," *New York Times*, 26 Oct. 1936, 2.

12. Editorial, *Pittsburgh Courier*, 26 May 1934.

13. Harold Ickes to Roy Wilkins, 31 Aug. 1933, in FDR Papers, President's Official File, Group 93, Box 1, FDRL.

14. For the influence of interracialists such as Foreman, Weaver, and Hastie, see Sullivan, *Days of Hope*, 23–67.

15. Brown, "Negroes for Roosevelt," FDRL.

16. Sitkoff, *New Deal for Blacks*, 90–91; "New Deal Starts Negro Vote Drive," *New York Times*, 3 Sept. 1936, 10.

17. Sitkoff, *New Deal for Blacks*, 84–101; Weiss, *Farewell to the Party of Lincoln*, 185.

18. Julian Harris, "Whites Oust Negro under NRA in South," *New York Times*, 27 Aug. 1933, E6.

19. "No New Deal Seen for Negro Labor," *New York Times*, 9 Jan. 1934, 13.

20. "In Defense of the Humble," *New York Times*, 19 Aug. 1933, 10. For more on the campaign for equal wages within the NRA, see Sullivan, *Days of Hope*, 43–52.

21. "The Surrender of F.E.R.A.," *Opportunity*, Dec. 1934, 359.

22. "The Wages of Wretchedness," *Opportunity*, June 1935, 166–67.

23. Alphonzo Harris to Louis Howe, 31 Aug. 1933, in FDR Papers, President's Official File, Group 93, Box 1, FDRL.

24. Ickes to Wilkins, 31 Aug. 1933, in ibid. For more on the appointment of Foreman, see Sullivan, *Days of Hope*, 24–40.

25. James Hoey to Louis Howe, 17 Oct. 1933, in FDR Papers, President's Official File, Group 93, Box 1, FDRL.

26. "The Negro and Federal Jobs," *New York Age*, 27 May 1933, copy in ibid.

27. Lester Walton to Louis Howe, 24 May 1933, in ibid.

28. "The Negro and Federal Jobs."

29. Weiss, *Farewell to the Party of Lincoln*, 157.

30. Eleanor Roosevelt, "The Negro and Social Change," *Opportunity*, Jan. 1936, 22.

31. On Roosevelt and liberalism, see Kirby, *Black Americans in the Roosevelt Era: Liberalism and Race* (1980), 76–96. For southern opposition to Eleanor Roosevelt, see Sullivan, *Days of Hope*, 158–61.

32. "Ickes Tells Negroes of New Deal's Help," *New York Times*, 30 June 1936, 10.

33. Sitkoff, *New Deal for Blacks*, 66–68.

34. Franklin D. Roosevelt, "Informal Extemporaneous Remarks to State Works Progress Administrators," 17 June 1935, in *Public Papers and Addresses*, 4:262.

35. Sitkoff, *New Deal for Blacks*, 70.

36. On Hopkins and antidiscriminatory policies, see Sullivan, *Days of Hope*, 281; and Badger, *New Deal*, 207–8.

37. Sitkoff, *New Deal for Blacks*, 72–78. On Alexander, see Kirby, *Black Americans*, 49–62; and Sullivan, *Days of Hope*, 24–35.

38. National Colored Committee, "Has the Roosevelt New Deal Helped the Colored Citizen?" (1936), in FDR Papers, President's Official File, Group 93, Box 2, FDRL.

39. Although several scholars express competing ideas on the Popular Front's composition, its development in 1935 most commonly refers to a change in the Communist Party ideology. Before Nazism became a grave threat, Communists, who occupied a small minority in America, expressed a radical "third period" ideology based on revolutionary dogma. Distancing themselves from socialists and anyone else who did not advocate their fiery brand of Marxism, the CP in the early 1930s was riddled with factional squabbles and internal dissension. But by 1935, the Popular Front aligned Communists, socialists, civil rights advocates, intellectuals, New Dealers, and other left-wing organizations in the antifascist campaign. The most recent interpretation of the Popular Front as a larger "historical bloc," revealing a laborite mentality among all groups and in several cultural genres, is Denning's *The Cultural Front: The Laboring of American Culture in the Twentieth Century* (1997). For the influence of Communism on the civil rights movement in the South, see Gilmore, *Defying Dixie*.

40. Katznelson, Geiger, and Kryder, "Limiting Liberalism," 285.

41. Leuchtenburg, *White House Looks South*, 59.

42. For Roosevelt's personal feelings on race, see ibid., 56–57. For the influence of southerners, see ibid., 46–60, 134–40; and Sitkoff, *New Deal for Blacks*, 102–23.

43. Franklin D. Roosevelt, "Address before the Federal Council of Churches of Christ in America: 'The Right to a More Abundant Life,'" 6 Dec. 1933, in *Public Papers and Addresses*, 2:519.

44. Charles Houston to Franklin Roosevelt, Apr. 26, 1935; J. E. Spingarn to Franklin Roosevelt, 19 Jan. 1938; James Weldon Johnson to Franklin Roosevelt, 24 Jan. 1938; and Oscar DePriest to Franklin Roosevelt, 8 June 1934, all in FDR Papers, President's Official File, Group 93b, Box 7, FDRL. On the antilynching bill see Leuchtenburg, *White House Looks South*, 57–58; and Sitkoff, *New Deal for Blacks*, 268–97.

45. Walter White to Franklin Roosevelt, 24 Apr. 1935 and attached Senate poll; Walter White, "U.S. Department of (White) Justice," *Crisis*, Oct. 1935; Memorandum from Walter White to Franklin Roosevelt, 2 Jan. 1936; and Walter White to Marvin McIntyre, 15 Feb. 1938, all in FDR Papers, President's Official File 93b, Box 7, FDRL.

46. William Hassett to David Niles, 24 June 1938, and Franklin Roosevelt to Walter White, 25 June 1938, in FDR Papers, President's Personal File No. 1337, NAACP, 1937–44, FDRL.

47. Stephen Early to Malvina Scheider, 5 Aug. 1935, in FDR Papers, President's Secretarial File, Box 173, FDRL.

48. Eleanor Roosevelt to Stephen Early, 8 Aug. 1935, in FDR Papers, President's Personal File No. 1336, NAACP, 1932–36, FDRL.

49. McMahon, *Reconsidering Roosevelt*.

50. Gold, "Intellectual Road to Fascism," 10–11.

51. Mumford quoted in Alexander, *Here the Country Lies*, 203.

52. Matthews, "Arts and the People," 319.

53. McKinzie, *New Deal for Artists*, 6.

54. Under Hoover, the Emergency Relief and Construction Act did authorize the government to allocate money to the states for the purpose of relief, either direct or work relief. The Reconstruction Finance Corporation, the main organ allocating money, however, was considered to be a banking agency (paying more attention to the financial condition of the states which needed help), and little was accomplished in the area of work relief. McDonald, *Federal Relief Administration*, 16.

55. Penkower, *Federal Writers' Project*, 9; McDonald, *Federal Relief Administration*, 27–29.

56. Matthews, "Arts and the People," 321.

57. Mangione, *Dream and the Deal*, 33.

58. McKinzie, *New Deal for Artists*, 5–8.

59. Leuchtenburg, *Franklin D. Roosevelt*, 125; Mangione, *Dream and the Deal*, 40.

60. Borglum quoted in Sherwood, *Roosevelt and Hopkins*, 58.

61. Matthews, "Arts and the People," 318–20.

62. McKinzie, *New Deal for Artists*, 78–80; Matthews, "Arts and the People," 322–23.

63. Alexander, *Here the Country Lies*, 220.

64. Mangione, *Dream and the Deal*, 49, 53–58.

65. One estimation states that by 1940, 160 million people had attended a quarter of a million performances by orchestras, bands, chamber, and operatic groups. Alexander, *Here the Country Lies*, 206.

66. Alfred Jones, "Search for a Useable American Past," 718.

Chapter 2

1. Foreword to National Service Bureau, "A List of Negro Plays," Mar. 1938, Box 937, FTP-LC.

2. Throughout this chapter, I have provided opening performance dates for plays and musicals. Play titles in quotations are those that had no prior performance information and were submitted to the Play Bureau for FTP use. Although most of the plays performed by the FTP were published, some were not.

3. "Ickes Pleased after Seeing 'The Mikado,'" *Chicago Defender*, 31 Dec. 1938, 7.

4. Flanagan, *Arena*, 60; Ross, "Role of Blacks," 40.

5. Survey of Audience Play Preferences, and Audience Survey Report on *The Mikado*, 26 Jan. 1937, in RG 69, Entry 907, Box 254, NA.

6. Interview with Clarence Muse by Lorraine Brown, 4 Jan. 1976, Perris, Calif., in GMUSC.

7. Flanagan, *Arena*, 7.

8. Ross, "Role of Blacks," 38.

9. Harry Hopkins, "Government Aid during the Depression to Professional, Technical and Other Service Workers," Box 28, FTP-LC.

10. Flanagan worked with Baker during his last year at Harvard; when he left to teach at Yale, he opened his first dramatic season with Flanagan's play *Incense*.

11. Matthews, *Federal Theatre*, 14–17.

12. Ibid., 18–19.

13. Flanagan, *Arena*, 3–5; Matthews, *Federal Theatre*, 10.

14. Flanagan, *Arena*, 18–19.

15. Interview with Robert Schnitzer and Marcella Cisney by John O'Connor, 17 Nov. 1975, Westport, Conn., in GMUSC.

16. "Woman 'Dictator' Runs Federal Theatre Project," *New York News*, 6 June 1937, in RG 69, Entry 875, Box 138, NA.

17. "Little Woman with a Big Job," *New York Woman*, 17 Mar. 1937, in ibid.

18. "Federal Theatre: Something of What It's Been Doing under Mrs. Flanagan's Leadership," 22 May 1937, in ibid.

19. Flanagan, *Arena*, 20.

20. Matthews, *Federal Theatre*, 38–39; O'Connor and Brown, *Free, Adult, Uncensored*, 7–25.

21. Ross, "Role of Blacks," 40.

22. Fraden, *Blueprints for a Black Federal Theatre*, 4.

23. First Meeting of Regional Directors, FTP, 8 Oct. 1935, in RG 69, Entry 890, Box 210, NA.

24. Highlights of the First Production Conference of the New York City Unit of the Federal Theatre, 22–24 July 1936, in Box 1, FTP-LC.

25. For Flanagan's racial progressivism, see Fraden, *Blueprints for a Black Federal Theatre*, 45–46; and Ross, "Role of Blacks," 42.

26. Fraden, *Blueprints for a Black Federal Theatre*, 54–55.

27. Ross, "Role of Blacks," 38.

28. Schwartz et al., *Voices from the Federal Theatre*, 22.

29. Most recently, Karen Sotiropoulos has explored the cultural politics of Williams and Walker in her book, *Staging Race: Black Performers in Turn of the Century America* (2006).

30. Woll, *Black Musical Theatre*, 23–28; Sotiropoulos, *Staging Race*, 189–90.

31. Mitchell, *Black Drama*, 69–70.

32. Woll, *Black Musical Theatre*, 54; Fraden, "National Negro Theater," 30.

33. Walker, "Krigwa," 348.

34. Ibid., 353–54.

35. Houseman, *Run-Through*, 178.

36. W. E. B. Du Bois, "Krigwa Players Little Negro Theatre," *Crisis*, July 1926, 134.

37. Alain Locke, "Steps toward the Negro Theatre," *Crisis*, Dec. 1922, 66.

38. W. E. B. Du Bois, "Criteria of Negro Art," *Crisis*, Oct. 1926, 297. For a detailed discussion of the debates among black intellectuals concerning black theater in the 1910s and 1920s, see Fraden, *Blueprints for a Black Federal Theatre*, chap. 2.

39. Mitchell, *Black Drama*, 76.

40. Krasner, *Beautiful Pageant*, 247.

41. Fraden, *Blueprints for a Black Federal Theatre*, 59; Woll, *Black Musical Theatre*, 58–75.

42. John Lyman, "A Negro Theatre," *Opportunity*, Jan. 1934, 15.

43. Plum, "Rose McClendon"; Grant, "Negro in Dramatic Art," 26.

44. Houseman, *Run-Through*, 178; Fraden, *Blueprints for a Black Federal Theatre*, 96–97.

45. Houseman quoted in the *Amsterdam News*, 23 Nov. 1935, in RG 69, Entry 876, Box 142, NA.

46. Houseman, *Run-Through*, 180–81.

47. Interview with John Houseman by John O'Connor and Mae Mallory Krulak, 11 May 1976, New York, N.Y., in GMUSC.

48. Interview with John Randolph by Diane Bowers, 28 May 1976, Hollywood, Calif., in GMUSC.

49. Interview with Hallie Jonas by Diane Bowers, 29 May 1976, Hollywood, Calif., and interview with Augusta Weissburger Schenker by Mae Mallory Krulak, 2 Mar. 1977, New York, N.Y., in GMUSC.

50. J. F. McDougald, "The Federal Government and the Negro Theatre," *Opportunity*, May 1936, 135.

51. Ross, "Role of Blacks," 41. When the project was first established, FTP historian Lorraine Brown indicates, there were sixteen Negro Units. Brown, "Story Yet to Be Told," 70.

52. Anne Powell, "The Negro in the Federal Theatre," *Crisis*, Nov. 1936, 341.

53. Ross, "Role of Blacks," 47.

54. By the end of the project, there were 851 black employees in the FTP, with half working on the New York City project alone. Other cities such as Chicago, San Francisco, and Boston boasted approximately 100 employees, while New Jersey, a smaller state, only employed 23 black FTP workers. It is important to note that these statistics were a result of a series of WPA budget cuts that affected a number of black employees. There were most likely many more than 851 black FTP workers in earlier years, as this report was written when the entire FTP was about to be abolished.

55. Interview with Muse by Brown, 4 Jan. 1976, in GMUSC.

56. Interview with Carlton Moss by Lorraine Brown, 6 Aug. 1976, Hollywood, Calif., in GMUSC.

57. Interview with John Silvera by Lorraine Brown, 11 July 1977, Fairfax, Va., in GMUSC.

58. Edward Lawson, "The Negro Actor on Broadway," *Opportunity*, Nov. 1938, 331.

59. Play Bureau, "Negro Plays," undated, in Box 937, FTP-LC.

60. Interview with Emmet Lavery by John O'Connor, 17 Oct. 1977, Encino, Calif., in GMUSC.

61. Interview with Francis Bosworth by Karen Wickre, 29 Sept. 1978, Gywnedd, Pa., in GMUSC.

62. Interview with Converse Tyler by John O'Connor, 15 Dec. 1975, Silver Spring, Md., in GMUSC.

63. Interview with Harold Berman by Karen Wickre, 16 Nov. 1977, Washington, D.C., in GMUSC.

64. Interview with Ben Russak by Lorraine Brown, 19 Feb. 1976, New York, N.Y., in GMUSC.

65. Interview with Berman by Wickre, 16 Nov. 1977, GMUSC.

66. Interview with Bosworth by Wickre, 29 Sept. 1978, in GMUSC.

67. Interview with Tyler by O'Connor, 15 Dec. 1975, in GMUSC.

68. Interview with Berman by Wickre, 16 Nov. 1977, in GMUSC.

69. Hill and Hatch, *History of African American Theatre*, 188; Andrews, Foster, and Harris, *Oxford Companion to African American Literature*, 241-42; Stephens, "Anti-Lynch Plays," 330.

70. Brown-Guillory, *Wines in the Wilderness*, 11-15.

71. Ibid., 61; Stephens, "Anti-Lynch Plays," 330.

72. Hill and Hatch, *History of African American Theatre*, 221-22, 263.

73. Ibid., 331-49; interview with Abram Hill by Lorraine Brown, 2 Feb. 1977, New York, N.Y., in GMUSC.

74. Quinn, *Representative American Plays*, 847-48.

75. Andrews, Foster, and Harris, *Oxford Companion to African American Literature*, 285.

76. Coyle and Damaser, *Six Early American Plays, 1798-1890*, 160, 157-60.

77. Interview with Silvera by Lorraine Brown, 11 July 1977, in GMUSC.

78. Interview with Russak by Lorraine Brown, 19 Feb. 1976, in GMUSC.

79. John Rimassa commenting on "Enchanted Figures," 6 May 1936, in RG 69, Entry 892, Box 229, NA.

80. C. C. Lawrence commenting on "Laugh Sing and Pray," 16 Nov. 1936, in ibid.

81. C. C. Lawrence commenting on "Broke: Six Dramatic Recitations for a Negro Theatre," in ibid.

82. Leonard Sachs commenting on "Angelo Herndon Jones," undated, in ibid.

83. John Silvera commenting on "The Big Timer," 8 Aug. 1937, in ibid.

84. Nathan Spiegel commenting on "Singing Piedmont," 11 Jan. 1936, and John Rimassa commenting on "Laugh Sing and Pray," 27 Oct. 1936, in ibid.

85. Otis Lucas commenting on "Laugh Sing and Pray," 23 Oct. 1936, in ibid.

86. C. C. Lawrence commenting on "Laugh Sing and Pray," 16 Nov. 1936, in ibid.

87. Leonard Sacks commenting on "The Christian Slave," undated, in ibid.

88. Converse Tyler commenting on "Heaven's My Home," 2 Oct. 1936, in ibid.

89. Reader unknown commenting on "Nobody Knows," 24 Sept. 1936, in ibid.

90. Judson O'Donnell commenting on "Nobody Knows," undated, in ibid.

91. John Rimassa commenting on "Safe," 20 July 1936, in ibid.

92. C. C. Lawrence commenting on "Safe," undated, in ibid.

93. Charles Gaskill commenting on "Safe," 29 June 1936, in ibid.

94. John Silvera commenting on "Hell's Half Acre," 5 Aug. 1937, in ibid.

95. Metrah Willie commenting on "The Octoroon," 24 May 1937, in ibid.

96. Alexander Cutner commenting on "The Dark Tide," 18 Oct. 1936, in ibid.

97. Willie commenting on "The Octoroon," 24 May 1937, in ibid.

98. Reader unknown commenting on "The Nigger," undated, in ibid.

99. Herbert Hutner commenting on "Rich Harlem," 23 July 1936, in ibid.

100. Rimassa commenting on "Enchanted Figures," 6 May 1936, in ibid.

101. Leonard Sacks commenting on "Boy Chillen," undated, in ibid.

102. Reader unknown commenting on "Boy Chillen," undated, in ibid.

103. Reader unknown commenting on "Old Man Pete," undated, in ibid.

104. National Service Bureau, "A List of Negro Plays," Mar. 1938, 12, 4, in Box 937, FTP-LC.

105. Ibid., 10.

106. Ibid., 20, 1.

107. Ibid., 8.

108. Fraden, *Blueprints for a Black Federal Theatre*, 115. On the controversy surrounding some of these projects, see 88–135. For more information on the content of these plays, see Jeanne-Marie Miller, "Successful Federal Theatre Dramas"

109. Walter White to Sherwood Anderson, 20 Apr. 1938, in Part 10: Peonage, Labor, and the New Deal, 1913–1939, Reel 8, Frame 138, NAACP (microfilm).

110. Memorandum to Executives from George B. Murphy Jr., 22 May 1939, in ibid., Frame 316; John Silvera to Walter White, 4 Apr. 1938, in ibid., Frame 125.

111. Abram Hill to Walter White, 28 Apr. 1938, in ibid., Frame 158.

112. Roy Wilkins to Emmet Lavery, 11 Apr. 1939, in ibid., Frame 288.

113. Emmett Lavery to Roy Wilkins, 14 Apr. 1939, in ibid., Frame 295.

114. Roy Wilkins to Emmett Lavery, 15 Apr. 1939, in ibid., Frame 293.

115. Lavery to Wilkins, 14 Apr. 1939; Fraden, *Blueprints for a Black Federal Theatre*, 159–60.

116. Lawson, "The Negro Actor on Broadway," *Opportunity*, Nov. 1938, 333.

117. Matthews, *Federal Theatre*, 77.

118. Ibid., 78.

119. Ibid., 119–22.

120. Ibid., 201.

121. Ibid., 205. For a further description of the Dies Committee hearings see ibid., 198–235; Flanagan, *Arena*, 335–48; and Saunders, "The Dies Committee."

122. Hearings before a Special House Committee on Un-American Activities on H. Res. 282, *Investigation of Un-American Propaganda Activities in the U.S.*, 75th Cong., 3rd Sess. (1938), 1:842–44 (House Un-American Activities Committee Hearings).

123. Ibid., 1:857–60.

124. Ibid., 4:2873–84.

125. Flanagan, *Arena*, 204–5.

126. Fraden, *Blueprints for a Black Federal Theatre*, 189.

127. Interview with Lavery by O'Connor, 17 Oct. 1977, in GMUSC.

128. Interview with Max Pollock by Lorraine Brown, 8 Jan. 1976, Los Angeles, Calif., in GMUSC.

129. Survey of Audience Play Preferences, and Audience Survey Report on "The Mikado," 26 Jan. 1937, in RG 69, Entry 907, Box 254, NA.

130. Interview with Duncan Whiteside by Karen Wickre, 13 Aug. 1978, Oxford, Mich., in GMUSC.

131. Director's Notes by Harry Minturn, in Production Report of "The Mikado," 25 Sept. 1938, in RG 69, Entry 937, Box 460, NA. Also see Set Design Notes and Costume Notes, in ibid.

132. "Exclusive to 'Pic' Magazine," 20 Mar. 1939, in RG 69, Entry 862, Box 108, NA.

133. Several publicity documents contain cast information. See "Exclusive to 'Pic' Magazine," 21 Mar. 1939, in ibid.; FTP for New York City, Program Notes on the "Swing Mikado," undated, in RG 69, Entry 960, Box 538, NA. Also see Fraden, *Blueprints for a Black Federal Theatre*, 189.

134. Quoted in Hayter, *Gilbert and Sullivan*, 47.

135. I use the term "quasi-Japanese" because although the set and costumes were changed to the Pacific locale, the script stayed mostly true to the Japanese setting. Traces of orientalism permeated the show, as did "Japanese" mannerisms.

136. Hayter, *Gilbert and Sullivan*, 60.

137. "Mikado" in 20th Week, 6 Feb. 1939, in RG 69, Entry 862, Box 108, NA.

138. "The Mikado" script #9, 11 May 1939, in National Service Bureau, Box 712, FTP-LC.

139. It is important to note that *Macbeth*'s Haitian setting had a more defined logic than the *Swing Mikado*. As Orson Welles explained, "The stormy career of Christophe, who became the 'Negro King of Haiti' and ended by killing himself when his cruelty led to a revolt, forms a striking parallel to the history of MacBeth." Houseman, *Run-Through*, 198.

140. Interview with Whiteside by Wickre, 13 Aug. 1978, in GMUSC.

141. Ibid.

142. Gail Borden, "Negro Unit Jazzes Up Opera 'Mikado,'" *Chicago Daily Times*, 26 Sept. 1938, clipping in Production Report on "The Mikado," 25 Sept. 1938, in RG 69, Entry 937, Box 460, NA.

143. Ibid.

144. Cecil Smith, *Chicago Tribune*, Sept. 26, 1938, clipping in Production Report on "The Mikado," 25 Sept. 1938, in ibid.

145. Nahum Daneil Brasher, "'The Mikado' Rates as Season's Best," *Chicago Defender*, 1 Oct. 1938, and Ted Watson, "'Mikado' Staged in 'Swing Style,'" *Pittsburgh Courier*, 6 Oct. 1938, clippings in ibid.

146. Ben Burns, "WPA Negro Unit Swings 'The Mikado' at the Great Northern Theatre," *Daily Record*, 27 Sept. 1938, clipping in ibid.

147. Aston Stevens, "Just a Twist of Swing in This Ethiopera," *Chicago Evening American*, 26 Sept. 1938, clipping in ibid.

148. Lloyd Lewis, "Mikado Malayed," *Chicago Daily News*, 26 Sept. 1938, clipping in ibid.

149. Borden, "Negro Unit Jazzes Up Opera 'Mikado,'" in ibid.

150. Katherine Irvin, "All Colored Cast Scores in Swing Version of 'Mikado,'" *Chicago Sunday Bee*, 2 Oct. 1938, clipping in ibid.

151. Brasher, "'The Mikado' Rates as Season's Best," in ibid.

152. Sallye Bell, "'Mikado' Scores in Chicago," Associated Negro Press, 28 Sept. 1938, clipping in ibid.

153. Lewis, "Mikado Malayed," in ibid.

154. Burns, "WPA Negro Unit Swings," in ibid.

155. Borden, "Negro Unit Jazzes Up Opera 'Mikado,'" in ibid.

156. Dorothy Day, "This 'Mikado' Unconvincing," *Herald and Examiner*, 29 Sept. 1938, clipping in ibid.

157. "Becomes Hit of the Season" (press release), *Chicago Tribune*, 1 Jan. 1939, clipping in ibid.

158. C. J. Bulliet, "Negro 'Mikado' Is Season's Major Hit: Tom-Tom 'Mikado' Frenzied Theatre" (press release), *Chicago Daily News*, 19 Jan. 1939, clipping in ibid.

159. Flanagan, *Arena*, 134.

160. For more on the McGhee dismissal see "Narrative Report of Events Leading to Dismissal of John McGhee as Regional and State Director of Federal Theatre Project," in RG 69, Entry 839, Box 15, NA.

161. Fraden, *Blueprints for a Black Federal Theatre*, 192; Flanagan, *Arena*, 146–47; Vanillo, "Battle of the Black Mikados," 153.

162. Brooks Atkinson, "The Play: Chicago Unit of the Federal Theatre Comes in Swinging the Gilbert and Sullivan 'Mikado,'" *New York Times*, 3 Mar. 1939, and John Anderson, "Swing Mikado Stomps In, Running High and Wide," *Stage and Screen*, 2 Mar. 1939, clippings in RG 69, Entry 877, Box 157, NA.

163. John Mason Brown, "'The Swing Mikado' Comes to Broadway," *New York Post*, 2 Mar. 1939, clipping in ibid.

164. John Cambridge, "Swing 'Mikado' Is New Federal Theatre Triumph," *Daily Worker*, 2 Mar. 1939, clipping in ibid.

165. The tactics of Mike Todd in trying to obtain the *Swing Mikado* and then replicating it for his own production were criticized by many *Swing Mikado* participants. Midwest play bureau director Dan Farran claims that he threw Todd out three times backstage because Todd was making notes on costumes and other parts of the show. Interview with Don Farran by John O'Connor, 3 Jan. 1976, Hollywood, Calif., in GMUSC.

166. Hearing before the House Subcommittee of the Committee on Appropriations on HR Res. 209 and 246, *Further Additional Appropriations for Work Relief, Fiscal Year, 1939*, 76th Cong., 1st Sess. (1939), 143–50.

167. Ibid.; Matthews, *Federal Theatre*, 260.

168. "Dilemma Facing '2-a-Day' Players; 'Swing Mikado' Commersh Deal On," *Variety*, 12 Apr. 1939, 50.

169. Fraden, *Blueprints for a Black Federal Theatre*, 194; Flanagan, *Arena*, 147–48; Vanillo, "Battle of the Black Mikados," 153–57; Woll, *Black Musical Theatre*, 183–84.

170. Matthews, *Federal Theatre*, 275–93.

Chapter 3

1. Sterling Brown, "The Problems of the Negro Writer," Official Proceedings, Second National Negro Congress, Philadelphia, Pa., 15–17 Oct. 1937.

2. Schomburg, "The Negro Digs Up His Past," in Locke, *New Negro*, 231, 237.

3. For recent studies of the FWP, see Hirsch, *Portrait of America: A Cultural History of the Federal Writers' Project* (2003); Bold, *The WPA Guides: Mapping America* (1999); Sporn, *Against Itself: The Federal Theater and Writers' Projects in the Midwest* (1995).

4. Hirsch, *Portrait of America*, 9.

5. Yetman, "Background of the Slave Narrative," 542–43, 548; Penkower, *Federal Writers' Project*, 1718. For additional perspective on the slave interviews see Musher's 2001 *Ameri-

can Quarterly article, "Contesting 'the Way the Almighty Wants It': Crafting Memories of Ex-Slaves in the Slave Narrative Collection."

6. Penkower, *Federal Writers' Project*, 10–16; Mangione, *Dream and the Deal*, 29–39.

7. Penkower, *Federal Writers' Project*, 22–26.

8. Unlike other historians, Norman Yetman contends that the FERA ex-slave narratives were not merely continued under the WPA; rather he argues that ex-slave narratives were "undertaken spontaneously" by black employees of the FWP and approved on a state-by-state basis. National headquarters did not officially recognize the collection as a project until 1937. Yetman, "Background of the Slave Narrative," 548–51.

9. As an administrator, however, Alsberg had many shortcomings; Baker appointed novelist and English professor George Cronyn and *New York Times* journalist Reed Harris as Alsberg's assistants. Although all three of these men had a similar passion for the written word, they displayed different management techniques in administering the American Guides. Former FWP editor Jerre Mangione contends that it was the clashing temperaments of Alsberg and Cronyn that contributed to poor administration in the Washington FWP office. Mangione, *Dream and the Deal*, 59.

10. Henry Alsberg, "Writers and the Government," *Saturday Review of Literature*, 4 Jan. 1936, 9.

11. On Harris, see Robert Cohen, *When the Old Left Was Young: Student Radicals and America's First Mass Student Movement, 1929–1941* (1993), 55–72. Mangione, *Dream and the Deal*, 59–66; Hirsch, *Portrait of America*, 107–40.

12. Penkower, *Federal Writers' Project*, 30; Mangione, *Dream and the Deal*, 97–98.

13. Penkower, *Federal Writers' Project*, 58–59.

14. Mangione, *Dream and the Deal*, 109.

15. Blair Bolles, "The Federal Writers' Project," *Saturday Review of Literature*, 9 July 1938, 4.

16. Penkower, *Federal Writers' Project*, 62.

17. Ibid., 73.

18. E. Current-Garcia, "Writers in the Sticks'" *Prairie Schooner* 12 (Winter 1938), 297.

19. Ibid., 300.

20. Penkower, *Federal Writers' Project*, 73, 39–42.

21. Henry Alsberg to Aubrey Williams, 16 Dec. 1935, in RG 69, Entry 2, Box 1, NA.

22. Ibid.

23. Gabbin, *Sterling A. Brown*, 15–22.

24. Ibid., 38–44. For additional insight on Brown and the Harlem Renaissance, see Hirsch, *Portrait of America*, 115–22.

25. Gabbin, *Sterling A. Brown*, 22–33.

26. Brown and Sanders, *Son's Return*, xii.

27. Quoted in Wright, "New Negro Poet," 97.

28. Gabbin, *Sterling A. Brown*, 49–51.

29. Ibid., 5.

30. Sterling Brown to Mr. Munson, 9 Jan. 1940, in Box A9, FWP-LC.

31. Sterling Brown to Horace Mann Bond, 12 Sept. 1936, in Sterling Brown Papers, Box 51, Correspondence Folder, MSRC.

32. Sterling Brown to Elmer Anderson Carter, 14 Apr. 1936, in ibid.

33. Gabbin, *Sterling A. Brown*, 69; Mangione, *Dream and the Deal*, 258–59.

34. Henry Alsberg to James Egan, 3 Dec. 1936, in RG 69, Entry 11, Box 2, NA.

35. David Williamson to Henry Alsberg, 8 Dec. 1936, in RG 69, Entry 27, Box 1, NA.

36. Office of Negro Affairs to W. T. Couch, 19 Oct. 1938, in ibid.

37. Edwin Bjorkman to Sterling Brown, 11 Jan. 1936, in ibid.

38. Hirsch, *Portrait of America*, 124. For a more detailed description of the relationship between Bjorkman and Couch and their attempts to incorporate black Americans into the guidebook, see Bold, *WPA Guides*, 123–61.

39. Hirsch, *Portrait of America*, 124.

40. Bjorkman to Brown, 5 Mar. 1937, in RG 69, Entry 27, Box 1, NA.

41. Rowell, "'Let Me Be with Ole Jazzbo,'" 801.

42. Maurice Hore to Henry Alsberg, 7 Dec. 1936, in RG 69, Entry 27, Box 1, NA.

43. William Myers to Sterling Brown, 5 Feb. 1937, in ibid.

44. "Notes on Negro Material in the State Guides," 11 Aug. 1936, in ibid.

45. Laura Middletown and Augusts Ladson to Harry Hopkins, 13 July 1937, in ibid. The reason that black workers were unequally affected by relief cuts is that most black workers comprised the nonrelief quota. Black writers who were educated did not often qualify for relief, making them most susceptible to budget cuts. At first the government justified high quotas for professional people not on relief to provide jobs for clerical workers and researchers. Penkower, *Federal Writers' Project*, 62–63.

46. Office of Negro Affairs to Couch, 19 Oct. 1938, in RG 69, Entry 27, Box 1, NA.

47. Penkower, *Federal Writers' Project*, 67.

48. "Notes on Negro Material in the State Guides," 11 Aug. 1936, in RG 69, Entry 27, Box 1, NA.

49. WPA press release, 6 Mar. 1939, in ibid.

50. Elkins, *Slavery*, 9–11.

51. For an analysis of black historians writing on slavery, see John David Smith's 1980 *Journal of Negro History* article, "A Different View of Slavery: Black Historians Attack the Proslavery Argument, 1890–1920."

52. For some discussion of Brown and the state guides see Hirsch, *Portrait of America*, 115–31; and Penkower, *Federal Writers' Project*, 140–43.

53. Editor unknown, "Arkansas: Folklore Subjects," 12 Feb. 1937, in Box A 23, FWP-LC.

54. All copy cataloged as "editorial comments regarding the Negro" was written by Brown and his assistants (and sometimes by folklore editor Ben Botkin), yet many reports do not list a particular author for comments. Editor unknown, "Texas: Negro Material," 8 May 1937, in Box A 443, and editor unknown, "Illinois: Folklore," 15 Oct. 1936, in Box A 113, FWP-LC.

55. Sterling Brown, "South Carolina: Beaufort and the Sea Islands," 24 Mar. 1937, in Box A 397, and editor unknown, "Alabama: Birmingham," 14 Mar. 1938, in Box A 18, FWP-LC.

56. Rowell, "Let Me Be with Ole Jazzbo," 802.

57. B. B., "Pennsylvania: Harrisburg," 6 Sept. 1938, in Box A 390, FWP-LC; FWP, *Pennsylvania*, 238.

58. Sterling Brown, "Illinois: East St. Louis," 13 July 1937, in Box A 113, FWP-LC.

59. FWP, *Illinois*, 313.

60. Glaucia Roberts, "Ohio: Toledo," 24 Sept. 1938, in Box A 371, FWP-LC; FWP, *Ohio Guide*, 326–29.

61. Editor unknown, "Alabama: Florence," 25 Sept. 1937, in Box A 18, FWP-LC.

62. FWP, *Alabama*, 184–85.

63. Jackson, introduction to FWP, *WPA Guide to 1930s Alabama*, xvi.

64. This memo was undated, but it appears to be written in the early stages of the FWP. Here, Brown reported that a large number of states had not yet submitted reports on the status of Negro Studies. Sterling Brown, "Summary of Work on Negro Life and History," undated, in RG 69, Entry 27, Box 1, NA.

65. FWP, *Arizona*, 254–55; G. B. R., "Arizona: Tucson," 7 Mar. 1939, in Box A 21, FWP-LC.

66. G. B. R., "Arizona: Nogales," 7 Oct. 1938, in ibid.

67. Henry Alsberg to State Directors of the FWP, 15 June 1937, in RG 69, Entry 11, Box 2, NA.

68. G. W. Cronyn to Myrtle Miles, 5 Nov. 1936, in RG 69, Entry 27, Box 1, NA.

69. Gabbin, *Sterling A. Brown*, 79. When Roberts wrote of three people in the office, I assume that she was referring to Brown, Eugene Holmes, and herself, the three most frequent editors on state copy materials. The initials B. B. also appear on some documents, and I assume this is folklore editor Benjamin Botkin, although Botkin was not serving the FWP solely as staff in the Negro Affairs division. Glaucia B. Roberts, "Existing Conditions in the Office on Negro Affairs," Nov. 1938, in RG 69, Entry 27, Box 2, NA.

70. Eugene Holmes, "Pennsylvania: Philadelphia," 10 Nov. 1938, in Box A 390, FWP-LC.

71. FWP, *Pennsylvania*, 47, 69, 111–12. These descriptions of black life in Pennsylvania would receive even further elaboration in the WPA guide to Philadelphia, published in 1937, which devoted significant attention to black schools, neighborhoods, authors, and the abolition movement, among other topics. See FWP, *WPA Guide to Philadelphia* (1988).

72. Sterling Brown, "The Negro in Indianapolis," 22 Apr. 1937, in Box A 130, FWP-LC.

73. Glaucia Roberts, "Indiana: Cities of the Calumet," 22 Sept. 1938, in ibid.; FWP, *Indiana*, 75, 167.

74. G. B. R., "Texas: History," 26 July 1939, in Box A 443, FWP-LC; FWP, *Texas*, 49. Writers, however, did not take Glaucia Roberts's suggestion to include the fact that Texas was in the worst condition of any state during Reconstruction, although they did make small changes that relieved blacks of blame for the period. The statement about Texas being in the worst condition of any state was reportedly made by an inspector general of the Freedmen's Bureau who found that "Whites and Negroes were everywhere, lawless and starving." Editors took this account from Du Bois's *Black Reconstruction* (1936).

75. G. B. R., "South Carolina: Education," 22 Mar. 1938 and 18 Apr. 1939, in Box A 397, FWP-LC.

76. FWP, *South Carolina: A Guide*, 94.

77. Edgar, introduction to FWP, *South Carolina: The WPA Guide*, v–vi.

78. G. B. R., "Virginia: Alexandria," 9 Mar. 1939, in Box A 486, FWP-LC.

79. Sterling Brown to George Cronyn, 25 Sept. 1936, in Box A 209, FWP-LC; FWP, *Mississippi*, 120–25.

80. Eugene Holmes, "Arkansas: Agriculture and Farm Life," 20 Aug. 1938, in Box A 23, FWP-LC.

81. FWP, *Arkansas*, 102.

82. FWP, *South Carolina: A Guide*, 53–54.

83. FWP, *Texas*, 97–98.

84. FWP, *Alabama*, 184.

85. Ibid., 221.

86. Ibid.

87. FWP, *Mississippi*, 30.

88. Ibid., 22.

89. Gene Holcolmb, "Introductory Essay: The Mississippi Negro," 20 Nov. 193?, in Box A 209, FWP-LC. Also, for some discussion of the Mississippi guide, see Gabbin, *Sterling A. Brown*, 76.

90. Hirsch, *Portrait of America*, 125, 123.

91. Jackson, introduction to FWP, *WPA Guide to 1930s Alabama*, xii.

92. Gabbin, *Sterling A. Brown*, 75; Cronyn to Miles, 5 Nov. 1936, in RG 69, Entry 27, Box 1, NA; Henry Alsberg to Myrtle Miles, 24 Sept. 1936, in RG 69, Entry 11, Box 2, NA.

93. Myrtle Miles to G. W. Cronyn, 4 Oct. 1937, in Box A 18, FWP-LC.

94. Ibid.

95. Hirsch, *Portrait of America*, 124; Sterling Brown, "South Carolina: Beaufort and the Sea Islands," 24 Mar. 1937, in Box A 397, FWP-LC.

96. Hirsch, *Portrait of America*, 124–25; Gabbin, *Sterling A. Brown*, 75–76; FWP, *South Carolina: A Guide*, 169.

97. Gabbin, *Sterling A. Brown*, 75.

98. FWP, *Ohio Guide*, 151.

99. Ibid., 81.

100. Sterling Brown, "The Negro Author and His Publisher," *Quarterly Review of Higher Education among Negroes* 9.3 (July 1941): 146.

101. Sterling Brown, "The Negro in Washington," in FWP, *Washington: City and Capital*, 89, 90.

102. "Distributing the WPA Guides," *Publishers' Weekly*, 11 May 1940, 1836.

103. "The Completion of the American Guide Series," *Publishers' Weekly*, 3 May 1941, 1815.

104. "Distributing the WPA Guides," 1838–39.

105. Albert Horlings, "Guidebooks to America," *New Republic*, 13 Apr. 1942, 501.

106. Penkower, *Federal Writers' Project*, 139.

107. "Presenting America," *Publishers' Weekly*, 3 May 1941, 1828; "WPA Writers Produce," *Publishers' Weekly*, 21 Aug. 1937, 569; Charles I. Glicksberg, "The Federal Writers' Project," *South Atlantic Quarterly* 37 (Apr. 1938): 164.

108. Horlings, "Guidebooks to America," 501.

109. Robert Cantwell, "America and the Writers' Project," *New Republic*, 26 Apr. 1939, 325.

110. Frederick Gutheim, "America in the Guide Books," *Saturday Review of Literature*, 14 June 1941, 5.

111. Bernard De Voto, "New England via the WPA," *Saturday Review of Literature*, 14 May 1938, 3.

112. Eleanor Touhey, "The American Baedekers," *Library Journal*, 15 Apr. 1941, 340; Horlings, "Guidebooks to America," 501.

113. Touhey, "American Baedekers," 340; Bolles, "The Federal Writers' Project," *Saturday Review of Literature*, 9 July 1938, 18.

114. Jared Putnam, "Guides to America," *Nation*, 24 Dec. 1938, 694–95.

115. Bolles, "Federal Writers' Project," 18.

116. "Federal Writers Dig into History of Race in Virginia; Pull Out Forgotten Plums Of

Prowess, Achievement," *Chicago Defender*, 4 June 1938, 6; "Contributions of Race to Growth of New Orleans Recorded by WPA," *Chicago Defender*, 18 June 1938, 7.

117. Henry R. Jenkins, "A Guide to North Carolina," *Opportunity*, Oct. 1940, 313.

118. D. W. Brogan, "Inside America," *London Spectator*, Nov. 1941, 507–8.

119. It is not clear in this letter whether Brown is referring to the larger WPA project focused on the collection of ex-slave narratives inaugurated in April 1937.

120. Sterling Brown to Walter White, 22 Dec. 1937, in Part 10 "Peonage, Labor, and the New Deal, 1913–1939," Reel 8, Frame 116, NAACP (microfilm). The other projects Brown listed included "Portrait of the Negro as an American" (PNAM), the history of black Americans in Virginia, the history of black Americans in Louisiana, *The Social and Economic Life of the Negro in Greater Little Rock*, and *Negroes in New York*. All of these, except for PNAM, were published in some form (the last two with different titles), some by the Writers' Program, which was the FWP's successor in the individual states.

121. It is most likely that plans to collect additional documents on black history were under way from the beginning of the project, as FWP employees researched materials for *The Negro in Virginia* for several years. Because Alsberg established an office of Negro Studies to combat discrimination in the project, it is probable that Brown initiated additional studies foreseeing the inadequacy of the guidebooks (but also capitalizing on the government's willingness to fund these studies). The heading "Negro Studies Project" is one listed in the Library of Congress finding aids; it is unclear whether the Library of Congress designated this as a separate study under the FWP, rather than a way to catalog documents once the project ended.

122. FWP, "Negro Studies Project, 1722–1939," in Boxes A 873, A 882, FWP-LC. Almost all states included in this project took an interest in interviewing blacks about slavery, folklore, and other subjects.

123. Hirsch, *Portrait of America*, 544–48; Mangione, *Dream and the Deal*, 259–61; Penkower, *Federal Writers' Project*, 145–47.

124. Glasco, *WPA History of the Negro in Pittsburgh*.

125. The first dated outlines for PNAM begin in the summer of 1937, "Material Collected for the Proposed Book," 30 July 1937, in Box A860, FWP-PNAM. A memo directed to the Library of Congress requested that the library process materials "prepared in the states before August 31, 1939" for deposit. This included the PNAM materials. "Supplementary Documentation on the Work of the Various Units of the Library of Congress Project," in RG 69, Entry 27, Box 1, NA.

126. Sterling Brown, 9 Mar. 1937, in Box A 860, "Outlines" folder, FWP-PNAM.

127. Sterling Brown to Mr. Munson, 9 Jan. 1940, in Box A9, FWP-LC.

128. Ibid.

129. Monroe Work, "Inventions by Negroes," Negro Year Book, 1931–32, in Box A 859, Chap. 15, "The Negro in Business" folders, FWP-PNAM; Rev. J. H. Brown, "A Short History of Madame C. J. Walker," 16 Nov. 1937, in ibid.

130. A. W. Brown, "Men of Yesterday and Today: Biographies of Notable Negroes of Washington, D.C. and Historical Homes," undated, in Box A 859, Chap. 17, "Negro Spokesmen" folders, FWP-PNAM.

131. A. Brown, "Harvard's Bill Lewis," undated, in Box A 858, Chap. 7 "In Sports" folders, FWP-PNAM; Evan J. Albright, "*Vita*: William Henry Lewis; Brief Life of a Football Pioneer, 1868–1949," *Harvard Magazine*, Nov.–Dec. 2005, 44–45.

132. George Gore, "Negro Journalism: An Essay," Greencastle, Ind., 1922, in Box A 858,

"In Arts" folders, FWP-PNAM; New York FWP, "The Negro Theater and Its History in New York," undated, in Box A 858, Chap. 9, "In Theater" folders, FWP-PNAM.

133. Cook quoted in Monroe Work, Negro Year Book, 1931–1932, "The Negro in Music," in Box A 858, Chap. 10, "In Music" folders, FWP-PNAM.

134. Eugene Holmes, "The Harlem Cabaret," undated, in Box A 858, Chap. 12, "The Negro Has a Good Time" folders, FWP-PNAM.

135. Ibid.

136. A. Brown, "Letters of Lydia Marie Child: Cases of Negro fugitives, abolitionist conductors for the U.G.R. and other references of interest pertaining to the cause of Negro Freedom," undated, in Box A 856, Chap. 2, "Struggle for Freedom" folders, FWP-PNAM.

137. Author unknown, "White Anti-Slavery Workers," undated, in ibid.

138. For historians using the Slave Narrative Collection, see Yetman's 1984 *American Quarterly* article, "Ex-Slave Interviews and the Historiography of Slavery."

139. Author unknown, "Black Abolitionists," undated, in Box A 856, Chap. 2, "Struggle for Freedom" folders, FWP-PNAM.

140. Ibid.

141. A. Brown, "Incidents in the Lives of Slaves," undated, in Box A 856, Chap. 1, "A Picture of Slavery" folders, FWP-PNAM.

142. Author unknown, excerpt from George Carleton, *The Suppressed Book about Slavery! Prepared for Publication in 1857* . . . (New York: Carleton, 1864), undated, in ibid.; author unknown, excerpt from Darius Lyman, a former resident of the South, *Leaven for Doughfaces; or, Threescore and Ten Parables Touching Slavery* (Cincinnati: Bangs and Co., 1856), undated, in ibid.

143. W. E. B. Du Bois, "Founding the Public School," in *Black Reconstruction in America* (1936), in Box A 858, Chap. 6, "At School" folders, FWP-PNAM.

144. Ulysses Lee, "Washington's 1919 Race Riots," *Washington Times*, 30 June 1919, in Box A 859, Chap. 13, "The Negro Has a Hard Time" folders, FWP-PNAM.

145. E. F. Driskell (PNAM writer), article taken from the *Miami Post*, author unknown (written either 20 Aug. 1937 or 23 July 1937), in ibid.

146. Martha Gruening, "'Fiddle Faddle' to the Old South," *Brooklyn Daily Eagle*, 16 May 1937, in ibid.

147. Penkower, *Federal Writers' Project*, 146. There is some discrepancy on when Brown left the FWP. Joanne Gabbin claims that Brown resigned around the spring of 1940 (Gabbin, *Sterling A. Brown*, 79–80), yet in one letter written in January 1939, Brown wrote that he was "no longer on the pay-roll, unfortunately" (Sterling Brown to Charles Jones, 14 Jan. 1939, in Sterling Brown Papers, Box 51, Correspondence Folder, MSRC).

148. Sterling Brown to Charles Jones, 8 Aug. 1939, in Sterling Brown Papers, MSRC.

149. Penkower, *Federal Writers' Project*, 199.

150. Mangione, *Dream and the Deal*, 293. Mangione claims that De Sola testified when he was cast out by FTP employees who derided him for leaving the CP; ibid., 301.

151. Penkower, *Federal Writers' Project*, 181–86 (quote on 181); Mangione, *Dream and the Deal*, 84.

152. Mangione, *Dream and the Deal*, 318–19.

153. Hearings before a Special House Committee on Un-American Activities on HR Res. 282, *Investigation of Un-American Propaganda Activities in the U.S.*, 75th Cong., 3rd Sess. (1938), 4:2741–45; Wright, "The Ethics of Living Jim Crow," in Thompson et al., *American Stuff*, 39–52.

154. Eda Lou Walton, "A Federal Writers' Anthology," *New York Times*, 29 Aug. 1937, 80.

155. Jerre Mangione contends that the FWP proved to be a fertile ground for Wright as a creative artist, as he made use of project time to work on *Native Son* (1940). According to Mangione, Henry Alsberg had a "secret creative writing unit" composed of ten writers, including Wright and Claude McKay, who were permitted to work on their own materials as long as they reported to the New York Project office once a week with proof of their productivity. Mangione stipulates that it was the "pressures of his [Alsberg's] conscience" that prompted him to allow for creative writing, albeit on a very small scale. Mangione, *Dream and the Deal*, 245.

156. William B. Smith, "Review and Comment," *New Masses*, 14 Sept. 1937, 24.

157. Mangione, *Dream and the Deal*, 245.

158. *Congressional Record* 84 (1939), pt. 4, 3931.

159. Ibid., 3930–33; Mangione, *Dream and the Deal*, 4–5; FWP, *Washington: City and Capital*, 880, 68–90.

160. Brown does not specify the college where Preston was dean, saying only that he was "dean of a Negro college in Florida." Sterling Brown to Henry Alsberg, "Statements Concerning Congressman Keefe's Speech," 10 Apr. 1939, in Sterling Brown Papers, Box 51, Correspondence Folder, MSRC.

161. Ibid. Here, Brown stated that he never received word that Keefe had tried to telephone him and that he did not respond to Keefe's letter "because I could add nothing to the information already sent to him on the case, information sent from this office." Brown stated that he did apologize to Keefe for neglecting his interests.

162. "NAACP Opposes State Control of Arts Projects," in Part 10, "Peonage, Labor, and the New Deal, 1913–1939," Reel 8, Frame 302, NAACP-LC.

163. Penkower, *Federal Writers' Project*, 234–37; Mangione, *Dream and the Deal*, 329–48.

164. Sterling Brown to Charles Jones, 14 Jan. 1939, in Brown Papers, Box 51, Correspondence Folder, MSRC.

165. Doris Kravis to Walter White, 10 Dec. 1938, in Box C-298, NAACP-LC.

166. Walter White to Franklin Roosevelt, 7 June 1939, in Sterling Brown Papers, Box 51, Third Party Folder, MSRC.

167. Penkower, *Federal Writers' Project*, 66.

168. Rowell, "Let Me Be with Ole Jazzbo," 803.

169. Alain Locke to the Hon. Frederick Taylor, 10 May 1939, Brown Papers, Box 51, Third Party Folder, MSRC.

Chapter 4

1. Franklin Roosevelt to William Thompkins, 26 June 1940, in FDR Papers, President's Personal File No. 3634, National Colored Democratic Association, FDRL.

2. Milton Starr, "Report on Negro Morale," 1942, in RG 208, Entry ED, Box 6, NA.

3. Chandler Owen to Franklin Roosevelt, 6 June 1941, in FDR Papers, President's Official File, Group 93, Box 4, FDRL.

4. "An Open Letter to President Roosevelt: An Editorial," *Crisis*, Jan. 1943, in ibid., Box 5, FDRL.

5. For a discussion of the media and war propaganda, see Steele, *Propaganda in an Open Society: The Roosevelt Administration and the Media, 1933–1941* (1985); and Steele's 1984 *Journal of American History* article, "The Great Debate: Roosevelt, the Media, and the Coming of the War, 1940–1941."

6. Sterling and Kittress, *Stay Tuned*, 87; Hilmes, *Radio Voices*, 29; Savage, *Broadcasting Freedom*, 6.

7. Doherty, *Projections of War*, 8–11.

8. Archibald MacLeish to Lewis Carliner, 2 Feb. 1942, in RG 208, Entry 7, Box 25, NA.

9. For Grable's influence, see Westbrook's 1990 *American Quarterly* article, "'I Want a Girl, Just like the Girl That Married Harry James': American Women on the Problem of Political Obligation in World War II." For black participation in wartime culture, see Erenberg, *Swingin' the Dream: Big Band Jazz and the Rebirth of American Culture* (1998); Stowe, *Swing Changes: Big Band Jazz in New Deal America (1994)*; Tucker, *Swing Shift: "All Girl" Bands of the 1940s* (2000).

10. Holt, *Problem of Race*, 108–13. For Louis and issues of racial transcendence, also see M. Jill Dupont, "'The Self in the Ring, the Self in Society': Boxing and American Culture from Jack Johnson to Joe Louis" (2000), 327–401.

11. Dalfiume, *Desegregation of the U.S. Armed Forces*, 44–63; Wynn, *Afro-American and the Second World War*, 21–38.

12. Winkler, *Politics of Propaganda*, 42–49, 65–72. On the development of the OWI and its internal dissension, see Weinberg's 1968 *Journal of American History* article, "What to Tell America: The Writer's Quarrel in the Office of War Information"; Steele's 1970 *American Historical Review* article, "Preparing the Public for War: Efforts to Establish a National Propaganda Agency, 1940–41." For the impact of the Southern congressional voting on New Deal policy, see Katznelson, Geiger, and Kryder's 1993 *Political Science Quarterly* article, "Limiting Liberalism: The Southern Veto in Congress, 1933–1950." For OWI's racial ideologies in regard to motion pictures see Cripps, *Making Movies Black: The Hollywood Message Movie from World War II to the Civil Rights Era* (1993); Koppes and Black, *Hollywood Goes to War: How Politics, Profits and Propaganda Shaped World War II Movies* (1987); and Doherty, *Projections of War*.

13. A. Philip Randolph to Henry L. Stimson, 4 June 1941, in RG 107, Entry 99, Box 3, NA.

14. The Office of Facts and Figures (OFF) would become incorporated into the OWI in June 1942 under the direction of Elmer Davis. MacLeish served as assistant director in charge of the Policy Development Branch.

15. Archibald MacLeish to Frances Biddle, 24 Apr. 1942, quoting memo by unknown person, and MacLeish to an unknown party, 24 Apr. 1942, in RG 208, Entry 7, Box 3, NA.

16. For some of MacLeish's statements on race, see Drabeck and Ellis, *Archibald MacLeish*, 131, 165–66. For MacLeish's role as librarian of Congress and OFF director, particularly pertaining to his ideological position on propaganda, see Gary, *Nervous Liberals*, 131–73. MacLeish's more general biography is Donaldson, *Archibald MacLeish: An American Life* (1992). For recent analysis of the March on Washington see Gilmore, *Defying Dixie*, 356–69.

17. Bureau of Intelligence, OWI, "Survey of Intelligence Materials, Supplement to Survey No. 25," 14 July 1942, 10, in Box 52, Archibald MacLeish Papers, LC.

18. Bureau of Special Services, OWI, "Opinions about Inter-Racial Tension," 25 Aug. 1943, 4, in RG 107, Entry 188, Box 230, NA; Armed Forces HQ to Office of the Undersecretary of War, 16 June 1944, in RG 107, Entry 141, Box 236, NA.

19. Philleo Nash to Leo Rosten, "The Need for a Negro Policy within OWI," 8 Jan. 1943, in RG 208, Entry E-27, Box 40, NA.

20. John Levirt Kelly to George A. Barnes, 18 May 1942, in RG 208, Entry 5, Box 3, NA.

21. Caroline Blake to Archibald MacLeish, 14 Feb. 1942, in ibid.

22. John Hammond to Agnes Meyer, 28 Jan. 1945, in RG 107, Entry 188, Box 181, NA.

23. Lillian Smith, "Portrait of the Deep South—Speaking to Negroes on Morale," n.d., in RG 107, Entry 188, Box 240, NA. Apparently, this poem was meant to be performed, as it appeared with stage directions in the southern literary magazine *South Today* in the spring of 1942, reprinted in White and Sugg Jr., *From the Mountain*, 110–15. Smith was one of the editors of this progressive journal.

24. Roy Wilkins to Archibald MacLeish, 27 Mar. 1942, in RG 208, Entry 5, Box 3, NA.

25. W. H. Jernagin to the U.S. Attorney General, 20 Apr. 1942, in RG 107, Entry 188, Box 223, NA.

26. Southern Negro Youth Congress, "Washington Memo: A Report of Interviews with Federal Agencies," 28–30 May 1942, in ibid.

27. Mary McLeod Bethune to Henry L. Stimson, 14 Oct. 1941, in RG 107, Entry 188, Box 183, NA.

28. Robert Huse, "Minutes of the Board Meeting," 14 Nov. 1942, in Box 53, MacLeish Papers, LC.

29. Milton Starr, "Suggestions for Improvement of Negro Morale," n.d., in RG 208, Entry 3D, Box 6, NA.

30. Nash to Rosten, "The Need for a Negro Policy within OWI," in RG 208, NA.

31. Theodore M. Berry to Elmer Davis, 24 July 1942, in RG 208, Entry 1, Box 8, NA.

32. Ibid.

33. Ibid.

34. Walter White to Elmer Davis, 8 Dec. 1942, and William Hastie to Walter White, 8 Dec. 1942, in ibid.

35. White to Davis, 15 Jan. 1943, in ibid.

36. Milton Starr, "Report on Negro Morale," 1942, in RG 208, Entry ED, Box 6, NA.

37. Theodore Berry to Walter White, 17 Dec. 1942, in RG 208 Entry 1, Box 8, NA.

38. Elmer Davis to Walter White, 18 Dec. 1942, in ibid. For further discussion of the relationship between Berry, Starr, and other OFF/OWI officials, see Savage, *Broadcasting Freedom*, 111–21.

39. William Hastie to the Under Secretary of War, 22 Sept. 1942, in RG 107, Entry 99, Box 3, NA.

40. Due to Hastie's outspokenness on combating segregation, the War Department formed a review board, the Advisory Committee on Negro Troop Policies, chaired by Assistant Secretary of War John McCloy, which did not include Hastie in its committee meetings. This committee eventually eclipsed Hastie as adviser on racial matters, with Truman Gibson, Hastie's assistant, as acting civilian aide. Gibson, in turn, aligned much more closely with the McCloy committee, and thus policies on race went from "confrontation to accommodation." Kryder, *Divided Arsenal*, 145–46. For the most thorough study of Hastie's experiences in the War Department, see McGuire, *He, Too, Spoke for Democracy: Judge Hastie, World War II, and the Black Soldier* (1988).

41. Eugene Katz to Gardner Cowles, "A Deputy for the Negro Problem?" 8 Feb. 1943, in RG 208, Entry 27, Box 40, NA.

42. Lawrence Cramer to Judge James Landis, 22 May 1942, in RG 208, Entry 222, Box 1079, NA.

43. Katz to Cowles, "A Deputy for the Negro Problem?" in RG 208, NA.

44. Truman Gibson to Maj. Gen. A. D. Surles, 9 Feb. 1943, in RG 107, Entry 188, Box 184, NA.

45. "Present Tensions Involved in the Negro Question," 1942, in RG 208, Entry 222, Box 1079, NA.

46. Ibid. For a study of both private and public uses of radio for racial programming during the war years, see Savage, *Broadcasting Freedom*. Other studies of radio's significance during the war years include Hilmes, *Radio Voices: American Broadcasting, 1922–1952* (1997), 230–70; and Barlow, *Voice Over: The Making of Black Radio* (1999), 67–89.

47. "Present Tensions Involved in the Negro Question," in RG 208, NA.

48. William Alexander to John Herrick, 20 Mar. 1942, in RG 208, Entry 7, Box 10, NA.

49. Subcommittee of Pro-Democracy Organizations Round Table, "The Negro in America: Outline of Public Relations Campaign to Better Negro-White Relations," 10 Mar. 1942, in RG 208, Entry 5, Box 3, NA.

50. Bureau of Public Relations, n.d.; Fred Moore to Col. Frank Pearson, 7 July 1941; and William Hastie to Fred Moore, 9 Aug. 1941, all in RG 107, Entry 188, Box 183, NA.

51. D. P. Page to Judge William Hastie, 23 June 1941, in ibid.

52. Bird and Rubenstein, *Design for Victory*; Roeder, *Censored War*, 76–79.

53. Roeder, *Censored War*, 79.

54. Ibid., 45.

55. Milton Starr, "Report on Negro Morale," 1942, in RG 208, Entry ED, Box 6, NA. Starr also promotes the employment of black celebrities in a memo entitled "Suggestions for Improvement of Negro Morale," n.d., in RG 208, Entry 3D, Box 6, NA. For more on this policy, see "Program for War Information to Negroes," 1943, in RG 208, Entry E-27, Box 40, NA; and T. M. Berry to Ulric Bell, 25 May 1942, in RG 208, Entry 5, Box 3, NA.

56. For more on Johnson, see Roberts, *Papa Jack: Jack Johnson and the Era of White Hopes* (1983). For a discussion of Jack Johnson in relation to Louis, see Van Deburg, *Black Camelot*, 92–95; Astor, *". . . And a Credit to His Race,"* 47–58; Mead, *Champion—Joe Louis*, 19–30; and Holt, *Problem of Race*, 77–80. For the impact of Johnson as a symbol in the black community, see Levine, *Black Culture and Black Consciousness: Afro-American Folk Thought from Slavery to Freedom* (1977), 430–33.

57. Mead, *Champion—Joe Louis*, 52.

58. For description of public reactions to Louis in the press, see Sammons, *Beyond the Ring*, 96–129; Sammons's 1983 *Journal of Popular Culture* article, "Boxing as a Reflection of Society: The Southern Reaction to Joe Louis"; Wiggins's 1988 *Journal of Sport History* article, "Boxing's Sambo Twins: Racial Stereotypes in Jack Johnson and Joe Louis Newspaper Cartoons, 1908–1938"; Gilmore's 1983 *South Atlantic Quarterly* article, "The Myth, Legend, and Folklore of Joe Louis: The Impression of Sport on Society"; and Capeci and Wilkerson's 1983 *Journal of Sport History* article, "Multifarious Hero: Joe Louis, American Society, and Race Relations during World Crisis, 1935-1945."

59. Mead, *Champion—Joe Louis*, 57.

60. Angelou, *I Know Why the Caged Bird Sings*, 135.

61. Ibid., 136.

62. Richard Wright, "Joe Louis Uncovers Dynamite," *New Masses*, 8 Oct 1935, 18–19.

63. For the impact of Joe Louis on folk culture, see Levine, *Black Culture and Black Consciousness*, 433–39; and Angelou, *I Know Why the Caged Bird Sings*, 111–15. For a collection of songs relating to Louis, see *Joe Louis: An American Hero*, Rounder Records (2001),

274

with liner notes by Rena Kosersky and accompanying essay "Reflections on the Joe Louis Recordings" by William H. Wiggins Jr.

64. For a close analysis of the historical context of the Louis-Schmeling fight, see Erenberg, *The Greatest Fight of Our Generation: Louis vs. Schmeling* (2006); and Margolick, *Beyond Glory: Joe Louis vs. Max Schmeling and a World on the Brink* (2005).

65. *Pittsburgh Courier*, 13 (p. 5) and 20 June 1936, 1; *Washington Post*, 18 June 1936, 19.

66. *Washington Post*, 20 June 1936, 1.

67. *Amsterdam News*, 27 June 1936.

68. *Pittsburgh Courier*, 27 June 1936, 4.

69. *Amsterdam News*, 15 Aug. 1936.

70. Ibid.

71. *Amsterdam News*, 27 June 1936.

72. Ibid.

73. *New York Times*, 23 June 1938, 1.

74. *Pittsburgh Courier*, 25 June 1938, 2, 17.

75. Richard Wright, "High Tide in Harlem," *New Masses*, 5 July 1938, 18–20.

76. *Washington Post*, 23 June 1938, 18.

77. *Chicago Tribune*, 22 June 1938, 18.

78. *Life*, 17 June 1940, 55.

79. *Time*, 29 Sept. 1941, 64.

80. Mead, *Champion—Joe Louis*, 210.

81. Walter White, Letter to the Editor, *New York Herald Tribune*, 15 Dec. 1941, in Box A405, NAACP-LC.

82. *Amsterdam News*, 10 Jan. 1942, 14.

83. *Baltimore Afro-American*, 13 Jan. 1942, 22.

84. *Baltimore Afro-American*, 3 Jan. 1942, 2; *Pittsburgh Courier*, 29 Nov. 1941, 6.

85. Mead, *Champion—Joe Louis*, 212.

86. *New York Post*, 10 Jan. 1942, 12; *Washington Post*, 10 Jan. 1942, 21.

87. *New York Post*, 10 Jan. 1942, 12.

88. Paul Gallico, "The Private Life of Joe Louis," *Liberty*, 23 May 1942, 52, 54.

89. *Pittsburgh Courier*, 31 Jan. 1942, 17.

90. *Baltimore Afro-American*, 31 Jan. 1942, 22.

91. *Amsterdam News*, 24 Jan. 1942, 12.

92. F. H. Osborn to Walter White, 1 Oct. 1941; Walter White to Eleanor Roosevelt, 22 Sept. 1941; and Roy Wilkins to Walter White, 3 Oct. 1941, in Box A405, NAACP-LC; Joe Louis to Secretary Knox, 29 Sept. 1941, in RG 80, Entry 23, Box 37, NA.

93. Osborn to White, 1 Oct. 1941, in NAACP-LC. In March 1941, the Morale Branch was assigned to the War Department; previously it had been a division within the Office of the Adjutant General. This new morale organization would "operate directly under the Chief of Staff on a place of equality with the arms and other services." War Department Bureau of Public Relations, "New Morale Branch of the Army Established," 14 Mar. 1941, in RG 107, Entry 188, Box 248, NA.

94. Mead, *Champion—Joe Louis*, 217.

95. White to Eleanor Roosevelt, 22 Sept. 1941; Osborn to White, 1 Oct. 1941; and Wilkins to White, 3 Oct. 1941, in Box A405, NAACP-LC.

96. Cripps, *Making Movies Black*, 103.

97. Milton Starr, "Report on Negro Morale," 1942, in RG 208, Entry ED, Box 6, NA.

98. Mary McLeod Bethune to F. H. Osborne [*sic*], 1 June 1943, in RG 160, Entry 196A, Box 249, NA.

99. Walter White to Joe Louis, 24 Feb. 1940, in Box A405, NAACP-LC.

100. Bethune to Osborne, 1 June 1943, in RG 160, NA.

101. Edwin Henderson to William Hastie and Major Campbell Johnson, 23 Dec. 1941, in RG 107, Entry 188, Box 248, NA. It is interesting that of all the sports listed for interracial competition, boxing was the only one marked with an asterisk. The asterisk at the bottom of the page noted, "Despite the violent contact here and the high emotional contact of the activity it is often evident that instead of arousing antagonism, qualities of respect and sportsmanship are engendered on the part of the participants and spectators. There may be some 'boos' at first but the spirit of American fair play nearly always dominates in the end."

102. Carroll Fitzgerald to Director, Special Service Division, 27 Sept. 1943, in RG 107, Entry 188, Box 182, NA.

103. Truman Gibson to the Assistant Secretary of War, 31 Mar. 1944, in ibid.; Mead, *Champion—Joe Louis*, 230–32.

104. Fitzgerald to Director, 27 Sept. 1943, in RG 107, NA.

105. Harrie W. Pearson to Lt. Col. Frederick H. Weston, 28 Dec. 1943, in RG 160, Entry 196A, Box 248, NA.

106. S. Robert Lough to Theodore Bank, 4 Oct. 1943, in ibid.

107. Theodore Bank to Robert Lough, 13 Oct. 1943, in ibid.

108. Westbrook Pegler, "Fair Enough," *Atlanta Constitution*, 26 Jan. 1942, clipping in RG 208, Entry 5, Box 3, NA; "Capitol Comments," *The Call*, 25 Dec. 1942, Box A426, NAACP-LC.

109. Pegler, "Fair Enough," *Atlanta Constitution*, 26 Jan. 1942, NA.

110. *Baltimore Afro-American*, 24 Jan. 1942, 22, 2; *Pittsburgh Courier*, 24 Jan. 1942, 4.

111. *Pittsburgh Courier*, 17 July 1943, 19.

112. *New York Times*, 11 Oct. 1944, 25; "Louis on Tour," *Life*, 13 Sept. 1943, 34–35; *Daily Worker*, 12 Oct. 1944, 10.

113. Louis et al., *Joe Louis*, 177–80.

114. Pvt. F. K. Wint to Louis Lautier, 1943; and Lautier to Wint, 29 Dec. 1943, both in RG 107, Entry 188, Box 182, NA.

115. Pvt. Jimmy Bivens to Truman Gibson, 1944; and Gibson to Bivens, 22 Aug. 1944, both in ibid. Gibson indicated that no further tours were being organized, but that he had been following Bivens's career and would notify him of any new developments.

116. Truman Gibson to J. Harvey Kerns, 7 Aug. 1943, in ibid.

117. Herman Shumlin to F. H. Osborn, 1 Sept. 1943, and Osborn to Shumlin, 2 Sept. 1943, in RG 160, Entry 196A, Box 249, NA.

118. Mildred Osby to Truman Gibson, 22 July 1943, in RG 107, Entry 188, Box 182, NA.

119. Truman Gibson to Mildred Osby, 6 Aug. 1943, in ibid.

120. Louis et al., *Joe Louis*, 174.

121. Carl Byoir, "Joe Louis Named the War," *Collier's*, 16 May 1942, 14.

122. Roeder, *Censored War*, 44–47, 78. Interestingly, the poster quotes Louis as saying, "We're going to do our part . . . and we'll win because we're on God's side," changing Louis's speech as mentioned earlier.

123. *The Negro Soldier*, dir. Stuart Heisler (Signal Corps, 1944), videotape, in RG 111, control number 111-M-6022, NA. Film historian Thomas Cripps asserts that by 1944, *The Negro Soldier* had become "'mandatory' viewing for all continental replacement troops."

By the spring of 1945, "almost every soldier who passed through I&E's training program saw the film." Cripps, *Making Movies Black*, 112. See Cripps's *Making Movies Black*, 102–25, on the making of *The Negro Soldier*, for a full evaluation of the film's production.

124. Thomas Webster to Dowdal Davis, 18 Apr. 1944, in RG 107, Entry 91, Box 224, NA.

125. Langston Hughes, "Here's a Film Everyone Should See, Writes Defender Columnist," *Chicago Defender*, 26 Feb. 1944, 8.

126. Fred Maloy to Director, Special Services Division, Army Service Forces, 16 Oct. 1944, in RG 107, Entry 188, Box 182, NA.

127. Mead, *Champion—Joe Louis*, 234.

Chapter 5

1. Brig. Gen. B. O. Davis to Tom Lewis, 29 Apr. 1944; and Truman Gibson to Tom Lewis, May 1944, both in RG 330, Entry 1007, Box 6, NA.

2. Tom Lewis, "Victory through Air Power," address delivered before the Advertising Club, Los Angeles, Calif., 6 Feb. 1945, reprinted in National Association of Broadcasters newsletter, 9 Mar. 1945, in RG 330, Entry 384, Box 4, NA.

3. Studies of radio's wartime influence include Savage, *Broadcasting Freedom: Radio, War, and the Politics of Race, 1938–1948* (1999); Horton, *Radio Goes to War: The Cultural Politics of Propaganda during World War II* (2002); Smith, "Radio's 'Cultural Front,' 1938–1948," in Hilmes and Loviglio, *Radio Reader: Essays in the Cultural History of Radio* (2002); and Newman, *Radio Active* (2004). The only study focused solely on the AFRS is the excellent dissertation by DeLay, "An Historical Study of the Armed Forces Radio Service to 1946" (1951). Hilmes gives a brief summary of AFRS activities, including *Jubilee*, in *Radio Voices: American Broadcasting, 1922–1952* (1997), 259–64.

4. Ellison, *Shadow and Act*, xiv.

5. Sterling and Kittress, *Stay Tuned*, 87; Savage, *Broadcasting Freedom*, 6.

6. Susan J. Douglas, *Listening In*, 22–39.

7. Barlow, *Voice Over*, 23–25.

8. Ibid., 26–28.

9. Ely, *Adventures of Amos 'n' Andy*; Hilmes, *Radio Voices*, 81–96.

10. See Oliver's 1974 interview with Les Tomkins, http://www.jazzprofessional.com/interviews/SyOliver_1.htm.

11. MacDonald, *Don't Touch That Dial*, 327; Hilmes, *Radio Voices*, 76–81; Barlow, "Commercial and Noncommercial Radio," in Dates and Barlow, *Split Image*, 176–89.

12. "Present Tensions Involved in the Negro Question," 1942, in RG 208, Entry 222, Box 1079, NA.

13. Frank D. Griffin, "Commercial Radio Won't Hire Colored," *Baltimore Afro-American*, 23 Aug. 1941, 13.

14. "The AFRTS Story," n.d., in RG 330, Entry 384, Box 4, NA; AFRS Fact Sheet, 1 Apr. 1945, in RG 330, Entry 384, Box 16, NA; Robert Sherwood to Ted DeLay, 4 July 1950, RG 330, Entry 1007, Box 5, NA. For a brief discussion of the development of the AFRS and its programming see Hilmes, *Radio Voices*, 259–64.

15. NBC, RCA Victor Division, "A War Record: The Uses of Records in the War Effort," in RG 330, Entry 1007, Box 6, NA. The best sources on V-Discs are Sears, *V-Discs: A History and Discography* (1980) and Sears, *V-Discs: First Supplement* (1986).

16. DeLay, "An Historical Study," 86–89; Robert Beuse, "Tom Lewis: A Profile," n.d., in RG 330, Entry 384, Box 4, NA.

17. Sherwood to DeLay, 4 July 1950 in RG 330, NA; DeLay, "An Historical Study," 121–22.

18. NBC, "War Record," in RG 330, NA.

19. AFRS history, n.d., in RG 330, Entry 1007, Box 6, NA; DeLay, "An Historical Study," 115–16.

20. Research Branch, Special Services Division, "Radio Habits of Enlisted Men," 3 Sept. 1942, in RG 330, Entry 1007, Box 5, NA.

21. National Urban League, "The Negro and National Defense," 30 Mar. 1941, National Urban League Papers, Series 12, Box 14, LC; Savage, *Broadcasting Freedom*, 138, 160–68.

22. Truman Gibson to Maj. R. B. Lord, 20 Mar. 1941; Truman Gibson to R. B. Lord, 1 May 1941; and Truman Gibson to E. M. Kirby, 11 June 1941, all in RG 107, Entry 188, Box 183, NA.

23. J. Brechner to Truman Gibson, 25 June 1941, in RG 107, Entry 188, Box 240, NA.

24. William Hastie to Acting Director, BPR, 6 Aug. 1941, in ibid.

25. "Tentative General Outline for a Negro Program over NBC," n.d., in ibid.

26. C. H. Tobias to William H. Draper, 22 Apr. 1941; Fred Moore to William Hastie, 17 Apr. 1941; Arthur Little to William Hastie, 20 Dec. 1941; and William Heyward to William Hastie, 17 Dec. 1940, all in RG 107, Entry 188, Box 220, NA.

27. Noble Sissle, "Noble Sissle," n.d., in ibid.

28. Truman Gibson to Sol Hurok, 29 July 1941; and Truman Gibson to Hubert Delaney, 19 July 1941, both in RG 107, Entry 188, Box 240, NA.

29. Truman Gibson to Edna Thomas, 11 July 1941, in ibid.

30. Thomas to Gibson, 18 July 1941, in ibid.

31. Gibson to Press Relations Officer, 3 July 1941, in ibid.

32. John Sutherlin to Truman Gibson, 15 July 1941; Charles Simon to Truman Gibson, 11 July 1941; Jack Rudolph to Truman Gibson, 11 July 1941; Ridgley Hall to Truman Gibson, 11 July 1941; Glenn Jacoby to Truman Gibson, 8 July 1941; and George Bestor to Truman Gibson, 9 July 1941, all in RG 107, Entry 199, Box 240, NA. Also see Savage, *Broadcasting Freedom*, 137–38 for some discussion of this correspondence.

33. M. R. Cox to Truman Gibson, 12 July 1941, in RG 107, Entry 199, Box 240, NA.

34. "Negroes in the Army" series, program no. 1, first draft, n.d., in RG 107, Entry 188, Box 240, NA; "America's Negro Soldiers," script prepared by radio branch, BPR [1941], in RG 107, Entry 188, Box 240, NA. Although the latter script was not dated, all of the information in it corresponds with the notices Gibson and the BPR received regarding performers. It also includes the studio number of the broadcast, along with the final date, information that was sent out on a formal invitation to guests (War Department Invitation, in ibid.)

35. Isadora Smith, "Radio's Greatest All-Colored Show for NBC," *Pittsburgh Courier*, 9 Aug. 1941, 20.

36. "America's Negro Soldiers" [1941], in RG 107, NA. Savage presents a discussion of *America's Negro Soldiers* in the context of other War Department radio shows and films emphasizing black military contributions; see *Broadcasting Freedom*, 135–42.

37. "The Army's Radio 'Flop,'" *Pittsburgh Courier*, 23 Aug. 1941, 6.

38. Gill, *White Grease Paint*, 21–91.

39. Savage, *Broadcasting Freedom*, 109, 142.

40. Ibid., 63–105, 194–245.

41. "Program for War Information to Negroes," 1943, in RG 208, Entry E-27, Box 40, NA.

42. Ibid.

43. Special Service Division, Memorandum of Projected Initial Program Schedule (undated, although DeLay, "An Historical Study," 117, speculates it was "finished in late June 1942"), in RG 330, Entry 1007, Box 4, NA; Savage, *Broadcasting Freedom*, 102.

44. The rented studios of NBC, ABC, and CBS were used for *Jubilee*, as were the studios of C. P. MacGregor, Radio Recorders, and Universal Recorders. Richard Sears, who has studied the production of V-Disks, asserts that it was NBC that undertook the majority of recording through 1947. Lotz and Neuert, *The AFRS "Jubilee" Transcription Programs*, vii.

45. DeLay, "An Historical Study," 151–52, 161–62. DeLay does not explain why Holiner did not immediately produce the program.

46. William Mullen to Major Fogel, AFRS, 13 Mar. 1944, in RG 319, Entry 286, Box 306, NA.

47. Lt. Col. Robert E. Kearney, "AFRS Editorial Policy," 1 Aug. 1948, in RG 330, Entry 1007, Box 6, NA.

48. "Nine Most Popular AFRS Show as Selected by Station Staff," n.d., in ibid.

49. Weekly Activity Report, Program Mail Section, 1 Nov. 1943, in RG 319, Entry 285, Box 308, NA.

50. Weekly Activity Report, Program Mail Section, 28 Feb. 1944, in ibid.

51. Weekly Activity Reports, Program Mail Section, 1 Nov. 1943, 28 Feb. 1944, 10 Jan. 1944, and 20 Mar. 1944, in ibid.

52. Charles Vanda to Arthur Wilson, 4 Feb. 1943; and OAC Network Radio Program, 13 Dec. 1943, both in RG 330, Entry 1007, Box 6, NA; Program Schedule for Cairo, Egypt, 5 Sept. 1943, in RG 319, Entry 285, Box 308, NA; General Analysis of AFRS Operations, n.d., RG 330, Entry 1007, Box 6, NA.

53. "The Armed Forces Station," 26 Apr.–2 May 1943, in RG 319, Entry 285, Box 308, NA.

54. Stowe, *Swing Changes*, 73–74, 152–53. The definition of "swing" is incredibly porous and has been a central subject of debate among musicologists, historians, and jazz critics. For the purpose of discussing the *Jubilee* show, I employ definitions offered by David Stowe, who argues that swing is "a stage in the development of jazz characterized by written arrangements and performed by big bands—or small ensembles culled from those bands—during the 1930's and 1940's" (5). Another distinction he makes between swing and jazz is the "tightly structured" nature of swing compared to the largely improvisational nature of jazz; playing "functional dance music," swing bands were larger than jazz combos and focused more on "choirs" than individual lines played by one instrument (10). Stowe points out that this distinction was not recognized at the time swing was emerging precisely because "jazz" was such a fluid term. Many performers on the *Jubilee* show, and historians who refer to it, use the terms "swing" and "jazz" interchangeably (5). Another important distinction is that swing bore a larger connection to its commercialization and modes of performance—in large dance halls, on the radio—associated with specific ensembles and songs.

55. E. B. Rea, "Encored and Echoes," *Baltimore Afro-American*, 9 Dec. 1944, 6; Stowe, *Swing Changes*, 156–67. For a broader discussion of the obstacles black swing bands encountered before the war, see Erenberg, *Swingin' the Dream*, 150–78. Erenberg also describes fears there would be sex between black women and white servicemen in swing clubs during the war, 207–8.

56. Lotz and Neuert, *AFRS "Jubilee" Transcription Programs*, xii; Stowe, *Swing Changes*, 115–17.

57. Erenberg, *Swingin' the Dream*, 130–49; Stowe, *Swing Changes*, 64–72.

58. *Jubilee* #107, dubbed 6 Nov. 1944, NCPC 19579, in MPBRS-LC.

59. Lotz and Neuert, *AFRS "Jubilee," Jubilee* shows 1–4.

60. *Jubilee* #72, dubbed 27 Mar. 1944, RG 200G-2207; and *Jubilee* #60, dubbed 10 Jan. 1944, RG 200G-2156, in DRSNA.

61. *Jubilee* #55, dubbed Dec. 1943, RG 200G-2155, in DRSNA.

62. Denning, *Cultural Front*, 338–41.

63. *Jubilee* #60, RG 200G-2156, in DRSNA.

64. *Jubilee* #48, dubbed 25 Oct. 1943, RG 200G-2208, in DRSNA.

65. *Jubilee* #72, RG 200G-2207, in DRSNA.

66. *Jubilee* #101, dubbed 16 Oct. 1944, broadcast 27 Jan. 1945, RG 200G-2193, in DRSNA.

67. Denning, *Cultural Front*, 348–61.

68. *Jubilee* #101, RG 200G-2193; *Jubilee* #72, RG 200G-2207, in DRSNA.

69. *Jubilee* #29, dubbed 14 June 1943, NCPC 19538, in MPBRS-LC.

70. *Jubilee* #60, RG 200G-2156, in DRSNA.

71. *Jubilee* #55, RG 200G-2155, in DRSNA.

72. *Jubilee* #101, RG 200G-2193, in DRSNA.

73. *Jubilee* #89, dubbed 24 July 1944, RG 200G-2130, in DRSNA; Jubilee #73, dubbed 3 Apr. 1944, RG 200G-2211, in DRSNA.

74. *Jubilee* #89, RG 200G-2130, in DRSNA.

75. *Jubilee* #55, RG 200G-2155, in DRSNA.

76. *Jubilee* #73, RG 200G-2211, in DRSNA.

77. *Jubilee* #60, RG 200G-2156, in DRSNA.

78. *Jubilee* #29, NCPC 19538, in MPBRS-LC; *Jubilee* #89, RG 200G-2130, in DRSNA.

79. *Jubilee* #101, RG 200G-2193, in DRSNA.

80. Ibid.

81. *Jubilee* #60, RG 200G-2156, in DRSNA.

82. Erenberg, *Swingin' the Dream*, 129–49.

83. *Jubilee* #225 (probably broadcast late March 1947), NCPC 19692, in MPBRS-LC.

84. Although it appears Whitman's last recorded show was in the fall 1946, prerecorded broadcasts ran until the beginning of 1947, when others took over as MC. Programs featuring Whitman also were rerun in September and October 1948.

85. Although discographers Lotz and Neuert state that *Jubilee* was "discontinued" in late 1949, weekly broadcasts did run until 18 February 1950. One of these shows was previously recorded in its entirety, but it seems that the AFRS aired a few more programs (most featured prerecorded performances by Ellington and Basie in other venues) even after the operation had declared its ending. Lotz and Neuert, *AFRS "Jubilee" Transcription Programs*, xi.

86. Ibid.

Chapter 6

1. "Our Leading Movie Artists Air Views at AFRO Roundtable," *Baltimore Afro-American*, 9 Jan. 1943, 11.

2. "Government Information Manual for the Motion Picture Industry" (undated, although Koppes and Black, *Hollywood Goes to War*, 343, suggest it was written in the summer of 1942), in RG 208, Entry 6A, Box 3, NA.

3. See Cripps, *Making Movies Black: The Hollywood Message Movie from World War II to*

the Civil Rights Era (1993); Koppes and Black, *Hollywood Goes to War: How Politics, Profits, and Propaganda Shaped World War II Movies* (1987); Doherty, *Projections of War: Hollywood, American Culture, and World War II* (1993).

4. Cripps, *Making Movies Black*, ix.

5. Some major titles include Cripps, *Making Movies Black*; Koppes and Black, *Hollywood Goes to War*; Doherty, *Projections of War*; Buhle and Wagner, *Radical Hollywood: The Untold Story behind America's Favorite Movies* (2002); Erenberg and Hirsch, *The War in American Culture: Society and Consciousness during World War II* (1996); May, *The Big Tomorrow: Hollywood and the Politics of the American Way* (2000); Alpers, *Dictators, Democracy, and American Public Culture: Envisioning the Totalitarian Enemy, 1920s–1950s* (2003).

6. Walter Wagner to Gardner Cowles, 30 July 1942, in RG 208, Entry 1, Box 3, NA.

7. Theodore Berry to Elmer Davis, "Summary and Suggestions on Negro Morale Problems," in RG 208, Entry 1, Box 8, NA.

8. "Program for War Information to Negroes," n.d., in RG 208, Entry E-27, Box 40, NA.

9. Doherty, *Projections of War*, 8–11.

10. OWI, Bureau of Motion Pictures, Box A426, in NAACP-LC. For more on the structural relationship between the OWI and the motion picture industry, see "Memorandum on Cooperation between OWI and MPI," in RG 208, Entry E1, Box 3, NA; Untitled memo in regard to OWI clearance of motion pictures, 1943, in RG 208, Entry 6H, Box 1, NA; Lowell Mellett to David Bader, 22 Jan. 1943, in RG 208, Entry 264, Box 1431, NA. For relationship between the OWI and the War Department in regard to motion pictures, see Kakane, Goldwyn, and Mannix to Lowell Mellett, 8 Mar. 1943, in RG 208, Entry 264, Box 1446, NA.

11. Koppes and Black, *Hollywood Goes to War*, 51–60.

12. Myers, *Bureau of Motion Pictures*, 68–69.

13. Government Information Manual for the Motion Picture Industry, Summer 1942, in RG 208, NA.

14. Poynter quoted in Koppes and Black, *Hollywood Goes to War*, 88.

15. Ibid., 104–12. Koppes and Black indicate that although executives, such as those at Paramount, did not object to the OWI's "general themes," they did state that the OWI should not prevent the studios from exercising their own creative control and "refrain from suggesting 'details of treatment'" (111).

16. Government Information Manual for the Motion Picture Industry, Summer 1942, in RG 208, NA.

17. Koppes and Black, *Hollywood Goes to War*, 85.

18. Walter White to Lowell Mellett, 17 Aug. 1942, in Box A277, NAACP-LC.

19. E. J. Mannix to Lowell Mellett, 20 Aug. 1942, in RG 208, Entry 264, Box 1436, NA.

20. Koppes and Black, *Hollywood Goes to War*, 86–90; Cripps, *Making Movies Black*, 69–72.

21. Weinberg, "What to Tell America"; Koppes and Black, *Hollywood Goes to War*, 136, 134–38; Winkler, *The Politics of Propaganda*, 71, 63–72.

22. Koppes and Black, *Hollywood Goes to War*, 139–41.

23. This literature includes, but is not limited to, Bogle, *Toms, Coons, Mulattoes, Mammies, and Bucks* (1995); Cripps, *Slow Fade to Black* (1977); Cripps, *Making Movies Black* (1993); Guerrero, *Framing Blackness: The African American Image in Film* (1993); Massood, *Black City Cinema: African American Urban Experiences in Film* (2003); Robinson, *Forgeries of Memory and Meaning: Blacks and the Regimes of Race in American Theater and Film before World War II* (2007).

24. Robinson, *Forgeries of Memory and Meaning*, 373.

25. Rogin, *Blackface, White Noise*, 149.

26. Walter White to Lowell Mellett, 24 Dec. 1941, in Box A426, NAACP-LC.

27. Lowell Mellett to Walter White, 26 Dec. 1941, in ibid.

28. Memo on the Negro press, 31 Mar. 1942, in RG 208, Entry 3D, Box 6, NA; publicity bulletin, public relations of the motion picture industry, 18 July 1942, in Box A279, NAACP-LC.

29. Press bulletin, "Film Executives Pledge Better Roles for Negroes at Conference with NAACP Secretary," 31 July 1942, in Box A275, NAACP-LC.

30. Walter White to Jonathan Daniels, 11 Apr. 1940, in Box A274, NAACP-LC.

31. Jonathan Daniels to Walter White, 12 Apr. 1940, in ibid. For Daniels's views on race, see Edgerton, *Speak Now against the Day: The Generation before the Civil Rights Movement in the South* (1994), 258–59.

32. James Chappell to Walter White, 13 Apr. 1940, in Box A274, NAACP-LC.

33. Grover Hall to Walter White, 14 Apr. 1940, in ibid.

34. Edgerton, *Speak Now against the Day*, 292, 250–51.

35. *Crisis* quoted in Doherty, *Projections of War*, 208.

36. May, *Big Tomorrow*, 142; Cripps, *Making Movies Black*, 35. For a further examination of the relationship between Hollywood and the Communist Party, see Buhle and Wagner, *Radical Hollywood*.

37. Cripps, *Making Movies Black*, 53. Chap. 2, 35–63, more fully elaborates on the relationship between Hollywood liberals and Walter White.

38. Sidney Buchman to Darryl Zanuck, 24 July 1942, in Box A280, NAACP-LC.

39. Cliff Work to Darryl Zanuck, 24 July 1942, in ibid.

40. Buddy DeSylva to Darryl Zanuck, 27 July 1942, in ibid.

41. "Hollywood Executives to Support Better Jobs Policy," *Chicago Defender*, 29 Aug. 1942, 23; "Better Movie Roles Promised," *Pittsburgh Courier*, 29 Aug. 1942, 21; "Col. Zanuck Urges Speed for Program," *Baltimore Afro-American*, 29 Aug. 1942, 10.

42. Billy Rowe, "Col. Zanuck Opened War for White and Willkie; Made Stars," *Pittsburgh Courier*, 31 Oct. 1942, 21.

43. Alice Key, "The Hollywood Situation," *Pittsburgh Courier*, 24 Oct. 1942, 20.

44. "Good Scenario Writers Cites as Urgent Need," *Pittsburgh Courier*, 17 Oct. 1942, 21.

45. "Another Group Speaks on the Question Negroes in Pictures," *Chicago Defender*, 19 Sept. 1942, 20.

46. Billy Rowe, "Film Celebrities Tell Billy Rowe What They Think," *Pittsburgh Courier*, 24 Oct. 1942, 20.

47. Billy Rowe, "Humphrey Bogart, John Garfield, Director Bacon Score Film Roles Given Negroes; Pledge Support," *Pittsburgh Courier*, 26 Sept. 1942, 20.

48. Clarence Muse, "Noted Screen Actor Thinks Performers Have Been Ignored," *Pittsburgh Courier*, 12 Sept. 1942, 20.

49. Harry Levette, "Movie Stars Most Successful in Fighting Their Own Battle for Recognition and Having Films Censored," *Baltimore Afro-American*, 5 Sept. 1942, 10.

50. "Our Leading Movie Artists Air Views at AFRO Roundtable," *Baltimore Afro-American*, 9 Jan. 1943, 11.

51. Ibid.

52. Walter White requested several copies of the *Afro-American* article; see Walter White

to Carl Murphy, 12 Mar. 1943, in Box A279, NAACP-LC. For a fuller discussion of White's attitude towards the West Coast actors, see Cripps, *Making Movies Black*, 46–49.

53. Buele and Wagner, *Radical Hollywood*, 189; Cripps, *Making Movies Black*, 81; Aschenbrenner, *Katherine Dunham*, 124–26.

54. Minnelli and Arce, *I Remember It Well*, 121, 126.

55. Naremore, "Uptown Folk: Blackness and Entertainment in *Cabin in the Sky*," in Gabbard, *Representing Jazz*, 169–92.

56. Massood, *Black City Cinema*, 30–38.

57. Naremore, "Uptown Folk," 171.

58. Minnelli and Arce, *I Remember It Well*, 121–22.

59. Kraft, *On My Way to the Theater*, 161.

60. "Says Studio Wants Crude, Corny Themes, Wants His Name Left Off Screen Credits of Film," *Baltimore Afro-American*, 13 Feb. 1943, 8.

61. Cripps, *Making Movies Black*, 83–84.

62. Massood, *Black City Cinema*, 32.

63. Peg Fenwick, Review of *Cabin in the Sky*, 19 Jan. 1943, in RG 208, Entry 567, Box 3513, NA.

64. Lillian Berquist, Review of *Thanks Pal (Stormy Weather)*, 11 Jan. 1943, in RG 208, Entry 567, Box 3526, NA.

65. Ulric Bell to Phil Hamlet, 11 Feb. 1943, in RG 208, Entry 567, Box 3513, NA.

66. Walter White to Edwin Embree, 13 Feb. 1943, in Box A279, NAACP-LC.

67. Marc Connelly to Walter White, 17 Nov. 1942, in Box A274, NAACP-LC.

68. Walter White to A. P. Tureaud, 17 July 1943, in ibid.

69. A. P. Tureaud to Walter White, 15 July 1943, in ibid.

70. Walter White to Darryl Zanuck, 2 July 1943, in Box A280, NAACP-LC.

71. Peter Furst to Walter White, 31 May 1943, in Box A277, NAACP-LC.

72. Porter Roberts, "Praise and Criticism," *Chicago Defender*, 22 May 1943, 18.

73. "Term 'Cabin' Film Downright Criminal," *Baltimore Afro-American*, 13 Mar. 1943, 10.

74. "Says Studio Wants Crude, Corny Themes," *Baltimore Afro-American*, 13 Feb. 1943.

75. Leo Roa, "Success of 'Cabin in the Sky' Seen as a Boon to Colored Stars in Films," *Baltimore Afro-American*, 13 Feb. 1943, 8.

76. Billy Rowe, "Courier Reporter at Private Showing," *Pittsburgh Courier*, 31 Oct. 1942, 20.

77. "'Stormy Weather' Rated a 'Sender,'" *Pittsburgh Courier*, 31 July 1943, 20.

78. Rowe, "Courier Reporter at Private Showing," *Pittsburgh Courier*, 31 Oct. 1942, 20.

79. "Ethel Waters, Crap-Shooter in MGM's 'Cabin in the Sky,'" *Baltimore Afro-American*, 3 Apr. 1943, 8.

80. Paul T. Mitchell, *Motion Picture Herald*, 14 Aug. 1943.

81. H. Goldson, *Motion Picture Herald*, 4 Sept. 1943.

82. W. R. Pyle, *Motion Picture Herald*, 30 Oct. 1943.

83. J. L. Cooper, *Motion Picture Herald*, 6 Nov. 1943.

84. J. D. Leger, *Motion Picture Herald*, 25 Mar. 1944.

85. Charles Richelieu, *Motion Picture Herald*, 24 July 1943.

86. For an explanation of the transformation of American theater in the nineteenth century, see Levine, *Highbrow/Lowbrow: The Emergence of Cultural Hierarchy in America* (1988), 11–81.

87. Government Information Manual for the Motion Picture Industry, Summer 1942, in RG 208, NA. For further discussion of the multiethnic platoon, see Alpers, *Dictators, Democracy, and American Public Culture: Envisioning the Totalitarian Enemy, 1920s–1950s* (2003), 157–87; and Slotkin, *Gunfighter Nation: The Myth of the Frontier in Twentieth-Century America* (1992), 313–43.

88. *Bataan Patrol* script review by Robert Andrews, 2 Oct. 1942, in RG 208, Entry E567, Box 3511, NA.

89. *Bataan* review by unknown author, 8 Apr. 1942, in ibid.

90. Statement by Walter White, 2 June 1942, in Box A275, NAACP-LC.

91. *Sahara*, dir. Zoltan Korda, Columbia, 1943.

92. *Sahara* review by unknown author, 1 Feb. 1943, in RG 208, Entry 567, Box 3524, NA.

93. *Sahara* review by unknown author, 8 July 1943, in ibid.

94. Ulric Bell to Robert Riskin, 8 July 1943, in ibid.

95. Ulric Bell to B. B. Kahane, 1 Nov. 1943, in ibid.

96. Government Information Manual for the Motion Picture Industry, Summer 1942, in RG 208, NA.

97. "Columbia Pictures Praised for Ingram in 'Sahara,'" in Box A275, NAACP-LC.

98. Charles Brooks, *Motion Picture Herald*, 26 Feb. 1944; F. R. Crist, *Motion Picture Herald*, 2 Oct. 1943.

99. Arthur Dame, *Motion Picture Herald*, 20 Nov. 1943.

100. S. L. George, *Motion Picture Herald*, 20 Nov. 1943.

101. O. E. Simon, *Motion Picture Herald*, 15 Jan. 1943.

102. D. L. Craddock, *Motion Picture Herald*, 15 Jan. 1944.

103. Benton Roy, *Motion Picture Herald*, 22 Apr. 1944.

104. Phil Carter, "'Bataan' Another Great War Film," *Pittsburgh Courier*, 13 Mar. 1943, 21.

105. "Deeds of Our Boys in Argonne Overlooked, Not So in Bataan," *Baltimore Afro-American*, 13 Mar. 1943, 10.

106. "Take Segregation and Like It," *Baltimore Afro-American*, 13 Mar. 1943, 6.

107. "Patterson Calls 30,000 Whites but No Colored," *Baltimore Afro-American*, 13 Mar. 1943, 1–2.

108. "Bias Will Prevail Says Air Official," *Pittsburgh Courier*, 27 Mar. 1943, 5.

109. "Success of Cabin in the Sky Seen as a Boon to Colored Stars in Films," and "Only One of 15 War Plant Employees in Baltimore Colored," *Baltimore Afro-American*, 13 Feb. 1943, 8, 7.

110. Cripps, *Making Movies Black*, 73. Although Cripps does not describe exactly how *Lifeboat* transformed from the ideas of the original three producers to its final stage, he relates that the film "suffered most from the continuing problem of how to maintain political coherence in the rough and tumble of movie lot operations while struggling against survivals of past practice." Cripps, *Making Movies Black*, 73.

111. *Lifeboat*, dir. Alfred Hitchcock, 20th Century Fox, 1943.

112. *Lifeboat* review by unknown author, 27 July 1942, in RG 208, Entry 567, Box 3520, NA.

113. Peg Fenwick, *Lifeboat* review, 21 Dec. 1943, in ibid.

114. Ibid.

115. Memorandum to Mr. Wilkins from Mr. Jones, 20 Jan. 1943, in Box A275, NAACP-LC.

116. Roy Wilkins to William Goetz, 17 Feb. 1944, in ibid.

117. Harry Levette, "Canada Less Has 'Uncle Tom' Phrases Cut from Script in Fox's 'Lifeboat,'" *Baltimore Afro-American*, 11 Sept. 1943, 10.

118. Harry Levette, "Lee's 'Lifeboat' Role Is Best Yet for Colored," *Baltimore Afro-American*, 13 Nov. 1943, 8.

119. "Author at Odds with 20th over Filming of 'Lifeboat,'" *Baltimore Afro-American*, 29 Jan. 1944, 8.

120. *Ox-Bow Incident* review by unknown author, 19 Dec. 1942, in RG 208, Entry 567, Box 3523, NA.

121. Walter White to William Goetz, 4 Dec. 1942, in Box A279, NAACP-LC.

122. Marguerite Cartwright to Walter White, n.d., in ibid.

123. Mayme Musselman, *Motion Picture Herald*, 13 Nov. 1943; E. M. Freiburger, *Motion Picture Herald*, 13 Nov. 1943.

124. Arthur Dame, *Motion Picture Herald*, 20 Nov. 1943.

125. For the careers of Lee, Wilson, and Ingram, see Gill, *White Grease Paint on Black Performers: A Study of the Federal Theatre, 1935–1939* (1988).

126. Langston Hughes, "Here's a Film Everyone Should See," *Chicago Defender*, 26 Feb. 1944, 8.

127. F. Leslie Clark to Dowdall Davis, 16 Apr. 1944, in RG 107, Entry 91, Box 224, NA.

128. *Chicago Defender*, 1 Apr. 1944, 8.

129. Hughes, "Here's a Film Everyone Should See," *Chicago Defender*, 26 Feb. 1944.

130. For more on *The Negro Soldier*, see Cripps, *Making Movies Black*, 102–25; and Cripps and Culbert's 1979 *American Quarterly* article "*The Negro Soldier* (1944): Film Propaganda in Black and White."

131. *Pittsburgh Courier*, 8 July 1944, 13.

132. Cripps, *Making Movies Black*, 120.

133. Herman Hill, "Claims Exhibitors Refuse to Show Racial Unity Film," *Pittsburgh Courier*, 8 Apr. 1944, 13.

134. Cripps, *Making Movies Black*, 112–14.

135. *Baltimore Afro-American*, 10 July 1943, 8.

136. "Dixie Theatres Cut Negro Scenes from Pix," *Pittsburgh Courier*, 22 July 1944, 13.

137. Doherty, *Projections of War*, 221–23.

138. Koppes and Black, *Hollywood Goes to War*, 323. This statistic differs from the earlier record of 1,652 scripts because the latter refers to a longer period, between 1942 and 1945.

139. "Producers Aware of Ten Per Cent Box Office Total," *Pittsburgh Courier*, 21 Oct. 1944, 13; Billy Rowe, "Even Film Talent Feels New Demand for Negro Stars," *Pittsburgh Courier*, 26 June 1943, 20.

140. "Writers to Demand Change in Policy of Film Industry," *Pittsburgh Courier*, 25 Mar. 1944, 13; "Stars Ask Just Treatment of Race in Show Business," *Pittsburgh Courier*, 3 June 1944, 13; "Actors Condemn Casting of Negro in Clown Roles," *Pittsburgh Courier*, 22 July 1944, 13.

141. "Writers to Demand Change in Policy Of Film Industry," *Pittsburgh Courier*, 25 Mar. 1944.

142. Herman Hill, "Three Movie Lots to Avoid Racial Slurs in Films," *Pittsburgh Courier*, 15 July 1944, 13.

Epilogue

1. Quoted in McCullough, *Truman*, 589.

2. Leuchtenburg, *White House Looks South*, 206. For further discussion of Truman's racial policy see ibid., 147–225.

3. Ibid., 225.

4. Brownell with Burke, *Advising Ike*, 190.

5. Burk, *Eisenhower Administration and Black Civil Rights*, 262–63.

6. Dudziak, *Cold War Civil Rights*.

7. For a complete analysis of the State Department tours, see Von Eschen, *Satchmo Blows Up the World: Jazz Ambassadors Play the Cold War* (2004); on Armstrong's resistance, see ibid., 58–91. For additional analysis of the controversy surrounding Baker and Robeson, see Biondi, *To Stand and Fight: The Struggle for Civil Rights in Postwar New York City* (2003), 155–60, 186–90; and Dudziak, *Cold War Civil Rights*, 61–78.

8. Von Eschen, *Satchmo Blows Up the World*, 148–84 (quote on 160).

9. Cripps, *Making Movies Black*, 261.

10. For a discussion of racial themes within the larger context of Cold War films, see May, *The Big Tomorrow: Hollywood and the Politics of the American Way* (2000), 175–213.

11. Quoted in Lipsitz, *Time Passages*, 121.

12. Short and Clark, *History of American Bandstand*, 7; Ward, *Just My Soul Responding*, 164–69.

13. Daniel, *Lost Revolutions*, 148. For an analysis of cultural exchange during the civil rights era, see Ward, *Just My Soul Responding*.

14. Ibid., 323–36.

15. Larry Neal, "The Black Arts Movement," *Drama Review* 12 (Summer 1968): 39.

16. Smethurst, *Black Arts Movement*. William Van Deburg offers an excellent study of the relationship between culture and political ideology in the Black Power movement, in *A New Day in Babylon: the Black Power Movement and American Culture, 1965–1975* (1992).

17. Dyson, "Be Like Mike?: Michael Jordan and the Pedagogy of Desire," 66.

18. *Do The Right Thing*, dir. Spike Lee, Universal, 1989.

19. Angelou, *On the Pulse of Morning*, 10–11.

BIBLIOGRAPHY

Manuscript Collections

Fairfax, Virginia
    George Mason University Special Collections and Archives
        American Theater Collection, Federal Theatre Project oral interviews
Hyde Park, New York
    Franklin D. Roosevelt Presidential Library
        Hallie Flanagan-Davis Papers
        Harry Hopkins Papers
        Lowell Mellett Papers
        Eleanor Roosevelt Pamphlet Collection
        Franklin D. Roosevelt Papers
            President's Official File
            President's Personal File
            President's Secretarial File
        White House Office of Social Entertainment Papers
Washington, D.C.
    Library of Congress
        Division of Motion Picture, Broadcasting, and Recorded Sound
            Jubilee recordings
        Manuscript Division
            Records of the Federal Theatre Project, Works Progress Administration
            Records of the Federal Writers' Project, Works Progress Administration
            Special Studies and Projects, Federal Writers' Project Papers
            Archibald MacLeish Papers
            Papers of the National Association for the Advancement of Colored People
            Papers of the National Urban League
    Moorland-Spingarn Research Center, Howard University
        Sterling Brown Papers
    National Archives
        RG 69, Records of the Work Projects Administration
        RG 80, General Records of the Department of the Navy
        RG 107, Records of the Office of the Secretary of War
        RG 111, Records of the Office of the Chief Signal Officer
        RG 160, Records of Headquarters, Army Service Forces
        RG 200G, Division of Recorded Sound, *Jubilee* recordings
        RG 208, Records of the Office of War Information
        RG 319, Records of the Army Staff
        RG 330, Records of the Office of the Secretary of Defense

Contemporary Journals and Periodicals
Collier's
Crisis
Journal of Negro History
Liberty
Life
Motion Picture Herald
Nation
New Masses
New Republic
Opportunity
Prairie Schooner
Public Opinion Quarterly
Publishers' Weekly
Quarterly Review of Higher Education among Negroes
Saturday Review of Literature
South Atlantic Quarterly
Time
Variety

Government Documents

U.S. Congress. House. Committee on Un-American Activities. *Investigation of Un-American Propaganda Activities in the U.S.* 75th Cong., 3rd Sess., 1938.
———. Subcommittee of the Committee on Appropriations. *Further Additional Appropriations for Work Relief, Fiscal Year, 1939.* 76th Cong., 1st Sess., 1939.
U.S. Congress. Senate. *Congressional Record.* 76th Cong., 4th Sess., 1939. Vol. 84.

Newspapers
Amsterdam News
Atlanta Constitution
Baltimore Afro-American
Chicago Defender
Chicago Tribune
Daily Worker
London Spectator
New York News
New York Post
New York Times
New York Woman
Pittsburgh Courier
Washington Post

Books, Articles, Dissertations, and Unpublished Papers

Abramson, Doris. *Negro Playwrights in the American Theatre, 1925–1959.* New York: Columbia University Press, 1969.
Alexander, Charles. *Here the Country Lies: Nationalism and the Arts in Twentieth-Century America.* Bloomington: Indiana University Press, 1980.

Alpers, Benjamin. *Dictators, Democracy, and American Public Culture: Envisioning the Totalitarian Enemy, 1920s–1950s*. Chapel Hill: University of North Carolina Press, 2003.

Andrews, William, Frances Smith Foster, and Trudier Harris, eds. *The Oxford Companion to African American Literature*. New York: Oxford University Press, 1997.

Angelou, Maya. *I Know Why the Caged Bird Sings*. New York: Bantam Books, 1993.

———. *On the Pulse of Morning*. New York: Random House, 1993.

Aschenbrenner, Joyce. *Katherine Dunham: Dancing a Life*. Urbana: University of Illinois Press, 2002.

Astor, Gerald. *". . . And a Credit to His Race": The Hard Life and Times of Joseph Louis Barrow*. New York: Saturday Review Press, 1974.

Badger, Anthony. *The New Deal: The Depression Years, 1933–1940*. Chicago: Ivan Dee, 1989.

Balogh, Brian. *Chain Reaction: Expert Debate and Public Participation in American Commercial Nuclear Power, 1945–1974*. Cambridge: Cambridge University Press, 1991.

Barlow, William. *Voice Over: The Making of Black Radio*. Philadelphia: Temple University Press, 1999.

Batiste, Stephanie L. "Darkening Mirrors: Otherness and Subjectivity in African-American Performance during the Depression Era." Ph.D. diss., George Washington University, 2003.

Binkiewicz, Donna M. *Federalizing the Muse: United States Arts Policy and the National Endowment for the Arts, 1965–1980*. Chapel Hill: University of North Carolina Press, 2004.

Biondi, Martha. *To Stand and Fight: The Struggle for Civil Rights in Postwar New York City*. Cambridge, Mass.: Harvard University Press, 2003.

Bird, William L., and Harry Rubenstein. *Design for Victory: World War II Posters on the American Home Front*. New York: Princeton Architectural Press, 1998.

Bogle, Thomas. *Toms, Coons, Mulattoes, Mammies, and Bucks*. New York: Continuum, 1995.

Bold, Christine. *The WPA Guides: Mapping America*. Jackson: University Press of Mississippi, 1999.

Borgwardt, Elizabeth. *A New Deal for the World: America's Vision for Human Rights*. Cambridge, Mass.: Belknap Press, 2005.

Boyle, Kevin. *Arc of Justice: A Saga of Race, Civil Rights, and Murder in the Jazz Age*. New York: Henry Holt, 2004.

Brinkley, Alan. *The End of Reform: New Deal Liberalism in Recession and War*. New York: Vintage Books, 1995.

Brown, Lorraine. "A Story Yet to Be Told: The Federal Theatre Research Project." *Black Scholar* 10 (July–August 1979): 70–78.

Brown, Sterling, and Mark A. Sanders. *A Son's Return: Selected Essays of Sterling Brown*. Boston: Northeastern University Press, 1996.

Brownell, Herbert, with John P. Burke. *Advising Ike: The Memoirs of Attorney General Herbert Brownell*. Lawrence: University Press of Kansas, 1993.

Brown-Guillory, Elizabeth, ed. *Wines in the Wilderness: Plays by African American Women from the Harlem Renaissance to the Present*. Westport, Conn.: Greenwood Press, 1990.

Buhle, Paul, and Dave Wagner. *Radical Hollywood: The Untold Story behind America's Favorite Movies*. New York: New Press, 2002.

Burk, Robert Frederick. *The Eisenhower Administration and Black Civil Rights*. Knoxville: University of Tennessee Press, 1984.

Canaday, Margot. "Building a Straight State: Sexuality and Social Citizenship under the 1944 G.I. Bill." *Journal of American History* 90 (December 2003): 935–57.

Capeci, Dominic J., Jr., and Martha Wilkerson. "Multifarious Hero: Joe Louis, American Society, and Race Relations during World Crisis, 1935–1945." *Journal of Sport History* 10 (Winter 1983): 5–25.

Carter, Dan T. "Legacy of Rage: George Wallace and the Transformation of American Politics." *Journal of Southern History* 62 (February 1996): 3–26.

———. *The Politics of Rage: George Wallace, the Origins of the New Conservatism, and the Transformation of American Politics.* Baton Rouge: Louisiana State University Press, 2000.

———. *Scottsboro: A Tragedy of the American South.* Baton Rouge: Louisiana State University Press, 1969.

Chen, Anthony. "'The Hitlerian Rule of Quotas': Racial Conservatism and the Politics of Fair Employment Legislation in New York State, 1941–1945." *Journal of American History* 92 (March 2006): 1238–64.

Cohen, Harvey G. "Improvising across the Lines: Duke Ellington's America." Ph.D. diss., University of Maryland–College Park, 2002.

Cohen, Lizbeth. *Making a New Deal: Industrial Workers in Chicago, 1919–1939.* Cambridge: Cambridge University Press, 1990.

Cohen, Robert. *When the Old Left Was Young: Student Radicals and America's First Mass Student Movement, 1929–1941.* New York: Oxford University Press, 1993.

Coyle, William, and Harvey Damaser, eds. *Six Early American Plays, 1798–1890.* Columbus, Ohio: Charles E. Merrill, 1968.

Cripps, Thomas. *Making Movies Black: The Hollywood Message Movie from World War II to the Civil Rights Era.* New York: Oxford University Press, 1993.

———. *Slow Fade to Black.* New York: Oxford University Press, 1977.

Cripps, Thomas, and David Culbert. "*The Negro Solider* (1944): Film Propaganda in Black and White." *American Quarterly* 31 (Winter 1979): 616–40.

Cruse, Harold. *The Crisis of the Negro Intellectual.* New York: Quill, 1984.

Dalfiume, Richard. *Desegregation of the U.S. Armed Forces: Fighting on Two Fronts, 1939–1953.* Columbia: University of Missouri Press, 1969.

———. "The 'Forgotten Years' of the Negro Revolution." *Journal of American History* 60 (June 1968): 90–106.

Daniel, Pete. *Lost Revolutions: The South in the 1950s.* Chapel Hill: University of North Carolina Press, 2000.

Dates, Jannette, and William Barlow, eds. *Split Image: African Americans in the Mass Media.* Washington, D.C.: Howard University Press, 1990.

DeLay, Ted, Jr. "An Historical Study of the Armed Forces Radio Service to 1946." Ph.D. diss., University of Southern California, 1951.

Denning, Michael. *The Cultural Front: The Laboring of American Culture in the Twentieth Century.* New York: Verso, 1997.

Doherty, Thomas. *Projections of War: Hollywood, American Culture, and World War II.* New York: Columbia University Press, 1993.

Donaldson, Scott. *Archibald MacLeish: An American Life.* Boston: Houghton Mifflin, 1992.

Douglas, Ann. *Terrible Honesty: Mongrel Manhattan in the 1920s.* New York: Farrar, Straus, and Giroux, 1995.

Douglas, Susan J. *Listening In: Radio and the American Imagination, from Amos 'n' Andy and Edward R. Murrow to Wolfman Jack and Howard Stern.* New York: Times Books, 1999.

Drabeck, Bernard, and Helen Ellis, eds. *Archibald MacLeish: Reflections.* Amherst: University of Massachusetts Press, 1986.

Du Bois, W. E. B. *Black Reconstruction in America: An Essay toward a History of the Part Which Black Folk Played in the Attempt to Reconstruct Democracy in America, 1860–1880.* New York: Atheneum, 1977.

Dudziak, Mary L. *Cold War Civil Rights: Race and the Image of American Democracy.* Princeton: Princeton University Press, 2000.

Dupont, M. Jill. "'The Self in the Ring, the Self in Society': Boxing and American Culture from Jack Johnson to Joe Louis." Ph.D. diss., University of Chicago, 2000.

Dyson, Michael Eric. "Be Like Mike?: Michael Jordan and the Pedagogy of Desire." *Cultural Studies* 7 (January 1993): 64–72.

Edgerton, John. *Speak Now against the Day: The Generation before the Civil Rights Movement in the South.* New York: Knopf, 1994.

Elkins, Stanley. *Slavery: A Problem in American Institutional and Intellectual Life.* Chicago: University of Chicago Press, 1968.

Ellison, Ralph. *Shadow and Act.* New York: Vintage Books, 1972.

Ely, Melvin Patrick. *The Adventures of Amos 'n' Andy: A Social History of an American Phenomenon.* New York: Free Press, 1991.

Erenberg, Lewis. *The Greatest Fight of Our Generation: Louis vs. Schmeling.* New York: Oxford University Press, 2006.

———. *Swingin' the Dream: Big Band Jazz and the Rebirth of American Culture.* Chicago: University of Chicago Press, 1998.

Erenberg, Lewis, and Susan Hirsch, eds. *The War in American Culture: Society and Consciousness during World War II.* Chicago: University of Chicago Press, 1996.

Federal Writers' Project. *Alabama: A Guide to the Deep South.* New York: Richard Smith, 1941.

———. *Arizona: A State Guide.* New York: Hastings House, 1972.

———. *Arkansas: A Guide to the State.* New York: Hastings House, 1941.

———. *Illinois: A Descriptive and Historical Guide.* Chicago: A. C. McClurg, 1939.

———. *Indiana: A Guide to the Hoosier State.* New York: Oxford University Press, 1973.

———. *Mississippi: A Guide to the Magnolia State.* New York: Viking Press, 1938.

———. *The Negro in New York: An Informal Social History.* Edited by Roi Ottley and W. J. Weatherby. New York: New York Public Library and Oceana, 1967.

———. *The Ohio Guide.* New York: Oxford University Press, 1962.

———. *Pennsylvania: A Guide to the Keystone State.* Philadelphia: University of Pennsylvania Press, 1940.

———. *South Carolina: A Guide to the Palmetto State.* New York: Oxford University Press, 1976.

———. *South Carolina: The WPA Guide to the Palmetto State.* Columbia: University of South Carolina Press, 1988.

———. *Texas: A Guide to the Lone Star State.* New York: Hastings House, 1974.

———. *Washington: City and Capital.* Washington, D.C.: Government Printing Office, 1937.

———. *The WPA Guide to 1930s Alabama.* Tuscaloosa: University of Alabama Press, 2000.

————. *WPA Guide to Philadelphia: A Guide to the Nation's Birthplace*. Philadelphia: University of Pennsylvania Press, 1988.

Feldstein, Ruth. "'I Don't Trust You Anymore': Nina Simone, Culture, and Black Activism in the 1960s." *Journal of American History* 91 (March 2005): 1349–79.

Flanagan, Hallie. *Arena: The History of the Federal Theatre*. New York: Benjamin Blom, 1940.

Fleischhauer, Carl, and Beverly W. Brannan, eds. *Documenting America, 1935–1943*. Berkeley: University of California Press, 1988.

Fraden, Rena. *Blueprints for a Black Federal Theatre, 1935–1939*. Cambridge: Cambridge University Press, 1994.

————. "A National Negro Theater That Never Was: Making It Real, Uphill All the Way." *American Visions* 9 (October/November 1994): 26–28, 30–33.

Gabbard, Krin, ed. *Representing Jazz*. Durham: Duke University Press, 1995.

Gabbin, Joanne V. *Sterling A. Brown: Building the Black Aesthetic Tradition*. Westport, Conn.: Greenwood Press, 1985.

Garabedian, Steven. "Reds, Whites, and the Blues: Lawrence Gellert, 'Negro Songs of Protest,' and the Left-Wing Folk-Song Revival of the 1930s and 1940s." *American Quarterly* 57 (March 2005): 179–206.

Gary, Brett. *The Nervous Liberals: Propaganda Anxieties from World War I to the Cold War*. New York: Columbia University Press, 1999.

Gerstle, Gary. *American Crucible: Race and Nation in the Twentieth Century*. Princeton: Princeton University Press, 2001.

————. "The Protean Character of American Liberalism." *American Historical Review* 4 (October 1994): 1043–73.

————. "Race and the Myth of the Liberal Consensus." *Journal of American History* 82 (September 1995): 579–86.

Gerstle, Gary, and Steve Fraser, eds. *The Rise and Fall of the New Deal Order, 1930–1980*. Princeton: Princeton University Press, 1989.

Gill, Glenda. *White Grease Paint on Black Performers: A Study of the Federal Theatre, 1935–1939*. New York: Peter Lang, 1988.

Gilmore, Al-Tony. "The Myth, Legend, and Folklore of Joe Louis: The Impression of Sport on Society." *South Atlantic Quarterly* 82 (Summer 1983): 256–68.

Gilmore, Glenda Elizabeth. *Defying Dixie: The Radical Roots of Civil Rights, 1919–1950*. New York: W. W. Norton, 2008.

Glasco, Laurence A., ed. *The WPA History of the Negro in Pittsburgh*. Pittsburgh: University of Pittsburgh Press, 2004.

Gold, Michael. "The Intellectual Road to Fascism." *New Masses* 7 (September 1931): 10–11.

Gordon, Colin. *New Deals: Business, Labor, and Politics in America, 1920–1935*. Cambridge: Cambridge University Press, 1994.

Gordon, Linda. "Black and White Visions of Welfare: Women's Welfare Activism, 1890–1945." *Journal of American History* 78 (September 1991): 559–90.

————. "Dorothea Lange: Photographer as Agricultural Sociologist." *Journal of American History* 93 (December 2006): 698–727.

————. *Pitied but Not Entitled: Single Mothers and the History of Welfare, 1890–1935*. New York: Free Press, 1994.

Graham, Hugh Davis. *The Civil Rights Era: Origins and Development of National Policy, 1960–1972*. New York: Oxford University Press, 1990.

Grant, George C. "The Negro in Dramatic Art." *Journal of Negro History* 17 (January 1932):
19–29.

Guerrero, Ed. *Framing Blackness: The African American Image in Film*. Philadelphia:
Temple University Press, 1993.

Hale, Grace. "Everyone Is a Negro: Racial Rebellion from the Blues to the Folk Music
Revival." Lecture given at the University of South Carolina, September 14, 2006.

———. *Making Whiteness: The Culture of Segregation in the South, 1880–1940*. New York:
Pantheon Books, 1998.

Hall, Jacquelyn Dowd. "The Long Civil Rights Movement and the Political Uses of the
Past." *Journal of American History* 91 (March 2005): 1233–63.

Hayter, Charles. *Gilbert and Sullivan*. London: Macmillan, 1987.

Heclo, Hugh. "The In-and-Outer System: A Critical Assessment." *Political Science
Quarterly* 1 (Spring 1998): 37–56.

Herzstein, Robert Edwin. *Roosevelt and Hitler: Prelude to War*. New York: Paragon House,
1989.

———. *The War That Hitler Won: The Most Infamous Propaganda Campaign in History*.
New York: Putnam, 1978.

Hill, Errol, and James V. Hatch, eds. *A History of African American Theatre*. Cambridge:
Cambridge University Press, 2003.

Hilmes, Michele. *Radio Voices: American Broadcasting, 1922–1952*. Minneapolis: University
of Minnesota Press, 1997.

Hilmes, Michele, and Jason Loviglio, eds. *Radio Reader: Essays in the Cultural History of
Radio*. New York: Routledge, 2002.

Hirsch, Jerrold. *Portrait of America: A Cultural History of the Federal Writers' Project*.
Chapel Hill: University of North Carolina Press, 2003.

Holt, Thomas C. *The Problem of Race in the 21st Century*. Cambridge, Mass.: Harvard
University Press, 2000.

Horton, Gerd. *Radio Goes to War: The Cultural Politics of Propaganda during World War II*.
Berkeley: University of California Press, 2002.

Houseman, John. *Run-Through: A Memoir*. New York: Simon and Schuster, 1972.

Huggins, Nathan Irvin. *Harlem Renaissance*. New York: Oxford University Press, 2007.

Hutchinson, George. *The Harlem Renaissance in Black and White*. Cambridge, Mass.:
Harvard University Press, 1995.

Isserman, Maurice. *Which Side Were You On? The American Communist Party during the
Second World War*. Middletown, Conn.: Wesleyan University Press, 1982.

Jacobson, Matthew Frye. *Whiteness of a Different Color: European Immigrants and the
Alchemy of Race*. Cambridge, Mass.: Harvard University Press, 1998.

Jones, Alfred Haworth. "The Search for a Useable American Past in the New Deal Era."
American Quarterly 23 (December 1971): 710–24.

Katznelson, Ira, Kim Geiger, and Daniel Kryder. "Limiting Liberalism: The Southern Veto
in Congress, 1933 1950." *Political Science Quarterly* 108 (Summer 1993): 283–306.

Kazin, Alfred. *On Native Grounds: An Interpretation of American Literature*. New York:
Reynal and Hitchcock, 1942.

Kelley, Robin D. G. *Hammer and Hoe: Alabama Communists during the Great Depression*.
Chapel Hill: University of North Carolina Press, 1990.

———. *Race Rebels: Culture, Politics, and the Black Working Class*. New York: Free Press,
1996.

Kessler-Harris, Alice. *In Pursuit of Equity: Women, Men, and the Quest for Economic Citizenship in Twentieth Century America*. New York: Oxford University Press, 2001.

———. "In the Nation's Image: The Gendered Limits of Social Citizenship in the Depression Era." *Journal of American History* 86 (December 1999): 1251–79.

Kirby, John. *Black Americans in the Roosevelt Era: Liberalism and Race*. Knoxville: University of Tennessee Press, 1980.

Koppes, Clayton R., and Gregory D. Black. *Hollywood Goes to War: How Politics, Profits and Propaganda Shaped World War II Movies*. Berkeley: I. B. Tauris, 1987.

Korstad, Robert, and Nelson Lichtenstein. "Opportunities Found and Lost: Labor, Radicals, and the Early Civil Rights Movement." *Journal of American History* 75 (December 1988): 786–811.

Kraft, Hy. *On My Way to the Theater*. New York: Macmillan, 1971.

Krasner, David. *A Beautiful Pageant: African American Theatre, Drama, and Performance in the Harlem Renaissance, 1910–1927*. New York: Palgrave, 2002.

Kryder, Daniel. *Divided Arsenal: Race and the American State during World War II*. Cambridge: Cambridge University Press, 2000.

Leuchtenburg, William E. *Franklin D. Roosevelt and the New Deal, 1932–1940*. New York: Harper and Row, 1963.

———. *The White House Looks South: Franklin D. Roosevelt, Harry S. Truman, Lyndon B. Johnson*. Baton Rouge: Louisiana State University Press, 2005.

Levine, Lawrence W. *Black Culture and Black Consciousness: Afro-American Folk Thought from Slavery to Freedom*. New York: Oxford University Press, 1977.

———. *Highbrow/Lowbrow: The Emergence of Cultural Hierarchy in America*. Cambridge, Mass.: Harvard University Press, 1988.

———. *The Opening of the American Mind: Canons, Culture, and History*. Boston: Beacon Press, 1996.

———. *The Unpredictable Past: Explorations in American Cultural History*. New York: Oxford, 1993.

Levine, Lawrence W., and Cornelia R. Levine. *The People and the President: America's Conversation with FDR*. Boston: Beacon Press, 2002.

Levine, Lawrence W., and Robert Middlekauff, eds. *The National Temper: Readings in American Culture and Society*. New York: Harcourt Brace, 1972.

Lewis, David Levering. *When Harlem Was in Vogue*. New York: Penguin, 1997.

Lhamon, W. T., Jr. *Raising Cain: Blackface Performance from Jim Crow to Hip Hop*. Cambridge, Mass.: Harvard University Press, 1998.

Lichtenstein, Nelson. *Labor's War at Home: The CIO in World War II*. Cambridge: Cambridge University Press, 1982.

———, ed. *American Capitalism: Social Thought and Political Economy in the Twentieth Century*. Philadelphia: University of Pennsylvania Press, 2006.

Lipsitz, George. *Time Passages: Collective Memory and American Popular Culture*. Minneapolis: University of Minnesota Press, 1990.

Locke, Alain, ed. *The New Negro: An Interpretation*. New York: Johnson Reprint, 1968.

Lott, Eric. *Love and Theft: Blackface Minstrelsy and the American Working Class*. New York: Oxford University Press, 1993.

Lotz, Rainer E., and Ulrich Neuert. *The AFRS "Jubilee" Transcription Programs: An Exploratory Discography*. Frankfurt: Norbert Rueker, 1985.

Louis, Joe, with Erna Rust and Art Rust Jr. *Joe Louis: My Life*. New York: Harcourt Brace, 1978.

MacDonald, J. Fred. *Don't Touch That Dial: Programming in American Life from 1920 to 1960*. Chicago: Nelson Hall, 1979.

Maney, Patrick J. *The Roosevelt Presence: A Biography of Franklin Delano Roosevelt*. New York: Twayne, 1992.

———. *The Roosevelt Presence: The Life and Legacy of FDR*. Berkeley: University of California Press, 1998.

Mangione, Jerre. *The Dream and the Deal: The Federal Writers' Project, 1935–1943*. Boston: Little, Brown, 1972.

Margolick, David. *Beyond Glory: Joe Louis vs. Max Schmeling and a World on the Brink*. New York: Knopf, 2005.

Martin, Waldo. *No Coward Soldiers: Black Cultural Politics in Postwar America*. Cambridge, Mass.: Harvard University Press, 2005.

Massood, Paula J. *Black City Cinema: African American Urban Experiences in Film*. Philadelphia: Temple University Press, 2003.

Matthews, Jane De Hart. "Arts and the People: The New Deal Quest for Cultural Democracy." *Journal of American History* 62 (September 1975): 316–39.

———. *The Federal Theatre, 1935–1939: Plays, Relief, and Politics*. Princeton: Princeton University Press, 1967.

Maxwell, William J. *New Negro, Old Left: African American Writing and Communism between the Wars*. New York: Columbia University Press, 1999.

May, Lary. *The Big Tomorrow: Hollywood and the Politics of the American Way*. Chicago: University of Chicago Press, 2000.

McCullough, David. *Truman*. New York: Simon and Schuster, 1992.

McDonald, William F. *Federal Relief Administration and the Arts*. Columbus: Ohio State University Press, 1969.

McFadden, Margaret. "'America's Boyfriend Who Can't Get a Date': Gender, Race, and the Cultural Work of the Jack Benny Program, 1932–1946." *Journal of American History* 80 (June 1993): 113–34.

McGuire, Phillip. *He, Too, Spoke for Democracy: Judge Hastie, World War II, and the Black Soldier*. New York: Greenwood Press, 1988.

McKinzie, Richard D. *The New Deal for Artists*. Princeton: Princeton University Press, 1973.

McMahon, Kevin J. *Reconsidering Roosevelt on Race: How the Presidency Paved the Road to Brown*. Chicago: University of Chicago Press, 2004.

Mead, Chris. *Champion—Joe Louis, Black Hero in White America*. New York: Scribner, 1985.

Miller, Jeanne-Marie A. "Successful Federal Theatre Dramas by Black Playwrights." *Black Scholar* 10 (July–August 1979): 79–82.

Minnelli, Vincente, with Hector Arce. *I Remember It Well*. New York: Doubleday, 1974.

Mitchell, Loften. *Black Drama: The Story of the American Negro in the Theatre*. New York: Hawthorn, 1967.

Musher, Sharon Ann. "Contesting 'the Way the Almighty Wants It': Crafting Memories of Ex-Slaves in the Slave Narrative Collection." *American Quarterly* 53 (March 2001): 1–31.

Myers, James M. *The Bureau of Motion Pictures and Its Influence on Film Content during World War II: The Reasons for Its Failure*. New York: Edwin Mellen, 1998.

Naison, Mark. *Communists in Harlem in the Great Depression*. Urbana: University of Illinois Press, 1983.

Newman, Kathy M. *Radio Active: Advertising and Consumer Activism, 1935–1947*. Berkeley: University of California Press, 2004.

O'Connor, John, and Lorraine Brown, eds. *Free, Adult, Uncensored: The Living History of the Federal Theatre Project*. Washington: New Republic Books, 1978.

Pells, Richard H. *Radical Visions and American Dreams: Culture and Social Thought in the Depression Years*. New York: Harper and Row, 1974.

Penkower, Monty Noam. *The Federal Writers' Project: A Study in Government Patronage of the Arts*. Urbana: University of Illinois Press, 1977.

Plum, Jay. "Rose McClendon and the Black Units of the Federal Theatre Project: A Lost Contribution." *Theatre Survey* 33 (November 1992): 144–53.

Poole, John R. "Making a Tree from Thirst: Acquiescence and Defiance in the Negro Federal Theatre Project in Birmingham, Alabama." *Theatre History Studies* 21 (June 2001): 27–42.

Quinn, Arthur Hobson, ed. *Representative American Plays*. New York: Appleton-Century-Crofts, 1953.

Roberts, Randy. *Papa Jack: Jack Johnson and the Era of White Hopes*. New York: Free Press, 1983.

Robinson, Cedric. *Black Marxism: The Making of the Black Radical Tradition*. London: Zed, 1983.

———. *Forgeries of Memory and Meaning: Blacks and the Regimes of Race in American Theater and Film before World War II*. Chapel Hill: University of North Carolina Press, 2007.

Roeder, George H., Jr. *The Censored War: American Visual Experience during World War II*. New Haven: Yale University Press, 1993.

Roediger, David. *The Wages of Whiteness: Race and the Making of the American Working Class*. New York: Verso, 1991.

Rogin, Michael. *Blackface, White Noise: Jewish Immigrants in the Hollywood Melting Pot*. Berkeley: University of California Press, 1996.

Roosevelt, Eleanor. *This I Remember*. New York: Harper and Brothers, 1949.

Roosevelt, Franklin D. *The Public Papers and Addresses of Franklin D. Roosevelt*. Vol. 2: *The Year of Crisis, 1933*. New York: Random House, 1938.

Rose, Tricia. *Black Noise: Rap Music and Black Culture in Contemporary America*. Hanover, N.H.: Wesleyan University Press, 1994.

Rosenzweig, Roy. *Eight Hours for What We Will: Workers and Leisure in an Industrial City, 1870–1920*. Cambridge and New York: Cambridge University Press, 1983.

Rosenzweig, Roy, and Barbara Melosh. "Government and the Arts: Voices from the New Deal Era." *Journal of American History* 77 (September 1990): 596–608.

Rosenzweig, Roy, and David Thelen. *The Presence of the Past: Popular Uses of History in American Life*. New York: Columbia University Press, 1998.

Rosenzweig, Roy, et al., eds. *Government and the Arts in Thirties America: A Guide to Oral Histories and Other Research Material*. Fairfax, Va.: George Mason University Press, 1986.

Ross, Ronald. "The Role of Blacks in the Federal Theatre, 1935–1939." *Journal of Negro History* 59 (January 1974): 38–50.

Rowell, Charles H. "'Let Me Be with Ole Jazzbo': An Interview with Sterling A. Brown." *Callaloo* 21 (1998): 789–809.

Sammons, Jeffrey T. *Beyond the Ring: The Role of Boxing in American Society*. Urbana: University of Illinois Press, 1988.

———. "Boxing as a Reflection of Society: The Southern Reaction to Joe Louis." *Journal of Popular Culture* 16 (Spring 1983): 23–33.

Saunders, D. A. "The Dies Committee: First Phase." *Public Opinion Quarterly* 3 (April 1939): 223–38.

Savage, Barbara. *Broadcasting Freedom: Radio, War, and the Politics of Race, 1938–1948*. Chapel Hill: University of North Carolina Press, 1999.

Schwartz, Bonnie Nelson, ed., and the Educational Film Center. *Voices from the Federal Theatre*. Madison: University of Wisconsin Press, 2003.

Sears, Richard. *V-Discs: A History and Discography*. Westport, Conn.: Greenwood Press, 1980.

———. *V-Discs: First Supplement*. Westport, Conn.: Greenwood Press, 1986.

Sherwood, Robert E. *Roosevelt and Hopkins: An Intimate History*. New York: Harper and Brothers, 1948.

Short, Michael, and Dick Clark. *The History of American Bandstand*. New York: Ballantine Books, 1985.

Singh, Nikhil Pal. *Black Is a Country: Race and the Unfinished Struggle for Democracy*. Cambridge, Mass.: Harvard University Press, 2004.

Sitkoff, Harvard. "Harry Truman and the Election of 1948: The Coming of Age of Civil Rights in American Politics." *Journal of Southern History* 37 (November 1971): 597–616.

———. *A New Deal for Blacks: The Emergence of Civil Rights as a National Issue*. New York: Oxford University Press, 1978.

———. "Racial Militancy and Interracial Violence in the Second World War." *Journal of American History* 58 (December 1971): 661–81.

———, ed. *Fifty Years Later: The New Deal Evaluated*. New York: McGraw-Hill, 1985.

Sklaroff, Lauren Rebecca. "Constructing G.I. Joe Louis: Cultural Solutions to the 'Negro Problem' during World War II." *Journal of American History* 89 (December 2002): 958–83.

———. "Joe Louis and the Construction of a Black American Hero." Paper delivered at the annual meeting of the American Studies Association, Detroit, Michigan, October 2000.

———. "Variety for the Servicemen: The *Jubilee* Show and the Paradox of Racializing Radio during World War II." *American Quarterly* 56 (December 2004): 945–73.

Skocpol, Theda. *Protecting Soldiers and Mothers: The Political Origins of Social Policy in the United States*. Cambridge, Mass.: Belknap Press, 1992.

Skowronek, Steven. *Building a New American State: The Expansion of National Administrative Capacities*. New York: Cambridge University Press, 1982.

Slotkin, Richard. *Gunfighter Nation: The Myth of the Frontier in Twentieth-Century America*. New York: Atheneum, 1992.

Smethurst, James Edward. *The Black Arts Movement: Literary Nationalism in the 1960s and 1970s*. Chapel Hill: University of North Carolina Press, 2005.

Smith, John David. "A Different View of Slavery: Black Historians Attack the Proslavery Argument, 1890–1920." *Journal of Negro History* 65 (Autumn 1980): 298–311.

Smith, Judith. "Radio's 'Cultural Front,' 1938–1948." In *Radio Reader: Essays in the Cultural History of Radio*, edited by Michele Hilmes and Jason Loviglio, 209–30. New York: Routledge, 2002.

Sotiropoulos, Karen. *Staging Race: Black Performers in Turn of the Century America*. Cambridge, Mass.: Harvard University Press, 2006.

Sporn, Paul. *Against Itself: The Federal Theater and Writers' Projects in the Midwest*. Detroit: Wayne State University Press, 1995.

Steele, Richard. "The Great Debate: Roosevelt, the Media, and the Coming of the War, 1940–1941." *Journal of American History* 71 (June 1984): 69–92.

———. "Preparing the Public for War: Efforts to Establish a National Propaganda Agency, 1940–41." *American Historical Review* 75 (October 1970): 1640–53.

———. *Propaganda in an Open Society: The Roosevelt Administration and the Media, 1933–1941*. Westport, Conn.: Greenwood Press, 1985.

Stephens, Judith L. "Anti-Lynch Plays by African American Women: Race, Gender, and Social Protest in American Drama." *African American Review* 2 (Summer 1992): 329–39.

Sterling, Christopher H., and John M. Kittress. *Stay Tuned: A Concise History of American Broadcasting*. Belmont, CA: Wadsworth, 1990.

Stott, William. *Documentary Expression and Thirties America*. New York: Oxford University Press, 1973.

Stowe, David. *Swing Changes: Big Band Jazz in New Deal America*. Cambridge, Mass.: Harvard University Press, 1994.

Sullivan, Patricia. *Days of Hope: Race and Democracy in the New Deal Era*. Chapel Hill: University of North Carolina Press, 1996.

Susman, Warren. *Culture as History: The Transformation of American Society in the Twentieth Century*. Washington, D.C.: Smithsonian Press, 2003.

Terrill, Tom E., and Jerrold Hirsch, eds. *Such as Us: Southern Voices of the Thirties*. Chapel Hill: University of North Carolina Press, 1978.

Thompson, Jim, et al. *American Stuff: An Anthology of Prose and Verse by Members of the Federal Writers' Project with Sixteen Prints by the Federal Arts Project*. New York: Viking Press, 1937.

Toll, Robert. *Blacking Up: The Minstrel Show in Nineteenth-Century America*. New York: Oxford University Press, 1974.

Tucker, Sherrie. *Swing Shift: "All Girl" Bands of the 1940s*. Durham: Duke University Press, 2000.

Van Deburg, William L. *Black Camelot: African-American Culture Heroes in Their Times, 1960–1980*. Chicago: University of Chicago Press, 1997.

———. *A New Day in Babylon: The Black Power Movement and American Culture, 1965–1975*. Chicago: University of Chicago Press, 1992.

Vanillo, Stephen M. "The Battle of the Black Mikados." *Black American Literature Forum* 16 (Winter 1982): 153–57.

Von Eschen, Penny. *Satchmo Blows Up the World: Jazz Ambassadors Play the Cold War*. Cambridge, Mass.: Harvard University Press, 2004.

Wald, Alan. *The New York Intellectuals: The Rise and Decline of the Anti-Stalinist Left from the 1930s to the 1980s*. Chapel Hill: University of North Carolina Press, 1987.

Walker, Ethel Pitts. "Krigwa, a Theater by, for, and about Black People." *Theatre Journal* 40 (October 1988): 347–56.

Ward, Brian. *Just My Soul Responding: Rhythm and Blues, Black Consciousness, and Race Relations*. Berkeley: University of California Press, 1998.

Weinberg, Sydney. "What to Tell America: The Writers' Quarrel in the Office of War Information." *Journal of American History* 55 (June 1968): 73–89.

Weir, Margaret, Ann Shola Orloff, and Theda Skocpol, eds. *The Politics of Social Policy in the United States*. Princeton: Princeton University Press, 1988.

Weiss, Nancy. *Farewell to the Party of Lincoln: Black Politics in the Age of FDR*. Princeton: Princeton University Press, 1983.

West, Ron. "Others, Adults, Censored: The Federal Theatre Project's Black Lysistrata Cancellation." *Theatre Survey* 37:2 (November 1996): 93–116.

Westbrook, Robert. "'I Want a Girl, Just like the Girl That Married Harry James': American Women on the Problem of Political Obligation in World War II." *American Quarterly* 42 (December 1990): 587–614.

White, E. B. *Charlotte's Web*. New York: Harper Collins, 1952.

White, Helen, and Redding S. Sugg Jr., eds. *From the Mountain: Selections from "Pseudopodia" (1936), "The North Georgia Review" (1937–1941), and "South Today" (1942–1945)*. Edited by Lillian Smith and Paula Snelling. Memphis: Memphis State University Press, 1972.

Wiggins, William H., Jr. "Boxing's Sambo Twins: Racial Stereotypes in Jack Johnson and Joe Louis Newspaper Cartoons, 1908–1938." *Journal of Sport History* 15 (Winter 1988): 242–53.

Winkler, Allan M. *The Politics of Propaganda: The Office of War Information, 1942–1945*. New Haven: Yale University Press, 1978.

Witham, Barry B. "Censorship in the Federal Theatre." *Theatre History Studies* 17 (June 1997): 3–14.

Woll, Allen. *Black Musical Theatre: From Coontown to Dreamgirls*. Baton Rouge: Louisiana State University Press, 1989.

Wright, John S. "The New Negro Poet and the Nachal Man: Sterling Brown's Folk Odyssey." *Black American Literature Forum* 23 (Spring 1989): 95–105.

Writers' Program. *Survey of Negroes in Little Rock and North Little Rock*. Little Rock: Urban League of Greater Little Rock, 1941.

Wynn, Neil. *The Afro-American and the Second World War*. London: Paul Elek, 1979.

Yetman, Norman. "The Background of the Slave Narrative Collection." *American Quarterly* 19 (Fall 1967): 534–53.

———. "Ex-Slave Interviews and the Historiography of Slavery." *American Quarterly* 36 (1984): 181–210.

INDEX

Page numbers in italics refer to illustrations.

Abbott, George. *See* 47 Workshop

Abbott, Lawrence, 87. *See also* American Guide Series

Abbott and Costello, 165. *See also* Lewis, Tom

Abel, Lionel, 88. *See also* American Guide Series—individual guides: New York

Agricultural Adjustment Administration (AAA), 17

Aiken, Conrad, 88

The Aldrich Family, 165. *See also* Lewis, Tom

Alexander, Will, 23–24, 25–26, 257 (n. 37). *See also* Farm Security Administration

Algren, Nelson, 88. *See also* American Guide Series—individual guides: Illinois

All-American Newsreel, 136. *See also* Starr, Milton

Allen, Gracie, 189. See also *Jubilee*

Alsberg, Henry, 32, 138, 265 (n. 9), 269 (n. 121), 271 (nn. 155, 160); as FWP Director, 31, 86–87, 118, 119, 265 (n. 9); and Sterling Brown, 81, 84, 89–91, 99; American Guide Series, 84–85, 87, 93, 99, 103; and Dies committee, 115–16; and House Subcommittee on Appropriations, 117. *See also* American Guide Series; Brown, Sterling; Dies committee; Federal Writers' Project

American Bandstand, 245

American Federation of Musicians, 62, 179

American Guide Series, 4, 8, 35, 79, 80, 86–89, 120, 235, 249, 265 (n. 9), 266 (nn. 38, 52), 267 (n. 71), 268 (n. 89), 269 (n. 121); and Sterling Brown, 12, 34, 81–85, 89, 92–118; reviews of, 102, 106–8; Dies committee, 115–16

—individual guides: Alabama, 93, 96, 97, 98, 99, 102, 103; Arizona, 94; Arkansas, 101; California, 88; Connecticut, 85; Delaware, 94, 104; Florida, 88, 95, 97, 109; Idaho, 88; Illinois, 88, 95, 98; Indiana, 84, 94, 97, 100; Kentucky, 84; Louisiana, 89, 95; Maine, 94; Massachusetts, 88; Michigan, 97, 118; Mississippi, 101, 102, 103, 107, 268 (n. 89); Missouri, 106; Montana, 88, 94, 115; Nebraska, 89, 97; Nevada, 93; New Hampshire, 95; New Jersey, 115, 260 (n. 54); New Orleans, 95, 106, 107; New York, 88, 95; North Carolina, 88, 93, 94, 97, 107, 108; North Dakota, 94; Ohio, 88, 97, 98, 104; Oklahoma, 94; Pennsylvania, 89, 97, 100, 109; Rhode Island, 94; South Carolina, 95, 96, 100, 101, 103, 104; Tennessee, 97; Texas, 97, 100, 102, 267 (n. 74); Utah, 94; Vermont, 94; Virginia, 95, 97, 100, 101, 105; Washington, 94; Washington, D.C., 105, 106, 107, 117, 118. *See also* Brown, Sterling; Federal Writers' Project

American Negro Theatre, 52. *See also* Hill, Abram

American Stuff, 116. *See also* Dies committee

"America's Negro Soldiers," 13, 125, 159, 161, 172–75, 176, 191, 278 (n. 36)

Amos 'n' Andy, 126, 162

Anderson, Eddie "Rochester," 140; in *Jubilee*, 167, 177, 180; in *Cabin in the Sky*, 212. See also *Cabin in the Sky*; *Jubilee*

Anderson, Ivie, 182, 184. See also *Jubilee*

Anderson, Marian, 15, 205; in *Jubilee*, 167, 170; in "America's Negro Soldiers," 172.

See also "America's Negro Soldiers";
Jubilee

Androcles and the Lion, 61, 64, 234

Angelou, Maya, 250; on Joe Louis, 141–42

Anticommunism, 9, 64, 115, 244. *See also* Communism

Antilynching bill, 24, 52, 60, 234, 258 (n. 44); and Eleanor Roosevelt, 1, 22; and Franklin Roosevelt, 26–27

Armed Forces Radio Service (AFRS), 13, 125, 159, *164*, *165*, *176*, 194, 277 (nn. 3, 14), 280 (n. 85). See also *Jubilee*; Lewis, Tom

Armstrong, Louis, 14, 163; goodwill tours, 127, 243, 286 (n. 7); on *Jubilee*, 160, 167, 189. See also *Jubilee*

Army Special Services Division (ASSD), 147, 166

Audience Research, Inc. *See* Lewis, Tom

Baedeker guidebooks, 85–86

Baker, George Pierce, 31, 37, 259 (n. 10). *See also* Flanagan, Hallie; 47 Workshop

Baker, Jacob, 30, 85–86, 116, 265 (n. 9). *See also* Dies committee; Federal Emergency Relief Administration

Baker, Josephine, 45, 243, 286 (n. 7)

Baltimore Afro-American, 227–28, 237; on Joe Louis, 144–45, 150; on *Jubilee*, 179; on Hollywood, 193, 208–9; on *Cabin in the Sky*, 219–20; on *Lifeboat*, 231–32

Basie, Count: on Joe Louis, 142; in *Jubilee*, 180, 182, 188, 190, 191, 280 (n. 85)

Bataan, 194–96, 222–23, *223*, 225, 229, 232, 234–35, 238–39, 245; response to, 223–24, 226–28; and censorship, 237

Bell, Ulrich, 125, 201, 218, 226. *See also* American Guide Series—individual guides: Kentucky; Office of War Information

Bellow, Saul, 88. *See also* American Guide Series—individual guides: Illinois

Benny, Jack, 126, 189

Berry, Chuck, 245

Berry, Theodore, 135–37, 156, 197. *See also* National Association of the Advancement of Colored People; Office of Facts and Figures

Bethune, Mary McLeod, 22, 24, 134, 146, 147, *210*

Biddle, Frances, 29, 131

Biddle, George, 29–30

Big White Fog, 34, 36, 59, 173

Birth of a Nation, 202

Bjorkman, Edwin, 88, 93–94, 266 (n. 38). *See also* American Guide Series—individual guides: North Carolina

Black Arts Movement, 4, 35, 246–47

Black Cabinet, 24. *See also* Bethune, Mary McLeod; Brown, Sterling; Gibson, Truman; Moss, Carlton; Weaver, Robert

Black Nationalism, 244, 246–47

Black patriotism, 12, 127, 134, 153, 226

Black Power, 247, 286 (n. 16)

Black Republicanism, 16

Black voting, 8, 16–17, 19, 26, 28, 242, 246

Bodenheim, Maxwell, 88. *See also* American Guide Series—individual guides: New York

Bogart, Humphrey, 51, 208; in *Sahara*, 224, *225*, 238

Bond, Horace Mann, 92, 95. *See also* American Guide Series—individual guides: Louisiana

Bontemps, Arna, 109, 120. *See also* American Guide Series—individual guides: Illinois

Bosworth, Francis, 50, 51. *See also* National Play Bureau

Botkin, Benjamin A., 87, 97, 266 (n. 54), 267 (n. 69). *See also* American Guide Series

Brechner, J., 168–69. *See also* Bureau of Public Relations; U.S. Department of War

Brooks, Van Wyck, 31, 37. *See also* 47 Workshop

Brother Mose, 58

Brown, James, 246, 247

Brown, Sterling, 6, 24, 108, 119, 121, 136, 247, 250, 269 (n. 119), 271 (n. 160); as FWP Director of Negro Affairs, 6–7, 12, 34–35, 80, 81–84, 120, 138, 269 (n. 121), 270 (n. 147); American Guide Series, 12, 34, 92–106, 266 (nn. 52, 54), 267 (nn. 64,

69); and Dies committee, 83, 114–16; background, 89–91, 265 (n. 24); and PNAM, 110–14, 269 (n. 120); and House Subcommittee on Appropriations, 117–18, 271 (n. 161). *See also* American Guide Series; Dies committee; House Subcommittee on Appropriations; Federal Writers' Project; "Portrait of the Negro as an American"

Brown, Theodore, 48. *See also* Federal Theatre Project; Negro Unit, Seattle

"Brown Bomber." *See* Louis, Joe

Brownell, Herbert, 242

Bunche, Ralph, 91

Bureau of Motion Pictures (BMP), 193–94, 196, 198–99, 201, 211, 218, 223, 226, 230–31, 233–34, 238. *See also* Mellett, Lowell; Office of War Information

Bureau of Public Relations (BPR), 134, 139, 149, 168–69, 225, 278 (n. 34). *See also* U.S. Department of War

Burns, George, 189

Cabin in the Sky, 13, 160, 181, 184, 194–96, 210–20; response to, 218–20, 228

Cagney, James, 206

Cahill, Holger, 30–31. *See also* Federal Art Project

Caliver, Ambrose, 174, 175. *See also* "Freedom's People"

Calloway, Cab, 140, 180, 237; and Joe Louis, 142; in *Stormy Weather*, 216

Carnera, Primo, 141. *See also* Louis, Joe

Carpenter, Thelma, 184–85, 186

Carter, Ben, 193, 209

Cavalcade of the American Negro, 106, 109. *See also* Federal Writers' Project

Civilian Conservation Corps (CCC), 17, 19, 24, 41, 52

Civil Rights Act of 1957, 242

Civil Rights Act of 1964, 244

Civil Works Administration (CWA), 29–30, 85; Public Works of Art Project (PWAP), 29, 30

Civil Works Authority, 85

Clark, Dick. See *American Bandstand*

Clinton, William Jefferson, 250

Cohen, Octavus Roy. See *Come Seven*

Coleman, Ralf, 48. *See also* Federal Theatre Project

Columbia Broadcasting System (CBS), 129, 132, 161. *See also* Davis, Elmer; Hammond, John

Come Seven, 60

Command Performance, 176, 178

Commission on Interracial Cooperation, 23

Communism, 9–10, 25, 59, 62–64, 114–15, 117–18, 173, 244, 257 (n. 39); Communist Left, 9, 25; Communist Party (CPUSA), 9, 25, 36, 114–15, 180, 206, 257 (n. 39), 270 (n. 150). *See also* Dies committee; House Un-American Activities Committee

Congress of Industrial Organizations (CIO), 25

Conn, Billy. See Louis, Joe

Conroy, Jack, 109. *See also* American Guide Series—individual guides: Illinois

Cooke, Sam, 246

Coordinator of Government Films. *See* Mellett, Lowell

Costigan-Wagner Bill. *See* Antilynching bill

Cotton Club, 188, 212

Couch, William, 94, 266 (n. 38). *See also* American Guide Series—individual guides: North Carolina

Court-packing, 62

Crane, Russak, and Company. *See* Russak, Ben

Crisis, 11, 43, 44, 47, 52, 139; and Sterling Brown, 90; on World War II involvement, 124. *See also* Krigwa Players

Cronyn, George, 86, 87, 99, 103, 265 (n. 9). *See also* American Guide Series

Crosby, Bing, 179, 189, *190*

Crosby, Bob, 189

Cullen, Countee, 46, 52–53, 90

Cultural apparatus, 2, 8, 10, 53, 239; and Sterling Brown, 82–83; wartime, 124–25, 138, 194

Cultural self-determination, 6, 246

"The Dark Tide," 56

Davis, Allison, 90, 92, 95. *See also* Ameri-

can Guide Series—individual guides:
Louisiana

Davis, Ben, 180. *See also* Communism

Davis, Benjamin O., Sr., 140, 159, 169

Davis, Bette, 169, 206

Davis, Elmer, 3, 129, *130*, 130, 136, 272
(n. 14). *See also* Columbia Broadcasting
System; Office of War Information

Davis, J. Frank, 89. *See also* American
Guide Series—individual guides: Texas

Davis, James, 62

Democratic Party, 12, 16–17, 19, 21, 24–26,
243; African Americans in, 12, 19, 22;
southerners in, 19, 26, 200, 241; conservatives in, 62

Dempsey, Jack, 146

DePriest, Oscar, 26, 103, 111. *See also* "Portrait of the Negro as an American"

De Sola, Ralph, 114, 270 (n. 150). *See also*
Communism

DeSylva, Buddy, 207

Dies, Martin. *See* Dies committee

Dies committee, 62–64, 76, 79, 83, 114–17,
262 (n. 121)

Donegan, Dorothy, 188–89, 238

Dorsey, Tommy, 162, 178

Do The Right Thing, 249

Drew, Charles, 90

*Drums and Shadows: Survival Studies
among the Georgia Coastal Negroes*, 109,
118

Du Bois, W. E. B., 44, 50, 96, 113, 153, 174,
221, 267 (n. 74). See also *Freedom's
People*; Krigwa Players

Du Bose, Louise Jones, 100. *See also* Federal Writers' Project; Liberalism, racial

Dunham, Katherine, 211, 214, 216–17. See
also *Cabin in the Sky*

Edwards, Harry, 45, 47–48. *See also* Federal
Theatre Project; Negro Unit

Eisenhower, Dwight, 242–43

Elections: presidential, of 1932, 16, 17, 28;
presidential, of 1936, 16, 19, 21, 26, 27;
congressional, of 1938, 62; presidential,
of 1948, 241

Ellington, Duke, 127, 161, 180, 214, 250;

goodwill tours, 14, 243; on *Jubilee*,
159, 177, 178, 180, 182, 188, 190–91, 280
(n. 85). See also *Jubilee*

Ellis, Maurice, 170, 173

Ellison, Ralph, 88, 95, 160–61

Emergency Relief Act of 1933, 29

Emergency Relief Act of 1935, 42

Emergency Relief Appropriation Act, 30

Ericson, Marvin, 78. See also *Swing Mikado*

Executive Order 9182. *See* Office of War
Information

Fair Employment Practices Commission
(FEPC), 125, 241

Farm Security Administration (FSA), 23–
24. *See also* Alexander, Will

Federal Art Project (fine arts project), 30–
31. *See also* Cahill, Holger

Federal Arts Project (FAP), 1, 2, 4–5, 8,
11, 12, 28, 80, 87, 95; establishment of,
18, 30–32, 42; pressure from Congress
on, 35, 61, 118, 120–21; integration in,
80; end of, 114, 119; and transition to
wartime, 124–26, 138. *See also* Brown,
Sterling; Federal Theatre Project; Federal Writers' Project; Flanagan, Hallie;
Works Progress Administration

Federal Emergency Relief Administration
(FERA), 20, 23, 29, 30; and American
Guide Series, 84, 85–87, 265 (n. 8). *See
also* American Guide Series; Hopkins,
Harry

Federal Music Project (FMP), 15, 31

Federal Theatre Project (FTP), 1, 2, 4, 8, 53,
55, 82, 91–92, 97, 121, 123, 162, 165, 170,
173, 224, 234, 247, 259 (n. 2); pressure
from Congress on, 12, 35–36, 51, 61–64,
114–18, 270 (n. 150); establishment of,
35–42, 45, 47; racial progressivism of,
42, 45, 47–49, 57–62, 64–65, 260 (n. 54);
end of, 62, 79, 119. *See also* Dies committee; Federal Arts Project; Flanagan,
Hallie; Moss, Carlton; Negro Unit; Play
Bureau; *Swing Mikado*

Federal Writers' Project (FWP), 5, 31, 52,
79–80, 91, 107, 125, 126, 201, 235, 247,
249, 264 (n. 3), 265 (n. 9), 269 (nn. 120,

121), 271 (n. 155); racial progressivism
of, 1, 80, 83, 92, 104, 106–7, 109–10, 120;
Negro Affairs division, 10, 12, 81–84,
88, 90–92, 94–99, 104–5, 110, 120, 267
(n. 69); pressure from Congress on, 83,
114–17, 123; and slave narratives, 84–86,
93, 109, 112–13, 265 (n. 8), 269 (nn. 119,
122), 270 (n. 138); end of, 118–20. *See also*
Alsberg, Henry; American Guide Series;
Brown, Sterling; Dies committee; "Portrait of the Negro as an American"
Fischer, Vardis, 88
Five Arts Project, 60. *See also* Works
Project Administration
Flanagan, Hallie, 3, 37, *38*, 51, 62, 64, 74,
75, 91, 116, 119, 259 (nn. 10, 25); back-
ground, 31–32, 35, 37–39; forming FTP,
40–41; and Negro Units, 41–42, 45; and
Dies committee, 63. *See also* Federal
Theatre Project; 47 Workshop
Fonda, Henry, 207–8
Foreman, Clark, 18, 21–22, 25, 256 (n. 14),
257 (n. 24); opposition to, 20, 138. *See
also* U.S. Department of the Interior
47 Workshop, 31, 37
Frankfurter, Felix, 137
Franklin, Aretha, 247
Freedom's People, 174, 177. *See also* Caliver,
Ambrose; Du Bois, W. E. B.
"Freedom's People," 175
French, Paul, 89. *See also* American Guide
Series—individual guides: Pennsylvania
Frost, Robert, 90, 250

Gaer, Joseph, 87. *See also* American Guide
Series
Gardner, Ava, 189–90
Garveyism, 56, 59, 173
Gershwin, George, 184
Gibson, Truman, 24, 138, 237, 273 (n. 40),
276 (n. 115); and Joe Louis, 150–52, 156,
278 (n. 34); on Armed Forces Radio Ser-
vice, 159; *Jubilee*, 168–71. *See also* Bureau
of Public Relations; *Jubilee*; Louis, Joe;
U.S. Department of War
Gilbert and Sullivan, 12; influences on
Swing Mikado, 33, 36, 64–66, 68–69, 70–

71, 72, 79. See also *The Mikado; Swing
Mikado*
Gillespie, Dizzy, 190, 243
The Golden Hillbilly Vocalist, 177. *See also*
Armed Forces Radio Service
GOP. *See* Republican Party
Grable, Betty, 127, 272 (n. 9)
Green, Eddie, 167, 170, 171, 172, 180, *181,
190*. See also *Jubilee*
The Green Pastures, 59, 181, 205, 213

Haiti, 49, 58, 61, 173, 234
Hammond, John, 132, 180. *See also* Colum-
bia Broadcasting System
Harlem Experimental Theatre, 45. *See also*
McClendon, Rose
Harlem Renaissance, 4, 5, 52, 90, 247, 254
(n. 11), 265 (n. 24)
Harrington, Francis Clark, *76*, 78. *See also*
Works Progress Administration
Harris, Reed, 86, 265 (n. 9). *See also* Ameri-
can Guide Series
Hastie, William, 24, 90, 136, 147, 170; in
Department of the Interior, 18, 256
(n. 14); in War Department, 137–38, 167–
69, 273 (n. 40).
Hatcher, Harlan, 88. *See also* American
Guide Series—individual guides: Ohio
"Hell's Half Acre." *See* Hill, Abram
Hill, Abram, 52, 55, 60
Hitchcock, Alfred. See *Lifeboat*
Holiner, Mann, 166, 175–78, *176*, 279
(n. 44). See also *Jubilee*
Holly, Buddy, 245
Hollywood Anti-Nazi League, 206
Hollywood Victory Committee, 165
Hollywood Writers Mobilization, 51
Holmes, Eugene: work on American Guide
Series, 93, 100, 101, 267 (n. 69); work
on PNAM, 110, 112. *See also* American
Guide Series; "Portrait of the Negro as
an American"
Hoover, Herbert, 16–17, 258 (n. 54)
Hope, Bob, 127
Hopkins, Harry, 28, 75, 89, 95; as FERA
director, 20, 23, 257 (n. 36); as WPA
director, 23, 29, 30, 62, 78, 89; and FTP,

37, 39, 40. *See also* Federal Emergency Relief Administration; Works Progress Administration

Hopper, James, 88

Hore, Maurice, 94

Horne, Lena, 127, 237; in *Jubilee*, 159–60, 177–79, *181*, 185–86, 188, 191; in *Stormy Weather*, *187*, 211, 215–16, *217*, 217; in *Cabin in the Sky*, 212, *213*, 214, 216–18. See also *Cabin in the Sky; Jubilee; Stormy Weather*

Hot Mikado, 76, 78, 79. *See also* Todd, Michael

Houseman, John, 44, 46–47, 50, 91, 125, 138, 165; and "voodoo" *Macbeth*, 64, 69–70. *See also* Federal Theatre Project; *Macbeth*; Negro Unit

House Subcommittee on Appropriations, 76, 117, 121. *See also* Woodrum, Clifton

House Un-American Activities Committee (HUAC), 2, 9, 35–36, 51, 62. *See also* Communism; Dies committee

Houston, Charles Hamilton, 26

Howe, Louis, 20, 21

Hughes, Langston, 45, 52–54, 90, 155, 235–36, 247

Hull, Cordell, 130

Hurston, Zora Neale, 88, 109. *See also* American Guide Series—individual guides: Florida

Hymn to the Rising Sun, 59

Ickes, Harold, 3, 12, 18, 20–23, 26, 33. *See also* U.S. Department of the Interior

Ingram, Rex, 49, 125, 227, 234; in *Jubilee*, 181; in *Cabin in the Sky*, 220; in *Sahara*, 224, *225*, 227; in *Bataan*, 227. See also *Jubilee; Lifeboat; Sahara*

International Labor Defense, 25

James, Ida, 178, 184, 185, 188–89. See also *Jubilee*

Jim Crow. *See* Segregation

Jitterbug, 70, *71*, 77

Johnson, Jack, 140, 143, 247, 274 (n. 56)

Johnson, James Weldon, 26

Jones, Charles. *See* National Urban League

Jubilee, 6, 7, 13, 79, 157, 159, 164, 166, 173, 177–92, *181*, *190*, 196–97, 211, 214, 235, 243–44, 277 (n. 3), 279 (nn. 44, 54), 280 (n. 85); creation of, 159, 167, 175–76; on racism, 160–61; and politics, 171, 175, 178; response to, 178–79. *See also* Armed Forces Radio Service; Holiner, Mann

Jump for Joy, 180. *See also* Ellington, Duke

Keefe, Frank, 117–18, 271 (n. 161). *See also* House Subcommittee on Appropriations

Kellock, Katherine, 85. *See also* American Guide Series

Kerr, Florence, 75, 77, 78

Knox, Frank, 130

Krigwa Players, 35, 43–44, 52. See also *Crisis*; Du Bois, W. E. B.

Ku Klux Klan, 113, 134

Ladson, Augustus, 95. *See also* American Guide Series—individual guides: South Carolina

Lafayette Players, 35, 43–44

La Guardia, Fiorello, 75, 170

Lavery, Emmet, 50, 51, 60–61, 64. *See also* National Service Bureau

Lawson, John Howard, 206, 224. See also *Sahara*

Leadbelly, 177, 180, 191

Lee, Canada, 47, 173, 234, 285 (n. 125); in FTP, 49; in *Sahara*, 125; in *Lifeboat*, 125, *229*, 229, 231–32; in *Jubilee*, 170

Lee, Spike. See *Do The Right Thing*

Lee, Ulysses, 93, 110. *See also* "Portrait of the Negro as an American"

Lewis, Roscoe, 95, 109, 110. *See also* American Guide Series—individual guides: Virginia; *The Negro in Virginia*; "Portrait of the Negro as an American"

Lewis, Tom, 159, *165*, 165, 166. *See also* Armed Forces Radio Service; *Jubilee*

Liberalism: white, 3, 10, 18, 22, 27, 50, 129, 130, 214; racial, 9, 11, 95, 100, 116, 125, 195, 208, 244, 246; black response to, 24; New Deal, 24, 126, 129, 130, 194, 201, 254 (n. 17); and Joe Louis, 127, 139, 156; and

Hollywood, 196, 208; and Eisenhower, 242; in the South, 261

Lifeboat, 125, 216, 228–30, *229*, 232, 234, 284 (n. 110); reaction to, 230–32

Lindy-Hop, 70

Little Richard, 245

Living Newspaper, 41

Locke, Alain, 44, 90, 121, 174

Logan, Rayford, 24, 91

Lomax, John, 87. *See also* American Guide Series

Lombard, Carole, 206

Louis, Joe, 14, *128*, 129, *149*, 159, 169, 172, 174, 175, 197, 235, 274 (n. 56); as Army propaganda, 1, 7, 13, 129, 140–41, 144–46, 149, 151–56, *154*, 276 (n. 122); in American Guide Series, 103; in "Portrait of the Negro as an American," 111; importance to African Americans, 127–29, 141–46, 150, 156, 272 (n. 10), 274 (n. 63); Carnera bout, 141; Schmeling bouts, 142–44, 154–55, 275 (n. 64); Baer bout, 145; in Army, 145–52; press response to, 150, 274 (n. 58); troop response to, 151; in *The Negro Soldier*, 153–55; and Army awards, 155–56; on *Jubilee*, 167

Louis Armstrong Show. *See* Armstrong, Louis

Lowell, Harold, 198. *See also* Office of War Information

Lunceford, Jimmie, 140, 180, 191

Lynching, 25–27, 44, 54–56, 63, 141, 232–34. *See also* Antilynching bill

Macbeth, 35, 49, 64, 65, 70, 125, 173, 263 (n. 139). *See also* Welles, Orson

MacLeish, Archibald, 3, 126, 129, 134; with OFF, 126, 131–33, 134, 139, 272 (nn. 14, 16). *See also* Office of Facts and Figures

Mail Call, 175, 176, 178

Mangione, Jerre, 88, 115–16, 265 (n. 9), 270 (n. 150), 271 (n. 155). *See also* American Guide Series—individual guides: Nebraska

March on Washington. *See* Randolph, A. Philip

Marshall, George, 172

McClendon, Rose, 45–46, 92

McDaniel, Hattie, 208, 209, *210*, 218; on *Jubilee*, 188

McGee, John, 40, 75, 264 (n. 160). *See also* American Guide Series—individual guides: Illinois

McKay, Claude, 88, 90, 95, 109, 271 (n. 155)

McQueen, Butterfly, 185–86

McVae, Jack, 189–90

Mellett, Lowell, 126, 129, 198–201, 203. *See also* Bureau of Motion Pictures

Merriam, Harold, 88. *See also* American Guide Series—individual guides: Montana

Metro-Goldwyn-Mayer (MGM), 199–200, 207, 211, 218–20, 222

Meyer, William, 94. *See also* American Guide Series—individual guides: Indiana

Micheaux, Oscar, 202, 221

Middleton, Laura, 95. *See also* American Guide Series—individual guides: South Carolina

The Mikado, 35, 64–66, 68–70, 73, 78

Mikado in Swing, 78

Miles, Myrtle, 99, 103. *See also* American Guide Series—individual guides: Alabama

Miller, Dorie, 140

Miller, Kelly, 18, 21, 90

Mills, Florence, 45. See also *Shuffle Along*

Minnelli, Vincente. *See Cabin in the Sky*

Minstrel, 49, 70, 73, 102, 111, 112, 144, 170, 249; stereotypes, 2, 6, 35, 45, 68, 73, 78, 244; minstrelsy, 6, 42–43, 70, 111, 162, 195, 202–3, 254 (n. 15); songs, 15; shows, 42, 104, 170, 248; in Hollywood, 180, 215. See also *Amos 'n' Andy*

Minturn, Harry, 35, 64–66, 75. *See also* Federal Theatre Project; *Swing Mikado*

Montgomery, Mabel, 100, 103–4. *See also* American Guide Series—individual guides: South Carolina

Morale Branch, 145–46, 151, 275 (n. 93). *See also* U.S. Department of War

Moreland, Mantan, 181, 193, 202

Moss, Carlton, 24, 46, 73, 162, 247; with

FTP, 2, 45, 47–49; with FAP, 6; *The Negro Soldier*, 125, 154–55, 236–37; *Teamwork*, 236. *See also* Federal Theatre Project; *The Negro Soldier*; Negro Unit

Motion Picture Board of Censors, 237

Muse, Clarence, 36, 48–49, *49*, 207–9. *See also* Federal Theatre Project; Negro Unit, Los Angeles

Nash, Philleo, 132, 134. *See also* Office of War Information

National Association for the Advancement of Colored People (NAACP), 2, 4, 18, 22, 26, 43, 108, 118, 235, 246; and Hollywood, 13, 195–96, 200, 202, 205–6, 208–10; criticism of Hoover, 16; on Clark Foreman, 20; on wage discrimination, 20; on lynching, 27; criticism of FTP plays, 60–61; response to World War II, 135; on Joe Louis, 144, 145–46; on *Jubilee*, 160; on *Stormy Weather*, 215, 219; on *Cabin in the Sky*, 218–19; on *Bataan*, 224, 226–27; on *Sahara*, 226; on *Lifeboat*, 231; on *The Ox-Bow Incident*, 233–34. See also *Crisis*; White, Walter; Wilkins, Roy

National Broadcasting Company (NBC), 46, 68, 161–63, 168, 170, 172, 174, 279 (n. 44)

National Play Bureau, 50. *See also* Bosworth, Francis; Tyler, Converse

National Recovery Administration (NRA), 17–19, 20–21, 113

National Service Bureau, 50, 58, 60, 64

National Urban League, 22, 95, 119, 132, 155, 167, 176

National Youth Administration (NYA), 23–24, 95; Negro Affairs, 22, *210*. *See also* Bethune, Mary McLeod; Williams, Aubrey

Navy Relief Society, 144–46, 152. *See also* Louis, Joe

Neal, Larry, 247. *See also* Black Arts Movement

Negro Actors Guild (NAG), 169, 170, 173

The Negro and National Defense, 167, 172

Negroes and the War, 124, 200

"Negroes in the Army," 171

The Negro Hour, 162

The Negro in New York, 109. *See also* Ottley, Roi

"The Negro in Pittsburgh," 109. *See also* American Guidebook Series—individual guides: Pennsylvania

The Negro in Virginia, 83, 95, 107, 109–10, 118, 269 (n. 121). *See also* Lewis, Roscoe

"The Negro in Washington," 105–6, 117–18. *See also* Federal Writers' Project

The Negro Soldier, 125, 196, 229, 235–37, 276 (n. 123), 285 (n. 130); and Joe Louis, 153, 155; response to, 236–39. *See also* Moss, Carlton

Negro Studies, 4, 105, 108, 267 (n. 64), 269 (n. 121)

Negro Unit, 2, 7, 12, 33–36, 41–49, 57–65, 80, 91–92, 109, 138, 162, 165, 221, 234, 236, 260 (n. 51); Chicago, 12, 47, 64, 65, 66, 75, 260 (n. 54); New York City, 35, 46–48, *48*, *58*, 62, 64, 91, 109, 125, 162, 234, 236, 260 (n. 54); Los Angeles, 36, 47, 48, *49*; Seattle, 47, 48; Newark, 47, 60; establishment of, 50–53, 57. *See also* Federal Theatre Project; Moss, Carleton; Muse, Clarence

New Negro, 4–5, 43–45, 54, 91

Newsom, John, 118. *See also* American Guide Series—individual guides: Michigan

Norris, George, 89

Odum, Howard, 174

Office of Coordinator of Information, 126. *See also* Sherwood, Robert

Office of Education, 174–75. *See also* Caliver, Ambrose

Office of Facts and Figures (OFF), 126, 131, 132, 135, 139, 197, 272 (nn. 14, 16), 273 (n. 38). *See also* MacLeish, Archibald

Office of Government Reports, 198

Office of War Information (OWI), 10, 126, 134, 156, 165, 206, 273 (n. 38); racial progressivism of, 1, 4, 13, 123, 125, 129–32, 135–40, 163, 166, 175, 194, 203, 272 (n. 14); and Hollywood, 13, 193, 194,

197–201, 202, 203, 210–11, 222, 238, 281 (nn. 10, 15); and State Department, 130; end of, 194; establishment of, 197, 272 (n. 12), 273 (n. 38); pressure from Congress, 201; on *Bataan*, 223–24; on *Sahara*, 226; on *Lifeboat*, 229. *See also* Bureau of Motion Pictures; Davis, Elmer; MacLeish, Archibald; Mellett, Lowell; Starr, Milton

Oliver, Sy, 162, 277 (n. 10)

O'Neill, Eugene, 37, 43. *See also* 47 Workshop

Opportunity, 11, 43, 44, 52, 90, 92, 167; on FERA, 20; play reviews, 45, 50, 61; on guidebooks, 107

Osborn, F. H., 146, 151, 177. *See also* Morale Branch; U.S. Department of War

Ottley, Roi, 52, 95, 109. *See also* American Guide Series—individual guides: New York

Owens, Jesse, 103, 111, 155

The Ox-Bow Incident, 232; response to, 233–34

Paramount Pictures. *See* DeSylva, Buddy

Patterson, Robert, 137, 168–70, 172, 173. *See also* U.S. Department of War

Pearl Harbor, 118, 123, 125, 144, 145

Pittsburgh Courier, 18, 139, 228; on Joe Louis, 143, 144–45, 150; on "America's Negro Soldiers," 172, 173; on Hollywood, 207, 208, 219, 237; on *Cabin in the Sky*, 220; on *Bataan*, 227

Play Bureau, 7, 34–36, 50–55, 57–60, 97, 110, 259 (n. 2), 264 (n. 165). *See also* Federal Theatre Project

Play Production Board, 60

Poitier, Sidney, 239

Poll tax, 1, 22, 24, 241

Popular Front, 9, 24, 25, 114, 179, 182, 184, 257 (n. 39)

"Portrait of the Negro as an American" (PNAM), 82, 84, 110–14, 119, 269 (nn. 120, 125). *See also* Brown, Sterling; Holmes, Eugene; Lee, Ulysses; Lewis, Roscoe; Wright, Richard

Poynter, Nelson, 198, 199, 201

Presidential Commission on Civil Rights. *See* Truman, Harry

Presley, Elvis, 245

Public Use of Arts Committee, 119

Public Works Administration (PWA), 22

Public Works of Art Project (PWAP). *See* Civil Works Administration (CWA)

Rainey, Ma, 184

Ramsay, Eudora, 109. *See also* American Guide Series—individual guides: Virginia

Randolph, A. Philip, 131, 140, 151–52

Randolph, John, 47, 51. *See also* House Un-American Activities Committee

Red Mikado, 78.

Republican Party, 16–19, 25, 62, 199, 200, 241. *See also* Black Republicanism

Rexroth, Kenneth, 88

Rice, Elmer, 40

Richardson, Robert, 168

Roberts, Glaucia B., 93, 99, 100, 267 (nn. 69, 74)

Robeson, Paul, 45, 111, 140, 172, 243, 286 (n. 7). *See also* *Shuffle Along*

Robinson, Bill "Bojangles," 140, 207; in *Hot Mikado, 76*, 79; in *Jubilee, 160*, 167, 171; in *Stormy Weather*, 215, *217*. *See also* *Hot Mikado; Jubilee; Stormy Weather*

Robinson, Edwin, 90

Robinson, Jackie, 150

Robinson, Sugar Ray, 147, 148

Rocco, Maurice, 188

Rogers, Timmie, 182, 183

Roosevelt, Eleanor, 39, 75, *76*, 119, 257 (n. 31); on civil rights, 1, 12, 18, 22–23; and Walter White, 27; and Joe Louis, 145–46

Roosevelt, Franklin D., 1, 5, 6, 11, 15, 21, 28–30, 39, 89, 119, 165, 198, 242, 249, 250, 255 (n. 23), 257 (n. 31), 258 (n. 42); inclusion of blacks in New Deal, 1–4, 8, 16, 23–24, 25, 245; intransigence on civil rights, 10, 17, 18, 20, 21, 25–26, 125, 241; racial liberalism, 12; inclusion of blacks in wartime, 13, 123, 194, 245; black voting for, 16; black support of,

309

17–18, 19, 20, 25, 26; on antilynching
bill, 26–27; court-packing, 62; opposition to, 116, 124–25, 201. *See also* Black
voting; Elections: presidential, of 1932;
Elections: presidential, of 1936; Roosevelt, Eleanor

Rourke, Constance, 31

Roxborough, John, 141. *See also* Louis, Joe

Royse, Morton, 87. *See also* American
Guide Series

Run Little Chillun, 48, 59

Russak, Ben, 51, 53

Sahara, 125, 194–96, 224–26, *225*, 229, 232,
234, 235, 237–39; reaction to, 226–28

Saxon, Lyle, 89. *See also* American Guide
Series—individual guides: Louisiana

Schmeling, Max, 127–28, 142–44, 154–55,
275 (n. 64). *See also* Louis, Joe

Schomburg, Arthur, 82

Schrank, Joseph. See *Cabin in the Sky*

Scottsboro trial, 25, 58, 108, 113, 173

Screen Actors Guild, 208

Screen Writers Guild, 51

Segregation, 4, 18, 26, 116, 133, 135, 137,
138, 162, 171, 173, 179, 193, 206, 218, 242,
248, 273 (n. 40); culture of, 6; in Armed
Forces, 13, 137, 148, 155–56, 171, 227–28,
239; in New Deal programs, 42, 94; in
American Guide Series, 100–101, 105,
108; in PNAM, 113; defense of, 129; in
wartime programs, 132, 134, 163, 184; in
Hollywood, 195, 216, 218, 223, 227, 228,
230, 235–36, 237

Selznick, David, 204, 205, 206

Sensations of 1945. See Calloway, Cab

Shelton, Edward, 52

Sherwood, Robert, 126, 165

Shuffle Along, 44–45, 66, 169

Silvera, John, 33, 49, 53, 54, 55, 60

Sinatra, Frank, 179, 189

Sissle, Noble, 44, 169, 170, 173. See also
Shuffle Along

Skelton, Red, 208

Slave Narrative Collection. *See* Federal
Writers' Project

Smith, Bessie, 184

Smith, Gus, 47. *See also* Federal Theatre
Project; Negro Unit, New York City

Smith, Lillian, 132–33

Smith, Walker. *See* Robinson, Sugar Ray

Sokoloff, Nikolai, 31. *See also* Federal
Music Project (FMP)

Southern Christian Leadership Conference (SCLC), 246

Southern Commission for Human Welfare, 23

Southern Negro Youth Congress (SNYC),
134

Southern Tenant Farmers Union, 23

Spingarn, J. E., 26. *See also* National Association for the Advancement of Colored
People

Stage Door Canteen, 235, 237

Starnes, Joseph, 63

Starr, Milton, 123, 134, 136, 137, 140, 273
(n. 38), 274 (n. 55). See also *All-American
Newsreel*; Office of War Information

Steinbeck, John. See *Lifeboat*

Stevedore, 36, 58, 59, 63–64, 117, 173, 234

Stevens, Thomas Wood, 40

Still, William Grant, 215, 219. See also
Stormy Weather

Stimson, Henry, 129, 130, 134, 171. *See also*
U.S. Department of War

Stone, Gene, 51. *See also* House
Un-American Activities Committee

Stormy Weather, 13, 160, 181, *187*, 194–96,
210–11, 214–18, *217*, 237; response to,
218–20

Stowe, Harriet Beecher, 53, 54

Student Nonviolent Coordinating Committee (SNCC), 246

Sullivan, Maxine, 180

Swerling, Jo, 229. See also *Lifeboat; The
Negro Soldier*

Swincopation, 36, 65, 71, 74

Swing Mikado, 8, 12, 33–37, 40, 64–72, *67*,
71, *76*, *77*, 196, 218, 221, 244, 263 (n. 139),
264 (n. 165); reaction to, 33, 72–76; anti-
New Deal reaction, 77–78; subsequent
versions, 78–79

Taylor, Fredrick. *See* House Subcommittee on Appropriations

Teamwork. See Moss, Carleton

Teddy Wilson Sextet. *See* Wilson, Teddy

Tennessee Johnson, 199–200

Tennessee Valley Authority (TVA), 19, 98

Theatre Alliance. *See* Rice, Elmer

Thomas, Edna, 125, 172; with FTP, 45, 49; with Negro Actors Guild, 170, 173. *See also* "America's Negro Soldiers"; Federal Theatre Project; *Haiti*; *Macbeth*; Negro Actors Guild; Negro Unit

Todd, Michael, 76. See also *Hot Mikado*

Tommy Dorsey Show, 178

Toomer, Jean, 90

To Secure These Rights. See Truman, Harry

Town Meeting, 174

Triple-A, 62

A Trip to Coontown, 42. *See also* Minstrel

The Truck, 70

Truman, Harry, 25, 194, 241–42, 286 (n. 2)

Tureaud, A. P., 219. See also *Cabin in the Sky*; National Association for the Advancement of Colored People

Turpentine, 34, 47. *See also* Federal Theatre Project

Tuskegee Institute, 93, 137, 173

Twentieth Century Fox. *See* Zanuck, Darryl

Tyler, Converse, 51, 52, 54. *See also* National Play Bureau

Ulio, J. A., 131

Ulrich, Bernard, 78. See also *Swing Mikado*

Unemployed Writers Union, 85

U.S. Department of Justice, 27

U.S. Department of the Interior, 18, 20, 33, 119. *See also* Foreman, Clark; Ickes, Harold

U.S. Department of the Treasury, 24, 30, 140

U.S. Department of War, 192, 203, 281 (n. 10); racial progressivism, 1, 110, 123, 125, 129, 137, 139–40, 273 (n. 40); and "America's Negro Soldiers," 13, 125, 173–74, 191, 278 (n. 36); and Joe Louis, 13, 145–46, 151, 156; and *The Negro Soldier*, 155, 229, 236–37; and *Jubilee*, 159, 166–68, 171, 176, 180, 191; and *Teamwork*, 236. *See also* Armed Forces Radio Service; Bureau of Public Relations; Morale Branch; Stimson, Henry

U.S. Office of the Treasury, 20

U.S. State Department, 14, 130, 243, 244, 286 (n. 7)

Universal Studios. *See* Work, Cliff

University of Chicago Round Table, 174. *See also* National Broadcasting Company

Urban League. *See* National Urban League

Vanda, Charles, 166, 176. *See also* Armed Forces Radio Service; Columbia Broadcasting System

V-Discs, 164, 277 (n. 15)

Verdi, Francis, 63. *See also* Dies committee

Walker, George, 42

Walker, Margaret, 88. *See also* American Guide Series—individual guides: Illinois; Federal Writers' Project

Walk Together, Chillun, 58, 58

Waller, Fats. See *Stormy Weather*

Wanger, Walter, 197, 204, 206

Ward, Theodore. See *Big White Fog*

Waters, Ethel, 140, 160, 163, 167; in *Cabin in the Sky*, 211–12, *213*, 214, 220

Wayne, John, 208

Weaver, Robert, 18, 20, 24, 256 (n. 14). *See also* U.S. Department of the Interior

Welles, Orson, 46, 50; "Voodoo" *Macbeth*, 64, 69–70, 170, 173, 263 (n. 139). See also *Macbeth*

White, Josh, 177, 183. See also *Jubilee*

White, Walter, 32, 108, 119, 140, 204; on unequal wages, 20; and Eleanor Roosevelt, 22, 27; on antilynching bill, 26, 27; and WPA, 60; on Joe Louis, 127, 144, 146; on Hollywood, 135–36, 200, 203, 205–8, 282 (nn. 37, 53); on *Stormy Weather*, 210, 215, 219; on *Cabin in the Sky*, 210, 218–19; on *Bataan*, 224, 226; on *Sahara*, 226; on *The Ox-Bow Incident*, 233. *See also* Antilynching bill; National Association for the Advancement of Colored People

Whiteman, Paul, 162, 169

Whitman, Ernest, 180–82, *181*, 184–85, 188–90, 280 (n. 84). *See also Jubilee*

Widom, Leonard "Bud," 190. *See also* Armed Forces Radio Service

Wilkins, Roy, 18, 133, 139; response to *Come Seven*, 60–61; response to *Lifeboat*, 231; response to *The Ox-Bow Incident*, 233. *See also* National Association for the Advancement of Colored People

Williams, Aubrey, 23, 26, 259 (n. 29). *See also* National Youth Administration

Williams, Bert, 42, 162

Williamson, David, 93. *See also* Federal Writers' Project

Willkie, Wendell, 206; on Joe Louis, 145

Wilson, Dooley, 234; in *Jubilee*, 181; in *Cabin in the Sky*, 211

Wilson, Frank, 45, 59; in *Jubilee*, 170. *See also* Federal Theatre Project; *Jubilee*; Negro Unit

Wilson, Teddy, 180, 182

Women's Interest Section of the Bureau of Public Relations, 134. *See also* Bethune, Mary McLeod

Woodrum, Clifton, 76–77. *See also* House Subcommittee on Appropriations

Woodrum Committee, 117. *See also* House Subcommittee on Appropriations

Woodson, Carter, 96, 111, 174. *See also* "Portrait of the Negro as an American"

Woodward, Ellen, 116. *See also* Dies committee

Work, Cliff, 207

Workers' Alliance, 62, 114. *See also* Popular Front

Work Relief and Special Projects. *See* Baker, Jacob

Works Progress Administration (WPA), 8, 10, 41, 60, 75, 77, 79, 87, 109; racial progressivism of, 1, 2, 23–24, 60, 83, 85; establishment of, 30, 39; pressure from Congress on, 62, 74, 76, 116; and Sterling Brown, 89, 93, 269 (n. 119); end of, 119; and *Jubilee*, 175. *See also* American Guidebook Series; Baker, Jacob; Federal Arts Project; Federal Music Project; Federal Theatre Project; Federal Writers' Project; Harrington, Francis Clark; Hopkins, Harry

World War I, 85, 132, 146, 169, 172, 216, 218; propaganda, 124

Wright, Richard, 174, 250; and FWP, 88, 95, 271 (n. 155); and PNAM, 110; and Dies committee, 116–17; on Joe Louis, 142–43. *See also* Federal Writers' Project; "Portrait of the Negro as an American"

Writers' Project. *See* Federal Writers' Project

Writers Union, 85

Writers' Unit of the War Services Subdivision of the WPA, 119

Writers' War Board, 238–39

Yerby, Frank, 95. *See also* American Guide Series—individual guides: Illinois; Federal Writers' Project

Zanuck, Darryl, 206–7, 215, 219, 234